Repositioning Restorative Justice

edited by

Lode Walgrave

WILLAN
PUBLISHING

Published by

Willan Publishing
Culmcott House
Mill Street, Uffculme
Cullompton, Devon
EX15 3AT, UK
Tel: +44(0)1884 840337
Fax: +44(0)1884 840251
e-mail: info@willanpublishing.co.uk
website: www.willanpublishing.co.uk

Published simultaneously in the USA and Canada by

Willan Publishing
c/o ISBS, 5824 N.E. Hassalo St,
Portland, Oregon 97213-3644, USA
Tel: +001(0)503 287 3093
Fax: +001(0)503 280 8832
e-mail: info@isbs.com
website: www.isbs.com

© the editor and contributors 2003

First published 2003

ISBN 1-84392-016-6 (paperback)
ISBN 1-84392-017-4 (hardback)

British Library Cataloguing-in-Publication Data
A catalogue record for this book is available from the British Library

Printed by T.J. International, Padstow, Cornwall
Project management by Deer Park Productions, Tavistock, Devon
Typeset by GCS, Leighton Buzzard, Beds.

Contents

Introduction

Lode Walgrave

The boom in restorative justice

Twenty years ago, 'restorative justice' was a barely known notion, indicating some isolated experiments with anecdotical significance only and some sympathetic utopian ideas advanced by a few academics. It has now grown to become a crucial field of renovating practices and empirical evaluation, a central issue in theoretical and socio-ethical reflection, and an unavoidable theme in debates on juvenile and criminal justice reform all over the world. In most countries, restorative practices are taking their place in the mainstream of responses to crime. International organisations advise further exploration of the restorative track in the hope of finding socially constructive renovating responses to crime. Restorative justice has also become a buzz-word. Practitioners and researchers get easier funding when they label their activities as such. Politicians refer to restorative justice to enhance the acceptability of their plans.

Several factors and dynamics may have assisted the breakthrough of restorative justice. Socio-cultural understreams – such as communitarianism and emancipation movements of indigenous people, victims' movements, feminist approaches to crime and criminal justice, and critical criminology – have all inspired the development of the restorative option in doing justice. These understreams have found fertile soil in the increasing awareness among the public and policy-makers that the traditional punitive responses to crime have ended up in a dead end, and that they do not offer prospects of more safety and more peace in society and communities – thus not providing relief for victims and/or reasonable reintegration opportunities for offenders. But this recognition rests also on the appealing potentials of the restorative approach itself. This has become more and more obvious in recent decades, thanks to the quality and the creativity of enlightened practitioners, the open minds of judges and visionary policy-makers, empirical feedback, and theoretical and socio-ethical underpinning by academics. They have all benefited enormously from intensive and constructive interaction, which has been facilitated by conferences and meetings.

International conferences on restorative justice

An important series of such conferences is organised by the International network for Research on Restorative Justice for Juveniles. Since 1997, the network has set up international conferences in Leuven (hosted by Lode Walgrave), Fort Lauderdale (hosted by Gordon Bazemore and Mara Schiff) and in Tübingen (hosted by Hans Jürgen Kerner and Elmar Weitekamp). Each has brought together most of the top scholars in the field, as well as advanced practitioners and enlightened policy-makers. They have created an ideal forum for debate on the methodological, empirical, theoretical, socio-ethical and juridical issues involved in restorative justice and for their implications for practice and policy. The conferences so far have undoubtedly initiated further scientific debates and empirical work, have resulted in influential publications and have had a direct impact on policy options.

The fifth conference in the series was held in Leuven, 16–19 September 2001. It registered 227 participants from 26 different countries from all continents of the world. More than 70 papers were presented and discussed. Though the events of 11 September necessitated the forced absence of some prominent scholars (which was more than deplorable), the meeting was nevertheless a great success again, offering in a friendly atmosphere very stimulating presentations and intensive and constructive debate.

Why 'repositioning restorative justice?'

The theme of the conference, 'repositioning restorative justice', was inspired by both satisfaction and concern. Satisfaction, because restorative justice appears to open ways of dealing with the aftermath of crime which are more satisfactory for the victims, more constructive for communities and society, and more reintegrative for the offenders. The feasibility of the restorative approach clearly goes far beyond what was originally believed. An increasing stream of empirical evidence shows significantly more satisfaction in those victims who participated in mediation or restorative conferencing. The offenders do understand better what they have done, accept more easily the consequences and display a tendency towards less reoffending. When confronted with various methods of responding, the public's attitude towards restorative responses is generally favourable. Restorative responses also seem not to lead to more public danger or disorder. On the contrary, the few indications as yet available suggest that this shift could result in a decrease in feelings of being unsafe and an increase in trust more generally.

But there is also reason for concern. As a buzz-word, restorative justice is sometimes misunderstood and even misused. Paradoxically, one could even say that the most important threat to restorative justice is the enthusiasm with which it is being accepted. Enthusiasm leads to poorly thought-out implementation, an overestimation of possibilities, negligence of legal rights, the blurring of the concepts and confusion with regards to the aims and limits of restorative justice.

It is therefore time to make an inventory of what has been achieved in terms of the experience, knowledge and visions of restorative justice. Hence the conference's title 'Repositioning Restorative Justice'. 'Repositioning' suggests a kind of self-confidence: restorative justice takes its position in the belief it has much to offer communities which are often imbued by a fear of crime and societies which are in need of new and socially more constructive responses to crime. At the same time, however, 'repositioning restorative justice' suggests a task, a programme to be carried out, possibly even an exercise in modesty. Restorative justice must seek to clarify its position and to accept its limitation. So, for example, evidence has made it clear that a restorative approach can be successfully applied after very serious crimes, but is unclear how far it can be applied, and how it would relate to punishment. Some consider restorative justice as nothing more than another type of punishment, while others claim it as a genuinely new paradigm. The underlying question is whether the deliberate infliction of pain (the essence of punishment) is socio-ethically intrinsically different from a possible imposition to repair, which is by its very nature intrinsically restorative.

During the last century, rehabilitation was the predominant aim for juvenile offenders. Pure rehabilitation, however, is now being supplemented or even replaced by a more strict, norm-enforcing approach. What are the potentials of the restorative approach here? Can it help to avoid a shift downwards to a more punitive reaction to youthful offending? Some fear that a priority for reparation would be detrimental to the possible rehabilitation and/or reintegration of the young; others simply consider reparation as another, more effective way forward; and yet still others seek to combine both methods while respecting the essentials of each.

This, of course, raises questions with regard to the general relationship between restorative justice and the treatment of offenders: to what extent can restorative justice include preventive aims? While restorative justice has been advanced as a method of crime prevention, is this not far too ambitious? One could also limit one's understanding of restorative justice to being a reactive response to a crime already committed and that, by adding preventive aims, one would make its objective too broad and uncontrollable.

A crucial task for restorative justice in the coming years is locating its position in relation to the law. The participatory philosophy of restorative justice – which aims at the maximum possible openness in informal dialogues and processes – is indeed difficult to combine with a need for formalisation and legalisation. But now that restorative justice is achieving mainstream status in the response to crime, it is imperative we find out how to juxtapose informal processes with the legal safeguards con-stitutional democracies demand.

Repositioning restorative justice also means its functions and results must be confronted systematically with the facts. Systematic empirical research is needed to examine whether restorative justice really does achieve the ambitions it has set for itself. Its potential to resolve conflicts both outside and inside the traditional judicial context therefore needs to be explored.

Publications

These and other themes were debated at the fifth international conference on restorative justice. The conference resulted in two volumes, both published by Willan Publishing. The first, published in 2002, is entitled *Restorative Justice and the Law*, and has chapters by Gordon Bazemore and Sandra O'Brien, Hans Boutellier, John Braithwaite, Adam Crawford, Jim Dignan, Antony Duff, George Pavlich, Daniel Van Ness, Ido Weijers and Lode Walgrave. The chapters were ordered in advance as keynotes to the conference with the aim of producing a coherent publication on the relationship between restorative justice and the law. The other volume is this one – *Repositioning Restorative Justice*. This volume contains a selection of revised keynote speeches and other papers which were presented at the Leuven conference. They have been selected for their intrinsic quality and because they all make an original contribution to the debate on how to reposition restorative justice in relation to mainstream responses to crime, punishment and rehabilitation, and to legal dispositions.

The volume comprises four parts. The first ('Discussing the Principles of Restorative Justice') concerns itself with the theory. Especially through its confrontation with the punishment paradigm, this part explores the essentials of restorative justice. The second part ('Evaluating Aspects of Restorative Practices') aims at positioning restorative justice in relation to what happens in the field. The third part ('Extending the Scope of Restorative Approaches') explores practices in fields that have not traditionally been included in the restorative reach. Finally, the fourth part ('Positioning Restorative Justice in Several Countries') describes how various countries have tried to include the restorative approach in their practices and legislation. It will be apparent, however, that the division among the chapters is rather arbitrary. Many of the chapters could have been included in other parts as they deal with two or more subjects. For example, the principles are described through the experiences of a particular country; countries organise their practices on the basis of principled choices; the evaluations carried out by countries are based on certain principles and the options for extending the scope of restorative justice are evaluated empirically; and so on.

Nevertheless, taken together the chapters make clear that those involved in restorative justice are gradually finding the contours of what restorative justice is and what it is not, what it can be expected to achieve and what it can not achieve. After a period of unbounded enthusiasm, which sometimes led to great confusion and even to dubious misuses of the restorative justice label, it seems that practitioners, academics and policy-makers are on their way to identifying a specific 'hard core' of restorative justice, with its intrinsic potentials and weaknesses. They seem to be working to 'reposition' restorative justice and thereby to save it from being yet another trendy phrase filled with so many dispersed notions and dubious practices that it would be emptied of its specifically renovating meaning.

A debt of many thanks is owed to all those who contributed to the conference. It was they who made it another thought-provoking yet enjoyable event. The authors of the chapters published here are to be congratulated on producing contributions that will help to further the thinking and practice of restorative justice. I would also like to thank the staff secretary of the criminology department at K.U. Leuven, and especially Andrea Ons for administrative support at the conference and for the final touches to this manuscript. It only remains for me to express my appreciation for the work of the publisher, Brian Willan, and of his staff. It is a pleasure to work with them.

Lode Walgrave
Leuven, June 2003

Notes on contributors

John Blad is Associate Professor in criminal law and criminology at the Erasmus University of Rotterdam. The focus of much of his earlier work has been on the (im)possibility of abolitionism (of criminal law) and on the problems of (decriminalising) euthanasia or 'physician-assisted suicide'. He is the main editor of the Dutch *Journal for Restorative Justice* (*Tijdschrift voor Herstelrecht*).

Valerie Braithwaite, Eliza Ahmed, Brenda Morrison and **Monika Reinhart** have worked together on the 'Life at School' Project in Canberra, Australia. All hold positions in the Research School of Social Sciences at the Australian National University, where Valerie Braithwaite is a senior fellow, Eliza Ahmed is a research fellow, Brenda Morrison is a postdoctoral fellow and Monika Reinhart is a data analyst. The research team is affiliated to the Centre for Restorative Justice, where Brenda Morrison is Acting Director.

Mia Claes is a social worker who worked for several years as a mediator for juveniles in a pilot project. Since 1998 she has been in charge of implementing the project in the whole of Flanders. She now co-ordinates a team that coaches eleven mediation projects throughout Flanders. **Frans Spiesschaert, Catherine Van Dijk** and **Sigrid Van Grunderbeeck** are part of the Inter-university Research Group on Restorative Justice. Thanks also to An Nuytiens and Tine Vanthuyne for their help with this chapter.

Isabelle Delens-Ravier is Visiting Lecturer and Research Assistant, Department of Criminal Law and Criminology at UC Leuven, Inter-university Children's Rights Attraction Pole, Federal Office for Scientific, Technical and Cultural Affairs.

Ottmar Hagemann is a sociologist from the University of Hamburg, where his dissertation was on the coping processes of victims. He has recently conducted international comparative criminological research at the University of Greifswald. His main interests are abolitionism, the penal system, victimology and restorative justice, and qualitative methodology.

Nathan Harris is Lecturer at the Institute of Criminology, University of Cambridge. He is currently working on an evaluation of conferencing in Belgium with colleagues at the Katholieke Universiteit Leuven. In addition to restorative justice, his primary interests are the moral emotions and their role in processes of social regulation.

Ida Hydle is Associate Professor at the Department of Health and Sports at Agder University College in the south of Norway. She has doctoral degrees in medicine and social anthropology and does research within the field of restorative justice.

Anne Lemonne is Research Assistant at the University of Copenhagen. She is currently working on a research project entitled 'Social Analysis of Restorative Justice: Comparisons between Belgium and Denmark'.

Grazia Mannozzi is Professor of Criminal Law at the Law Faculty of Como, University of Insubria (Italy). Her primary research interests include restorative justice and the sentencing process. Since May 2000 she has been charged by the Italian Consiglio Superiore della Magistratura with criminal justice training for Italian judges and for justices of the peace. Since January 2002 she has worked as honorary judge at the Court for the Enforcement of Sanctions of Venice.

Gabrielle Maxwell is Acting Director of the Crime and Justice Research Centre at Victoria University of Wellington. She was previously a senior research fellow at the Institute of Criminology, Victoria University of Wellington and a lecturer in psychology at the University of Otago. Her current research focuses on youth justice, restorative justice and family violence. **Venezia Kingi**, **Jeremy Robertson** and **Tracy Anderson** are all part of the team working in association with the Crime and Justice

Research Centre at Victoria University of Wellington. Their research focuses on youth justice, restorative justice, family violence, women in prison, crime prevention, victims and programmes for offenders.

Buyi Mbambo holds an MA in social science from the University of Natal, South Africa. She has been a pioneer in developing a family preservation model for South Africa. She currently works for a UN technical assistance project for the government of South Africa. **Ann Skelton** has a BA LLB degree and is an advocate. She chaired the committee that drafted the Child Justice Bill and currently co-ordinates the Child Justice Project – a UN technical assistance project for the government of South Africa.

Paul McCold is the Director of Research for the International Institute for Restorative Practices, Bethlehem, PA, where he is currently developing university curriculum materials on restorative justice as well as conducting research on a variety of restorative practices. Paul represents the Friends World Committee on Consultation of the Religious Society of Friends at the Alliance of Non-Governmental Organisations (NGOs) on Crime Prevention and Criminal Justice (NY).

Allison Morris was, until recently, Professor of Criminology and Director of the Institute of Criminology at Victoria University of Wellington. She is now an independent researcher and is currently writing up the second New Zealand National Survey of Crime Victims and is involved in an evaluation of restorative justice conferences for adults.

Vesna Nikolic-Ristanovic is Senior Researcher at the Institute for Criminological and Sociological Research in Belgrade (Serbia), President of the Victimology Society of Serbia and Visiting Professor at Keele University (England). She has published largely on criminal and war victimisation in the former Yugoslavia.

Inge Vanfraechem works at the Catholic University of Leuven on a research project with regard to family group conferences in Flanders. She is chair of the Research Committee of the European Forum for Victim–Offender Mediation and Restorative Justice.

Jolien Willemsens studied criminology at the Catholic University of Leuven, where she also completed an MA in European criminology. She currently runs the Secretariat of the European Forum for Victim–Offender Mediation and Restorative Justice.

Martin Wright was Director, Howard League for Penal Reform, and Policy Officer, Victim Support. His books include *Making Good* (1982), *Justice for Victims and Offenders* (2nd edn. 1996) and *Restoring Respect for Justice* (1999).

Toshio Yoshida is Professor of Criminal Law and Criminology, Faculty of Law, and Director of the Graduate School of Law, Hokkai-Gakuen University (Sapporo, Japan). He has special interests in the areas of restorative justice, criminal responsibility and medical ethics. He studied in Sapporo and as a student in the German Academic Scholarship Programme in Hamburg (1973–5), and was also a visiting scholar at University of Cologne (1988–9) and the Max-Planck Institute for Foreign and International Criminal Law in Freiburg (1995, 1998 and 2001). He has published several articles in German and English.

Figures and tables

Figures

Tables

Part I

Discussing the Principles of Restorative Justice

Chapter 1

Is it time to question the concept of punishment?

Martin Wright

The catalogue of punishments inflicted on human beings, usually by men, is a long and shameful one. They are often far more barbarically inventive than anything perpetrated by the malefactors themselves, for example, outlawry, transportation, branding, mutilation by cutting off the tongue or hands, the scold's bridle, burning, boiling in oil, flogging and death. All these have been abolished in the civilised world (some not until the mid-twentieth century), but solitary confinement is still widely practised. It is often hard to see where lies the borderline, if there is one, between legally permitted punishments and torture. Reviewing the killing, torture, separation of families and general misery inflicted in the name of law enforcement, the Dutch criminologist, Louk Hulsman, in a speech to the Howard League for Penal Reform in 1976, said that the three greatest causes of human misery throughout the ages have been famine and pestilence, war and the criminal justice system. Restorative justice is an attempt to find a better way.

Making pain humane

As people began to be squeamish about the grosser forms of physical punishment, the response was not to question the use of punishment but to find a punishment which was doubly invisible, first, because it was psychological and left no marks and, secondly, because it took place in a remote penal colony or behind high walls. Today we have sensory deprivation in 'supermax' security prisons, out of public view. All too often it drives people to insanity, self-harm or suicide. As the futility of all this dawned on the Victorians and their successors, prisons were given fig-leaves of respectability: the silence rule went, prisoners were allowed to do useful if uninspiring work and given wages for it (usually mere pocket money). Prison regimes began to include rehabilitation, with some education and training for some prisoners, but generally only for a few hours a week.

Prisons are inherently costly (in financial as well as human terms), so that even in rich countries they seldom provide enough work or education, and in less 'developed' countries gross overcrowding is common. Imprisonment is sometimes described as 'incapacitation': the word is ambiguous, since it means that the incarcerated person is rendered incapable not only of committing further crimes (except those which can be organised from within prison) but also, all too often, of living a normal working life after release.

Just as prison is ambivalent, trying to show a humane side to liberal public opinion while appeasing hard-liners, so is rehabilitation: to satisfy demands for severity, its advocates claim that it includes some punishment because 'it's very tough really', or 'anger management courses are very demanding'. It may also be unintentionally punitive, for example, through deprivation of liberty in a place of detention with a euphemistic name such as correctional institution. The claimed rehabilitative intentions can mean that fewer safeguards are in place than if the institution were overtly punitive. According to Garland (2000), however, recent developments have eroded the ' "civilised" attitude towards crime of the educated middle classes'. They themselves may have been more directly affected by crime, and hence 'less supportive of penal-welfarism and more supportive of punitive responses to crime' (p. 357). Be that as it may, mass-circulation media, either influencing public opinion or reflecting it, have taken a generally punitive stance, and politicians have felt that tough rhetoric would be popular. This means that their agenda is no longer the same as that of the professional groups who want to produce tangible results (Garland 2000: 350–1, 368–9). Examples from England are the introduction of minimum sentences for certain repeated offences, in the Crime (Sentences) Act 1997, and the renaming of community service orders as community punishment sentences, in the Criminal Justice and Court Services Act 2000. These moves fail to take account of evidence that the public is not as punitive as is often assumed, as will be discussed below.

But the more punitive, the less rehabilitative, and vice versa. In other words, the more deliberately painful a measure is, the less likely it is to persuade and enable the offender to change his or her offending behaviour; and a measure which attempts to help will be less painful, even though it involves an element of coercion which many offenders will find unpleasant. Also, the more punitive, the harder to uncover the truth. The 'wall of silence' met by investigators in the inquiry into the Hatfield rail crash is one example (*Independent*, 23 January 2001; others are given by Wright 1999: 41–2).

Terminological confusion

All punishment, in the normal sense of the word, is intended to cause pain and fear, and in some cases incapacitation. Some writers use the word 'punishment' as if it were synonymous with 'sentencing' (Daly 2000); others, correctly in my view, restrict its use to sanctions intended to inflict pain (Christie 1982).

We need to distinguish, first, what it is (its definition, and its description, which may not always tally with the definition) and, secondly, what we call it (its name). The intention of the person causing the injury or imposing the sanction does matter. The infliction of pain is not always punitive. The sufferer may endure pain voluntarily, as in the case of undergoing surgery, taking part in athletics – or writing a book! Even without consent, the way in which the same sanction is presented can make a difference. An offender will respond differently if he or she has to work alone, or with other offenders, or with staff or volunteers working alongside him or her, or if he or she is told 'Scrub that floor and don't let me catch you talking to the patients', or 'The hospital is short-staffed, so the patients would really appreciate it if as part of your community service you scrubbed the floor, and you are welcome to have a cup of tea with them afterwards'. In the former, the offender will feel that the intention is primarily to make him or her suffer; in the latter, the unpleasantness of coercion is still present, but it is likely to be moderated, and possibly outweighed, by a feeling that he or she is being treated with respect and doing work which is appreciated. Preferably, of course, the work will be of a kind which uses more of the offender's talents than scrubbing floors or picking up litter.

'Punishment' has become an ambiguous term, because it may be used to mean any of the following:

1. A measure primarily intended to hurt, described by Christie (1982) as 'pain delivery'.

2. A measure primarily intended to rehabilitate or contain. It may often also be painful, but this is not the primary aim. It is sometimes said that rehabilitative measures are in fact punitive, because sometimes they take place in penal institutions and may involve indeterminate sentences which are out of proportion to the offence. This objection is, however, as illogical as it would be to say that imprisonment is rehabilitative because some prisons offer rehabilitative programmes to some of their prisoners.

3. A measure primarily intended as reparation. Whether it is painful or enjoyable is irrelevant. There is much anecdotal evidence of offenders enjoying their community service; a small number even continue it voluntarily because they felt appreciated and their self-esteem was enhanced; this is probably valuable, but to call it punishment seems a clear misnomer.

4. A general term for any kind of sentence. This seems unhelpful because it uses a word with a punitive root to refer to measures which, as we have seen, are not necessarily punitive. Daly defines punishment as anything that is unpleasant, a burden or an imposition of some sort on an offender (2000: 39). This may well be a widely held concept; one informed lay commentator, for example, expresses what is probably a common assumption when she writes that 'the guilty deserve to suffer' but also that punishment 'can properly take the form of the offender making some reparation to his victim, and/or the community, in order to help restore his relations with them' (Windsor 1991: 6, 9).

If all these are described by the same term, confusion is inevitable. It would make for greater clarity in academic debate if we avoided the term, and used a word such as 'sanction' as the general term for any imposed measure, with adjectives to distinguish the various kinds according to their primary purpose; the existence of subsidiary aims or unintended side-effects (when the description of what it is really like does not tally with the definition or the name) could of course be acknowledged. It is true that any measure imposed by authority is backed up by coercion which some will find irksome: it may be more unpleasant than intended, and safeguards are therefore needed. But if the *name* expresses the intention, it will make clear to those who implement sanctions that this is the ideal to be aimed for. There is no objection to the task itself being burdensome and requiring effort on the offender's part, but the pain of coercion will be minimised, and the ultimate aim will be voluntary compliance. We could speak, instead, of:

- 'punitive sanctions', to describe measures which intend to hurt, and fail if they don't. They may be symbolic, when the criterion for 'success' is pain or denunciation, or instrumental, where the usual measure is a reduction in reoffending;

- 'rehabilitative sanctions', which are intended to help; if they cause pain it is unintentional, and any loss of liberty should be minimised;
- those which are ambivalent about their aims can be described, for example, as 'punitive/rehabilitative sanctions';
- 'reparative sanctions', intended to help the victim and often the offender also. They may involve loss of liberty or money but this should be by consent if possible (again, safeguards are needed). Since pain is not the aim, they can succeed even when they are enjoyed and continued voluntarily;
- 'containment', intended to protect the public. This may include restriction of liberty, such as disqualification from running a company or driving a car, or deprivation of liberty, i.e. detention. Institutional regimes should as far as possible be reparative, not punitive, and should not 'incapacitate' people for normal lives after release.

In the remainder of this chapter, 'punishment' will be used only where the authors quoted have used it. The word 'sanction' implies a measure imposed on a wrongdoer by an individual (e.g. a parent or a gang leader) or an authority (e.g. a school or a court). There are other possibilities, as we shall see, such as voluntary action by the wrongdoer, and 'natural consequences' of the deed (Wright 1982), of which more below.

The desirability of punitive sanctions

This chapter will consider two recent writings on punishment: a review article by Duff (1996) and a paper by Daly (2000), drawing on Duff's work. It will argue that it is impossible to impose punitive sanctions consistently and proportionately, that they are not the only or the most effective way of achieving their aims and that they have unacceptable side-effects; it is questionable whether an ethical policy for punitive sanctions is possible. Restorative justice should therefore be developed as an alternative.

Duff (1996) is one of those (like Sir Walter Moberly 1968) who lists many cogent objections to punishment but cannot quite follow them to the logical conclusion and reject it as a basic principle. He rightly points out, for example, that 'To justify a system of punishment, we must … show not only that it does good (and does more good than harm) but also that no available alternative practice could be expected to bring about as much or more good, at lower (or no higher) cost' (Duff 1996: 4–5). At times it almost seems as if he, like Daly, is using 'punishment' to refer to any imposed sanction, but he makes clear that he includes 'the delivery of pain' (p. 89).

Duff puts forward two main arguments: that punishment is 'communicative' and that it encourages repentance and penance, which are conducive to possible reconciliation and forgiveness. We communicate how serious the crime is by how heavily we punish the offender, according to Duff (1996: 56). He questions why it should be 'the *state's* task to administer censure through a formal system of punishment: why not just leave it to other individuals (most obviously the victim or her friends) to censure the wrongdoer?' (pp. 60, 34, emphasis in original). He also admits that setting the absolute levels of punishment is another problem: 'How long is "lengthy"?' (p. 66).

According to him, the response to wrongdoing should be 'communicative', involving two-way communication, and forward-looking, aiming to induce repentance and reparation, which ideally the offender imposes on him or herself. Advocates of restorative justice would certainly agree, because as Daly (2000: 42) says, it sounds very much like the conferencing process; but surely such processes should be distinguished from punishment, not subsumed within that term? As regards communication, punitive sanctions are certainly 'expressive' of indignation or condemnation (Duff 1996: 32); but apart from that, as any child who has been hit on the knuckles with a ruler knows, they are likely to block communication, by making the offender too afraid or too resentful to speak or to listen. Duff says that punishment is to bring offenders to realise the social desirability of obedience to law. The aim is unexceptionable, but is this an effective or justifiable way of trying to achieve it?

The question then is: how best to induce repentance, or metanoia (change of mind)? Here Duff (and Daly, as we shall see) find themselves trapped in the punitive tradition: having said that they would like offenders to undertake penitence or reparation voluntarily, they propose to *impose* it as punishment. The trouble with this is that repentance, if it is to mean anything, has to come from within, inspired by empathy for the other person. But punitive sanctions are more likely to produce resistance, resentment and attempts to avoid the pain; they inhibit learning rather than promote it. Von Hirsch questions whether the state should 'use its coercive powers to seek to induce moral sentiments of repentance' (quoted by Daly 2000: 47); he might also have asked whether, if it does so, the state is any more likely to succeed than Glendower in Shakespeare's *Henry IV Part I*:

> *Glendower:* I can call spirits from the vasty deep.
> *Hotspur:* Why, so can I, or so can any man;

But will they come when you do call for them?
Just as the offender's repentance cannot be coerced, neither can the victim's trust that it is freely expressed (Davis, quoted by Daly 2000: 48).

Duff's aim is 'to induce the pain of condemnation and of recognised guilt' (quoted by Daly 2000: 42); but in restorative justice, the aim is not the pain for its own sake, but the empathy with the person harmed. It can indeed be painful to feel empathy for someone whom one has hurt; but this is different from the pain inflicted by an authority; when it comes from within, it encourages the offender to relieve it through words or actions, and this in turn can make the victim feel less angry, and more likely to accept an apology or other reparation, sometimes enabling him or her to forgive.

Duff asks whether censure requires hard treatment: could not the communication be purely symbolic? If its aim is to acknowledge the damage to the victim, this can also sometimes be achieved by apology and restoration or reparation ... or by informal community action. Why punishment and not victim-oriented compensation (Duff 1996: 34, 39, 80)? This is indeed the restorativist case, and it is not clear why Duff suggests that the infliction of pain would assist the process, especially as he quotes Von Hirsch as saying that punishment itself does not profess to deter 'the most recalcitrant' but to give 'ordinary persons good reasons for compliance', which is just what the restorative process claims to do. He says that it is because the victim has been *wronged*, and is owed at least an apology, which 'must involve a repentant recognition of wrongdoing'; 'communicative punishments' aim to 'bring the offender to a repentant understanding of his wrongdoing' (pp. 80–1). He admits that 'punishment can of course all too often be, in intention or in fact, mere "pain delivery"' and that 'similarly, blame or censure ... can too often be merely exclusionary or dismissive'. Duff claims that 'neither blame nor punishment need be like this' (p. 82), but the contention of this chapter is that the use of the term 'punishment' makes this more likely by appearing to legitimate it. If sanctions are clearly labelled according to their intention, as restorative, rehabilitative or indeed communicative, it will be clearer that pain as pain is not acceptable, and pain as side-effect should be minimised.

This is the crux: the restorative case is that the infliction of pain because it is painful is likely to be counterproductive; if the aim is to increase awareness, understanding and empathy, the measures should be designed for that purpose. If they succeed they may prove painful, but the pain will come from *within* the offender, and that is what is needed in order to generate repentance and the willingness to apologise and make reparation. None of this can be guaranteed, of course, and more thought needs to be given to procedures which are to some degree restorative; they can be followed when the full process cannot be used or is not complied with.

Turning now to Kathleen Daly's recent discussion of punishment and restorative justice, in Heather Strang and John Braithwaite's collection *Restorative Justice: Philosophy to Practice* (2000). If I may crudely summarise Daly's argument, she seems to be saying that:

- 'We should embrace (not eliminate) the concept of "punishment" as the main activity of the state's response to crime' (p. 34);
- restorative justice is punishment;
- that's as it should be.

Of course she expresses it much more elegantly than that, in a series of clearly argued propositions. She invites discussion and debate, and this chapter is a response to that invitation. She accepts that there are basic differences between traditional and restorative justice, singling out four: victims as peripheral or central, focus on punishing/treating the offender or repairing the harm, community represented by the state or participating more actively, and an adversarial process or a dialogue (p. 36). But she suggests that restorative justice processes should be seen not as alternatives to punishment, but as alternative punishments.

So, first, why does Daly consider punitive sanctions desirable? One reason is that they are necessary in order to vindicate the victim's worth (p. 39), and that the offender can atone only by willingly submitting to punishment (Garvey, quoted by Daly 2000: 50, n. 10). But Daly herself recognises the value of the restorative justice process (p. 46), which seems to vindicate the victim's worth much more clearly than inflicting pain on the offender. She is also able to claim that punishment is desirable because she is using the definition of it which includes non-punitive measures; she does have a place for painful measures, but stresses that in her definition punishment doesn't have to be humiliating, harming or degrading, and need not involve prison – rather like the housemaid who told her mistress that she had an illegitimate baby, but pleaded in mitigation that 'It's only a little one, Ma'am'.

Secondly, Daly says that restorative justice is punishment because it 'combines retribution and rehabilitation' (p. 35), but there are two problems with this. One is that, if by retribution she means deliberate infliction of pain, this is incompatible with restorative justice as most of its advocates understand it; the second is that we cannot 'serve two masters': one of the two contradictory aims will have to take precedence. It is true that restorative actions require effort, psychological or physical, and may be 'burdensome'; but that is not the same as the infliction of pain for its own sake.

Hence, Daly asserts that restorative justice is punishment (in her extended use of the word). She says that it combines retributive, rehabilitative and restorative principles (p. 45). She is referring to the use of conferencing, of which she approves (pp. 45–6). We need to separate the processes. If the court *orders* that a case be referred to a conference, I think it would be clearer to describe that as a 'restorative sanction'; if the case is *routinely* referred to a conference, that is not a sanction, but part of the process. Furthermore, the outcome will then normally be agreed by those concerned, so it seems inappropriate to call it a sanction, let alone a punishment.

Daly's third point is that restorative justice *should* be punishment. But just as rehabilitation and deterrence are contradictory aims (Wright 1999: 6), so are reparation and proportionality; the idea of restorative justice is that any reparative acts by the offender are if possible agreed by the victim and the offender. They therefore are not necessarily proportionate to the seriousness if the victim does not feel this to be necessary; it may be thought that there should be a safeguard against demands by victims for excessive reparation, although this does not appear to have been a problem in practice. Restorative justice practices, according to Daly, 'are concerned with sanctions or outcomes that are proportionate *and* that also "make things right" '(p. 35, emphasis in original). But these aims are also in conflict, and certainly the sanction should not be increased in the name of proportionality, as the Clotworthy case described in the same volume shows (Morris and Young 2000: 11–13, see also Mason 2000: 4–6). After a very serious offence in which the offender, Clotworthy, demanded money at knife-point and stabbed the victim six times, he explained to the victim that he had been drunk but had not touched alcohol since the offence. The victim told the offender that he himself had been to prison, which 'did not do him much good', and they agreed that instead the offender would pay a large sum towards the cost of cosmetic surgery; but the Crown appealed, and the Court of Appeal ruled that this was 'inadequate', and sent the offender to prison for three years, substantially reducing the amount he was able to pay. Thus a punitive sanction replaced a restorative one, and went clearly against the victim's wishes.

The Court of Appeal stated that it was not opposed to the idea of restorative justice, but that in cases of serious violence it must be 'balanced against other sentencing policies' – i.e. outweighed by retributive ones. This is an example of 'authoritarian' restorative justice (Wright 2000: 21–3), and could be described as punitive. Similarly, it is reported that in some cases family group conferences in New Zealand include a punitive element, even including imprisonment (McElrea 1995); to that extent, I would argue, they too are not restorative.

Daly makes the further point that 'commonsense understandings of a just response to crime' include 'punishing wrongdoers', and that restorative justice advocates would be wise to work with them in building interest in the idea, because to excise the idea of punishment 'may not be strategic politically' (p. 45). This is a purely pragmatic argument, not a principled one, and in any case it ignores the fact that 'commonsense' is also attracted to the idea that the offender should make amends in a constructive way, as we shall see in a moment.

What's wrong with punitive sanctions?

In this section we will consider the argument that punitive public opinion requires sanctions to be severe; other conventional justifications for punitive sanctions; and the claim that proportionality and fairness in sentencing are achievable.

Public opinion

First, it is necessary to question the common assumption that public opinion insists on punitive sanctions. Several opinion polls in various countries show that ideas such as reparation to the victim or the community are very popular. One large survey found that 93% thought that offenders should have to 'make good the consequences of their crime wherever possible' (cited by Wright 1989: 267). The British Crime Survey found that a minority of victims wanted 'their' offenders imprisoned: for 'mugging', 31% preferred prison, as against 62% who preferred a non-custodial sanction; 43% would have accepted an opportunity for mediation. For burglary with entry: 34% wanted prison, 48% a non-custodial measure, and 47% would have accepted mediation (Mattinson and Mirrlees-Black 2000: 69, 70, 42).

It is true however that there is a culture of violence in some parts of British society, perhaps reinforced by, for example, children's comics such as the *Beano*, in which children's escapades routinely end with physical punishment by an adult (see, for example, *Beano* 15 November 1980: 5; 12 December 1981: 18). Several European countries have prohibited physical punishment by parents, since Sweden intorduced the reform in 1979 (EPOCH Worldwide 1996); in Scotland there is a current proposal to prohibit it up to the age of 3, but in England even that small step has aroused strong opposition to such infringement of the parents' 'rights' and the government in 2001 refused to introduce a ban (*Independent* 8 November 2001); children's rights are being ignored by the punitive lobby.

It has to be conceded, also, that through the millennia there has been a persistent tendency of humans to impose punitive sanctions on each other: either alone or combined with reparation (but in some cases allowing them to be replaced by compensation). In the Judaeo-Christian tradition, there are widely quoted precepts about 'an eye for an eye and a tooth for a tooth', and so on, but it is generally accepted that these injunctions are setting limits to the amount of compensation that can be demanded. The ideal of peace and harmony (*shalom*) is expressed more strongly (Hoyles 1986; Zehr 1995). In the New Testament a non-violent doctrine was taken further. To many, 'Turn the other cheek' seems at first too idealistic; but when one considers the effects of blood feuds and international tit-for-tat retaliation, it appears obviously practical. Similarly 'Do not return evil for evil, but drive out evil with good' is very much in harmony with the principles advocated in this chapter.

Hindu teaching also starts from a punitive standpoint, with many punishments from reprimands, fines and shaming to mutilation and death (Tähtinen 1982: 14–15). But here too there are limitations. There is an element of 'virtue is its own reward' and the converse: those whose speech and mind are pure get *dharma* (socio-ethical good), *artha* (economic good) and *kâma* (psycho-hedonistic good), while sin results in karmic social consequences and punishment (pp. 9, 16). There is a need for penance and expiation (*prâyaúcitta*), but this is seen as replacing or at least mitigating punishment, not as being induced by it: 'It seems that expiation soothes and palliates the retributive punitive feelings in society and modifies the seriousness of punishment ... To a great extent the desire of "hitting back" at the offender has been *replaced* by the rite of expiation' (p. 39, italics added). If a learned person breaks the law, punishment should not be excessive; Tähtinen notes drily that the rules were mostly written by Brahmins (p. 44).

This tradition has also been developed in a spirit of non-violence, notably by Mahatma Gandhi. He stresses the significance of harm rather than law-breaking: 'Crime which really matters is a serious moral crime no matter whether it is in harmony with the existing laws or against them', and the worst is structural violence such as corrupt bureaucracy (or, he might have added, exploitative industry and commerce). He even questions the state's right to impose rehabilitation: 'Has society a moral right to rehabilitate an individual to adjust to an unjust society?' Punishment aggravates criminal tendencies: 'Moral crime has to be eradicated by moral means', and Gandhi reiterates the importance of expiation (Tähtinen 1982: 47–8).

There are also parallels with Islam. The Quran is explicit about cutting off hands of thieves (e.g. V: 39), but at least one Islamic scholar has argued, with examples from other Quranic texts, that this should not be taken literally (just as, he might have added, Christians interpret the injunction 'If thy right hand offend thee, cut it off, and cast it from thee' (Matthew 5: 29) as hyperbole). Certainly the Quran also teaches repentance, mercy and forgiveness (see also Wright 1999: 167–8).

Conventional justifications for punitive sanctions

The main justifications for punitive sanctions may be grouped under the headings utilitarian, symbolic, or both.

Consequentialist, utilitarian

This is the basic 'behaviourist' response: if you do that, I will do something that hurts you. But it only works under certain circumstances – for example, when the wrongdoer believes that he or she is likely to be detected, and that the pain inflicted will outweigh the 'reward' brought by the deed.

Even if it works, it does so for the wrong reason: fear. 'If the law and the authorities win [by using "legitimate" violence], this is a bad victory, because it is achieved by the very means which are pronounced illegiti- mate ... the other side – the criminals – is using it' (Fatić 1995: 201). Or, as Marshall Rosenberg, the psychologist and advocate of 'non-violent communication' (NVC) has put it, the first reason for punishment is that we want someone to act differently, and for this it sometimes works, but sometimes instead provokes resistance; we should also ask ourselves, however, 'What do I want this person's reasons to be for doing what I'm asking?' We do not want him or her to act from fear, guilt, shame or to buy love, but willingly, so as to enrich life for him or herself and others. 'NVC ... fosters a level of moral development based on autonomy and independence, whereby we acknowledge responsibility for our own actions and are aware that our own well-being and that of others are one and the same' (Rosenberg 1998, 1999). Duff (1996: 5, emphasis in original) similarly queries 'Is the goal simply that fewer crimes are committed, or does it matter *why* ... : whether for instance people obey the law only through fear ...'

The side-effects of punitive sanctions are well known, though often ignored in theoretical debates. They will be considered below. Also widely ignored is the ethical aspect. Punitive sanctions consist of the infliction of pain by the state on a citizen; if this can be justified at all, it can surely only be, first, when it can be shown to achieve a desired (and acceptable) effect and secondly when, this effect cannot be achieved in another way that does not cause damage.

The utilitarian argument seldom stops to ask 'useful for what?' but assumes that it should aim at the reduction of crime; crime reduction can however be achieved in other ways, and compensating or otherwise helping the victim is just as desirable an intention (Fatić 1995: 34–5). For the victim, seeing the truth acknowledged can be more important than seeing the offender dealt with severely and, as we have seen, these outcomes often have to be traded against each other; as Nils Christie (pers. comm. 2001) has said, the conventional criminal justice process could hardly have been better designed to prevent the acknowledgement of the facts that are most important to the participants. Even accepting the conventional aim, most penal institutions are far from utilitarian: 'The reality of prison life has nothing to do with any corrective, training or otherwise rehabilitative policies. Prisoners are beaten, raped, killed and commit suicide in "training" and "educational" facilities while under "protection" of the state'; utilitarianism 'deliberately shuts its eyes to the social realities' (Fatić 1995: 87). Still more fundamental is the basic moral principle on which social action should be based: according to Ryder (2001) it should be to reduce the pain of others, and to be consistent it would aim to minimise not only crime but the infliction of pain by the state on its citizens. Ryder, however, does not directly address the question of punishment; he states that certain pain-causing actions, such as bullying, should be prosecuted (p. 84), and that wrongdoing by the police should be severely punished (p. 89), which seems at odds with his principle.

Penal measures also have a less desirable utility: crimes sell newspapers and attract television viewers, and it is the exceptional and frightening ones and the apparently 'lenient' sentences which are defined as 'news' and given the biggest headlines. In reacting to the fear that this produces among the public, politicians have, as we have noted, discovered the usefulness of tough rhetoric in giving the impression that they are 'doing something' about it.

Punishment as symbol: the impossibility of proportionality and the chimera of consistency

The second main justification of punitive sanctions is that they demonstrate that certain acts are unacceptable. The idea is that punishments should be consistent and proportionate to the seriousness of the offence; but this is possible only in a rough-and-ready way. Sentencers are supposed to take account of so many competing factors that the scales of justice should have at least four dishes, in which deterrence, rehabilitation, retribution and containment would be weighed against each other; and the use of victim impact statements in some countries means that a fifth should be added, representing the seriousness of the harm from the victim's point of view. But everyone finds it convenient to ignore the fact that to achieve both logic and consistency is unachievable. As I have tried to show (Wright 1999):

- *Harm – pain.* It is not possible to quantify wrongdoing and, if it were, there is no way logically to equate the seriousness of a particular crime with a particular punitive sanction. As Fatić (1995: 72) has said, 'institutions of criminal justice are basically incompetent to determine the exact amount of desert and therefore also the corresponding exact amount of retributive punishment'; in fact, he says (p. 75), ' "desert" is nothing different from the reproach or dislike that the public feels for the offender'.
- *Pain for A – pain for B.* The same punishment has different effects on different people, and the system usually exaggerates these differences by sending the more privileged offenders to the less unpleasant prisons. Prison is a trauma for some, an occupational hazard for others. Likewise fines: even with unit fines, the loss of one day's income has a different impact on a person earning £5,000 and one earning £50,000 (Duff 1996: 59; cf. Wright 1999: Chs. 5 and 6).
- *Short prison – long probation.* There is no way of integrating different sanctions into a single scale: no one can say that one week in prison is more or less severe than x months or years of probation, or y amount of fines. Where is the crossover point?
- *Deterrence – proportionality.* The less a person has to lose, and the more desperate he or she is, the harsher are the punitive sanctions needed to deter them from even a small crime like stealing food. For a person of status, the conviction alone is deterrence enough. In any case, no one knows how much punitive sanction is necessary to deter a particular person or the public at large; and to increase penalties is more symbolic than effective.
- *Mercy – proportionality.* Sentencers often feel the need to reduce the sentence in the light of extraneous factors, such as the fact that the offender had a good army record, or is suffering because she killed her best friend in a road crash, or rescued a child from drowning while awaiting trial, or is pregnant; or to increase it because there have been other similar offences recently, or for reasons they would not admit such as the colour of the offender's skin.
- *Exemplary punitive sanctions are unjust.* Even if it were possible to determine a just punitive sanction for a particular offender, to increase it in order to 'make an example' of him or her is as unjust, and precisely in proportion as it is exemplary (Lord Justice Asquith, quoted in Wright 1982: 191).

Both types of punitive sanction

A third group of objections apply to both utilitarian and symbolic punitive sanctions. They inevitably tend to make the offender think of him or herself, not of the victim. They are not very effective in deterring offenders, but once the offence has been committed, they deter them from admitting their actions: in order to try to avoid them, offenders are less likely to confess or, if convicted, they try to minimise the harm rather than acknowledge its full impact on the victim:

- *Side-effects of punitive sanctions.* Even attempts to make punitive sanctions less harsh can have insidious results. In prisons it is harder to provide constructive activity such as education and training, which are usually available only to a minority of prisoners. But if humane judges believe that prisons are rehabilitative, they are less reluctant to send offenders there. The same applies to facilities such as mother-and-baby units, which serve only to provide a choice of evils: to bring up a child in prison or to separate it from its mother. (Prisons also separate children from their fathers, of course.) It could even be said of restorative justice in prisons. Care must therefore be taken to make all these constructive activities available in the community. Punitive sanctions have other obvious undesirable side-effects: they tend to provoke resentment, and often superficial compliance; they stigmatise people, making it harder to obtain accommodation and work.
- *Collateral damage.* Punitive sanctions also have an impact on the offender's family, and sometimes on the victim (as the Clotworthy case, discussed earlier, shows). This is unfair and counterproductive, especially when it has an adverse effect on children.

Restorativists do however need to address some problems, such as whether reparation should (or can) be proportionate; whether responses to similar kinds of harm should be similar to each other; and, if restraint is needed to protect the public from an offender, how to decide whether deprivation of liberty is necessary or whether restriction is enough; and in either case, how to determine the length.

For all these reasons, despite the best efforts of scholars such as David Thomas, Nigel Walker, Andrew von Hirsch and others, it is hard to see how the philosophical contradictions can be overcome (Wright 1999). The conclusion is, as Fatić (1995: 192, 255) says, that 'punishment in principle is morally unjustified'; and 'the answer to moral concerns about infliction of pain is not to rationalise punishment but to eliminate it'. Hoyles, writing from a Christian perspective, agrees: 'The ultimate penal reform must be the abolition of punishment' (1986: 139). Not only specific punitive sanctions, but punishment itself, would be recognised as 'cruel, inhuman and degrading'.

The first step, then, is to label sanctions according to their intentions; the second is to eliminate those whose primary intention is pain delivery; and the third is to make the actuality match the name as far as possible, especially by maximising the degree of voluntary compliance. Restorative measures may well be experienced as difficult and even burdensome, but they should not inflict pain for its own sake.

Managing without punitive sanctions

If punitive sanctions are unacceptable and ineffective, it is necessary to propose how people can be persuaded to behave decently to each other, and how to react when they do not. As Fatić (1995: 255) puts it, the theory 'has to explain what mechanism would provide a social control equivalent for punishment'.

Such a social policy would have four main strands. It would be based on encouragement to behave well rather than threats to inflict pain for misconduct; when a person caused harm the primary response would be to try to repair it as far as possible; people would be made aware of the 'natural consequences' which follow from harmful acts, rather than threatened penalties; and restriction or deprivation of liberty would be kept as a last resort when there was a serious risk of serious harm which could be prevented in no other way. Each of the last three becomes necessary only when the preceding one did not succeed.

Prevention

The first is somewhat Utopian: it supposes, first, that a society is possible in which everyone has a fair opportunity to make the most of him or herself and a fair share of material and spiritual resources, and that if such a society were attainable, people would not harm each other or try to obtain more than their share.

But even before that idealistic transformation of society, there is much that can be done to reduce crime by programmes which are not based on state intervention but involve 'the organisations, institutions and individuals of civil society' (Garland 1996: 451). Garland gives examples of ways of making crime harder to commit, such as employing parking-lot supervisors, providing late-night buses and advising retailers about security (p. 451; see also Wright 1982: Ch. 9). A complementary approach is the involvement of young people in more constructive activities: early examples were the Wincroft Youth Project (Smith *et al.* 1972) and the

French programme for keeping them occupied during the schools' summer vacation (King 1988).

Restorative justice is not limited to the criminal justice system. It is based on thinking and acting for others (and for oneself, as side-effect). There are initiatives to start it in schools, with methods such as circle time, peer mediation and a problem-solving approach to discipline and bullying (Highfield Junior School 1997). It can also be used in the workplace, families (not only in relation to divorce or separation), old people's homes or when problems arise between doctors and patients or police and citizens.

Repair

This is the basic principle underlying restorative justice; it includes making up for the harm as far as possible, dialogue with the victim (if there is an identifiable one), involvement of the community and feedback to assist crime reduction policies. It will be elaborated below. What many victims want is acknowledgment of the truth of what happened to them; restorative justice, its advocates believe, offers an incentive to confession and disclosure, while punishment encourages concealment and denial.

Natural consequences

The idea that 'virtue is its own reward' is mirrored by the idea that 'wrongdoing is its own punishment' (Wright 1982: 255–8, 262–3). As Fatić (1995) argues, everyday life in society basically depends on each person's trust in others not to cause harm, and crime is a betrayal of that trust. Initially, therefore, the offender loses people's trust, but the aim must be to enable him or her to regain it – not because of a belief in human goodness but because individuals *need* trust, and 'will be best off by accepting the moral norms arising from the principle of refraining from punitive infliction of pain as pain, of justice and vengeance, and from the adoption of reconciliatory and restorative values' (Fatić 1995: 220). At its simplest, if someone tells lies, people will not believe him or her; someone found acquiring goods dishonestly will have them confiscated. An employee who betrays trust may face dismissal – a preventive measure, although it could also be regarded as punitive – or may be allowed to remain so that he or she can repay what he or she took. They may be required to pay the costs of any hearing (for example when charged with attempts or crimes where there is no quantifiable loss), although this should not be disproportionate to the offence or to their means. People who cannot be trusted to drive a car, run a business or hold elected office can be disqualified from doing so, but given the opportunity to win back the trust they lost.

Those who have forfeited trust may be placed under supervision (or detention, if there is a substantial risk of serious violence – see below); but as in the other cases they should have the opportunity, and any necessary help, to make amends and regain the trust which they need, and which others need to give them.

Restriction of liberty

Even abolitionists concede that there are 'a dangerous few' who 'have committed a series of dangerous, violent acts [and] need to be protected from their own violent impulses as much as we need to be protected from them' (Morris 2000: 106). But they stress, first, that their numbers are extremely small; secondly, that their conditions must be very different from those in present-day prisons; and, thirdly, that a policy of locking up the dangerous can only be justified if society has done all it can to prevent people from becoming so violent, through measures such as education of children in non-violence, programmes for abusers and gun control (Morris 2000).

Conclusion: principles and procedures for intervention

From these principles it is possible to develop a model of reducing harm, and responding to it when it occurs (crime-handling, to use Fatić's term). There would be an opportunity for those concerned to respond voluntarily before any coercive measures were used. This could include the concept of 'sanctuary', as 'a place of refuge where the perpetrator of a serious offence could go and live for a while in safety until negotiations [about reparation] could begin' (Bianchi 1986: 123).

For victims, members of the community would offer support, especially where no offender was known; there should also be financial assistance where they needed it and the offender was unable to provide it. When the offender was known, there would be an opportunity for dialogue between them. The process would not aim at encouraging forgiveness, but at providing conditions in which it could more easily occur.

Offenders would be given the opportunity to take responsibility for their actions and make amends, and to regain trust by undertaking positive action for the victim, for the community or for their own future life as trustworthy members of the community.

Incidents would be handled by community organisations unless it was necessary to involve state agencies, and these would divert cases back to the community if possible. The community groups would use lay volunteers as far as possible. They would help not only in the apprehension of offenders and subsequent processes, but, for example, by forming 'circles of support' for vulnerable offenders (Heise *et al.* 2000; Native Counselling Services 2001), providing opportunities for them to make reparation, and managing victim–offender mediation services.

Last but not least, in a non-adversarial, non-punitive system people would speak more freely, and much could be learnt about the circumstances which make crime more likely: failures in parenting, in schools, in supervision of buildings and open spaces, in provision of work and recreation and many more. These could be relayed to local authorities with responsibility for crime reduction strategy, and ultimately to those who influence social policy. Society would 'eliminate the language of weapons' (Fatić 1995: 233) and commit itself not to fighting crime (or even terrorism) but to building peace. The pillory, mutilation, flogging and the death penalty would be followed into history by punishment itself, and restorative justice would make a significant contribution to social justice.

Acknowledgement

I am grateful to Margarita Zernova for some constructive criticisms.

References

Barton, C. (2000) 'Empowerment and Retribution in Criminal Justice', in H. Strang and J. Braithwaite (eds) *Restorative Justice: Philosophy to Practice.* Aldershot: Ashgate.

Bianchi, H. (1986) 'Abolition: Assensus and Sanctuary', in H. Bianchi and R. van Swaaningen (eds) *Abolitionism: Towards a Non-repressive Approach to Crime.* Amsterdam: Free University Press.

Christie, N. (1982) *Limits to Pain.* Oxford: Martin Robertson.

Daly, K. (2000) 'Revisiting the relationship between Retributive and Restorative Justice', in H. Strang and J. Braithwaite (eds) *Restorative Justice: Philosophy to Practice.* Aldershot: Ashgate.

Duff, R.A. (1996) 'Penal Communications: Recent Work in the Philosophy of Punishment', in M. Tonry (ed.) *Crime and Justice: A Review of Research.* Chicago: University of Chicago Press.

EPOCH Worldwide (1996) *Hitting People is Wrong – and Children are People too.* EPOCH Worldwide, 77 Holloway Road, London N7 8JZ, and Rädda Barnen, Stockholm.

Fatić, A. (1995) *Punishment and Restorative Crime-handling: A Social Theory of Trust* Aldershot: Avebury.

Garland, D. (1996) 'The Limits of the Sovereign State: Strategies of Crime Control in Contemporary Society', *British Journal of Criminology*, 36, pp. 445–71.

Garland, D. (2000) 'The culture of high crime societies: some preconditions of recent "law and order" policies' *British Journal of Criminology*, 40: 347–75.

Heise, E., Horner, L., Kierkgaard, H., Nigh, H. Peters Derry, I. and Yantzi, M. (2000) *Community Reintegration Project: Circles of Support and Accountability.* Mennonite Central Committee, Ontario: mcccos@look.ca

Highfield Junior School (1997) *Changing our School: Promoting Positive Behaviour* (P. Anderson, ed.). Highfield School, Torridge Way, Efford, Plymouth PL3 6JQ.

Hoyles, J.A. (1986) *Punishment in the Bible.* London: Epworth Press.

King, M. (1988) *How to Make Social Crime Prevention Work: The French Experience.* Nacro, 169 Clapham Road, London SW9 0PU.

Mason, Sir A. (2000) 'Restorative Justice: Courts and Civil Society', in H. Strang and J. Braithwaite (eds) *Restorative Justice: Philosophy to Practice.* Aldershot: Ashgate.

Mattinson, J. and Mirrlees-Black, C. (2000) *Attitudes to Crime and Criminal Justice: Findings from the 1998 British Crime Survey. Home Office Research Study* 200. London: Home Office (www.homeoffice.gov.uk/rds/index.htm)

McElrea, F.W.M. (1995) 'Accountability in the Community: Taking Responsibility for Offending.' Paper presented at the Legal Research Foundation's conference, 'Re-thinking Criminal Justice', Auckland, 12–13 May.

Moberly, Sir W. (1968) *The Ethics of Punishment.* London: Faber & Faber.

Morris, A. and Young, W. (2000) 'Reforming Criminal Justice: The Potential of Restorative Justice', in H. Strang and J. Braithwaite (eds), *Restorative Justice: Philosophy to Practice*, Aldershot: Ashgate.

Morris, R. (2000) 'But What About the Dangerous Few?', in W.G. West and R. Morris (eds) *The Case for Penal Abolition.* Toronto: Canadian Scholars' Press.

Native Counselling Services of Alberta (2001) *A Cost-benefit Analysis of Hollow Water's Holistic Circle Healing Process.* (lead researcher: Dr J. Couture). Aboriginal Corrections Policy Unit, Solicitor General of Canada, 340 Laurier Avenue West, Ottawa, Ontario, Canada K1A 0P8 (www.sgc.gc.ca).

Rosenberg, M. (1998) *Expressing and Receiving Anger Compassionately Using the Principles of NVC.* (audiotape). CNVC, PO Box 2662, Sherman, TX 75091, USA (www.cnvc.org).

Rosenberg, M. (1999) *Non-violent Communication: A Language of Compassion.* Del Mar, CA: PuddleDancer Press.

Ryder, R.D. (2001) *Painism: A Modern Morality.* London: Centaur Press.

Smith, C., Farrant, M.R. and Marchant, H.J. (1972) *The Wincroft Youth Project: A Social-work Programme in a Slum Area.* London: Tavistock.

Tähtinen, U. (1982) *Non-violent Theories of Punishment: Indian and Western.* Delhi: Motilal Banarsidass.

Windsor, A., Princess Royal (1991) *What is Punishment for and How does it Relate to the Concept of Community? Rede Lecture 1990.* Cambridge: Cambridge University Press.

Wright, M. (1982) *Making Good: Prisons, Punishment and Beyond.* London: Burnett Books.

Wright, M. (1989) 'What the Public Wants', in M. Wright and B. Galaway (eds) *Mediation and Criminal Justice: Victims, Offenders and Community.* London: Sage.

Wright, M. (1999) *Restoring Respect for Justice.* Winchester: Waterside Press.

Wright, M. (2000) 'Restorative Justice: for Whose Benefit?', in European Forum for *Victim–Offender Mediation and Restorative Justice* (ed.) *Victim–Offender Mediation in Europe: Making Restorative Justice Work.* Leuven: Leuven University Press.

Zehr, H. (1995) *Changing Lenses: A New Focus for Crime and Justice.* Scottdale, PA: Herald Press.

Chapter 2

Restorative justice: a discussion of punishment

Jolien Willemsens

Introduction

If restorative justice is to succeed in realising more than simply a few programmes on the periphery of the criminal justice system but, instead, to become the philosophy on which the whole justice system is based, it will have to deal with a number of legitimate questions, such as what place punishment would have in a justice system based on restorative justice. This issue has recently been the subject of fierce debate among restorative justice proponents. At first view, the debate has drawn a clear dividing line within the group of restorative justice protagonists: those who believe that punishment is part of restorative justice (e.g. Braithwaite, Duff, Daly, Barton and Dignan), and those who argue that punishment has no place at all in such a system (e.g. Wright and Walgrave). However, when we take a closer look at the content of this discussion, it seems almost to be mere bickering about words: what some call punishment, others call restorative sanctions.

In what follows, I present an overview of the different positions within this debate. However, these positions are strongly linked with views on how restorative justice should function as part of (or as alternative to) the criminal justice system. That is why this chapter begins with a short discussion of the present author's position on this issue. I support a model that calls for the maximum integration of restorative justice in the current justice system – a position that is also defended by Walgrave (e.g. 2001a) and Wright (e.g. 1996; see also this volume). What is key to this model is the position that restorative justice will modify the foundations of the criminal justice system. The basic organisation of the administration of justice would not be changed dramatically, but the basic values on which it operates would. The justice system would adopt one primary aim: the restoration of harm. Every action – from first contact with the police up until the after-care of inmates on their release from prison – would be geared towards maximising the possibilities for achieving restoration. This primary aim would be qualified by subsidiary aims or limiting factors. As Wright suggests: 'A subsidiary aim is one which is desirable, but is subordinate to the primary aim if the two are incompatible. A limiting factor is an operating condition which must not be overstepped in the pursuit of the aims' (1996: 140). Examples of subsidiary aims are denunciation, rehabilitation and deterrence. Limiting factors, on the other hand, are, for example, the protection of society and respect for human rights.

Informal conflict resolution would be sought in all cases that came to the attention of the criminal justice system – and this at all stages of the process. Participation would be voluntary. The process could take on different forms, depending on the needs of the parties: direct or indirect, between victim and offender only or with the communities of care taking part. A state authority would always supervise (not participate actively in) the process to ensure that the legal rights of the parties were respected. If an agreement could be reached before the decision to prosecute was taken, the public prosecutor could decide to drop the case. However, if the prosecutor considered that the public interest aspect of the case was too important, the case would be referred to court and the parties would be informed about the reasons for this decision. Therefore, courts would only be needed for those cases in which voluntary reparation was insufficient or not possible. This would include those cases in which the offender refused to make reparation voluntarily; no informal conflict resolution was possible (because victim or offender refused, because there was no individual victim or because the offender denied having committed the act); the agreement between victim and offender was insufficient to respond to the public concern at the crime; and in which it was necessary to impose restrictions or detention on the offender out of a need to protect the public.

The court would primarily concern itself with the public interest dimension of a case, for it is not only the victim whose rights and interests are at stake. The state must also consider the interests of potential future victims and those of the community as a whole. Crime transcends the purely individual: it disrupts public order, is a threat to public values and societal peace, is detrimental to the solidarity and mutual respect which are essential to community life, and it creates feelings of insecurity which diminish the quality of life. This means that an official representative of the community will always have the final say in the sentencing of an offender and must judge whether public interest requirements are satisfied. However, the agreement that was reached between victim and offender would always be taken into account, and due weight would be given to it by the court when determining sentence. It is believed public interest considerations will, in most cases, be well served by the process and the outcome of informal conflict resolution. By voluntarily accepting to participate in informal conflict resolution, offenders would acknowledge that a crime was committed contrary to the law. And by accepting responsibility for the wrongdoing and in undertaking to correct it, the offender would be able to express his or her willingness to live within the law in the future. Recognising the harm done confirms the value and rights of the victim. In other cases, however, the court might find that an additional measure was needed. Nevertheless, any measure taken by the court would also, primarily, be orientated towards restoration. It therefore would seem necessary that the sentencing stage was preceded by a phase of genuine two-way communication – a different kind of mediation in which the sentence most appropriate for the maximum achievement of restoration would be considered. Reasonable obligations which are understandable and achievable will contribute more to the restoration of peace and safety than obligations which go far beyond the offender's capacities. This communication process between the state and the offender – which would preferably be preceded by a communication process between the state authorities and the victim to discuss the 'private' aspects of the crime – would serve to ensure not only that the sentence would achieve the maximum degree of restoration but would also invite the offender to co-operate as much as possible voluntarily. In this way sentencing *could* be stripped of its purely coercive function, and the concept of reintegrative speech could have an important role to play in this process.

A limited notion of proportionality in sentencing could be introduced into this model. As Wright proposes:

> There would be a single quantum of the offence; if the victim demanded less for private reparation, more would be owed to the community in the court's order for public reparation. The victim would thus not be under pressure, because he or she would affect only the private/public distribution, not the total. There would still be questions about how much reparation a particular offence

merited, and about the equivalence of reparation through money and community service. But the human rights implications are less serious when it is a question of how much good a person should be required to do, rather than how much pain he or she should be required to suffer. (1980: 236)

Because of this (limited) notion of proportionality, and because of the state authority's supervision of the informal process, concerns for legal safeguards could be addressed. Under such a model there would be some important similarities between restorative justice and punitive justice. The crucial features they have in common are that they are both retrospective and that they both take the principle of the offender's accountability as the basis of their intervention. Within punitive justice, the intervention is based on the seriousness of the crime; in restorative justice it is based on the extent of the harm. But contrary to punitive justice, the sanction in a restorative justice system is not predetermined – it will depend on the needs and rights of the victim, the community and society for restoration. This means that under this model, sentencing is not only retrospective but even more so prospective in defining the content of the obligation.

Of course, such a model would require totally different court procedures from the ones we know today. Procedures would need to be more flexible to allow the victim and offender to agree on the 'private' aspect of the crime. The model would require a great amount of flexibility in sentencing in order to give due weight to the informal agreements reached between the parties, without being detrimental to the parties' legal and human rights. There would also need to be a great deal of communication and creativity to make sure the sentences did not take on the form of retributive punishment but a genuine measure on the road towards restoration. And, finally, the systems of communication within the criminal justice system would need to be changed radically – from being accusative and rejecting to being restorative and reintegrative.

Although this outline of a restorative model of justice is by far not complete and thus vulnerable to numerous objections, it should – in the context of this chapter – be sufficient to provide a context in which to see the author's position in the following discussion.

Punishment

The debate about the role of punishment within restorative justice has been hampered considerably by a lack of clarity about what is meant by the term 'punishment'.

Towards a definition of punishment

It is not an easy task to define punishment. Whole shelves of books have been written about the justifications for punishment, but definitions of what punishment (as used in the criminal justice context) is are very scarce. Some say that punishment is the intentional or deliberate infliction of pain or inconvenience on the offender legally convicted of a legally defined offence. This is the position taken by Wright (1996; see also this volume), who distinguishes among the *intentions* of the legal authorities. He argues that, whereas punishment is an intended deprivation, what is not punishment is intended to be constructive. However, according to others (among them Daly 2000), this is a dangerous line of thinking. She argues that some people may delude themselves into thinking that what they *intend* to do, which is not to punish, is in fact experienced that way by those at the receiving end. Daly (along with Duff 2001) would rather define punishment as anything that is unpleasant: a burden or imposition of some sort on the offender. Under this definition, I would agree it would be difficult to keep any notion of punishment out of the restorative justice discourse. For it is clear that many of the agreements reached in a mediation process will require a considerable investment of time or money from the offender, and will require serious, and possibly unpleasant, commitments. Even more fundamentally, the fact that the offender is confronted with the (harms done to the) victim is unpleasant in itself. This view has led several scholars to consider restorative justice as another form of punishment. One well-known example is Duff, who regards restorative justice interventions not as 'alternatives to punishment' but as 'alternative punishments' (cited in Walgrave 2001a).

In this chapter I regard punishment as every act which fulfils the following conditions:

1. At least two people are involved: the punisher and the punished.
2. The punisher deliberately causes a certain harm or unwanted treatment to happen to the punished.
3. The punisher has been authorised under a system of rules or laws, to harm the punished.
4. The punished has been judged by a representative of that authority to have done what is forbidden or to have failed to do what is required by some rule or law to which he or she is subject.
5. Whether the act is considered as punishment or not is dependent on what the punisher considers to be punishment and not on the opinion of the punished.

By adopting this definition of punishment, I have, of course, already taken a stance for the debate to come. From conditions 1, 3 and 4, for example, it follows that we exclude self-imposed punishment from our definition. These same conditions also imply that punishment entails one-way communication: a punishment is imposed by an authorised person (according to the law) against the will of the one being punished. We also limit our definition of punishment to state-imposed punishment and place the intent of the punisher at the centre of our definition.

Punishment not part of a criminal justice system based on restorative justice

No coercion, no punishment

The most straightforward position in this debate has clearly being taken by McCold (1999), who claims that accepting any form of coercion as being potentially restorative would completely shift restorative justice back to being a theory of retributivism. McCold totally rejects coerciveness in restorative justice and opts for a 'purist' model of restorative justice. In this model the potentialities of restorative justice are limited to forms of voluntary and informal conflict resolution. Any conflict that cannot be dealt with in such an informal process would be referred back to the traditional criminal justice system. There are some basic difficulties with this position. Limiting restorative justice to consensual informal processes runs the risk of confining it to a diversion model in which the traditional criminal justice system uses restorative programmes simply to reduce the caseloads of the courts. The message conveyed by such a model is that, ultimately, the traditional justice system is better at dispensing justice. Also, if the offender refused to participate in the restorative process, both the victim and community would be excluded from any form of restoration. This limitation on consensual, informal processes presents serious difficulties when we consider cases that do not lend themselves to such processes. According to Dignan, this is a serious mistake, 'since it represents a missed opportunity to consider how restorative justice thinking might contribute to a broader and more far-reaching programme of penal reform' (2001: 3).

A place for coercion, not punishment

Walgrave and Wright, however, see a basic difference between coerciveness and punitiveness. In Walgrave's view, restorative justice includes voluntary processes as well as coercive sanctions, although he stresses that the former will always have a higher restorative value since, through his or her willingness to participate, the offender expresses his or her understanding of the wrong and the harms done and his or her willingness to make up for them. This means that a justice system's first obligation is to maximise the possibilities for informal conflict resolution. What distinguishes coercive restorative sanctions from punishment is that the former are reasonable, restorative and respectful (Walgrave 2001a). Walgrave defines punishment as the intentional infliction of a deprivation, and he recognises four crucial elements in punishment: coerciveness, hard treatment, the intention to cause suffering and a correspondence between the infliction of pain and the wrong committed. These four elements fit easily into our definition of punishment. Walgrave contends that, if one of these elements is lacking, there is no punishment. Like Wright, Walgrave positions the punisher's intentions at the centre of the definition. This means that if a sanction is imposed with the intention of bringing about restoration instead of simply causing the offender to suffer, this sanction cannot be considered a punishment. The possible, and highly probable, unpleasantness of the sanction is regarded as a mere side-effect.

Walgrave proposes several reasons why coerced restorative sanctions are preferable to punitive or forced rehabilitative sanctions. First, he argues, is the simple material benefit: the mere fact that something is done for the victim and the community. However, it is clear that many victim- and community-orientated measures might well be imposed purely with a punitive intent. Secondly, he sees a reintegrative function in the imposition of restorative sanctions. He argues that:

> Even if offenders do not originally freely accept a restorative action, they may in the longer term understand the sanctions in a constructive way. That will increase their chances of being reaccepted by the community more than a retributive action would. This seems even to be true also in comparison with rehabilitative measures. (2001a: 23)

However, there is no reason why, at some point, an offender should not look back at his or her punitively imposed prison sentence or other sanction and see this as a turning point in his or her life, as the one thing the offender needed in order to be able to change his or her ways. Because of this change in behaviour, the offender could well be accepted back into the community. There does not, therefore, seem to be a valid reason to support this claim. Thirdly, Walgrave contends that a restorative sanction carried out in the community itself may have benefits for that community through, for example, the destruction of stereotypical images of the 'offender'. Again, however, there is no clear reason why this should not happen if community service were imposed with a punitive intent. The last reason Walgrave proposes is that punitive responses to crime have no moral or instrumental value. After summarising the ills of retributive and instrumentalist punishment, Walgrave concludes that 'Punitive justice stigmatises, excludes, responds to violence with counter violence and does not contribute to reconciliation or the peace' (2001a: 27). In the present author's view, this is a valid argument, as opposed to the three other arguments, which are not convincing. The most that could be said is that restorative sanctions probably have a *greater* potential to achieve these things. Based on the restorative justice model proposed earlier, an element could be added to Walgrave's reasoning, namely, that the process by which restorative sanctions and punishments are imposed are radically different.

As a possible counter-argument to Walgrave's conclusions, Daly contends that punishment should not necessarily be associated with humiliation, harm or degradation, unless 'one argues that any sanction imposed by a legal authority on a convicted (or admitted) offender is, by definition, harmful or unjust because the criminal justice system is unjust' (2000: 40). This suggests that, if we look at what at first might seem divergent definitions of punishment, Daly's and Walgrave's points of view might not be as different as originally thought. It could be that the difference between these positions is only a terminological one. Walgrave uses the word punishment in its negative sense; Daly, on the other hand, tries to divorce the word from its negative connotations to give it a more constructive meaning. Thus what Walgrave calls restorative sanctions, Daly calls punishment but, inherently, they do not disagree about what forms these measures should take: an imposition of some sort that is not deliberately (but probably is) burdensome to the offender but that is constructive and imposed with the intention to contribute to the overall achievement of restoration for the victims, offenders, their communities of care and society. Both would agree that the restorative value of these impositions is less than that of voluntarily accepted, informal methods of conflict resolution, and that we should therefore maximise the possibilities of using such processes while using restorative sanctions/punishments parsimoniously. This suggests that the debate about restorative sanctions versus punishment might be an empty one, unless we start looking at the content of, and the process by which, such impositions are made.

Walgrave (2001a) suggests that there are two basic problems with the punishment paradigm: namely, that the intentional infliction of pain cannot be justified ethically and the a priori assumption that offenders must suffer is destructive to social life. He argues that restorative sanctions are different because the infliction of pain 'is not intentional, but only a possible side-effect, and because the obligation is meant to be socially constructive, namely to contribute reasonably to the repair of the harm, suffering and social unrest caused by the crime' (2001a: 27–8). However, it could be claimed that the first part of this argument (which is also used by Wright 1996) is weak since it is clear that most restorative sanctions, although it is not their *primary* intention, will be painful or burdensome to the offender, and that, when imposing these sanctions, the imposer is well aware of the painful possibilities. The second part of the argument, however, is much stronger and more difficult to refute.

The second problem with the punishment paradigm, Walgrave contends, is that it makes a priori choice to punish offenders. However, if it is possible to serve the goals of criminal justice (e.g. the confirmation of social norms by censuring transgressions and/or positively influencing offenders) equally well without punishing, then this course of action should be the preferred method. From this it follows that, if it is possible to serve the goals of criminal justice without any form of coercion, this is also preferable. Walgrave argues correctly that the communicative aspect of the social response to crime is crucial, and that there are much more constructive ways to express censure of the criminal act than punishment:

[This a priori option for punishment] cramps the criminal justice communication in a way which is impeding for a possible dialogue in view of finding a constructive solution to the problem caused by crime... [It is essential that] the disapproval is communicated in such a way that it is understood and accepted by those concerned, i.e. the offender, who should be convinced to do what is necessary to re-instate his position as an integrated citizen and not to repeat the wrongful behaviour; the victim, who must feel supported in his victimisation and assured in his citizenship by the formal rejection of him being victimised, and the broader society which would see the social norm being re-confirmed. The settings in view of restoration are much more adequate for such communication, including moral disapproval and provoking repentance, than are the traditional punitive procedures and actions. (Walgrave 2001b: 5–6)

This position is supported by Dignan, who argues that there are three principal shortcomings to expressing censure through punishment. The first is the assumption that the degree of punishment imposed reflects the degree of disapprobation with the crime:

it does not *necessarily* follow that the severity of a sanction will (or should) express the stringency of blame that is attached to it. Nor does it follow that this is the way it is likely to be perceived by an offender. Indeed, the main objection to this line of argument is that it appears to be based on a rather crude form of instrumentalist reasoning that may well not be the most effective method of communicating censure to offenders or eliciting a constructive response from them. (Dignan 2001: 8)

The second shortcoming, is that the court-based format within which the censure is conveyed affords only limited opportunities for meaningful, censure-based communication and virtually no possibility for any constructive engagement on the part of either victim or offender. The third shortcoming is 'linked to Braithwaite's well-known critique of the potentially criminogenic consequences that may follow when the process of censuring an offender results in indelible, open-ended stigmatic shaming' (2001: 8).

Finally, Walgrave (2001a) sees important strategic reasons for maintaining a clear distinction between punishment and restoration. He is right in saying that punishment has become a container-notion; so many different ideas have been put under the label of punishment that it has become meaningless. It is, therefore, necessary to be very clear about what is and what is not punishment. And not simply for theoretical reasons – there are practical reasons why the distinction must be made clear. If we are not clear about what constitutes punishment, there is a very real risk (that has already become a reality) that many practices which are in fact not restorative will be called that way. Accepting so-called restorative punishment is also dangerous from a macro-social strategical standpoint because restorative ethics and practices would run the risk of gradually fading away in favour of a renewed accent on the punitive core of the traditional approach. On the other hand, Daly suggests that 'As a political and policy matter, it may be mistaken to excise the idea of punishment from a restorative justice process. It may not be strategic politically nor comprehensible culturally' (2000: 45). Moreover, she feels there is no real point in making a distinction between punishment and restorative justice:

> From the perspective of lawbreakers, the distinction will seem no different from (and just as disingenuous as) that between punishment and treatment. From the point of view of victims, it denies legitimate emotions of anger and resentment towards a lawbreaker and some sign of expiation. And from the point of view of the community, certain harms may appear to be condoned, not censured as wrong, if they are not punished (2000: 41).

However, it could be said that these arguments are not very convincing: through good communication offenders *could* see the difference. As proposed earlier, the sentencing stage should ideally be preceded by a phase of genuine two-way communication, during which measures to maximise the achievement of restoration would be discussed. Further, punishment does not allow victims to express their emotions of anger and resentment, and it often does little to redress the victims' personal loss or injury. Under the restorative model, however, victims *would* get a chance to express their feelings since they would be actively involved in the resolution of the conflict, and the sentences (or agreements) imposed would address their harms. Lastly, it is a misconception that, if offenders are not punished, people regard this as condoning wrongdoing. What society wants is a reaction – a reaction that should not necessarily be painful but constructive so as to minimise the risk of reoffending.

Punishment as part of a criminal justice system based on restorative justice

An uncertain, decentralised place for punishment

Braithwaite's approach to punishment is based upon the principle of parsimony: punishment should be limited to enable the offender to retain as much 'dominion' as possible. This approach is considered as comprising one of four elements of a republican theory of justice, which also includes checks on power, reprobation and reintegration. According to Braithwaite (2001), even if a punishment is less respectful of an offender than a restorative alternative, this does not mean we should never resort to it. However, when we do resort to such a punishment we should do so on consequentialist grounds (i.e. there is no other way of resisting injustice) and as respectfully as possible.

Quite surprisingly, it seems that both Zehr and Christie also acknowledge that a place remains for punishment. Christie has argued that if pain – intended as pain – is used, it should at least not be used with an ulterior purpose. Pain should be applied simply as punishment, not as a way of reaching some other goal, such as rehabilitation or social control. To apply pain utilitarianly is to be dishonest and to use people as commodities. Christie also urges that we inflict pain only under conditions that will reduce the level of the pain inflicted (cited in Zehr 1990: 209). Zehr seems to follow this position, saying that, if punishment cannot be eliminated entirely from a restorative approach, it should at least not be normative and its purposes should be carefully described. He goes on to say that, if we punish as a society, we must do so in a context that is just and deserving. Punishment must be viewed as fair and legitimate because we cannot experience justice unless justice provides a framework of meanings that make sense of experience. For the punishment to seem fair, the outcome and process need to relate to the original wrong. It seems that, at least at face value, Zehr makes some limited concessions to the just-desert proponents. However, he adds that the social context must also be viewed as fair, and that this raises larger questions of social, economic and political justice. Finally, he suggests that, if there is room for punishment in a restorative approach, its place should not be central: it would have to be applied under conditions which controlled and reduced the level of pain and in a context where restoration and healing were the goals. He concludes by saying that 'Perhaps there are possibilities for "restorative punishments". Having said that, however, I hasten to add that possibilities for destructive punishment are much more plentiful' (1990: 210). From the above it is clear that Zehr does not preclude the possibility of punishment (or does he mean restorative sanctions?). However, it is not clear where its place would be and what form it would take. It might well be Zehr should be grouped with Walgrave and Wright, but the limited information we have makes his position unclear.

Retributive punishment as an integral part of restoration

The stance others take is clearer. Duff contends that restoration and retributive punishments are not incompatible with each other. Further, he argues that restoration requires punishment in that the kind of restoration crime makes necessary can be brought about only through retributive punishment. For Duff, punishment is ideally 'a penance, that is, something which a wrongdoer imposes on [him or herself], as a painful burden to which [they] subject [themselves] because [they have] done wrong' (Duff 1992, cited in Daly 2000: 42). From this definition it is clear we have a totally different view of what constitutes punishment.

Duff (2001) begins his argument by saying that any discussion of restoration must be sensitive to the fact that the victim has been *wronged* as well as harmed. Moreover, crimes – while they are very often wrongs against an individual victim – also concern 'the public' because they infringe upon the values by which a community defines itself as a law-governed polity. It is, therefore, not just up to the victim and offender as private individuals to make provisions for an appropriate response but also, partly, up to the public. However, these considerations do not lead to the necessity for punishment but only to the necessity of state supervision over the resolution of conflicts.

Duff continues by saying that reparation must be burdensome if it is to serve its purpose because only then can it express a serious apology. He claims that if the reparation cost the wrongdoer nothing, it would be nothing more than an empty verbal apology. This could be construed as a misconception: it all depends on what the victim feels he or she needs in order to be restored. It might be, for example, that the victim wants some form of commitment from the offender that will cost him or her time or money – but this is not necessarily the case.

Duff continues his reasoning by saying that we should recognise criminal mediation and reparation as punitive, as a paradigm of punitive justice. He suggests that mediation in criminal justice fits in with standard definitions of punishment since punishment is something intentionally painful or burdensome imposed on the offender for the crime committed by some person or body with the authority to do so and with the intention to communicate censure for that crime: 'the aim is not to "deliver pain" or to make the offender suffer simply for its own sake, but it is to induce an appropriate kind of suffering – the suffering intrinsic to confronting and repenting one's own wrongdoing and to making reparation for it' (2001: 15). By adopting this definition, Duff basically equates mediation with a form of penal hard treatment. This, however, is not how most people would describe mediation. A mediation process gives the victims and offenders a chance to communicate about the crime and its consequences, and it aims to bring about restoration. Although the 'confrontation' with the victim might be painful for the offender, this is certainly not the intention. Most proponents of restoration would also agree that mediation cannot be imposed on the offender (nor on the victim for that matter). Adopting Duff's view, moreover, runs the risk of allowing the process to deteriorate into one in which the victim is once more used as a mere instrument in the 'treatment' of the offender. Finally, there are much more constructive ways to express censure for a crime than through punishment.

In Duff's view, criminal mediation takes place under the aegis of the criminal law and under the authority of the criminal court. The central role of the court would be to act as a guarantor of punitive justice. The court must determine that the defendant did indeed commit the offence, supervise the mediation process, approve its outcomes and deal with offenders who refuse to take part or to make the agreed reparation. Since the court has the role of protector of each party's rights and guardian of the public interest, Duff would work with court-appointed mediators 'who can speak with the voice and authority of the law and of the polity whose law it is' (2001: 19). The court would ensure that the offender is required to discuss and make reparation only for the crime proved against him or her. It could be said that in this Duff is correct in that it is important that the mediation process and its outcomes are supervised by a state authority to ensure that the legal and human rights of the parties have not been infringed upon and to safeguard the public interest dimension in crimes. However, this perhaps cannot be said of the court-appointed mediator: a mediator should be impartial – it should not be the role of the mediator to speak as a representative of society.

Duff anticipates some of the possible critiques of his reasoning. He predicts that some might argue that mediation and reparation cannot constitute punishment since punishment is imposed against (or regardless of) the offender's will, while mediation and reparation must be consensual. However, he argues, punishment can be self-imposed. He goes on to say that his claim that mediation and reparation should be seen as punishment is not only definitional but also that such a process can serve the aims of criminal punishment. First, he argues, mediation is a communicative process since it censures the offender for his or her crime and requires a burdensome reparation for that crime. He believes that punishment must be justified as a communicative enterprise between a state or community and its members, and he sees mediation as being such a communicative enterprise. Secondly, he argues that mediation is retributive in that it seeks to impose on or induce in the offender the suffering he or she deserves for the crime: 'What they deserve to suffer is not just "pain" or a "burden", but the particular kind of painful burden which is integral to the recognition of guilt: they deserve to suffer that because it is an appropriate response to their wrongdoing, and criminal mediation aims precisely to impose, to induce that kind of suffering' (2001: 17). Thirdly, the reparative burden the offender undertakes is a kind of penal hard treatment; it is intentionally burdensome independently of its communicative meaning. However, it is also an essential aspect of a communicative penal process because it is the means by which the offender can make apologetic reparation to the victim (and – according to Duff – as mentioned above, reparation must necessarily be burdensome if it is to express a serious apology). It is also a vehicle through which the offender can deepen and strengthen his or her own repentant under-standing of the wrong he or she has done. And, finally, although mediation is retributive (looking at the past), it is also future orientated since it aims at reconciling the victim and offender and at dissuading the offender from committing crimes in the future. It could be argued that this train of thought is based on a sequence of misconceptions – misconceptions that were outlined above. The only element of the argument with which we agree completely is the last – that mediation is future orientated.

Finally, if mediation is not possible or practicable, Duff suggests that the offender would likely undergo a punishment of the kind with which we are more familiar. Nevertheless, the sentencing process should still, if possible, be a formal analogue to the mediation process in which the victim and offender might take part. Moreover, the offender's punishment should resemble (in its meaning and purpose) the reparation to which mediation between the victim and offender often leads. On this last idea, we would agree. However, this is no longer a form of punishment as we defined it, since we regard punishment as a form of one-way com-munication, as something strictly imposed on the offender against his or her will. Moreover, Duff seems to believe that also formal sentences should aim at the restoration of harms. Again this leads us to suggest that the sentence is not a punishment.

Punishment as a precondition for restoration

According to Barton, '. . . blaming retribution, or even punitiveness, for the ills of the criminal justice system is largely beside the point. Punishment and retribution cannot be ruled out by any system of justice' (2000: 55). Rather, he sees the problems as lying within the fact that criminal justice silences, marginalises and disempowers the primary stakeholders in the dispute. He continues by saying that the chief weakness of the current justice system is the greatest strength of restorative justice interventions – which is not their rejection of punitiveness and retribution but their empowerment of communities that are best placed to address both the causes and consequences of crime.

Barton raises two difficulties with the claim that 'the problem with the criminal justice system is that it is punitive and that punishment doesn't work'. The first, he contends, is that most people regard punishment (certainly in the case of serious crimes) as an appropriate response to wrongdoing. To support this contention he draws on Umbreit's findings from surveys of crime victims in which it became clear that many victims wanted to hold the offender accountable for his or her actions and wanted the offender to know that he or she had done something wrong and that he or she had to pay for that. However, according to the author, these statements do not necessarily mean that victims of crime would prefer a form of penal hard treatment over some more constructive measure. What victims want is for something to happen which expresses disapprobation of the crime – which people, for convenience, call punishment. From research we also know that most people would prefer that these 'punishments' (by which – we would suggest – people actually mean measures) take on a constructive form.[1]

Barton also claims that the concept of justice seems to presuppose the idea of a punitive response – if not that of retribution in its 'just deserts' sense. This seems a very limited view on the notion of justice. For example, Bazemore and Walgrave (1999) consider justice as meaning at least three things: a feeling of equality, the optimal satisfaction of all parties and the legal protection of the individual against unwarranted intrusions by the state. This view about justice is supported here, and there seems to be no indication in this view of the necessity of a punitive response.

Barton (2000: 61) goes on to say that 'In practice, restorative justice responses incorporate punitive and retributive measures and elements in what appears to be optimum doses and degrees'. He claims this is rightly so since, otherwise, informal justice processes would never become part of accepted practice. He also feels that some appropriate level and form of punishment would enhance the effectiveness of the restorative justice response and that, without this, most parties would not come to any form of agreement. However, he does not appear to give any evidence to support his claim, and it is not clear what he means by 'punishment' in this context. Moreover, he feels that our liability on punishment is an ineliminable part of what defines us as mature and responsible members of the moral community. On the contrary we would say; if we were mature and responsible, we would be able to resolve conflicts constructively, without imposing pain in return for pain.

Finally, Barton feels that, instead of rejecting punishment and retribution, these should be complemented 'with genuine caring, acceptance and reintegration of the person, as opposed to stigmatising, rejecting or crushing them ...' (2000: 61). This, according to the view presented here, would give offenders a very contradictory message: first we stigmatise, reject and crush them by punishing them and then, afterwards, we try to show them genuine caring, acceptance and reintegration!

Punishment as a 'backup' for restorative measure:

In a recent paper, Dignan (2001) develops an alternative enforcement pyramid from the one proposed by Braithwaite.[2] According to Dignan's pyramid, the standard response for the vast majority of cases would be to deal with the matter by means of the most appropriate informal restorative process. This process would take place under some form of judicial oversight in order to protect the legal and human rights of all the parties concerned. If reparation is agreed and performed to the satisfaction of both parties, and if there is no evidence of a lengthy history of similar offences, that would be the end of the case – unless there was an important 'public element' to it: 'Recourse to the courts would not normally be allowed unless either the accused denied guilt, the victim was unwilling to participate, the parties were unable to reach agreement on the subject of reparation or the offender refused to make reparation as agreed' (Dignan 2001: 12). In such cases, the court would only have the power to impose a 'restoration order', which would take the form of compensation, reparation for the victim or community service.

In more serious cases, greater weight would be placed on the public interest aspect of the offence. This includes cases in which the offender unreasonably refused to make adequate amends and where there was a prolonged history of repeat offending followed by a refusal to make reparation. There would also here be the possibility for informal conflict resolution, but the court would add a certain amount of punishment to this. Dignan adds that:

If restorative justice is to furnish a more constructive form of 'replacement discourse' to counter the current repressive approach, it will be necessary to reformulate the existing range of punishments so that, as far as possible, every kind of penalty applies restorative justice principles in the pursuit of restorative outcomes. (2001: 12–13):

This suggests that Dignan calls punishment what we have been calling here restorative sanctions. In fact, Dignan's enforcement pyramid is very reminiscent of the model of restorative justice proposed in this chapter: he considers the primary aim of a punishment system to be the reparation of the harm caused by an offence and the promotion of restoration for victims, offenders and communities.

Concluding remarks

The debate about the place of punishment in restorative justice is hampered to a considerable extent by the definitions of punishment used. Some (Wright and Walgrave) regard punishment to be the intentional infliction of pain – putting the decision as to whether something is or is not punishment in the hands of the imposer. Others (Daly and Duff) regard punishment as anything that is considered by the offender to be a burden. A third position is taken by Barton and Dignan who adopt a very wide notion of punishment as any measure that is imposed on an offender. While Wright and Walgrave use the word punishment within its negative sense, others, such as Daly, want to give it a more positive, constructive meaning. However, when we look at the content and aims of what are termed restorative sanctions/punishments, the differences between these divergent views seem *almost* to disappear (with Duff as the main exception): an imposition of some sort which is not deliberately (but probably is) burdensome on the offender but which is, at the same time, constructive and imposed with the intention to contribute to the overall achievement of restoration for the victims, offenders, their communities of care and society. Restorative sanctions/punishments are not primarily intended to cause pain and suffering – their primary aim is to achieve restoration. They should be socially constructive in that they contribute in a reasonable manner to the repair of harm, suffering and social unrest caused by the crime. They should confirm social norms by censuring transgressions, and they should try to influence the offender in a positive way. They should be imposed in such a way as not to stigmatise the offender. Finally, this author feels that most would agree that the forum in which these restorative sanctions/punishment would be imposed should be changed drastically in order to allow respectful communication between all parties. Why, then, if the differences are so small should we use the term 'restorative sanctions' instead of 'punishments'? I would like to suggest that we use, for pragmatic reasons, restorative sanctions instead of the word 'punishment'. The first things that come to mind when we think of the word punishment are imprisonment, the infliction of pain, stigmatisation, exclusion and many more negative things. The negative associations with the word punishment are too strong, and I do not believe, as Daly suggests, that we can break this negative link. Punishment has become a 'container-notion'. Each time it is used we should ask what is meant by it to make sure we all understand it in the same way. So, certainly for scientific purposes it is necessary to differentiate between the two terms. On a more practical level, however, it is important we maintain those distinctions for there is a risk that non-restorative practices might be called restorative, which might result in the situation in which – one day – we would have to come to the conclusion that everything is called restorative, but that in the core, criminal justice is still punitive. It might well be that the difference in meaning will need stating many times before the notion 'restorative sanctions' becomes common parlance – but at least this will keep us focused on what we want and what we don't want, thereby increasing the chances of real change.

Notes

1. For an overview of such research, see Wright (1996: 154–6; also this volume).
2. Braithwaite refers to his enforcement pyramid as an integration of restorative, deterrent and incapacitative strategies. At the base of the pyramid stand informal restorative justice processes, available for well intended offenders who are willing to participate in these processes. On the second level is the principle of 'active deterrence'. This involves the strategic use of escalating threats in response to those who might be recalcitrant. At the top of the pyramid is incapacitation for the incompetent or irrational. For more see Braithwaite (1999).

References

Barton, C. (2000) 'Empowerment and Retribution in Criminal Justice', in H. Strang and J. Braithwaite (eds) *Restorative Justice: Philosophy to Practice.* Aldershot: Ashgate.

Bazemore, G. and Walgrave, L. (1999) 'Restorative Juvenile Justice: in Search of

Fundamentals and an Outline for Systemic Reform', in G. Bazemore and L. Walgrave (eds) *Restorative Juvenile Justice: Repairing the Harm of Youth Crime.* Monsey, NY: Willow Tree Press.

Braithwaite, J. (1999) 'Restorative Justice: Assessing Optimistic and Pessimistic Accounts', in M. Tonry (ed.) *Crime and Justice: An Annual Review of Research. Vol. 25.* Chicago, IL: University of Chicago Press.

Braithwaite, J. (2001) 'Principles of Restorative Justice.' Draft paper presented at the Toronto Symposium, May.

Daly, K. (2000) 'Revisiting the Relationship between Retributive and Restorative Justice', in H. Strang and J. Braithwaite (eds) *Restorative Justice: Philosophy to Practice.* Aldershot: Ashgate.

Dignan, J. (2001) 'Restorative Justice: Limiting Principles?' Paper presented at the Restorative Justice Seminar, Toronto, May.

Duff, R.A. (2001) 'Restoration and Retribution.' Paper presented at the Restorative Justice Seminar, Toronto, May.

McCold, P. (1999) 'Towards a Holistic Vision of Restorative Juvenile Justice: A Reply to Walgrave. Paper presented at the Third International Conference on Restorative Justice for Juveniles, Leuven.

Walgrave, L. (2001a) On Restoration and Punishment: Favourable Similarities and Fortunate Differences.' in G. Maxwell and A. Morris (eds) *Restoring Justice for Juveniles: Conferencing, Mediation, Circles.* Cambridge: Hart.

Walgrave, L. (2001b) 'Restoration and Punishment: Duet or Duel? In Search of Social Ethics for Restorative Justice.' Paper presented at the Toronto Symposium.

Wright, M. (1980) 'Can Mediation be an Alternative to Criminal Justice?' in J. Hudson and B. Galaway (eds) *Victims, Offenders, and Alternative Sanctions.* Lexington, MA: Heath.

Wright, M. (1996) *Justice for Victims and Offenders. A Restorative Response to Crime.* Winchester: Waterside Press.

Zehr, H. (1990) *Changing Lenses. A New Focus for Crime and Justice.* Scottdale, PA: Herald Press.

Chapter 3

Alternative conflict resolution and restorative justice: a discussion

Anne Lemonne

Introduction

The development of victim–offender mediation programmes has often been considered as a key element in the implementation of restorative justice, revealing what some authors have called a paradigm shift in the criminal justice system (Zher 1990; Messmer and Otto 1992; Galaway and Hudson 1996).

The idea of restorative justice emerged in the 1970s, in the increasing scepticism towards both retributive and rehabilitative models. Within this context, the theoretical arguments supporting the implementation of restorative justice programmes were very broad and included the devastating effect of the penal system on young offenders and the penal system's incapacity to handle an ever-increasing caseload. The arguments also included growing criticism of the judicial system for victimising the victims a second time, of the very limited role of the victim in the procedure and of the necessity to revive community participation in the handling of the (penal) conflicts. These arguments contributed to the promotion of new strategies of conflict resolution designed to be more beneficial to society as a whole by taking into account the needs of citizen (Messmer and Otto 1992; Snare 1995; Faget 1997).

In the European context, the *abolitionist* movement (led in particular by such Norwegian and Dutch criminologists as Christie, Hulsman, Bianchi and de Haan) provided the first theoretical framework for the promotion of alternative forms of dispute settlement, such as community boards and victim–offender mediation programmes (Bianchi and Van Swaaningen 1986).

In the 1990s the idea of restorative justice (based on such principles as reparation/reconciliation and the participation of the victim, offender and community in the process of conflict resolution – Galaway and Hudson 1996) progressively constituted the theoretical framework surrounding various initiatives implemented during the 1980s under various labels, operational philosophies, actors and levels of institutionalisation.

Victim–offender mediation programmes and family (or community) group conferencing are good examples of this kind of intervention. Additionally, some victim support programmes as well as community service orders can be considered as part of this movement towards restorative justice. Since then, various theoretical and ideological movements have been more or less associated with development of this model – for example, Braithwaite's theory of 'reintegrative shaming', feminist criminology, peace-making criminology, the victim movement, religious movements and so on. Braithwaite (1999), Marshall (1999), Crawford (2000), Walgrave (2000a), Weitekamp (2000) and Wright (2000) have compiled thorough reviews of this field and have discussed the slow emergence of the concept, the diversity of the roots that led to its development and the close relationship of restorative justice with other concepts or theories.

Evaluations of programmes in various European countries have often illustrated the gap between theoretical ambition and its practical implementation. For instance, restorative justice programmes have often been criticised for being implemented *unilaterally* (i.e. focusing only on the offender or on the victim), in the framework of the *previous aims* of the penal justice system (i.e. diversion, education and rehabilitation) and in an *authoritarian* way, without giving the conflict back to the people.

Moreover, victim–offender mediation programmes in particular, have been criticised for occupying a peripheral position within the field of criminal justice. Indeed, during the 1980s and at the beginning of the 1990s, the programmes implemented were usually small scale, targeting young first offenders who had committed petty crimes to divert them from the penal justice system. The minor influence these programmes had on the general functioning of the traditional system and their net-widening effects were often denounced. Indeed, such mediation programmes were regularly used in cases where penal prosecution would not have arisen.

The partial implementation of restorative justice in general, and of victim–offender mediation programmes in particular, has often been considered the result of a tension emerging from attempts to reconcile the programmes with the formal apparatus of penal justice. The decision to refer a case to mediation has regularly been made with little regard for the needs of the victims, the system being orientated towards the offender. Moreover, mediation programmes were often dependent on the criminal justice system for their funding and, hence, were inevitably subject to the goal of the traditional penal justice system. In this respect, it is important to stress that this gradual growth in implementation has given birth to different typologies of the restorative justice model. The one recently proposed by Wright (2000) – which distinguishes among unilateral, authoritarian and democratic versions of restorative justice – is one such example of this trend.

At the end of the 1990s, it seemed that restorative justice programmes were arousing renewed interest in western countries, and international recommendations were proffered in favour of the implementation of victim–offender mediation programmes at all stages of the penal procedure.[1] In the aftermath of this revival of interest, various governmental and non-governmental organisations have paid more attention to the extensive implementation of so-called 'restorative justice' programmes, to the point where restorative justice programmes have now been implemented at various stages of the penal justice procedure and for more serious cases – for example, at the community and police stage, before/after prosecution, after judgment, within the framework of detention and even, in the USA, in 'death row' (European Forum for Victim–Offender Mediation 2000; Umbreit and Vos 2000).

These developments are a clear witness to the various interests shown in the implementation of the restorative justice programmes. This diversity of interests explains, to some extent, the support given to these programmes in different countries, as well as their ambivalent nature (Snare 1995; Faget 1997; Braithwaite 1999; Crawford 2000). Hence, restorative justice has different meanings for the different actors involved (political and judicial actors, researchers, practitioners and society at large).[2]

In the Nordic countries, the *konfliktråd*[3] – where the victim and offender meet with a neutral mediator in the local environment – was implemented many years ago. Norway, for instance, has had a *konfliktråd* for twenty years now. In 1994, the Danish government also took the initiative to pilot a *konfliktråd*. In these two countries, the term 'restorative justice' is seldom used to refer to these programmes, the words 'mediation' or 'alternative conflict resolution' being preferred instead. It is to developments in criminal policy that have arisen in the light of some trends in the restorative justice movement that this chapter now turns.

Restorative justice: in search of a viable alternative to the traditional penal justice system

At the same time as governments have lent increasing support towards the implementation of new restorative justice programmes, researchers and practitioners have continued to reflect actively on the evolution of restorative justice, including its theoretical and practical reorientation as well as innovations in its development. In Europe, active collaboration and dialogue is maintained through the activities co-ordinated by the International Network for Research on Restorative Justice for Juveniles and the European Forum for Victim–Offender Mediation and Restorative Justice.

As discussed previously, the first restorative justice programmes – often victim–offender mediation programmes – tended to develop as 'diversionist' measures with respect to the penal justice system (Walgrave and Aertsen 1996). Examples of this kind are such programmes as community-based mediation and some diversion mediation programmes developed at the police stage or before prosecution. Within this framework, some adherents of the restorative justice approach continue to favour the development of voluntary settlements by all parties to a conflict and to limit as much as possible the state's intervention in the resolution of conflicts in order to retain the benefits of informal settlements. They recommend diverting as many cases as possible from the penal justice system and propose the development of programmes parallel to the traditional justice system (McCold 2000; Walgrave 1999, 2000a, 2000b).

However, at a theoretical level, the definition of restorative justice (as well as the most appropriate techniques, the actors and the procedures) is still being widely debated. According to Walgrave (2000a), these debates illustrate a tension between two fundamentally diverging trends that coexist within the restorative movement: the communitarian-diversionist model and the maximalist or fully fledged model.

In opposition to the diversionist model, a new trend has recently emerged within the restorative justice movement (Bazemore and Walgrave 1999; McCold 2000; Walgrave 1998, 1999, 2000a, 2000b). This trend questions the current core values of both the restorative and traditional justice systems and attempts to discover some of the essential principles that will allow the development of a fully fledged model (Walgrave 2000a). The adherents of this approach are concerned with the potential risks associated with diversionist techniques. They believe that such an approach will lead to a 'two-track system': victim–offender mediation programmes will be accepted on a large scale for minor offences or social conflict, whereas violent or more serious crimes will continue to be dealt with exclusively in the traditional system in a harsher and more punitive way – despite the fact that this is precisely the place where the *victims* are most in need of these programmes (Walgrave and Aertsen 1996; Walgrave 1999, 2000a). The development of a real alternative to the penal justice system (replacing rather than complementing the existing one over the long term) is the main concern of this model.

Adherents of the fully fledged model also believe that the handling of conflict through voluntary settlements between the victim (sometimes extended to the community) and the offender is not appropriate for all situations. Indeed, the value of mediation-orientated programmes is limited by the voluntary nature of these programmes, as well as by the ability of the parties concerned to arrive at an agreement. Hence, if one wants to develop a real alternative to the penal justice system, it is necessary to propose a model that takes into account all the cases that might need to be dealt with. When situations arise where the victim, offender and community cannot agree to a reparative solution to the problem, the state (reintroduced here as an actor in the process) should propose constructive solutions rather than react in a punitive manner, with the use of coercion if necessary. This should obviously be done with the guarantee of the due process of the law.

In order to facilitate the implementation of this alternative to the penal justice system, the adherents of this model have proposed other measures than mediation as means of achieving restorative justice (e.g. community service orders, the offender working for a victim compensation fund and so on). These measures could be used when a voluntary settlement could not be reached. They also argue for the necessity of reconsidering the role of society in this process (which is acknowledged as an actor potentially suffering harm as a result of an offence) and of the state's interventionist role (including coercion) in the restorative justice model.

As an example, Walgrave suggests that some offences are so serious they transcend their impact on local communities: 'Here, a coercive public intervention and sanction by the formal justice system may be considered necessary, possibly even on top of the settlement with the actual victims and the community' (2000a: 273). He goes on to suggest that the restorative justice aspect of the intervention in this example is not entirely lost – there is an opportunity to suggest voluntary restorative settlements, parallel to the judicial intervention. Further, the content of the imposed sanction could be restorative, and the prisons themselves could be reformed: 'If concerns for security necessitate it, the offender could be incapacitated through a forced stay in a closed facility, but restorative justice actions should be attempted from within the facility' (Walgrave 2000a: 273).

As shown by these examples, the adherents of this approach want to abandon the idea of a purely communitarian–diversionist model of restorative justice in favour of a fully-fledged, and maximalist model that would impact on the core of the penal justice system.[4]

As proposed by Walgrave (2000a), this change would necessitate opting for a definition of restorative justice more concerned with restorative *outcomes* (the restoration of the harm caused by the offender) than with the restorative *process* (whereby the parties to a particular offence try to deal collectively with the outcome of the offence). In this respect, it is worth noting that the adherents of maximalist restorative justice still believe that the process of conflict resolution by the parties involved should be prioritised because of its greater potential for restoration. However, they also believe that one important element of the restorative justice approach is its ability to counteract the negative effects of the traditional penal justice system on victims and offenders. Whether such strategies are appropriate will be discussed in more detail in the conclusion to this chapter.

While these trends form a lense through which one can situate the various positions within the restorative justice movement, it would be too simplistic to reduce restorative justice to these two trends alone. Nevertheless, they constitute important discourses in the restorative justice movement, as is illustrated by the position they have occupied in recent debates. They also provide a background against which we can investigate the implementation of alternative conflict resolution programmes in the Nordic countries. Hence the next section of this chapter focuses on the (victim–offender) mediation programme as implemented in Norway and Denmark. These two cases are of particular importance when discussing the notion of alternative conflict resolution – indeed, the two schemes have strong similarities as well as significant differences, a fact that illustrates well how programmes can take on different meanings when implemented in different contexts.

Mediation or alternative conflict resolution in Norway and Denmark

Norway: the development of an alternative to the penal justice system

In Norway, the first experimental mediation project was implemented in the municipality of Lier in 1981, as part of a broader project aimed at preventing juvenile offending. This pilot project, which was evaluated satisfactorily after two years, lead to the government proposal that Norwegian municipalities develop a *konfliktråd*. As this proposal resulted in only a few implementations, on 15 March 1991, Parliament passed an

Act to establish the mandatory nature of the *konfliktråd*. The programme (supervised by the civil division of the Ministry of Justice) was implemented gradually throughout the whole country during the period 1992–1994.

The philosophy behind the *konfliktråd* is closely associated with the ideas promoted by Nils Christie in his pioneer paper 'Conflict as Property' (1977), as well as in further contributions. Christie's work emphasises the need to find a valid alternative to the penal system, which is considered as stigmatising and too remote from the concerns of citizens. Moreover, Christie stresses that conflict should be placed back in the hands of the principal actors, who should then be allowed to resolve their own disputes. In this respect, participation is more important than outcome. He is thus less concerned with the determination of guilt than with solutions. Christie's basic idea is that people's inability to solve conflicts is a great loss for society as a whole: first for the victim through the anxiety generated by the crime; secondly, for the offender through the lack of an opportunity to repair; and, finally, for society in general because of the lack of opportunities to discuss standards, values and the law. For Christie, giving conflict back to the people is a means to revive and strengthen the local community.

The 1991 Act allows for a wide range of cases to be heard (mediation is possible in both civil and criminal cases) and mediation is accessible to the whole population. There is also no age limit with respect to the use of the programme. The public prosecuting authorities, the parties themselves and private institutions can all refer criminal cases to mediation. A mediator – a voluntary, paid person from the community – is then appointed to assist the parties in their negotiation but does not determine the content of the agreement. It is up to the parties themselves to solve the dispute (whether through compensation or not). Mediation is a voluntary process and the parties must meet in person. In criminal cases, the mediator approves the agreement and sends it to the public prosecutor, who then drops the charges (except in subsequent cases of serious breaches of the agreement). The 1991 Act has thus introduced the possibility of implementing a real alternative to the traditional penal system where the parties can solve the problem together with the help of an independent person from the local community.

In 1993, the Attorney General issued a circular in accordance with the 1991 Act that set out guidelines for prosecutors when referring cases to mediation. The guidelines state that cases should, in the main, be referred to mediation as an alternative to such sanctions as dismissal of criminal proceedings, fines or suspended sentences. In cases that qualify for immediate custody, mediation is not an alternative. Typical cases the

Attorney General recommended for mediation were theft, joy-riding and vandalism. Mediation was also recommended in some cases involving less serious violence, where the victim had not suffered severe injuries (Paus 2000). In limiting the number of cases for mediation, the possibility of developing a real alternative to the penal justice system was, hence, reduced considerably.

The Institute of Criminology in Oslo has carried out extensive research aimed at evaluating the implementation of the *konfliktråd* (Dullum 1996). This research has found that, despite the wide range of possibilities provided by the 1991 Act and the quite high number of cases dealt with in *konfliktråd* in one year (1995; 4,387 cases), the *konfliktråd* were mainly handling petty offences committed by (sometimes very) young offenders against adult victims, often in shops or at work. Indeed, of the cases dealt within a *konfliktråd* in 1995, only 6% were civil cases. For various reasons (such as the use of the *konfliktråd* for under the age of 15 who would not have been punished anyway and the use of mediation as an alternative to a waiver of prosecution), the *konfliktråd* has generated a net-widening effect. The tendency to use mediation as a means of deterring young offenders was seen by the researchers as a reflection of political and judicial interests. More recent literature has confirmed the overall trends identified in the earlier study (Kemeny 2000; Paus 2000).[5]

In 1999, a report submitted to the Minister of Justice proposed that mediation could be introduced as a voluntary option to court proceedings and to unconditional sentencing, particularly in cases of violence. The basic premise of such projects is that the negative impacts of judicial punishments can be avoided if opportunities are given to the offender to apologise, restore and atone for his or her wrongdoings. Such projects also go some way to fulfilling the victim's needs (Kemeny 2000). In introducing a proposal aimed at implementing mediation for more serious cases of violence as a voluntary option to prosecution in cases of unconditional sentencing, Norway has followed in the steps of other European countries. As is discussed below, such proposals go some way to meeting the philosophy of the Danish *konfliktråd*. Indeed, more than ten years after the first Norwegian experiment, the Danish government decided to introduce a *konfliktråd*. In Denmark, however, the introduction of these councils has never been considered as an alternative to the penal justice system.

Denmark: the development of mediation as a supplement to the penal justice system

Even though the possibility of developing a mediation initiative in Denmark had been discussed several times since the middle of the 1970s, it was only in 1994 that the *konfliktråd* was implemented. In Denmark, alternatives to imprisonment have been part of the debate about criminal policy since the middle of the 1970s and, in this context, the question concerning confrontation between victims and offenders was raised. However, despite earlier proposals, it was only through the framework of a large action plan introduced by the government under the name 'Bekæmpelse af vold' (voldspakke 1) that, among several initiatives aimed at combating violence, it was decided to introduce a pilot *konfliktråd* (Rentzmann and Reimann 1994; Raahave 1999). In the light of experiments carried out in other countries, the Danish government decided to conduct an experiment concerning the confrontation of violent young offenders with their victims. In contrast to other countries, however, it was decided to implement the measure as a preventative option to the traditional system of penal justice rather than as an alternative to it. The main reason for this was the mixed results obtained from similar experiments in other countries. As a tentative first step, the government established the *konfliktråd* as a pilot experiment in a few police districts. This experiment, which was supposed to be the first stage in the introduction of a permanent *konfliktråd*, was planned to run for a period of two years.

The aims were to give more responsibility to the young offenders and to prevent further violence. At the same time, the mediation process had the objective of allowing the victims to express their frustrations and fears and, consequently, of giving them an increased sense of security in their everyday lives.

In 1995–6, five *konfliktråd* were established in four police districts. Participation in a *konfliktråd* was voluntary for both the victim and the offender, and mediation was proposed as the method of confrontation. The meetings were regarded as a confidential, safe procedure, conducted competently and in an unbiased way by volunteering mediators. The responsibility for transferring cases to a mediator (when both victim and offender had agreed to receive more information about the *konfliktråd*) was given to the police. However, other institutions (such as the SSP – local school social welfare provision – police teams, employees in the prison service, leaders of youth schools), as well as the victims and offenders themselves, were also offered the possibility of referring cases to a *konfliktråd*. During that period, the experiment focused on juvenile offenders from 15 to 18/20 years old and their victims. The offender had to be a first-time offender or someone who had been punished previously but without having had a serious charge brought against him or her. In order to participate in a *konfliktråd*, the offender had to plead guilty and, in accordance with the governmental plan, could only be charged with one of the criminal acts as defined in Straffelovens S. 244 (i.e. less serious violent crimes) (Det Kriminælpræventive Råd 1996).

However, some conditions were rapidly revised. Older offenders (up to 21 years) were included, as well as young people with a criminal record – but only if a thorough evaluation of their case indicated they were suitable for mediation. The possibility of including other kinds of criminal acts in the experiment was also highlighted, as long as this would have an impact on the victim or offender. This broadening was, essentially, done in order to guarantee a sufficient number of cases for the pilot experiment.

The evaluation report (Det Kriminælpræventive Råd 1996) stressed that, after a few months of implementation and despite the widening of the criteria for eligibility, only a few cases were mediated within the *konfliktråd*. Indeed, only four mediations had been settled at the end of the second year. In particular, the report stressed that the implementation of the *konfliktråd* involved new working techniques and new ways of viewing criminal acts and their victims – inherent problems in the proper selection of cases that rendered its implementation difficult.

In May 1997, on the basis of the limited pilot experiment, the Danish Parliament (Folketinget) proposed a new, larger experiment as a pre-requisite for any further and permanent implementation of the *konfliktråd*. This second experiment was conceived as a three-year project to take place from 1997 to 2000. In September 1999, the Minister of Justice extended the experiment for another two years (i.e. until June 2002). The framework of the second experiment aims to reinforce the legal standing of victims of crime (Lov no. 349, 23 May 1997).

In this new experiment, there is no upper age limit for the offender (who has, however, to be at least 15 years old); the experiment now includes all forms of criminality that are suitable for mediation; and no residence criteria are required to participate in a *konfliktråd*. Moreover, confrontation within a *konfliktråd* is still an adjunct to the usual legal procedures, even though it is explicitly stated that, after a thorough evaluation of the case, the court may now decide to take into account involvement with a *konfliktråd* when determining the sentence (Det Kriminælpræventive Råd 1997).

In many respects, the new experiment confirms some of the tendencies that were already present in the first pilot experiment. For instance, the aim of the councils is still to be a forum for dialogue between the victim and offender, providing solutions to the victim's frustrations and anxieties. It will, at the same time, give the offender a greater sense of responsibility and (as a desired outcome) should discourage any further criminality. Other things the new experiment has in common with the old one are the possibility for an offender to participate in a *konfliktråd* even if he or she has previously been punished and the offender is still free to refuse the mediation process but, if he or she accepts it, he or she has to plead guilty. Again, it is still the police who transfer the cases to a mediator when both the victim and offender have agreed, and other institutions (as mentioned earlier) as well as the victims and offenders themselves, can formally suggest cases. The project is currently being implemented in three neighbouring police districts.

While the first pilot experiment was difficult to evaluate because of a lack of cases, the second experiment has involved a much larger number. A recent evaluation of the second experiment shows that the number of cases dealt within a *konfliktråd* since the beginning of the project has now risen to 75 (this had risen to over 100 cases by the summer of 2001). This evaluation has also demonstrated that, despite the progressive widening of the criteria for selection, the offender population subject to mediation in the *konfliktråd* is still 'young' and the cases handled remain primarily cases of violence (the majority being for assault). Despite the possibility of the community bringing its own cases to a *konfliktråd*, the police are still the principal referring body. Several factors have been identified that contribute to the difficulties in increasing the caseload. For example, it has been shown that the police do not transfer all cases that are suitable for mediation, and the offender and victim are not always willing to participate in the process.[6] These factors constitute the key problems many countries face when attempting to establish victim–offender programmes. Possibly they reflect the habitus[7] of the various actors involved in the implementation of the new measure (from government officials to the parties themselves), who are still geared towards the formal legal process and its outcomes – including the important issue of the legal guarantees provided by the state.

The evaluation has also given some indication of the reasons why some parties refuse to participate in a *konfliktråd*. The victims usually refuse because the process will take up too much time and/or because they consider that the 'usual' procedure is sufficient. Sometimes they are afraid to meet the offender, particualrly if they have had a prior relationship with him or her. From the offender's point of view, the main reasons for not participating are that they feel guilty, they find the procedure too formal or they do not believe in the benefits of mediation.

Interestingly, the evaluation has also shown that the satisfaction rate of the parties after participation in a *konfliktråd* is high. Some 90% of participants in a *konfliktråd* considered their involvement as being success-ful, and the supplementary nature of the procedure (as compared to the traditional penal system) moderated the decisions taken by some courts. Instances of courts dealing leniently with those who had participated in a *konfliktråd* should, nevertheless, not be generalised – indeed, such instances were very rare (Henriksen 1999, 2000; Rasmussen pers. comm.

2000). According to the evaluation, there are reasons for believing that the mediators handled the cases with neutrality, and that the parties voluntarily/freely discussed the issues they considered at stake in their conflict. The parties' own evaluations, as well as those supplied by the project leader, ratify this conclusion. Nevertheless, it is important to stress that no systematic analysis of the working practices, of the professional ideologies of the mediators or of the outcomes of the mediation process is currently available. The restorative nature of the process should therefore be investigated further before any final conclusion can be drawn.

Alternative conflict resolution programmes in the Nordic countries and the concept of restorative justice

The development of the Norwegian and Danish *konfliktråd* increased the participation of all parties in the process of solving conflicts while, at the same time, suggesting constructive solutions as to their settlement. The participation of all parties in the process of conflict resolution leading to a constructive/reparative solution is evident in both programmes. Indeed, a voluntary mediation process (where the parties can discuss together the outcomes of an offence and find a mutually suitable agreement with the help of a lay mediator from the community) has evidently been introduced.

Viewed narrowly, this model is a radical break with the aims and processes of traditional penal justice systems and can thus be considered an *alternative* model of conflict resolution. In both countries, the great satisfaction of all the parties participating in such a scheme is a witness to the potential of these programmes. This satisfaction should not be neglected in any evaluation of the implementation of such processes (Henriksen 2000; Rasmussen pers. comm. 2000; Paus 2000). In this respect, the implementation of the Danish and Norwegian *konfliktråd* is different from many other official experiments in Europe, where the mediation process is conducted by professionals who are closely related to the penal justice system and who do not always allow for a real meeting between the parties (Wright 2000).

However, when viewed in the larger context, the implementation of these programmes has not produced the expected paradigm shift. In Norway, the *konfliktråd*, (despite the wide-ranging possibilities on offer) has essentially been considered as a means of diverting cases that would not have been dealt with by the penal justice system. This programme not only leaves intact the main core of the penal justice system but one could also say that, in some respects, it complements it. In Denmark, the small number of cases dealt with (as well as the supplementary nature of the new measure) leads to the same conclusion. Thus, in introducing a victim–offender programme as an *adjunct* to the traditional penal justice system, the penal justice process (considered as a whole) still leads one to define crime as a conflict with the state, leading, therefore, to the imposition of a 'traditional' sentence by a judge. In the Danish programme, as opposed to the situation found in other countries, there seems to have been no intention to introduce a procedure that would have an impact on sentencing.[8]

Consequently, it is reasonable to conclude that the introduction of the Danish *konfliktråd* (which links the mediation programme to the traditional justice system) serves to complement the principles under-pinning the traditional system. This is especially true of the cases most frequently taken to *konfliktråd* (i.e. those involving minor violence) which, over the past ten years, have been dealt with more severely (Balvig 2000). In this regard, it would seem that the victim–offender mediation programme introduced in Denmark speaks eloquently of the need to integrate the restorative justice programme more fully into the broader criminal policy context.

This analysis of the concepts of mediation and alternative conflict resolution in these two countries has demonstrated their multifaceted nature.

In Norway (through the promotion of reparative measures and the settlement of conflicts by the parties themselves), alternative conflict resolution corresponds to the communitarian–diversionist position in the restorative justice movement. Accordingly, it is interesting to note that the Norwegian programme displays precisely these unintended effects denounced by adherents of the maximalist model of restorative justice. The use of such a programme has been accepted for petty (penal) cases and it has created a net-widening effect, without impinging on the main core of the penal justice system. The latter continues to deal with crime through the still-dominant retributive/rehabilitative model. Hence, while these programmes contradict the traditional justice system they do not compete with it.

The Danish model (which links the mediation programme to the traditional justice system) cannot be located easily along the communi-tarian–diversionist versus fully fledged/maximalist continuum. In this instance the community-based settlement does not constitute a means of diversion but, instead, is an explicit complement to the traditional system. This programme never really aimed to contradict and/or to compete with the penal justice system. Indeed, it seems that, in Denmark, the notion of restorative justice is still far from constituting a coherent framework for reform of the penal justice system. The term 'restorative justice' is never used in political discourse, and the programme does not have any associations with institutions that should be conducive to the philosophy of restorative justice (Justitsministeriet 2000). Currently, it seems that a more pragmatic and less structured ideology is emerging in Denmark – as in other European countries (Mary 2001). After a period of debate concerning less emphasis on punishment, less severe sentencing, the liberalisation of correction and a search for alternatives to imprisonment (Vestergaard 1991; Greve 1999; Balvig 2000), the public debate about violence resulted in the implementation of the *konfliktråd* and of several other initiatives – such as the fast handling of violent cases by the courts, treatment experiments for violent behaviour, youth contracts, efforts to get rid of street gangs and rapid interventions to deal with children and juveniles (including placements in secured units and the implementation of long-term courses of treatment) (Ekspertgruppen om ungdoms-kriminalitet 2001). An optimistic view would be that the *konfliktråd* has the potential to evolve into a form that could ultimately replace, or at least circumvent, the traditional penal system. Indeed, the final official decision to adopt this programme on a permanent basis has still to be taken. However, it is worth emphasising that should it be adopted on a permanent basis, broader changes in criminal policy would also be necessary. Consequently, it is only through the development of a restorative philosophy that less punitive trends would emerge in criminal justice – traditionally favoured in the Nordic countries.

Conclusion

This chapter has suggested the necessity to develop a fully-fledged or maximalist model of restorative justice that can have an impact on the core of the penal justice system. It has been argued that it is through such developments that a wider range of 'constructive' alternatives to punitive methods can be achieved and, hence, that a real alternative to the current penal justice system could be created. However, this argument is not without its caveats. The success of a restorative justice stance is closely related to the fact that victim-offender programmes should not be implemented simply as 'techniques' at various stages of the criminal justice system or without questioning the system they complement. However, this is, in fact, the trend in many countries (partly as a result of international recommendations) and as has been argued in the light of the Norwegian and Danish experiments, the introduction of mediation programmes reinforces and/or legitimises the current penal system.

In contrast, the action research projects introduced in some countries have a greater chance of succeeding in modifying the penal justice system because they are founded on theoretical principles that help keep them on the right track. However, it is generally well established that the penal justice system is extremely resistant to changes – new developments are often transformed to fit in with pre-existing measures (Mathiesen 1974).

Restorative justice measures should also be viewed within the wider penal and social policy area. For European criminologists, the most striking example of this need is perhaps the implementation of restorative programmes on death row in the USA. Indeed, as has been argued:

> If the state is truly interested in promoting restorative justice between killers and the families of their victims – as we think it should be – the first step it needs to take is to abolish the death penalty and stop promoting the false belief that capital punishment is an effective way to foster the healing of families of homicide victims. By its very nature, the death penalty is not about forgiveness … , finding common ground or reconciliation. Instead it embraces the polar opposites: retribution, hatred and denial of the offender's humanity. (Radelet and Borg 2000: 88–90)

Similar questions can be raised in Europe concerning the implementation of restorative justice in prisons. Indeed, it is necessary to evaluate the restorative justice philosophy in relation to wider punitive developments because this philosophy cannot be understood in an often dualistic and ambivalent criminal justice system (Crawford 2000). With an increasing tendency to use imprisonment and to criminalise social problems (Wacquant 1999),[9] one could argue that the implementation of this alternative system has to be done, first of all, in parallel with *depenalisation* (a widening of the range of non-imprisonable offences) and *decriminalisation* (a narrowing of the scope of criminal law – providing civil solutions rather than criminal outcomes) policies. 'As few prisoners as possible' would be an expression of this minimalist position (Christie 2001). Since the implementation of such policies at the core of the penal justice system is considered by some as 'the finishing touch' of a restorative policy (Peters *et al.* pers. comm. 2000), it is important to evaluate critically the implementation of restorative justice programmes at all stages of the criminal justice system in relation to both normative and managerialist claims (Crawford 2000).

The introduction of other forms of restorative measures/sanctions, proposed by adherents of the fully fledged or maximalist model, to compensate for the difficulties associated with the communitarian-diversionist model – despite repairing in all cases the harm caused by crime – raises problems inherent in the use of such notions such as 'victims' and 'offenders' and in the unwavering focus on the 'crime', and on the 'harm done'. In this respect, one should be careful not to replicate the inequities of the current penal justice system, even if the underlining philosophy is more reparative than punitive. As mentioned by Braithwaite and Parker (1999), restorative justice proponents 'sometimes fail to recognise the societal context of domination and structural inequality affecting victims and offenders'. It would be difficult to require an offender to restore the harm caused by his or her offence without, at the same time, addressing the victimisation that arises as a result of socio-economical inequalities.

Moreover, such factors as voluntariness or the suitability of cases for mediation can lead to discrimination because 'the offenders, who exist at the periphery or are most marginalised by the dominant moral community are less likely to have a stake in restorative justice processes' (Crawford 2000: 300) – and, therefore, to participate in voluntary mediation. Those less integrated into society could be subjected to enforced reparation – something that would reduce the value of restoration and that could easily be perceived as a punishment by the victims, offenders and the community.[10]

It is hence the contention here that particular attention should be paid to both the *quality* of the process *and* to the *definition of the values* underlying restorative justice practices. As noted by Boyes-Watson (2000), the quality of the process should mean that the issue of responsibility – and, in particular, our conception of individual guilt and the responsibility associated with the traditional system of law – should be understood both individually and collectively. The definition of the values underlying restorative justice should clarify the relationship between restorative justice, punitive trends and the structural causes of crime. Hence Braithwaite's suggestion (2000, 2001) that we should evaluate restorative justice programmes in the light of differing concepts about human rights should be considered further. As Braithwaite notes, particular attention should be paid by advocates of restorative justice to the Universal Declaration of Human Rights (especially art. 5: – 'no one shall be subjected to torture or to cruel, inhuman or degrading treatment or punishment'); to the International Covenants on Economic, Social and Cultural Rights; to the International Covenant on Civil and Political Rights and its second protocol; and so on.

We could conclude by arguing that, if the concept of alternative conflict resolution as implemented in the Nordic countries has its limitations, at the same time it clearly promotes the concept 'alternative'. It is only through the use of this concept that restorative justice can be of some value in the development of a less punitive and more constructive policy that is orientated towards victims, the community *and* offenders.

Acknowledgements

I would like to express my gratitude to Annika Snare for her support in the writing of this chapter. Additional thanks go to Dagmar Rasmussen and Lode Walgrave for valuable comments and suggestions in response to an earlier version of this Chapter. I am also grateful to the European Commission (Marie Curie Fellowship HPMF-CT-1999-00325) and to the University of Copenhagen for their financial support.

Notes

1. Umbreit and Vos (2000) report that there are at least 1,200 known programmes in North America and Europe. In addition, according to the general principles of the recommendation of the Council of Europe on mediation in penal matters, mediation should be a widely available service at all stages of the criminal justice process (Council of Europe 1999).
2. Examples include a willingness to reduce costs, to accelerate the penal justice system, to reduce the amount of imprisonment, to permit a response to criminality that the current criminal justice system cannot handle, to decrease the rate of recidivism, to improve the quality of life in general, to answer the needs of victims and so on.
3. Often translated as 'council of conflict' or 'mediation board'.
4. The idea of attacking the core of the penal justice system might seem more discursive than practical. However, recently some workers devised a research programme in order to investigate the principles of restorative justice as applied to the core of the penal justice system. The Belgians' projects 'Restorative Justice in Prison' and 'Mediation for Redress' are good examples of this (Walgrave and Aertsen 1996; Aertsen and Peters 1998; Aersten 2000; Peters *et al.* 1998, pers. comm. 2000).
5. In 1998, the mediation services dealt with 6,433 cases: 3,345 civil and 3,039 criminal. However, the police referred 65% of the civil cases, which mostly concerned offences in which the offender was below the age of 15. The main group of offenders comprised young boys between 15 and 17 years, the second largest group being 12–14-years-old. Private persons and firms were the 'victims'. The offences were still dominated by damage to property and shoplifting (Paus, 2000). The overall picture was thus similar to that of 1996, despite the participation of society in general and of mediation being used in more serious cases.

6. It seems the main difficulty in getting more cases can be attributed to the police, who do not always offer mediation to the offender and victim in cases 'technically' suitable for mediation (i.e. when the offender has pleaded guilty). Moreover, it could also be argued that the selection of cases suitable for mediation is also limited by the criteria imposed by the traditional penal justice system (i.e. when offenders have pleaded guilty).

7. The habitus is a system of durable dispositions acquired by an individual through the process of socialisation. These dispositions include the individual's attitudes and inclinations to perceive, feel, do and think which have been acquired by the individual during the course of his or her life. Together, these dispositions work as an unconscious principle that guides an individual's action, perception and reflexion (Bourdieu 1994).

8. As, for example, in the project, 'Mediation for Redress' (developed in Belgium) where, in the long run, the researchers aim to reorientate the traditional penal justice system (which is essentially punishment focused) to a more restorative philosophy (Walgrave and Aertsen 1996; Aertsen and Peters 1998; Aertsen 2000). These workers maintain that mediation is not only a possibility for dialogue between the offender and victim – 'horizontal communication' – but also that it constitutes an opportunity for communication between the judging magistrate and the parties – 'vertical communication'. For example, in this programme, the parties are asked to propose (in a written agreement) their position concerning a future sentence. In this respect this project aims to 'transcend the exclusively inter-individual level of the mediation and puts it in a social context' in giving the victim, offender and their relatives the chance to reflect on 'what is socially acceptable and unacceptable', taking their conflict as a starting point. The parties should feel that 'they play an active and constructive role in the criminal justice decision-making process', and 'pursuit of this vertical dialogue means that the citizens actively express their own, maybe deviant, norms and values and that the judge uses this as a test for the general rule'. It seems that no systematic research on the effects of mediation for redress in judiciary decision-making has been done until now. However, the proponents of this research have suggested that a 'Follow-up study of some samples points to a mitigating effect on the sentence when an agreement between victim and offender has been reached' (Aersten 2000).

9. There has been a rapid and continuing increase in incarceration rates in all member countries of the European Union during the last decade. During the period 1983–97, this increase was 6% in Denmark, 18% in Sweden, 28% in Belgium, 39% in France and 43% in England and Wales (*Statistiques penales annuelles du Conseil de l'Europe, Enquête* 1997). This increase is, however, less apparent than in the US. In the majority of European countries, and contrary to trend in the USA, the increase in the inmate population is due to the lengthening of detention terms rather than to an increase in the number of prison sentences. In France, from 1975 until the present, the unemployment rate has been parallel to detention rates. Changes in the economy in general – massive unemployment, increasing poverty and so on – correspond, therefore to changes in incarceration rates (Wacquant 1999: 96–7).

10. For a discussion of the concept of punishment and the community service order, see Walgrave (1999).

References

Aertsen, I. (2000) 'Victim–Offender in Belgium', in the European Forum for Victim–Offender Mediation and Restorative Justice (ed.) *Victim–Offender Mediation On Europe. Making Restorative Justice Work.* Leuven: Leuven University Press.

Aertsen, I. and Peters, T. (1998) 'Mediation for Reparation: the Victim's Perspective', *European Journal of Crime, Criminal Law and Criminal Justice*, 4(2): 106–24.

Balvig, F. (2000) *Det Voldsomme Samfund. Om vold som problem og fængsel som løsning. Fortid og nutid.* København: Jurist- og Økonomforbundets Forlag.

Bazemore, G. and Walgrave, L. (1999) 'Restorative Justice: in Search of Fundamentals and an Outline for Systemic Reform', in G. Bazemore and L. Walgrave (eds) *Restorative Juvenile Justice: Repairing the Harm of Youth Crime.* Monsey, NY: Criminal Justice Press.

Bianchi, H. and Van Swaaningen, R. (eds) (1986) *Abolitionism. Towards a Non-Repressive Approach to Crime.* Amsterdam: Free University Press.

Bourdieu, P. (1994) *Raisons pratiques. Sur la Théorie de l'action.* Paris: Editions du Seuil.

Boyes-Watson, C. (2000) 'Reflections on the Purist and Maximalists Models of Restorative Justice', *Contemporary Justice Review*, 3(4): 441-50.

Braithwaite, J. (1999) 'Restorative Justice: Assessing Optimistic and Pessimistic Accounts', in M. Tonry (ed.) *Crime and Justice. A Review of Research. Volume 25.* Chicago, IL: University of Chicago Press.

Braithwaite, J. (2000) 'Decomposing a Holistic Vision of Restorative Justice', *Contemporary Justice Review,* 3(4), 433–40.

Braithwaite, J. (2001) *Restorative Justice and Responsive Regulation.* Oxford: Oxford University Press.

Braithwaite, J. and Parker, C. (1999) 'Restorative Justice is Republican Justice', in G. Bazemore and L. Walgrave, (eds) *Restorative Juvenile Justice: Repairing the Harm of Youth Crime.* Monsey, NY: Criminal Justice Press.

Council of Europe (1999) *Recommendation no. R (99): 19 of the Committee of Ministers to Member States Concerning Mediation in Penal Matters.* Strasbourg.

Christie, N. (1977) 'Conflict as Property', *The British Journal of Criminology*, 17(1): 1–5.17.

Christie, N. (2001) *Crime Control as Industry.* London: Routledge.

Committee of Experts on Mediation in Penal Matters (1999) *Recommendation Concerning Mediation in Penal Matters.* CDPC (99). Strasbourg: Council of Europe, 15 September.

Crawford, A. (2000) 'Salient Themes towards a Victim Perspective and the Limitations of Restorative Justice: some Concluding Comments', in A.

Crawford and J. Goodey (eds) *Integrating a Victim Perspective within Criminal Justice*. Aldershot: Ashgate.

Det Kriminælpræventive Råd (1996) *To-årigt forsøg med konfliktråd*. København.

Det Kriminælpræventive Råd (1997) *Konfliktråd i Danmark. Design af en forsøgsordning 1997–2000*. København.

Dullum, J. (1996) 'The Norwegian Mediation Boards', *European Journal of Criminal Policy and Research*, 4(4): 86–94.

European Forum for Victim–Offender Mediation and Restorative Justice (ed.) (2000) *Victim–Offender Mediation in Europe. Making Restorative Justice Work*. Leuven: Leuven University Press.

Ekspertgruppen om ungdomskriminalitet (2001) *Rapport om ungdomskriminalitet*. København: Rigspolitiets Trykkeri.

Faget, J. (1997) *La Médiation. Essai de Politique pénale*. Ramonville Saint-Agne: Eres.

Galaway, B. and Hudson, J. (eds) (1996) *Restorative Justice: International Perspectives*. Amsterdam: Kugler.

Greve, V. (1999) 'Criminal Law in the 21st Century', in P. Blume (ed.) *Legal Issues at the Dawn of the New Millenium*. Københaven: DJØF Publishing.

Henriksen, C. (1999) *Arbejdsnotat. Evaluering a konfliktråd*. København: Samfundsanalyse.

Henriksen, C. (2000) *Midtvejesevaluering af Konfliktråd i Danmark*. København: Center for Alternative Samfundsanalyse.

Justitsministeriet Lovafdelingen (2000) Speech delivered at the conference on Victim–Offender Mediation, Tampere, 26–27 October.

Kemeny, S. (2000) 'Policy Developments and the Concept of Restorative Justice through Mediation', in the European Forum for Victim–Offender Mediation and Restorative Justice (ed.) *Victim–Offender Mediation in Europe. Making Restorative Justice Work*. Leuven: Leuven University Press.

Marshall, T. (1999) *Restorative Justice: An Overview*. London: Home Office Research Development and Statistics Directorate.

Mary, P. (2001) 'Pénalité et Gestion des Risques: vers une Justice *actuarielle* en Europe ?', *Déviance et Société*, 25(1): 33–51.

Mathiesen, T. (1974) 'The Politics of Abolition', *Scandinavian Studies of Criminology*, 4.

McCold, P. (2000) 'Toward a Holistic Vision of Restorative Juvenile Justice: A Reply to the Maximalist Model', *Contemporary Justice Review*, 3(4): 357–414

Messmer, H. and Otto, H. (eds) (1992) *Restorative Justice on Trial*. 'Dordrecht: Kluwer Academic.

Paus, K. (2000) 'Victim–Offender Mediation in Norway', in the European Forum for Victim–Offender Mediation and Restorative Justice (ed.) *Victim–Offender Mediation in Europe. Making Restorative Justice Work*. Leuven: Leuven University Press.

Peters, T., Snacken, S., Kellens, G. De Coninck, G. De Jaegher, K., Lauwaert, K., Maes, E. Stassart, E. Tubex, H. and Verhoeven, J. (1998) *Fondements pour une politique judiciaire et cohérente axée sur la réparation et sur la victime*. Leuven: Services Fédéraux chargés des Affaires Scientifiques, Techniques et Culturelles.

Raahave, D. (1999) *En komparativ analyse af den norske og danske konfliktrådsmodel.* *Speciale.* København: Det Juridiske Fakultet.

Radelet, M. and Borg, M. (2000) 'Comment on Umbreit and Vos. Restributive versus Restorative Justice', *Homicide Studies*, 4(4): 88–92.

Rentzmann, W. and Reimann, J. (1994) *Samfundstjeneste og ungdomskontrakter- og andre samfundssanktioner og foranstaltninger.* København: Jurist- og Økonomforbundets Forlag.

Snare, A. (1995) 'Hvorfor *konfliktrådsbehandling*?', in F. Balvig and A. Snare (eds) *Kriminalistisk Institut. Årbog 1994.* Københavns Universitet.

Umbreit, M. and Vos, B. (2000) 'Homicide Survivors Meet the Offender Prior to Execution. Restorative Justice through Dialogue'. *Homicide Studies*, 4(1): 63-87.

Vestergaard, J. (1990) 'Konfliktråd I graffiti-sager, hvori DSB er den skadelidte part', in *Kriminalistisk Instituts stencilserie.* Volume 56. København: Københavns Universitet.

Vestergaard, J. (1991) 'Juvenile Contract in Denmark: Paternalism Revisited', *Scandinavian Studies in Criminology Youth, Crime and Justice*, 12: 73–97.

Wacquant, L. (1999) *Les Prisons de la Misère*. Paris: Editions Raison d'agir.

Walgrave, L. (1998) 'What is at Stake in Restorative Justice for Juveniles?', in L.Walgrave (ed.) *Restorative Justice for Juveniles: Potentialities, Risks and Problems.* Leuven: Leuven University Press.

Walgrave, L. (1999) 'Community Service as a Cornerstone of a Systemic Restorative Response to (Juvenile) Crime', in G. Bazemore and L. Walgrave (eds) *Restorative Juvenile Justice: Repairing the Harm of Youth Crime.* Monsey, NY: Criminal Justice Press.

Walgrave, L. (2000a), 'Extending the Victim Perspective towards a Systemic Restorative Justice Alternative', in A. Crawford and J. Goodey (eds) *Integrating a Victim Perspective within Criminal Justice.* Aldershot: Ashgate.

Walgrave, L. (2000b) 'How Pure can a Maximalist Approach to Restorative Justice Remain? Or can a Purist Model of Restorative Justice become Maximalist?´, *Contemporary Justice Review,* 3(4): 415–32.

Walgrave, L. and Aertsen, I. (1996) 'Reintegrative Shaming and Restorative Justice', *European Journal on Criminal Policy and Research*, 4(4): 67–85.

Weitekamp, E. (2000) 'Research on Victim–Offender Mediation. Findings and Needs for the Future', in the European Forum for Victim-Offender Mediation and Restorative Justice (ed.) *Victim–Offender Mediation in Europe. Making Restorative Justice Work.* Leuven: Leuven University Press.

Wright, M. (2000) 'Restorative Justice: for whose Benefit?', in the European Forum for Victim–Offender Mediation and Restorative Justice (ed.) *Victim–Offender Mediation in Europe. Making Restorative Justice Work.* Leuven: Leuven University Press.

Zehr, H. (1990) *Changing Lenses.* Scottdale, PA: Herald Press.

Part II

Evaluating aspects of restorative practices

Chapter 4

A survey of assessment research on mediation and conferencing

Paul McCold

This chapter briefly overviews 30 years of evaluation research of restorative justice programmes[1] from 1971–2001 to see what evidence we can bring to bear on the probable truth or falsity of restorative justice as a credible response to crime and conflicts in society. The large volume of assessment research of restorative justice programmes makes it difficult to present the breadth of the research while still providing a useful overview in a single chapter. Therefore, I endeavour to follow the advice of Albert Einstein, who said 'make things as simple as possible, but no simpler.'

> Nothing can be 'proved' scientifically – experimental methods of inquiry are not methods of proof. Research methodology provides controlled methods to bring objective evidence to bear on the probable truth or falsity of relational propositions (Kerlinger 1973:1 55–156).

Public policy responses to crime should not be based upon the enthusiasm or popularity of programme advocates. The history of criminal justice reform efforts warrants healthy scepticism of enthusiasm (e.g. DARE in the USA). If a justice programme is effective, it should be possible to measure these effects. If programme advocates cannot objectively demonstrate the merits of a programme using sound empirical measures, they, too, deserve a large measure of scepticism. Confidence in a given programme's *effectiveness* becomes possible only when positive results are documented. Confidence in that programme's *model* is justified only after positive results have been replicated by independent evaluations.

What constitutes success? Comparisons of any new approach, such as restorative justice, must be measured against existing practice. While this may seem obvious, there is a tendency to compare new programmes to perfection and to criticise them when they fail to reach the ideal. To succeed, restorative justice does not need to be perfect. To be preferred, it need only demonstrate superiority, on average, to traditional adjudicatory approaches:

> [T]here are too many cases there to begin with that end up in dismissals and fines that are impossible to collect and they should be diverted in the very first place ... If you can somehow relay ... the cost of processing cases that end up going nowhere to no satisfactory result to any of the participants in the system, then you can show that mediation is not only worthwhile but absolutely necessary (MacWillie 1981: 34–5).

First, we consider what the data say about public satisfaction with the current justice approach to crime and compare this to public attitudes towards restorative approaches to crime. We will then consider the restorative justice programme assessment research.

Public and restorative justice

The USA has the largest, most expensive criminal justice system in the world. In spite of huge government spending on a variety of programmes and approaches, the American public remains an unsatisfied customer. In a randomly selected national sample of adults conducted in 2000, a Gallup Poll found only 24% of the American public expressed confidence in the criminal justice system (Gallup Organisation, Inc. 2000).

In 1998, Schulman, Ronca and Bucuvalas, Inc. (1999) surveyed a randomly selected sample of 4,015 adults in the nine northeastern states of the USA. Respondents were asked:

> A number of States are considering significant changes in the way the criminal justice system works. Without knowing any specific details, do you like the idea of totally revamping the way the system works, or do you feel the present system works well enough the way it is?

As shown in Figure 4.1, 75% favour revamping the system and only 16% felt the criminal justice system works well enough as it is. These rates were remarkably consistent across all nine states. Among the 224 crime victims whose offenders were caught – derived from the larger sample – less than half (48%) expressed satisfaction with the outcome of their case, and only 37% felt the prosecutor had taken their opinion into consideration.

In another question, respondents were asked:

In some communities, the victim has the opportunity, if he or she wants, to talk to the offender about why the offender committed the crime and whether the offender accepts the consequences of what he or she did. How important do you think it is to offer this kind of service to victims?

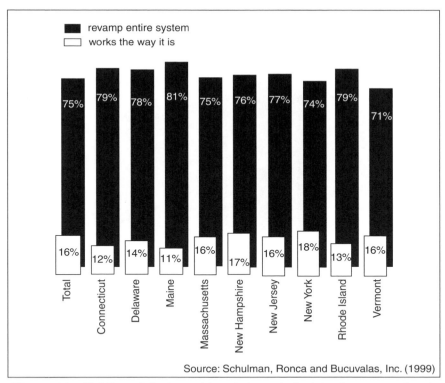

Figure 4.1. Public satisfaction with existing criminal justice system in nine northeastern states, USA.

As shown in Figure 4.2, both the public and crime victims across all nine states expressed high support for the idea of victim–offender encounters. This widespread public support for restorative approaches to crime has been replicated in surveys conducted in New Zealand, Great Britain and Germany.

From two random samples of 1,200 persons in New Zealand, Galaway (1984) concluded that the public would accept a reduction in imprisonment if it were offset by an increase in requiring offenders to make restitution to their victims. Based upon two national British Crime Surveys, Wright (1989) concluded that many members of the public, including victims, are ready to shift the whole basis of the public debate about criminal justice from whether to use harsh or lenient punishments,

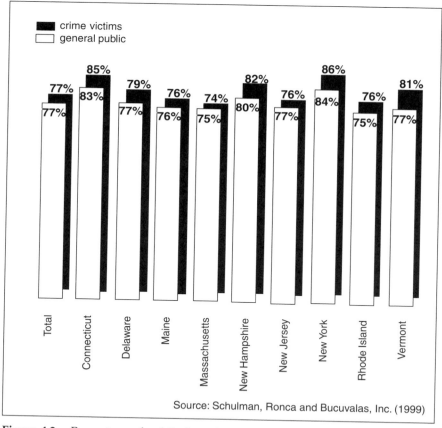

Figure 4.2. Percentage of public for voluntary victim-offender meetings in nine US northeastern states.

to the use of reparative sanctions instead of punishment. Walker and Hough (1988: 6) further concluded from these surveys that it is a myth that the public demands tough punishment: 'a majority thinks that restorative sanctions ...make more sense than retributive ones.' In his survey of the German public, Sessar (1999) concluded that the public at large displays an intrinsic acceptance of private conflict-solving following an offence and he also concluded that the concept of the public's strong punitive sentiments is a myth. In a survey of 2,177 randomly selected members of the public in Minnesota, Bae (1992) found strong public support for restitution as an alternative to incarceration for property offenders, and he too found that crime victims were less punitive than non-victims. Hudson and Galaway (1974) also found that crime victims who were aware that their involvement could lead to shortened or non-prison sentences were willing to accept this:

> Most important is the significance that has been attached to restitution by the public – and the victims! – when it comes to dealing with offenders. The impression is that whenever restitution is given precedence over punishment, it should be tried and applied before other instruments come into question; it is not or only rarely an additional sanction. This implies that in many instances, restitution substitutes not only for criminal sanctions but also for criminal procedures (Sessar 1999: 301).

In his recent overview of the research on restorative justice, Weitekamp (2000) could find no evidence that the public or crime victims are very retributive. He concludes: 'the acceptance for victim–offender mediation and restorative justice is high in most societies and should be no reason to hamper the spread of these ideas and [the] implementation [of] more programmes' (2000: 105). Public support for restorative approaches to justice is very high in the abstract, especially when compared to the known reality of existing justice systems. Public familiarity and attitudes about the actual practice of restorative justice is only beginning to develop. That public perception should be informed by the cumulative results from well conducted assessment research of individual programmes, the subject we turn to next.

Restorative justice programme samples

This chapter presents the results of surveying published assessments of primary restorative programmes – specifically, mediation and conferencing. This overview is necessarily limited in presenting the depth of the original research and should not be a substitute for a full reading of the source documents. Further, this survey is limited to programme assessments available in English. This sample frame may not be representative of the whole of such programmes, and may not be the best representation of specific programmes as they change over time. The results of programme assessments presented in this chapter can only be considered representative of mediation and conferencing programmes which have conducted and published the results of those assessments. This sampling frame probably over-represents the larger and better funded programmes (Hughes and Schneider 1989), and over-represents results of programmes at start-up, rather than programmes operating with the benefit of results from earlier evaluations.

What constitutes a restorative justice programme?

Primary restorative justice practices bring offenders and those directly affected by their behaviour together to agree mutually on a plan to repair the harm done. These practices include at least two distinctive versions of mediation – 'community mediation' and 'victim–offender mediation;' two distinctive versions of conferencing – 'family group conferencing' and 'community group conferencing'; and at least three distinct versions of peace-making circles (see McCold 1999). However, as of 2001, empirical research is only available on mediation and conferencing programmes (see Couture *et al.* 2001).

Community mediation centres (CMC) are local programmes that provide conciliation, mediation, arbitration or other types of alternative dispute resolution services for a wide range of criminal and civil conflicts and may include family mediation, divorce mediation, custody mediation, landlord/tenant mediation, consumer mediation, court-annexed arbitration, labour mediation, victim–offender mediation, school-based dispute resolution, inter-group dispute resolution, public policy dispute resolution mechanisms, peer mediation and other specialised efforts (ABA 1990). CMCs are often operated as adjuncts to law schools or court services and often are publicly funded. CMCs receive cases from schools, the police, prosecutors, probation or as walk-ins. Many criminal cases are referred to them because they involve parties with an ongoing relationship. Pre-mediation contact is normally by phone and limited to explaining the process and eliciting participation. Although these programmes initially relied heavily on trained community volunteer mediators, community mediation has become increasingly professionalised (McGillis and Mullen 1997).

Victim–offender mediation (VOM) as a distinct approach to mediation traces its beginning to victim offender reconciliation programmes (VORPs), which were initially rooted in the experience of Mennonite communities (Cordella 1991; Merry and Milner 1995: Part III). VORPs' concept of mediation dynamics is faith centred (Claassen and Zehr 1989). Programmes tend to use faith-based terms – such as shalom, atonement, reconciliation, obligation, responsibility, accountability, forgiveness and justification – to describe and understand the restorative justice process (Northey 1989; Zehr 1980). These faith-based concepts have gradually become secularised – combining CMC's techniques with VORP's focus on emotional healing of victims and offenders (McCold 1999).

VOM programmes are normally limited to criminal rather than civil cases. VOM programmes avoid cases where victim and offender are involved in ongoing relationships (McGillis and Mullen 1997: 16). VOM distinguishes itself from CMC, which it sees as too settlement driven. VOM de-emphasises reconciliation and emphasises victims' healing, offenders' accountability and the restoration of losses. Most VOM programmes differ from CMCs by their premediation in-person preparation of the parties and non-directive 'dialogue-driven' style of mediation (Umbreit 1994a, 1996a, 1997a, 1997b, 1998; cf. Umbreit 1978). The terms used by these programmes do distinguish VOMs from VORPs, but this survey does not attempt to do so – counting both types of programmes as victim–offender mediation.

Family group conferencing (FGC) began the third wave of restorative interventions by radically broadening the practice of restorative justice, moving it from a mediated one-on-one process to a group process involving a wider set of stakeholders than victim and offender. The Children, Young Persons and their Families Act 1989 revolutionised how New Zealand manages youth justice proceedings. Under political pressure to indigenise the legal system (Olsen *et al.* 1995; Hassall 1996; Pratt 1996), policy-makers devised FGCs to involve 'families in deciding what would be the most appropriate response to their young people's offending' (Maxwell and Morris 1993: v). They were introduced as both an alternative to court proceedings and as a guide for sentencers, and are used for serious and persistent young offenders (about 20% of young offenders). New Zealand's FGCs are unique among restorative programmes because offender participation in a conference is required by law and is enforceable by court authority.

FGCs are facilitated by youth justice co-ordinators, employees of the Department of Children, Young Persons and Family and are attended by the young offender, the offender's family (including the extended family), the victim, the victim's supporters, the police youth aid officer, the youth advocate and others whom the offender's family wishes to be present. Facilitators work with offenders' families in extensive pre-conference preparation. A centrepiece of New Zealand conferencing continues to be the 'family caucus': encouraging the offender's family to deliberate privately about how best to deal with the offending (McCold 2001).

Community group conferencing (CGC) was pioneered in Wagga Wagga, New South Wales in 1991, loosely based on New Zealand's FGCs (O'Connell 1998). Generally, professionals (for example, a police officer, school counsellor or social worker) facilitate conferences, either as part of a full-time position or as a consultant (Marsh and Crow 1998; Warner-Roberts and Masters 1999). Initial contact focuses on explaining the process and eliciting participation. Offenders are encouraged to take clear responsibility for their behaviour. Victims are encouraged to think about what they would like to say to the offender and what they would like to get out of the conference. Both are expected to nominate personal supporters to attend the conference, who are also contacted by the facilitator. CGCs are distinguishable from FGCs in three respects: (1) facilitators follow a scripted process; (2) CGCs have no private caucuses – victims remain present throughout the conference; and (3) CGCs focus on the incident, not on the offender's family. CGCs attempt to balance the number of victim and offender supporters and normally include a broader range of indirect victims and affected parties (O'Connell *et al.* 2000).

Comparing restorative programmes

Restorative justice programmes can be compared to each other – albeit not without some difficulty. This difficulty arises from three sources. First, there are different criteria for types of disputes deemed appropriate for the programme. Some programmes accept only juveniles under the age of criminal intent, while others work exclusively with adult felony cases. Some programmes are limited to offences against property, others focus primarily on crimes of violence. Some programmes prefer cases where the victim and offender have ongoing relationships, others work only with stranger crime. Some programmes include only criminal case referrals, others accept a wide variety of 'disputes' not limited to criminal cases.

The divergent case patterns (offence type and relationship) can be attributed directly to the referral sources used by programmes (Garofalo and Connelly 1980a: 428). An early survey of agencies with a victim–offender component in the USA (n = 79) found 43% private non-profit organisations, 21% probation, 17% state or county agencies and 7% court operated. Programme staff alone were used as mediators in 55% of programmes. In another 37% a combination of staff and volunteers was used, and in the remaining 8%, only volunteers served as mediators (Hughes and Schneider 1989: 224–5). Some programmes are operated by small non-profits organisations, others are large well financed programmes operated by government agencies. Various forms of sponsorship determine the proportion of referrals from the justice system and the proportion as walk-ins, the ability to develop stable case referrals, the neutral image of the programme, and the probability of obtaining long-term funding (Garofalo and Connelly 1980a).

The second difficulty in comparing cross-programme case attrition rates is that not all restorative programmes involved direct meeting of victims and offenders. Some mediation programmes provide indirect mediation (conciliation or shuttle-mediation) to some of their cases, others do not. Further, some conferencing programmes conduct conferences even when the victim declines to participate or for offences with no direct victim, using the family as indirect victims or substituting community volunteers as surrogate victims (Inkpen pers. comm. 2000).

The third difficulty in comparing restorative programmes is the different measurements and meanings of these measurements used in different evaluation contexts. From what counts as a case referral, to what counts as a recidivist event, there is little standardisation of process or outcome measures.

Programme size and service delivery rates

Assessment research varies from single-year programme evaluations to multi-year summaries of programmes for a whole country. To standardise comparison across assessment schemes, an annualised number of mediations/conferences was estimated for each programme sample. Because of the vast differences in the volume of cases processed, the restorative programme samples will be compared within size category: programmes with 100 or fewer per year, between 100 and 500 per year and samples larger than 500 per year. Increasing the number of cases processed is thought to decrease the amount of time that can be spent on each case and lower the cost per case (Garofalo and Connelly 1980a: 432). Programme auspices have also been found to affect the capacity and quality of programme service (Cook et al. 1980; Roehl and Cook 1982). The neighbourhood justice centres produced an equally high quality of justice as the small community dispute settlement projects. Their scale, however, has been radically different. Court-connected centres have helped thousands of citizens, while community-based programmes serve far fewer (Roehl and Cook 1989: 41).

Of annual caseloads for programmes processing 100 cases per year or fewer, community mediation centres and VOM programme assessments dominate prior to 1995, with annualised rates from as few as 9 conferences per year in Palm Island Australia, to 100 mediations per year in the two-site Scottish evaluation.

Even though these programmes process relatively few cases per year, the impact of the programme may be hidden behind the absolute numbers served. A small programme serving a small community or directed towards a small finite population may have a larger aggregate effect than a small programme serving a large metropolitan area. To control for these differences, a service delivery rate (mediations/conferences per year per 10,000 population base) was computed for each programme sample, as shown in Figure 4.3. Among the small programmes, the Rotterdam CMC provided the most intensive programme delivery to the residents of the target housing district with an astounding service delivery rate of 135. Sparwood, Canada, a small town in British Columbia (120) processed every juvenile arrest using a conference. Next most intensive service delivery rates are the tiny village of Palm Island, Australia (47), followed

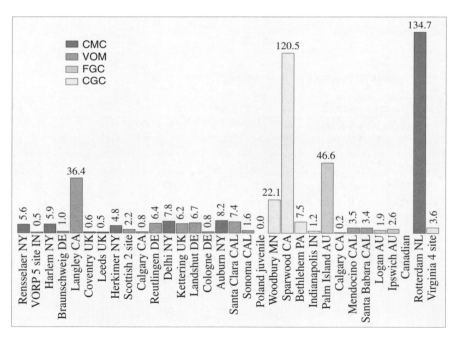

Figure 4.3. Estimated service delivery rates per 10,000 population, small programme samples.

by an early VOM programme in Langely, Canada (35), and the CGC programme in Woodbury, Minnesota (22). The remaining small programme samples had programme service delivery rates of less than 20 per year per 10,000 residents.

CMCs dominated the early evaluation samples among the mid-sized programme samples. Among mid-sized restorative programmes with 100–500 meetings per year, CMCs are among the largest, followed by Canberra's CGC programme, and Winnipeg, Canada's long-running VOM programme.

Programme service delivery rates for these mid-size programmes are shown in Figure 4.4. The 1975 CMC in Dorchester, Massachusetts (an inner-city Boston neighbourhood), stands out with more than 80 mediations per year per 10,000 population. Other highly intensive programmes are the initial Wagga Wagga CGC programme in Australia (43), New York's CMCs in Oneida (36) and Warrenton (33), followed by one of the three National Institute of Justice (NIJ) original pilot CMCs in Venice, California (25), a neighbourhood of Los Angeles. Since Canberra's CGC programme included a large number of conferences not included in the ReIntegrative Shaming Experiment (RISE) assessment (Inkpen pers. comm. 2000), the true programme service delivery rate is probably also

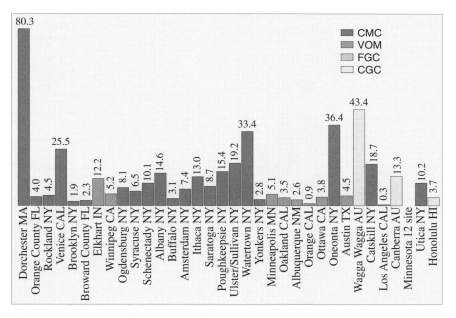

Figure 4.4. Estimated service delivery rates per 10,000 population, mid-size programme samples.

above 20. None of the other mid-sized programmes had rates above 20. In spite of processing a relatively large number of cases, most of the mid-size restorative justice programmes are providing alternatives to formal case processing for only a small fraction of potential cases.

Among the restorative justice programme samples with more than 500 mediations/conferences per year are individual CMCs, as well as state and national CMC, VOM and conferencing samples. France dominates among these, with more than 8,000 mediations per year nationally (Jullion 2000: 237, reported 8,782 mediation files opened in 1995), followed by New Zealand's nationally mandated programme of FCG, closely followed by Norway, Austria, Belgium and Finland's VOM programmes. Remarkably, the 1971 Night Prosecutor's CMC in Columbus, Ohio mediated as many cases as whole European countries.

As Figure 4.5 shows, the city-based programmes clearly provide more intensive programme delivery rates than state or national programmes. The large number of cases reported for France appears tiny when controlling for the population of the country. In contrast, Columbus, Ohio, CMC provided service at a rate of nearly 68 per 10,000 in its first year of operation. Other highly intensive programmes reported include Atlanta,

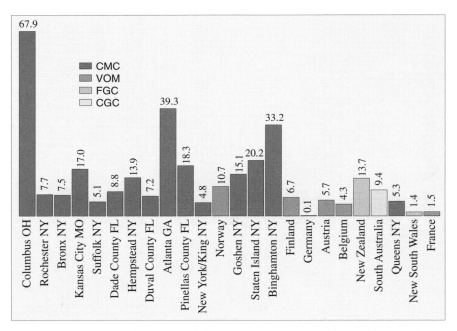

Figure 4.5. Estimated service delivery rates per 10,000 population, large programme samples.

Georgia (another NIJ original pilot) CMCs with a rate of 39, and New York's CMCs in Binghamton (33) and Staten Island (20). All the state and national aggregates have a programme service delivery rate of less than 20. Again, it is not expected that any large area aggregate can produce service intensities as high as programmes measured against city or neighbourhood populations.

If the comparison is limited to state and national programme aggregates, as shown in Figure 4.6, the largest is New York State's 28 community mediation programmes with nearly 16,000 mediations per year (although Miers 2001: 30 reported 33,600 mediations carried out in France during 1995). Germany's annual number of both adult and juvenile mediation is the smallest of these samples.

As before, the programme service intensities for these samples reveals a different pattern, as shown in Figure 4.7. New Zealand (13.7), Norway (10.7) and South Australia (9.4) have programme service intensities higher than New York State (8.7), followed by Finland and Austria. When measured by programme service delivery rate, the VOM programmes in Germany and France and the conferencing programme in New South Wales seem much less impressive.

A couple of examples will give concrete meaning to these service intensities. The total number of mediations in Germany during the period 1984–90 was 300 adult and 1,257 juvenile cases. By 1997, there were about

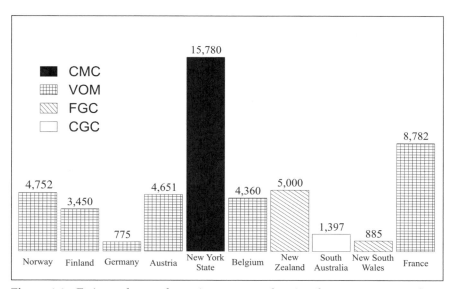

Figure 4.6 Estimated annual meetings, state and national programme samples. *Source*: Loschnig-Gspandl and Kilchling (1997: 58)

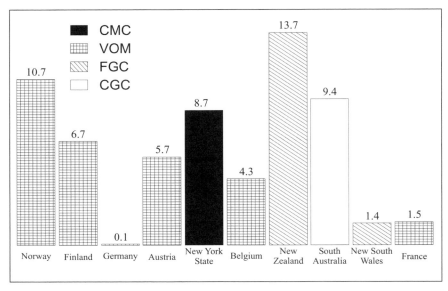

Figure 4.7. Estimated service delivery rates per 10,000 population, state and national programme samples.

2,000 cases mediated a year, representing 2–10% of all suitable cases (Loschnig-Gspandl and Kilchling 1997: 72). Hartmann (1992) estimated that the potential for VOM in Germany is about 16% of cases, or about 600,000 per year.

In spite of a low rate of service delivery for Germany of 0.1, the practice of restorative justice in the German justice system has not been trivial:

> 'VOM has reached a new quality as it can no longer be labelled as an "exceptional measure" suitable for juvenile offenders at best. Now it has been established as a regular part of legal reactions available to the Criminal Justice system in general.' (Loschnig-Gspandl and Kilchling 1997: 58)

In neighbouring Austria with a service delivery rate of 5.7, 73.4% of all juvenile offenders were diverted from court through mediation during 1992. As of 1995, 2,602 or 10% of all cases involving juvenile information were settled by mediation (Loschnig-Gspandl and Kilchling 1997: 70–1). New Zealand, with the highest service delivery rate of 13.7 mandates a family group conference for nearly 100% of their serious juvenile offenders, or about 20% of all young offenders (Maxwell and Morris 1993).

Programme case attrition rates

Case attrition rates are an important measure of any programme based on voluntary participation. Programmes which require offenders to participate will include a mixture of co-operative and unco-operative cases. If only the most co-operative and minor cases are selected for programme referral, better results can be expected than for programmes with high participation rates. Also, case attrition is an important measure of the efficiency with which restorative justice programmes divert cases from the court system. Regardless of how positive individual case outcomes may be, programmes with participation rates of less than 10% are inefficient.

Programme effectiveness is at least partly a function of case screening and case retention. Some crimes come to the attention of authorities; most are not reported and remain unserviced by the justice system. Among crimes with a known offender, a proportion will be referred to a restorative programme (referral rate). Of these, some offenders and some victims will decline to participate. The proportion of cases referred which participate (participation rate) will depend partly upon how carefully cases were screened at the referral process. Participation rates will be high if victim and offender have agreed to participate prior to programme referral, for example.

Among the cases participating in a restorative programme, some percent will reach an agreement (agreement rate). Of these, some proportion will be complied with and some will not (compliance rate). The current justice system has a comparable case-screening process (reporting rate, arrest rate, prosecution rate and conviction rate), controlled by justice professionals (police, prosecutor, judge). Since restorative justice insists on at least a limited choice to participate (participation or prosecution), attrition rates will be lower than involuntary participation rates of the formal justice system (with the exception of New Zealand's mandatory FGCs).

Programme participation rates

As discussed above, community mediation centres were implemented within the framework of alternative dispute resolution (ADR) which views mediation as a part of a continuum ranging from formal court adjudication to conciliation. In conciliation, parties resolve a dispute themselves directly, or with the assistance of an intermediary without meeting face to face during negotiations (McGillis and Mullen 1997; Yarn 1999).

Programme participation rates were compared among the CMCs, as shown in Figure 4.8. Direct participation rates range from a low of 7% of the cases referred in Buffalo, New York, to a high of 71% reported by Goshen, New York's programme. Direct mediation rates ranged from 50% of referrals in Buffalo, New York (receiving primarily consumer complaints), to 100% directly mediated in Goshen, New York (receiving primarily school referrals) and Brooklyn, New York (only adult custodial felony cases). Among this sample of CMCs direct participation rates average 43% and indirect participation rates average 13%.

Among the three original National Institute of Justice experimental CMCs of 1975, failure to gain the respondent's (offender) co-operation accounted for 30% of case referrals in Atlanta, Georgia, 35% in Kansas City, Missouri, and 47% in Venice, California. Garofalo and Connelly (1980a: 435) concluded 'centers that have systematic procedures for receiving cases … have relatively little trouble with no-shows or refusals to agree to mediation.'

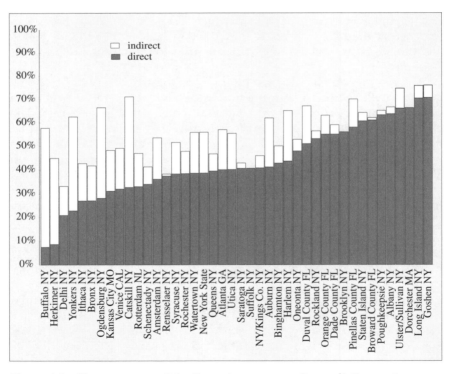

Figure 4.8. Programme participation rates – community mediation centres.

A more recent assessment of participation rates for CMCs based upon a total of 76,702 referrals to New York State's 28 CMCs is shown in Figure 4.9. In a majority (60%) of cases referred to the programme, victims and offenders participated in either direct mediation or indirect conciliation. Only 3% of the referrals were deemed inappropriate or not amenable to mediation. Offenders refused to participate in 8% of referrals, victims in 4%. Offenders failed to show at the scheduled mediation in 14% of referrals, victims in 8%. Offenders were the reason for non-participation in 27% of referrals, victims in 19%. Whether because of failure to contact, failure to show or refusing to participate, offenders were the sole reason for non-participation in 15% of referrals, victims in 7%.

Programme participation rates for the 35 victim–offender mediation programmes in the assessment sample is shown in Figure 4.10. Direct participation rates range from a low of 8% and 13% for two British programmes (Leeds and Coventry), to a high of 95% reported in the small Polish programme.

Indirect mediation or third-party conciliation is less likely to be an option among the sample of victim–offender mediation programmes than it was for the CMCs sample. This technique is most used by the three British VOMs, with indirect mediation rates of 57% for Kettering, 42% in Leeds and 40% in Coventry. Belgium also makes extensive use of

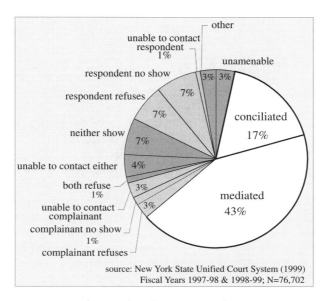

source: New York State Unified Court System (1999)
Fiscal Years 1997-98 & 1998-99; N=76,702

Figure 4.9. Disposition of case referrals in New York State community mediation centres.

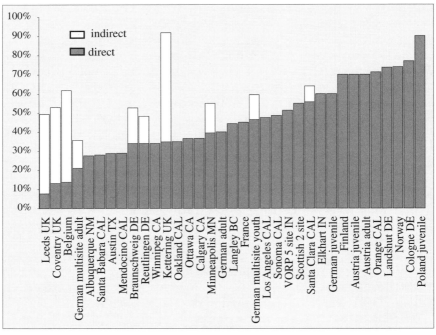

Figure 4.10. Programme participation rates – victim–offender mediation programmes.

conciliation with a rate of 48% indirect, compared to only 14% meeting face to face. It was not always clear in some assessment reports, especially those reporting more than 60% participation rates, what combination of direct and indirect mediation was being reported. Very high rates of programme participation may also be a result of the evaluation counting only cases where the parties had agreed to participate prior to their being referred to the programme (i.e. were pre-screened).

An assessment of German mediation programmes (Bilsky *et al.* 1991) compared cases mediated directly with those being settled without a mediator's intervention. Among the cases settled through direct participation of victim and offender, half were property offences and half were offences against the person. Among the cases settled informally, 85% were property and only 15% were personal offences. Researchers found no gender differences between conciliated and mediated cases. Parties who settled indirectly did not know each other more frequently than those participating in formal mediation (Bilsky *et al.* 1991: 522).

Direct and indirect mediation were also found to produce different intermediate outcomes as measured by participant perceptions. Umbreit and Warner-Roberts (1996) sampled 68 victims and 51 offenders among the referrals to the VOM programmes in Coventry and Leeds (UK) who participated in direct mediation, indirect mediation and court. As shown in Figure 4.11, offenders rated the satisfaction and fairness of indirect mediation as high or higher than direct mediation, and both higher than court. Victims rated indirect mediation as fair and as satisfying as court, but much less fair and satisfying than direct mediation. Both victims and offenders were more satisfied with the outcomes from direct mediation than indirect mediation, and both were more likely to rate their participation as voluntary for face to face mediation than third-party conciliation. Most significantly, victims whose cases were processed by court were more likely to report fearing revictimisation (33%) than victims whose cases were conciliated (21%), and were least likely to fear revictimisation after meeting their offender in direct mediation (11%).

Participation rates varied widely across the sample of conferencing assessments, as shown in Figure 4.12. Rates of participation for both victims and offenders range from a low of 33% among the violent cases

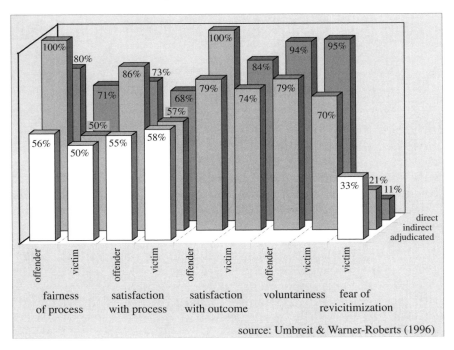

Figure 4.11. Participant perceptions of court, indirect and direct mediation (% responding positively).

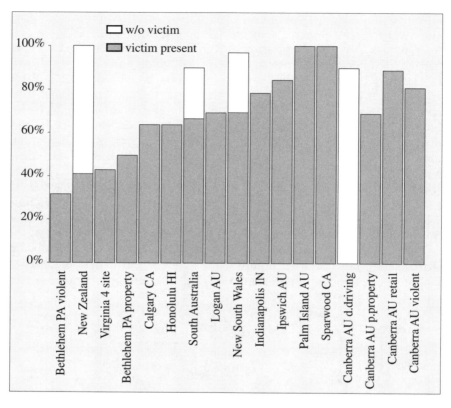

Figure 4.12. Programme participation rates – conferencing programmes.

in Bethlehem, Pennsylvania's programme to the Sparwood, British Columbia, Canada's programme which held a conference for every juvenile arrested, and conferencing in New Zealand where all serious juvenile offences are disposed with a conference, under court order if necessary (Maxwell and Morris 1993).

Many conferencing programmes only hold a conference if the victim agrees to participate, but conferences can be held without victim participation. Some programmes offer opportunities for victims to participate indirectly, by submitting a letter to be read. These victims do not take part in developing the reparation agreements. New Zealand, South Australia and New South Wales reported conferences held without the presence of the victim. The Canberra community group conferencing sample includes cases selected for the RISE experiment where offenders were found to be driving in excess of the legal limit of alcohol. Offences involving actual damage to property or persons were ineligible for the study so there was no victim in these cases. In some of these conferences, community volunteers acted as surrogate victims (Inkpen pers. comm. 2000).

One early assessment of VOM suggested that participation rates, at least for victims, were related to offender race. Gehm (1990) sampled 535 VORP referred cases during 1985, in which 53% of all potential cases never reached a meeting because the victim declined to participate (Gehm 1990: 179). Multivariate analysis found weak but significant correlations. Victim participation was inversely related to offence seriousness (felony mis-demeanour), positively related to offender being white (white–non-white), and more likely among institutional victims than among individual victims (Gehm 1990: 177). However, all three factors accounted for less than 7% of the variation in the victims' decision to participate (adjusted R^2 = .07) (Gehm 1990: 180).

No other assessments reported racial differences in participation or referral rates, but none have used multivariate methods to evaluate participation rates. Still Gehm's evidence of a racial bias is weak. A comparison of the racial and ethnic breakdowns of the population in the target areas for the three original National Institute of Justice field test-sites with the characteristics of disputants referred to those centres revealed few major divergences, although whites were over-represented among corporate respondents at all three centres (Cook et al. 1980).

Among adult custodial felony offences randomly assigned to court or mediation, two factors were found to be related to the victim's decision to participate, as shown in Figure 4.13. Participation rates for victims who had an ongoing relationship with their offender were about as high for mediation as for court (76–80%), while victims with no such relationship were less likely to participate in mediation than court (56–70%). Likewise, among cases where the offence was a one-time incident, victims are less likely to participate in mediation (59–74%) unlike cases which are the result of a repeat occurrence (83–77%). Victims and offenders from different racial or ethnic groups are less likely to have ongoing relationships and therefore the offence is less likely to be a repeat occurrence. Because victim–offender relationship and the degree of the dispute are related to the victim's decision to participate, race is likely to be spuriously related to participation rates.

Participation rates also differ by whether the dispute is related to personal or property harms. For example, the German assessment reported that attempts to settle conflicts associated with assault were more likely to fail than issues over property or money (Bilsky et al. 1991: 531).

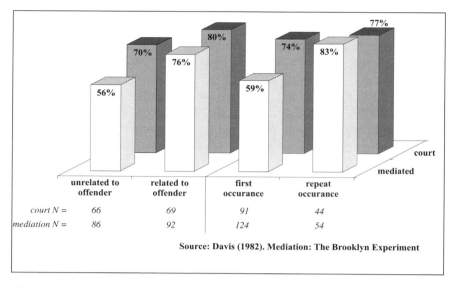

	unrelated to offender	related to offender	first occurance	repeat occurance
court N =	66	69	91	44
mediation N =	86	92	124	54

Source: Davis (1982). Mediation: The Brooklyn Experiment

Figure 4.13.   Victim participation rates by relationship and occurrence.

One reason appears to be the lower participation rate of crime victims in cases involving violence. Among the juvenile offenders and their victims, none of whom had ongoing relationships, randomly assigned to court or a conference in the Bethlehem Experiment (McCold and Wachtel 1998), participation rates were much lower for victims of violent offences than for property offences (43–88%), while offenders' participation was high for both violent and property offences (84–75%).

A consistent finding, from the initial to the most recent assessment of restorative justice programmes, is that when the parties come together, the success rate is high. In different settings and locales, under different sponsors and philosophies, a high proportion of participating cases 'have consistently ended in agreements satisfactory to the parties involved and upheld by both' (Roehl and Cook 1989: 33).

In their review of the research on mediation in 1991, Bilsky *et al.* (pp. 53–5) concluded there is:

> no general restriction with respect to the categories of social conflict that are suited to mediation ... practical limitations arise from lack of professional experience and expertise in mediation. While middle-range conflicts usually do not pose any problems to the mediator, this does not apply to more demanding conflicts as sexual offense for instance.

Programme agreement and compliance rates

Voluntary participation, the strength of restorative justice, is also the main limitation on case-processing capacity. Approximately half the cases referred to programmes never reach a hearing (either mediation or conciliation). 'Once a case reaches a hearing, though, the likelihood of effective resolution is high' (Roehl and Cook 1989: 33).

One explanation for the variation in participation rates, agreement rates and compliance rates between programmes is related to the type of cases and disputes handled by the programme. Within programmes, assessments reveal vastly different case attrition rates for different offence/dispute types, as shown in Figure 4.14. Assessments of early community mediation programmes revealed a pattern of these case attrition rates. Although property disputes proved comparatively difficult to get to mediation and to settle at mediation, they are more likely than interpersonal disputes to lead to stable agreements. As shown in Figure 4.15 Felstiner and Williams (1980) found violent cases were more likely to agree to participate and to reach agreement but less likely to comply with that agreement than property cases. Cases involving problems between parties with ongoing relationships were least likely to keep their agreements.

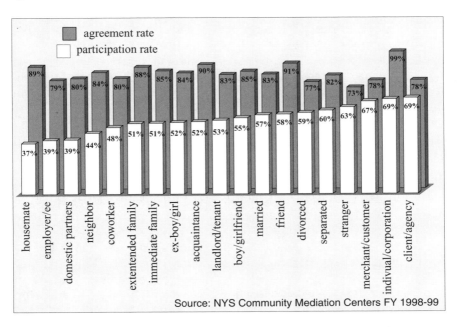

Source: NYS Community Mediation Centers FY 1998-99

Figure 4.14. Participation and agreement rates by disputant relationships.

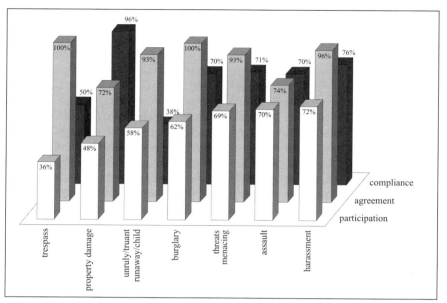

Figure 4.15. Participation, agreement and compliance rates by offence type.

Felstiner and Williams compared three types of disputes with escalating seriousness: (1) cases where the conflict was a 'one-shot dispute' not involving people with ongoing relations; (2) cases involving ongoing relations but without underlying emotional or behavioural problems; and (3) cases with ongoing relationships and an apparent underlying emotional and/or behavioural problem (*n* = 206). As shown in Figure 4.16, the higher the level of dispute the more likely it is to go to mediation, the more likely an agreement will be reached at mediation and the less likely a mediated agreement is to be kept (Felstiner and Williams 1980: ix).

In the research on the effects of mediation, one finding stands out – the worse the state of the parties' relationship with one another, the dimmer the prospects that mediation will succeed (Kressel and Pruitt 1985b; Kressel *et al.* 1989: 402). Programme case attrition rates differ within programmes by dispute/offence types and relationships between participants. Since each restorative justice programme has cases with a unique combination of these characteristics, it should not be surprising that they report such different processing rates. Between-programme comparison of participation rates and agreement rates reveals there is no relationship between programme participation rates and programme agreement rates, whether we count total or only direct participation. Conferencing

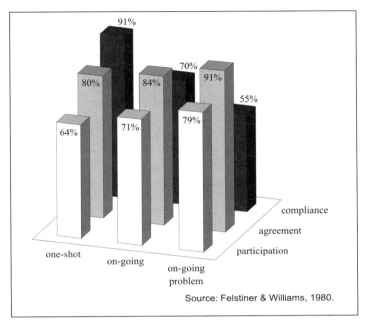

Figure 4.16. Participation, agreement and compliance rates by level of dispute.

programmes report consistently high agreement rates in spite of a wide range of reported participation rates. VOM programmes and CMCs vary in both participation rates and agreement rates, without a demonstrated relationship. Likewise, among the 28 restorative justice programmes reporting compliance rates, there was no clear relationship between compliance and participation rates. Most programmes report compliance rates above 85%, regardless of the participation rate. Both the Belgium VOM and New Zealand's FGCs reported low compliance rates, with vastly different participation rates (participation for offenders is mandatory in New Zealand).

Comparisons of agreement rates by compliance rates for the 27 programmes reporting both measures also failed to reveal a relationship. Eight programmes reported 100% agreement rates (VOMs in Los Angeles, Mendocino, and Santa Barbara, California; CGCs in Honolulu, HI, and both violent and property cases in Bethlehem, PA; and the two FGCs in Australia, Logan and Ipswich) and two programmes reported 100% compliance rates (CGC in Sparwood, California, and FGC in Ipswich, Australia). Only the performance of New Zealand could qualify as agreements which are 'easy to get but hard to keep'. Most programmes report both high agreement and high compliance rates.

Comparison of compliance rates between mediated agreements and court imposed community service or restitution has found mixed results. Supito Roy (1993) compared a VORP juvenile restitution programme providing victim–offender fact-to-face meetings with a court-based juvenile restitution programme without mediation. He found no significant differences in successful completion of restitution contracts, although offenders with prior offence history were less likely to compensate their victims fully under either scheme (Roy 1994: 30). Roy concluded compliance is as high for VOMs' voluntary agreements as for court-ordered restitution (1993: 52).

However, compliance with the decision has been found to be greater in mediated versus adjudicated cases in small claims (McEwen and Maiman 1981) and divorce and custody (Pearson *et al.* 1982; Person and Thoennes 1982, 1984; Roehl and Cook 1989: 34). Umbreit (1994: 111) compared restitution completion between juvenile offenders in the Minneapolis, MN, and Albuquerque, NM, VOM programmes ($n = 167$) with comparison groups matched by jurisdiction, age, race, gender, offence and amount of restitution ($n = 221$) and found higher compliance rates (77% and 93%) for the mediation samples compared to court (55% and 69%).

In summary, case attrition rates vary widely among mediation and conferencing programmes. Programme participation rates appear to be affected by the nature of the offence, relationship between the parties and the age of the offenders. There is no clear relationship between participation rates and agreement rates or compliance with agreements. There is mixed evidence supporting the easy-to-reach, hard-to-keep hypothesis, but both agreement rates and compliance rates are generally very high for all types of restorative practices surveyed – as high or higher than similar court cases.

Outcome measures

The case attrition data presented above can be considered either process measures or products of the programme. Typically, restorative programme assessments include measures of participant perceptions and satisfaction, which we turn to next. The final section considers what is known about the capacity of restorative programmes to reduce offender recidivism.

Participant perceptions

Restorative justice assessment research commonly surveys participants' perceptions of justice, their satisfaction with the process and their perceptions of the agreement reached. There is no accepted standard for measuring these intermediate restorative outcomes. The primary questions asked of participants include variations of the following:

- Satisfaction with the way their case was handled.
- Satisfaction with the outcome of their case.
- Satisfaction with the facilitator.
- Fairness of the process.
- Fairness of the outcome.
- Neutrality of the facilitator.
- Are they glad they participated?
- Would they recommend this programme to others?
- Would they participate again under similar circumstances?

These questions are asked of the victim and offender in mediation assessments and also of the parents of offenders or other participants in conferencing programmes. Some assessments do not report separate rates for victims and offenders, but report rates for 'disputants' (Dorchester and New York State). The metric used for these measures also varies between assessments, from rating on a scale from 1 to 10, to Likert scales with and without a neutral response, to forced yes/no choices. In order to create a standard comparison across assessments, all metrics were collapsed into affirmative responses and others (including neutral), and a percent responding affirmatively calculated. Because of the differences in questions asked, the question with the maximum rating of victims and offenders is used for programme comparisons. Programmes reporting mean satisfaction ratings, for example 8.0 on a scale of 1–10, were converted using the formula $(score - min)/(max - min)$ or $(8 - 1)/(10 - 1) = 78\%$. Thus, if all respondents rated the programme '1', the average would be '0%'; and if all rated it '10' the average would be 100%. Because the distribution of responses are likely skewed, these calculations can only be considered estimates of the actual percent responding positively. For example, all six victims surveyed in the Wagga Wagga, CGC programme rated their satisfaction as an 8 on a scale of 1–10, which is 100% satisfaction (all above 5.5). Without assessments reporting the distribution of responses, the mean score is at best a biased estimate of percent satisfaction. Where the distribution is reported, the rates are directly calculated from the data.

There were no substantial differences reported across case types in satisfaction with the overall experience at the three National Institute of Justice CMC pilot sites. Disputant satisfaction and agreement stability varied with case type, but case type effects were not particularly strong or widespread. Respondent satisfaction varied by case type, attributable mainly to the larger percentages of dissatisfied respondents in cases involving family disputes, neighbourhood nuisance and domestic assault/harassment. Complainant satisfaction also reflected these case type differences, but did not reach significance. Case type shows no influence on disputant satisfaction with the mediator or with the agreement terms. Agreement stability showed no effects of case type (Cook *et al.* 1980: 50).

Ideally, restorative justice programmes would transform the relationship between parties and produce equally high ratings from both victims and offenders. Programmes with much higher ratings from offenders than from victims might be considered offender focused, and vice versa. As shown in Figure 4.17, among the VOM programmes, most clump tightly around the line of victim–offender parity, with Santa Clara rating higher among offenders than among victims. Among the CMCs reporting both measures, the two Florida programmes which report relatively low satisfaction rates from offenders also report low ratings from victims.

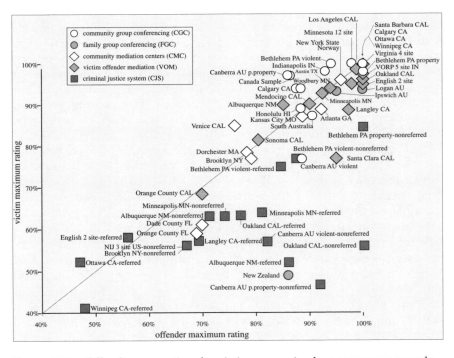

Figure 4.17. Offender perceptions by victim perception by programme sample.

Both victim and offender satisfaction in the conferencing programmes are much more closely clumped above 90%, with two exceptions. The youth violent offence sample from Canberra's RISE project was somewhat more preferred by offenders than victims, and New Zealand's FGCs were rated much less satisfactory by victims than by offenders. While legislation was been passed providing victims with certain rights in New Zealand FGCs and facilitator training has improved since these data were gathered (Maxwell and Morris 1999), it remains to be determined if victim participation or satisfaction has increased as a result.

All but three of the court samples are offender focused in that the process is more preferred by offenders than by victims. All but one restorative justice programme demonstrate a more balanced approach. The most obvious exception to this general trend is the case of New Zealand's Family GCs, which was lowest of all restorative programmes, and lower than all but two of the court samples as rated by participating victims. New Zealand's FCGs were also further from parity than all restorative programme samples and all but two of the court samples.

McCold and Wachtel (2000) compared victim and offender satisfaction and fairness ratings from conferencing and mediation assessments using comparable measurements to test a restorative practices typology. This typology predicts programmes which involve the victims' and offenders' communities of care will be more restorative than programmes which exclude direct participation of the families, and both will be perceived by participants as more restorative than court (McCold 2000). As predicted, victims and offenders rated conferencing programmes significantly higher than mediation and both higher than court on both satisfaction and fairness (McCold and Wachtel 2000).

These findings generally confirm the conclusions about restorative justice programmes made two decades ago: disputing parties typically hold positive views of restorative justice programmes; and they feel satisfied with the process and would return under similar circumstances in the future. Assessments involving different settings and types of disputes found disputants perceived the outcomes of mediation hearings to be significantly fairer than those of court proceedings.

Restorativeness and recidivism

Evaluating a new paradigm by the criteria of the old paradigms is inappropriate. Restorative justice offers advantages for victims, offenders, their families and communities, even if the practice is eventually shown to have no direct effect on offender recidivism rates. Offenders are expected to be held accountable for the consequences of their misbehaviour, but as a way to begin to address the offender's need to learn responsible behaviour. Holding offenders accountable in a reintegrative manner is expected to affect their future behaviour (Braithwaite 1989; Braithwaite and Mugford 1994), but changing that behaviour is not the primary purpose of restorative justice (McCold 2000): 'Mediation should first be judged on how well it resolves disputes between conflicting parties. Only after we … examined the immediate effects, do people find it satisfactory? are agreements durable? should we look beyond to potential broader effects?' (Roehl and Cook 1989: 32).

While reduction in recidivism is not the central goal, it remains relevant to the paradigm. The goals of restorative justice are to meet the real needs of victims, offenders and their communities created by the criminal act. Crime victims need to have their injuries acknowledged and to be reassured that the offence was not their fault. They need to feel a restoration of safety and to know that something is being done to prevent the future victimisation of themselves or others by the offender (Karmen 1990: 166, citing National Crime Survey). Communities of care and local communities also need to know that hurtful behaviour will not be tolerated and that concrete measures are being taken to hold offenders accountable to help prevent a reoccurrence of the offence (McCold 2000). Reducing offender recidivism is a measure of the capacity of restorative approaches to address one of the needs created by a criminal offence, and might be considered a secondary goal of restorative justice.

No significant differences have been found in recidivism rates (actual arrest of either party for a crime against the other) between mediated cases and those processed by the court (Davis *et al.* 1980; Davis 1982; Roehl and Cook 1982, 1989). Equally important, no programme assessment found rearrest rates higher than comparative court cases.

In an early assessment of VORP programmes in Indiana and Ohio, Roy compared recidivism rates among juveniles participating in VORP to a court-based juvenile restitution programme without mediation ($n = 48$). He found for youths with a prior offence history that the VORP had been effective in reducing their recidivism as long as they were under the programme supervision. After they were released from the programme, there was an increase in their subsequent offending (Roy 1993b: 52).

Umbreit's (1994) comparison of four VOM programmes in the USA included comparison of recidivism between VOM participants ($n = 160$) with matched samples from structured, court-administered restitution programmes ($n = 160$). While offenders participating in mediation had lower one-year rearrests (18%) than their court counterparts (27%), these differences were not statistically significant – a result consistent with other VOM assessments (Stead 1986; Dignan 1990; Marshall and Merry 1990; Pate 1990; Nugent and Paddock 1995, Wynne 1996).

Part of the difficulty in detecting possible effects of restorative justice on recidivism relates to differential case attrition. Disputes brought to the attention of authorities are not like cases which are not reported to authorities (the so-called 'dark figure of crime'). The differences introduce a 'reporting bias' into the sample. Next, those that are reported are screened as appropriate for programme referral or not. Cases selected for referral to a restorative justice programme are not the same as those not referred. For example, offences without an identifiable offender and victim may be excluded. This is the 'system selection bias.' Finally, as was demonstrated above, among those cases that are referred, not all will agree to participate. Offenders preferring court are not the same as those who participate; and cases in which the victim also agrees to participate are likely different from cases where they do not. This is the 'self-selection bias.' Several studies have found a self-selection bias among mediated cases that tends to inflate the degree of success (Roehl and Cook 1989: 36).

Recidivism is not independent of the decision to participate. Because of differential case attrition, results achieved in restorative justice programmes cannot be presumed to work as well with all referred cases, all known cases or all cases. Each represents a distinct sampling frame. The standard way to control for selection bias is through random assignment of cases to programmes. Random assignment does not remove the bias but assures that the differences between cases are equally distributed among groups. To date, there have been three published randomised assessments of restorative justice programmes.

The Brooklyn experiment began in 1977 and was conducted by the Vera Institute of Justice (Davis *et al.* 1980; 1982). A total of 465 adult custodial felony offence cases where victim and offender had prior relationship were selected for the experiment, primarily without prior contact with the parties. Thus, the sampling frame was the universe of such cases in that jurisdiction during the late 1970s, and the results should generalise to serious criminal cases between adults with prior relationships. Cases were randomly assigned to court ($n = 206$) or mediation ($n = 259$). Researchers conducted four-month follow-up interviews with complainants and police records checks for offender rearrests.

Among cases assigned to court, 81% participated in court, 19% failed to show. Among those assigned to mediation, 56% participated, 20% declined to participate and took their case to court, and 24% failed to participate in either court or mediation. As shown in Figure 4.18, victims whose cases were assigned to mediation reported fewer continuing problems (19%) than control group victims (28%), but they were more likely to have subsequently called the police about the respondent (12 versus 7%).

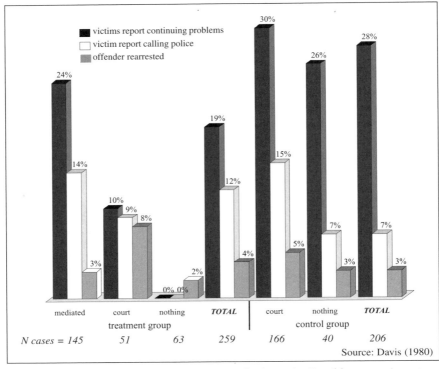

Figure 4.18. Reoffending rates at four months from the Brooklyn experiment.

This contradictory result becomes even more confusing when comparing outcomes by the treatment received rather than assigned. Victims participating in mediation were less likely to report continuing problems (24%) than those participating in court (30%), and about as likely to report having to call the police again (3 and 5%, respectively). Oddly, among those cases assigned to mediation that ended up in court, only 10% of victims reported continuing problems, in spite of their offenders being rearrested at a higher rate (8% compared to < 5%). Remarkably, none of the victims selected for mediation who did not participate in either court or mediation reported ongoing problems. Among both the treatment and control groups, cases receiving no services seemed to fair best. Davis (1982) concluded that mediation was no more effective than court adjudication in preventing recidivism.

It was nearly two decades until the next randomised assessment of a restorative justice programme – in this case community group conferencing. The Bethlehem experiment began in 1996 in northeastern Pennsylvania to evaluate the feasibility of police-facilitated CGC in a typical American city. A total of 140 property and 75 personal cases involving arrested first-time juvenile misdemeanour and summary offenders – 23% of all juvenile arrests during the period – were randomly assigned to court or conferencing without prior contact of the parties. Thus, the sampling frame was the universe of such cases in that jurisdiction during the 18 months of the experiment, and the results should generalise to all moderately serious first-time juveniles in mid-sized American cities. Researchers conducted 12-month follow-up interviews with victims, offenders and offenders' parents, and checked police records for rearrests. An additional recidivism comparison sample was selected from police records, matched by offence and offender prior history ($n = 227$).

Like the Brooklyn experiment, not all cases assigned to the treatment group actually participated in a conference, nor did all those assigned to court actually attend court. Among the 98 offenders assigned to court, 59% charged with crimes against a person and 70% charged with property offences received a court disposition (plea or hearing). Among cases assigned to a CGC, 32% of the violent cases and 50% of the property cases (both victim and offender) participated in a CGC. Among the 92 offenders assigned to CGC where either victim or offender declined to participate, 51% of the personal and 57% property cases received court dispositions. Among a matched set of juvenile offenders arrested but not selected for the study, 80% of 250 personal and 84% of 191 property offenders received court dispositions (McCold and Wachtel 1998: 86).

The Bethlehem experiment found no differences in the 12-month rearrest rates between court-assigned and CGC-assigned juvenile property or violent offenders. The rate for the combined treatment groups (participate and decline) was statistically the same as the rates for both control groups across both offence types. However, an interesting pattern in re-arrests was revealed when groups were compared by the actual treatment received. Among property offenders, the declined cases had a higher rate than the conference-attended cases through all but the last month, at which point they essentially converge (35–32%), as shown in Figure 4.19. The matched cases (29%) rate was lower, but not as low as the randomly assigned control cases (21%). Given the sample sizes, these differences could be due to chance.

However, the pattern of recidivism for offenders charged with a violent offence showed a strong divergent pattern that increased through the 12 months, as shown in Figure 4.20. Offenders who were willing to participate in a conference reoffended at a lower rate (20%), and offenders declining to participate reoffended at a rate much higher (48%) than the matched and experimental control groups (both at 35%).

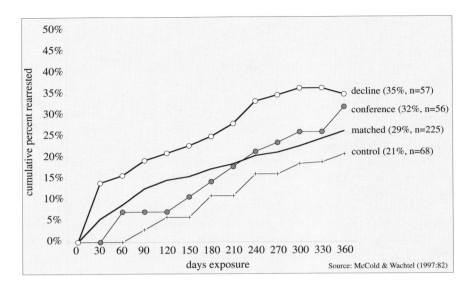

Figure 4.19. Re-arrest rates, juvenile property cases in the Bethlehem experiment.

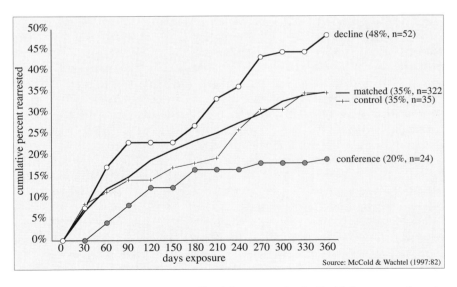

Figure 4.20. Re-arrest rates, juvenile violent cases in the Bethlehem experiment.

McCold and Wachtel (1998) concluded that offenders who are willing to participate in a restorative justice conference are less likely to reoffend than those for whom a conference could not be arranged. The difference in reoffending is more the result of the decision to participate than the participation itself. While this is encouraging for justifying case diversion, there are two implications in these findings for interpreting other research assessments that use comparison groups.

First, given the relative ease of constructing matched-cases samples and the difficulties involved in random assignment, matched-cases designs provide a more stable comparison group, especially where sample size is small. Secondly, comparing differences between non-referred and participating cases without including the 'referred but declined' cases does not tell us anything about programme effects, even if this difference is statistically significant. Participating offenders should always perform better than the comparison group since those participating are all co-operative (at least to a degree), while the comparison groups contain a mix of co-operative and unco-operative cases (McCold and Wachtel 1998).

To test the relationship between the decision to participate and rearrest rates, rearrest rates were compared for offenders assigned to a CGC but not participating between cases where the offender declined to participate and where the conference was not held because the victim refused to participate. As shown in Figure 4.21, the rearrest rates for offenders declining to participate were much higher than cases where the offender agreed, but the victim had declined to participate. Offenders who were willing to participate had lower recidivism even when they did not actually participate. Although the sample sizes were small, this evidence of a self-selection bias on the part of offenders is very strong – differences in reoffending are more a result of the offender's choice to participate than the effects of the programme. This finding confirmed the conclusion of the original Wagga Wagga study (Moore 1995) – that a large number of typical juvenile offences can be safely diverted from the justice system without increasing overall reoffending levels.

The ReIntegrative Shaming Experiment (RISE) in Canberra was specifically designed to detect the effect of police-facilitated CGC on offender recidivism for four offence types (juvenile personal property, juvenile retail theft, young violent offenders and 'drink driving' adults driving over the legal limit for alcohol). The Australian National Police facilitated nearly 1,300 community group conferences over a five-year period ending July 2000.

Offenders agreed to participate in a CGC prior to referral to RISE, so nearly all assigned a conference actually participated in one (90% drink driving, 69% personal property, 89% retail theft and 81% violent). Among

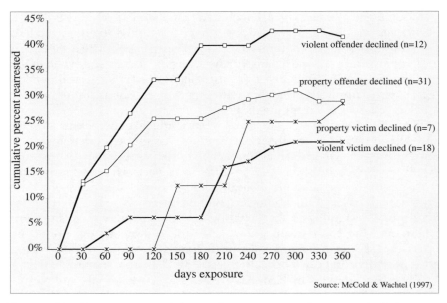

Figure 4.21. Re-arrest rates, violent and property cases by person declining.

the cases assigned to court, most participated in a court hearing (96% drink driving, 84% personal property, 89% retail theft and 90% violent) (Sherman *et al.* 2000: 9 fn.1). These high rates of cases receiving the correct treatment are necessary to maintain internal experimental validity (i.e. to conclude the programme caused the difference in outcomes) by distributing any system and self-selection bias present in the sample equivalently for both court and conference groups. The sampling frame is offenders who are willing to participate in a conference, and not all similarly charged offenders in that jurisdiction because the sample excludes unco-operative offenders prior to randomisation. This trade-off between internal validity and external validity (generalisability) means the RISE programme outcomes cannot be compared directly to other studies and the cases included in the experiment differ in systematic ways from typical cases.

Still, among the cases selected and across all four offence categories, both offenders and victims reported CGCs to be procedurally fairer than court, and victims expressed significantly higher satisfaction with conferences than with court (Sherman *et al.* 2000). Recidivism patterns of both juvenile personal property and shoplifting offenders revealed that the deterrent effect of conferencing and court was equivalent. More dramatically, reoffending rates by violent offenders dropped significantly among the CGC group by 38% in the 12 months following the conference (Sherman *et al.* 2000). This represents the first scientifically defensible evidence that CGCs can reduce recidivism, at least among violent offenders.

The 12-month rearrest prevalence rates reported by RISE are shown in Figure 4.22 as percentages. Prevalence rates will tend to be higher compared to the percent reoffending because of the multiple reoffending of individuals. None the less, the differences in post-treatment reoffending rates are substantial for violent and retail theft cases. Comparison of pre-conference offence prevalence rates with post-conference rates found significant reduction only for the violent cases. The RISE researchers conclude the effects of CGCs on offender recidivism depend upon crime type:

> Across the four experiments that make up RISE, very different results have emerged for the different offence categories. In the Youth Violence experiment, those offenders who were assigned to conference subsequently offended at substantially lower levels – 38 fewer offences per year per 100 offenders – than did the offenders assigned to court. This was not true for any of the other experiments (Sherman *et al.* 2000: 18).

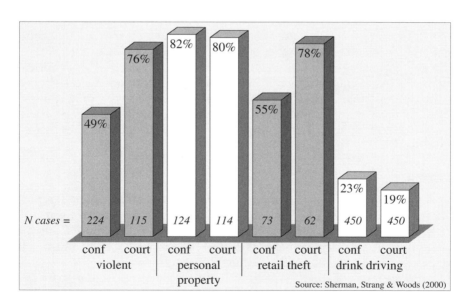

Figure 4.22. Twelve-month rearrest prevalence rates by offence type in the ReIntegrative Shaming Experiment (RISE).

The effect of restorative justice on recidivism are different for different types of offences. Results from assessments of restorative justice programmes which include cases of violence and interpersonal conflicts seem to indicate that restorative justice has greater crime reduction effects with serious rather than minor offences, personal rather than property offences, and offences with a direct victim involved (also see Braithwaite 2002: 40).

All three randomised experimental assessments of restorative justice programmes suffer from the inability to get unco-operative high recidivist offenders to participate in a mediation or conference. This has not been a problem for New Zealand, which mandates a FGC for nearly all serious juvenile offenders. Systematic research efforts did not accompany the implementation of New Zealand's sweeping 1989 national legislation, yet some research evidence is available on the effects. Far fewer young offenders appeared in court and received convictions in 1990 (2,587) compared to before the Act (10,000–13,000). Commitments of young people to institutions were cut by over 50%, from 262 in 1988 to 112 in 1990 (Maxwell and Morris 1993).

In a multivariate analysis of reoffending, Maxwell and Morris (2001) traced offenders participating in FGCs and categorised them in three groups: the non-reconvicted, the once-only reconvicted the multiple reconvicted. Using canonical discriminant analysis of 88 offenders, three factors were found that explain 75% of the differences between reconviction categories: (1) early childhood experiences; (2) the impact of the FGC; and (3) events after the FGC. They conclude that family group conferences can have an impact on future offending behaviour. However, having a conference is, by itself, unlikely to be effective. The critical variables that make for a successful FGC are whether or not the conference was a memorable event, evoked remorse and led to the young person meeting the victim, apologising and attempting to make amends. These factors remained significant, even when controlling for the other factors (Maxwell and Morris 2001: 253).

Summary

Results from the 98 restorative programme samples and 21 court samples surveyed provide strong empirical support for a few generalisations. Disputing parties typically hold positive views of restorative justice programmes; they feel satisfied with the process and would return if a dispute arose in the future. Studies involving different settings and types of disputes found disputants perceived the outcomes of restorative justice to be significantly fairer than those of court proceedings.

Different restorative justice models do not function equally well with all types of cases. Before we can begin better 'fitting the forum to the fuss' or draw conclusions about which of the variations in the processing of cases constitute 'best practices' for any type of case, programme assessments involving random assignment of different case types to different resolution processes are needed (Roehl and Cook 1989: 37). In the mean time, the practice of restorative justice remains more an art form than a science.

Conclusions

The following conclusions can be drawn:

1. There is no significant public opposition to restorative justice. There is a high degree of support among victims of crime and the public for offender reparation and for victims to have an opportunity to meet with their offender.
2. While participation rates vary widely from programme to programme, most victims and offenders will choose to participate given the opportunity. Offenders are somewhat less likely to participate than victims. Participation rates differ for type of offences, age of offender, type of victim, and the relationship between victim and offender. Many mediation programmes offer the option of indirect mediation (conciliation). Victims rate direct mediation higher than indirect mediation or court, and reported being less fearful when they meet their offender face to face.

   At least one conferencing programme, New Zealand, requires participation of qualifying juvenile offenders. This programme and some other conferencing programmes proceed with or without the attendance of the victim. Victim participation and satisfaction rating for New Zealand's youth justice family group conferencing was lower than for most restorative programmes.
3. Where victim and offender participate in restorative programmes, the rates of agreement and compliance with that agreement are very high. Victims and offenders with ongoing relationships produce agreements that are easy to get, but hard to keep. There is no consistent relationship between a programme's participation rate and either the agreement or compliance rates.
4. There is no intrinsic limitation to the type of dispute or disputants for which restorative justice can bring a reparative response and no empirical limitation reported in the evaluation research. Mediation and conferencing have reported successful resolutions in violent and property cases, adult felony and first-time juvenile cases, and between

strangers or among family members. For everything from consumer complaints to domestic violence, programme evaluations have documented the positive outcomes of restorative justice.

5. Justice does not need to be a trade-off between victims and offenders. Both victims and offenders rate restorative justice as more fair and satisfying than court. This is especially true for victims and models that directly involve communities of care. Several recent restorative justice programmes report fairness and satisfaction ratings from both offenders and victims above 95%.

6. Reoffending rates for offenders is no higher for restorative justice than it is for court adjudication. The effects of the programme on reoffending depend upon crime type and are related to participation rates. While there appears to be a strong self-selection effect for the voluntary programmes, reoffending following restorative justice processing seems to be reduced more among offences against the persons than property offences or victimless offences.

In spite of many programme assessments, research on restorative justice practice today is a mile wide but only an inch deep. Beyond documenting a self-selection effect on recidivism, few assessments have explored the relationships between case attrition and outcomes within or between programmes or case types. Evidence that certain cases produce agreements which are easy to get but hard to keep remains mixed. While conferencing programmes seem to produce higher outcomes on average than mediation, without multivariate assessments of programme and dispute characteristics, there is insufficient empirical basis for establishing 'best practices.' Until cross-programme cost-benefit analyses are available, no objective criteria exist for determining how best to 'fit the forum to the fuss.'

The logical limits of a voluntary approach remain undetermined. For example, how does compelling offender participation affect victim participation rates, participant perceptions, agreement compliance and offender recidivism? The low response of victims to mandatory FGCs suggests voluntariness of the process affects satisfaction rates, but New Zealand's programme is unique in this respect. Even on a voluntary basis, restorative justice remains an option available to very few in most places outside some countries in Europe.

The finding of larger recidivism effects for cases involving interpersonal violence raises an interesting question. Repeat victimisation needs to be distinguished from new victimisation to know how much of the reported lower reoffending is due to resolving the conflict thereby preventing an escalation of conflict between those particular disputants, and how much is due to reforming the general behaviour of the offender.

Finally, no studies have evaluated the effect of restorative justice on the nature and strength of social bonding within localities receiving intensive restorative services over an extended period, as is occurring in Rotterdam and some counties of New York State. The promise of aggregate reduction in the crime rate reported from Sparwood, British Columbia, has not been replicated elsewhere, nor was adequate pre-programme baseline data available to evaluate the system-wide implementation of programmes in Austria, Norway or New Zealand. Thus, the aggregate crime reduction potential of restorative justice remains unexamined.

None the less, the overall results from the empirical research demonstrate that restorative justice programmes consistently perform as well or better than traditional prosecution across countries, clients and programme types. Given these findings, restorative justice can be expected to continue to gain popular and political support. The future development of restorative justice should be accompanied by carefully controlled scientific assessments using standardised measures across a variety of settings and practices.

If research on restorative justice practice is to evolve, findings need to be comparable across programmes. Assessments need to report conditions for programme eligibility, the number of cases referred, the number of cases participating, reasons for non-participation, number and nature of agreements reached, and the rate of compliance with agreements. Results need to be disaggregated by offence type and disputant relationship. Programmes providing indirect conciliation and conferences without victim presence should report these data separately. Referred but non-participating cases need to be included in follow-up surveys and incorporated into the analyses of programme outcomes. Participant satisfaction/fairness findings reported should allow for computing percentage positive response.

Without concerted governmental guidance, programme assessments are likely to continue to reconfirm already well established findings while contributing little to the cumulative understanding of the practice of restorative justice.

Note

1. Excluded are assessments of restorative practices devoted to child welfare family interventions, since this specific application is beyond the scope of this chapter (see Burford and Hudson 2000).

References

Aertsen, I. (2000) 'Victim–Offender Mediation in Belgium', in the European Forum for Victim–Offender Mediation and Restorative Justice (ed.) *Victim–Offender Mediation in Europe: Making Restorative Justice Work.* Leuven: Leuven University Press.

American Bar Association. (1990) *Dispute Resolution Programme Directory 1990.* Washington, DC: American Bar Association Standing Committee on Dispute Resolution.

Bae, I. (1992) 'A Survey on Public Acceptance of Restitution as an Alternative to Incarceration for Property Offenders in Hennepin County, Minnesota, USA', in H. Messmer, and H.-U. Otto, (eds) *Restorative Justice on Trial: Pitfalls and Potentials of Victim–Offender Mediation – International Research Perspectives.* Dordrecht: Kluwer Academic Publishers.

Bannenberg, B. (2000) 'Victim–Offender Mediation in Germany', in the European Forum for Victim–Offender Mediation and Restorative Justice (ed.) *Victim–Offender Mediation in Europe: Making Restorative Justice Work.* Leuven: Leuven University Press.

Bilsky, W., Pfeiffer, H. and Trenczek, T. (1991) 'New Forms of Conflict Management in Juvenile Law: A Comparative Evaluation of the Brunswick Victim–Offender Reconciliation Programme', in G. Kaiser (eds) *Victims and Criminal Justice: Legal Protection, Restitution and Support. Criminological Research Reports* 51. Saarbrücken: Max-Planck Institute.

Bouwman, J. (1997) 'Sparwood Youth Assistance Programme.' Paper presented to 'Dawn or Dusk in Sentencing', CIAJ national conference, Montreal, 24–26, April.

Braithwaite, J. (1989) *Crime, Shame and Reintegration.* New York, NY: Cambridge University Press.

Braithwaite, J. (2002) *Restorative Justice and Responsive Regulation.* New York, NY: Oxford University Press.

Braithwaite, J. and Mugford, S. (1994) 'Conditions of Successful Reintegration Ceremonies', *British Journal of Criminology*, 34(2): 139–71.

Burford, G. and Hudson, J. (eds) (2000) *Family Group Conferencing in Child Welfare.* Monsey, NY: Willow Tree Press.

Calhoun, A. (2000a) *Calgary Community Conferencing: Participant Satisfaction: 1998–2000.* Calgary: Calgary Community Conferencing, Youth Probation Services [www.calgary communityconferencing.com/rande/satisfaction.html].

Calhoun, A. (2000b) *Calgary Community Conferencing: Activities and Outputs: January 1998 – July 2000.* Calgary: Calgary Community Conferencing, Youth Probation Services.

Chatterjee, J. (1999) *A Report on the Evaluation of RCMP Restorative Justice Initiative: Community Justice Forum as Seen by Participants.* Ottawa: Research and Evaluation Branch, Community Contract and Aboriginal Policing Services, Royal Canadian Mounted Police.

Citizens' Action on Crime (1980) *Waste, Delay and Ineffectiveness: An Economic Analysis of New York City's Criminal Justice System.* New York, NY: Citizens' Action on Crime.

Claassen, R. and Zehr, H. (1989) VORP Organizing: A Foundation in the Church. Elkhart, IN: Mennonite Central Committee, Office of Criminal Justice.

Coates, R. (1985) *Victim Meets Offender: An Evaluation of Victim–Offender Reconciliation Programmes.* Valparaiso, IN: PACT Institute of Justice.

Coates, R. (1990) 'Victim–Offender Reconciliation Programmes in North America: An Assessment', in G. Galaway and J. Hudson (eds) *Criminal Justice, Restitution, and Reconciliation.* Monsey, NY: Criminal Justice Press.

Coates, R. and Gehm, J. (1989) 'An Empirical Assessment', in M. Wright and B. Galaway (eds) *Mediation and Criminal Justice.* London: Sage.

Cook, R., Roehl, J. and Sheppard, D. (1980) *Neighborhood Justice Centers Field Test: Final Evaluation Report.* Washington, DC: Government Printing Office.

Cordella, J. (1991) 'Reconciliation and the Mutualist Model of Community', in H. Pepinsky, and R. Quinney, (eds) *Criminology as Peacemaking.* Bloomington, IN: Indiana University Press.

Couture, J., Parker, T., Couture, R. and Baboucane, P. (2001) *A Cost-Benefit Analysis of Hollow Water's Community Holistic Circle Healing Process.* Native Counseling Services of Alberta.

Czarnecka-Dzialuk, B. and Wojcik, D. (2000) 'Victim–Offender Mediation in Poland', in the European Forum for Victim–Offender Mediation and Restorative Justice (ed.) *Victim–Offender Mediation in Europe: Making Restorative Justice Work.* Leuven: Leuven University Press.

Daly, K. (2000) 'Ideals Meet Reality: Research results on Youth Justice Conferences in South Australia.' Paper presented to the fourth international conference on restorative justice for juveniles, Tuebingen, Germany, 1–4 October.

Daly, K. (2001a) 'Conferencing in Australia and New Zealand: Variations, Research Findings, and Prospects,' in A. Morris and G. Maxwell (eds). *Restorative Justice for Juveniles: Conferencing, Mediation and Circles.* Portland, OR: Hart Publishing.

Daly, K. (2001b) *Research on Conferencing. Technical Report 2.* South Australia Juvenile Justice.

Davis, G., Boucherat, J. and Watson, D. (1987) *A Preliminary Study of Victim–Offender Mediation and Reparation Schemes in England and Wales. Research and Planning Unit Paper* 42. London: Home Office.

Davis, R. (1982) 'Mediation: The Brooklyn Experiment', in R. Tomasic and M. Feeley (eds) *Neighborhood Justice – Assessment of an Emerging Idea.* New York, NY: Longman.

Davis, R., Tichane, M. and Grayson, D. (1980) *Mediation and Arbitration as Alternatives to Prosecution in Felony Arrest Cases: An Evaluation of the Brooklyn Dispute Resolution Center.* New York, NY: Vera Institute of Justice.

de Jong, W. (2001) 'Neighborhood-centered conflict mediation in the Netherlands: An Instrument for Social Cohesion – Part II', *Contemporary Justice Review,* 4(1): 49–58.

Dignan, J. (1990) *Repairing the Damage: An Evaluation of an Experimental Adult Reparation Scheme in Kettering, Northamptonshire.* Centre for Criminological and Legal Research, University of Sheffield.

Dignan, J. (1992) 'Repairing the Damage: Can Reparation be Made to Work in the Service of Diversion?', *British Journal of Criminology* 32: 453–72.

Dunkel, F. and Rössner, D. (1989) 'Law and Practice of Victim/Offender Agreements', in M. Wright and B. Galaway (eds) *Mediation and Criminal Justice: Victims, Offenders and Community.* London: Sage.

Evaluation Group (1980) *An Evaluation Report on the Suffolk County Community Mediation Center.* Glendale, NY: Evaluation Group, Inc.

Evje, A. and Cushman, R. (2000) *A Summary of the Evaluations of Six California Victim–Offender Reconciliation Programs. Report to the California Legislature.* The Judicial Council of California, Administrative Office of the Courts, Center for Families, Children and the Courts, May.

Felstiner, W. and Williams, L. (1980) *Community Mediation in Dorchester, Massachusetts.* Washington, DC: US Government Print Office.

Fercello, C. and Umbreit, M. (1998) *Client Evaluation of Family Group Conferencing in 12 Sites in the 1st Judicial District of Minnesota.* St Paul, MN: Center for Restorative Justice and Mediation.

Francey, C., Palenski, J.E., Roehl, J. and Jacobs, N. (1983) 'Evaluating Dispute Resolution Programmes', in M.R. Volpe *et al.* (eds) *Mediation in the Justice System – Conference Proceedings.* Chicago, IL: American Bar Association Special Committee on Resolution of Minor Disputes.

Galaway, B. (1984) 'A Survey of Public Acceptance of Restitution as an Alternative to Imprisonment for Property Offenders', *Australian and New Zealand Journal of Criminology,* 17(2): 108–17.

Gallup Organisation, Inc. (2000) *Reported in the Sourcebook of Criminal Justice Statistics* Albany, NY: University at Albany (www.albany.edu/sourcebook/).

Garofalo, J. and Connelly, K. (1980a) 'Dispute Resolution Centers. Part I. Major Features and Processes', *Criminal Justice Abstracts,* September: 416–39.

Garofalo, J. and Connelly, K. (1980b) 'Dispute Resolution Centers. Part II. Outcomes, Issues, and Future Directions', *Criminal Justice Abstracts,* December: 576–611.

Gehm, J.R. (1990) 'Mediated Victim–Offender Restitution Agreements: An Exploratory Analysis of Factors Related to Victim Participation', in B. Galaway, and J. Hudson (eds) *Criminal Justice, Restitution and Reconciliation.* Monsey, NY: Criminal Justice Press.

Grönfors, M. (1989a) 'Ideals and Reality in Community Mediation', in M. Wright, and B. Galaway (eds) *Mediation and Criminal Justice: Victims, Offenders and Community.* London: Sage.

Grönfors, M. (1989b) 'Mediation – Experiment in Finland', in P. Albrecht and O. Backes (eds) *Crime Prevention and Intervention: Legal and Ethical Problems.* New York, NY: Walter de Gruyter.

Grönfors, M. (1992) 'Mediation: A Romantic Ideal or a Workable Alternative?', in H. Messmer and H.-U. Otto (eds) *Restorative Justice on Trial: Pitfalls and Potentials of Victim–Offender Mediation – International Research Perspectives.* Dordrecht: Kluwer Academic.

Hartmann, A. (1992) 'Victim–Offender Reconciliation: Programme and Outcomes', in H. Messmer and H.-U. Otto (eds) *Restorative Justice on Trial: Pitfalls and Potentials of Victim–Offender Mediation – International Research Perspectives.* Dordrecht: Kluwer Academic.

Hassall, I. (1996) 'Origin and Development of Family Group Conferences' in J. Hudson, *et al.* (eds) *Family Group Conferences: Perspectives on Policy and Practice.* Monsey, NY: Criminal Justice Press.

Hayes, H. and Prinzler, T. (1998) *Making Amends: Final Evaluation of the Queensland Community Conferencing Pilot.* Brisbane: Department of Justice.

Henry, M. (1982) 'The New York Experience: The Community Dispute Resolution Centers Programme', in M. Volpe *et al.* (eds) *Mediation in the Criminal Justice System Conference Proceedings, May 20–21.* New York, NY: John Jay College of Criminal Justice.

Hudson, J. and Galaway, B. (1974) 'Undoing the wrong', *Social Work,* 19(3): 313–18.

Hughes, S. and Schneider, A. (1989) 'Victim–Offender Mediation: A Survey of Programme Characteristics and Perceptions of Effectiveness', *Crime and Delinquency,* 35: 2, 217–33.

Hughes, S. and Schneider, A. (1990) *Victim–Offender Mediation in the Juvenile Justice System.* Washington, DC: US Office of Juvenile Justice and Delinquency Prevention.

Iivari, J. (2000) 'Victim–Offender Mediation in Finland', in the European Forum for Victim–Offender Mediation and Restorative Justice (ed.) *Victim–Offender Mediation in Europe: Making Restorative Justice Work.* Leuven: Leuven University Press).

Jullion, D. (2000) 'Victim Offender Mediation in France', in the European Forum for Victim–Offender Mediation and Restorative Justice (ed.) *Victim–Offender Mediation in Europe: Making Restorative Justice Work.* Leuven: Leuven University Press.

Karmen, A. (1990) *Crime Victims: An Introduction to Victimology.* Belmont, CA: Wadsworth.

Kerlinger, F. (1973) *Foundations of Behavioral Research.* (2nd edn). New York, NY: Holt, Rinehart and Winston.

Kressel, K. and Pruitt, D. (1985) 'The Mediation of Social Conflict', *Journal of Social Issues,* 41(2), 179–19.

Kressel, K. *et al.* (1989) 'Conclusion: A Research Perspective on the Mediation of Social Conflict', in K. Kressel *et al.* (eds) *Mediation Research: The Process and Effectiveness of Third-party Intervention.* San Francisco: Jossey-Bass.

Loschnig-Gspandl, M. and Kilchling, M. (1997) 'Victim/Offender Mediation and Victim Compensation in Austria and Germany – Stocktaking and Perspectives for Future Research', *European Journal of Criminal Law and Criminal Justice,* 5(1): 58–78.

MacWillie, J. (1981) *The Price of Justice: The Cost of Arresting and Prosecuting Three Robbery Cases in Manhattan.* New York, NY: New York City Criminal Justice Coordinating Council.

Marshall, T. (1990) 'Results of Research from British Experiments in Restorative Justice', in B. Galaway and J. Hudson (eds) *Criminal Justice, Restitution, and Reconciliation.* Monsey, NY: Criminal Justice Press.

Marshal, T. and Merry, S. (1990) *Crime and Accountability.* London: Home Office.

Maxwell, G. (1993) 'Family Decision-making in Youth Justice: The New Zealand Model', in L. Atkinson and S.-A. Gerull (eds) *National Conference on Juvenile*

Justice. Conference Proceedings No. 22. Canberra: Australian Institute of Criminology.

Maxwell, G. and Morris, A. (1993) *Family, Victims and Culture: Youth Justice in New Zealand.* Wellington: Institute of Criminology, Victoria University of Wellington.

Maxwell, G. and Morris, A. (1994) 'The New Zealand Model of Family Group Conferences', in C. Alder and J. Wundersitz (eds) *Family Conferencing and Juvenile Justice: The Way Forward or Misplaced Optimism?.* Canberra: Australian Institute of Criminology.

Maxwell, G. and Morris, A. (1999) *Understanding Reoffending.* Wellington: Institute of Criminology, Vicoria University of Wellington.

Maxwell, G. and Morris, A. (2001) 'Family Group Conferences and Reoffending', in A. Morris and G. Maxwell (eds) *Restorative Justice for Juveniles: Conferencing, Mediation and Circles.* Portland, OR: Hart Publishing.

McCold, P. (1999) *Virginia Conferencing Project: Evaluation Results.* Pipersville, PA: Community Service Foundation.

McCold, P. (2000) 'Toward a Mid-range Theory of Restorative Criminal Justice: A Reply to the Maximalist Model', *Contemporary Justice Review*, 3(4): 357–414.

McCold, P. (2001) 'Primary Restorative Justice Practices', in A. Morris, A. and G. Maxwell, (eds), *Restorative Justice for Juveniles: Conferencing, Mediation and Circles.* Portland, OR: Hart Publishing.

McCold, P. and Wachtel, B. (1998) *Restorative Policing Experiment: The Bethlehem Pennsylvania Police Family Group Conferencing Project.* Washington, DC: US Printing Office.

McCold, P. and Wachtel, T. (2000) 'Restorative Justice Theory Validation.' Paper presented at the fourth international conference on restorative justice for juveniles, Tübingen, Germany, 1–4 October.

McEwen , C. and Maiman, R. (1982) 'Mediation and Arbitration: Their Promise and Performance as Alternatives to Courts', in P. Dubois (ed.) *The Analysis of Judicial Reform.* Lexington, MA: Lexington Books.

McGarrell, E., Olivares, K., Crawford, K. and Kroovand, N. (2000) *Returning to the Community: The Indianapolis Juvenile Restorative Justice Experiment.* Indianapolis, IN: Hudson Institute Crime Control Policy Center.

McGillis, D. and Mullen, J. (1997) *Neighborhood Justice Centers: An Analysis of Potential Models.* Washington, DC: US Government Printing Office).

Merry, S.E. and Milner, N. (eds) (1995) *The Possibility of Popular Justice: A Case Study of Community Mediation in the United States.* Ann Arbor, MI: University of Michigan Press.

Miers, D. (2001) *An International Review of Restorative Justice. Crime Reduction Research* Series Paper 10. London: Home Office.

Moore, D.B. (1995) A New Approach to Juvenile Justice: An Evaluation of Family Conferencing', in *A Report to the Criminology Research Council. Wagga Wagga*: Centre for Rural Social Research, Charles Sturt University-Riverina.

Morris, A. and Maxwell, G. (1993) 'Juvenile Justice in New Zealand: A new paradigm,' *Australian and New Zealand Journal of Criminology*, 26: 72–90.

Morris, A. and Maxwell, G. (1998) 'Restorative Justice in New Zealand: Family

Group Conferences as a Case Study', *Western Criminology Review* 1(1) (http://wcr. sonoma.edu/v1n1/morris.html).

Morris, A., Maxwell, G. and Robertson, J. (1993) 'Giving Victims a Voice: A New Zealand Experiment', *The Howard Journal,* 32(4): 304–21.

Mott McDonald Associates, Inc. (1979) *The Cost of Justice: An Analysis of Case Processing Costs in the Bronx.* Washington, DC: Criminal Justice System.

Netzig, L. and Trenczek, T. (1996) 'Restorative Justice as Participation: Theory, Law, Experience and Research', in B. Galaway and J. Hudson (eds) *Restorative Justice: International Perspectives.* Monsey, NY: Criminal Justice Press.

New York State Unified Court System (1985) *The Community Dispute Resolution Centers Program: A Progress Report: January 1, 1984 to March 31, 1985.* Albany, NY: New York State Unified Court System.

New York State Unified Court System (1999) *Dispute Resolution Centers Program. Annual Report for the Fiscal Year 1998–1999.* Albany, NY: Office of Alternative Dispute Resolution, Division of Court Operations, New York State Unified Court System.

Northey, W. (1989) 'Biblical/Theological Works Contributing to Restorative Justice: A Bibliographic Essay', in *New Perspectives on Crime and Justice.* 8. Akron, PA: Mennonite Central Committee Office of Criminal Justice.

Nugent, W. and Paddock, J. (1995) 'The Effect of Victim–Offender Mediation on Severity of Reoffence', *Mediation Quarterly,* 12(4), 353–67.

O'Connell, T. (1998) 'From Wagga Wagga to Minnesota', in *Conferencing: A New Response to Wrongdoing. Proceedings of the First North American Conference on Conferencing.* Bethlehem, PA: Real Justice.

O'Connell, T., Wachtel, B. and Wachtel, T. (1999) *Conferencing Handbook: The New Real Justice Training Manual.* Pipersville, PA: The Piper's Press.

Olsen, T., Maxwell, G. and Morris, A. (1995) 'Maori and Youth Justice in New Zealand', in K. Hazlehurst, (ed.) *Popular Justice and Community Regeneration.* London: Praeger.

Palk, G., Hayes, H. and Prenzler, T. (1998) 'Restorative Justice and Community Conferencing: Summary of Findings from a Pilot Study', *Current Issues in Criminal Justice,* 10(2), 138–55.

Pate, K. (1990) 'Victim–Young Offender Reconciliation as Alternative Measures Programmes in Canada', in B. Galaway and J. Hudson (eds) *Criminal Justice, Restitution, and Reconciliation.* Monsey, NY: Criminal Justice Press.

Paus, K. (2000) 'Victim–Offender Mediation in Norway', in the European Forum for Victim–Offender Mediation and Restorative Justice (ed.) *Victim–Offender Mediation in Europe: Making Restorative Justice Work.* Leuven: Leuven University Press.

Pearson, J. and Thoennes, N. (1982) 'Mediation and Divorce: The Benefits Outweigh the Costs', *The Family Advocate,* 4: 26–32.

Pearson, J. and Thoennes, N. (1984) 'A Preliminary Portrait of Client Reactions to Three Court Mediation Programmes', *Mediation Quarterly,* 3: 21–40.

Pearson, J., Thoennes, N. and Vanderkooi, L. (1982) 'The Decision to Mediate: Profiles of Individuals who Accept and Reject the Opportunity to Mediate Contested Child Custody and Visitation Issues', *Journal of Divorce,* 6: 17–35.

Pelikan, C. (2001) 'Victim–Offender Mediation in Austria', in the European Forum for Victim–Offender Mediation and Restorative Justice (ed.) *Victim–Offender Mediation in Europe: Making Restorative Justice Work*. Leuven: Leuven University Press).

Pratt, J. (1996) 'Colonization, Power and Silence: A History of Indigenous Justice in New Zealand Society', in B. Galaway and J. Hudson (eds) *Restorative Justice: International Perspectives*. Monsey, NY: Criminal Justice Press.

Ray, L. (1979) 'Intake and the Night Prosecutor's Programme – The Year in Review 1978'. in US House, Subcommittee on Courts, Civil Liberties, and the Administration of Justice, Committee on the Judiciary, and Subcommittee on Consumer Protection and Finance, Committee on Interstate and Foreign Commerce (Joint Hearings), *Resolution of Minor Disputes*. Washington, DC: US Government Printing Office.

Roehl, J. and Cook, R. (1982) 'Neighborhood Justice Centers Field Test', in R. Tomasic and M.M. Feeley (eds) *Neighborhood Justice – Assessment of an Emerging Idea*. New York, NY: Longman.

Roehl, J. and Cook, R. (1989) 'Mediation in interpersonal disputes: Effectiveness and Limitations', in K. Kressel, D. Pruit and Associates (eds) *Mediation Research: The Process and Effectiveness of Third-party Intervention*. (San Francisco: Jossey-Bass.

Rössner, D. (1996) 'Situation, Ethical Grounds and Criminal Political Perspective of Victim–Offender Reconciliation in Community', in B. Galaway and J. Hudson (eds) *Restorative Justice: International Perspectives*. Monsey, NY: Criminal Justice Press.

Roy, S. (1993a) 'Perspectives on Juvenile Delinquency', *Journal of Contemporary Criminal Justice*, 9(2): 81–167.

Roy, S. (1993b) 'Two Types of Juvenile Restitution programmes in two Midwestern Counties: A Comparative Study', *Federal Probation*, 57(4): 48–53.

Roy, S. (1994) 'Victim–Offender Reconciliation Programme for Juveniles in Elkhart County, Indiana: An exploratory study', *Justice Professional*, (8)2: 23–35.

Schöch, H. and Bannenberg, B. (1991) 'Victim–Offender Reconciliation in Germany: Stocktaking and Criminal Political Consequences' in G. Kaiser *et al.* (eds) *Victims and Criminal Justice: Legal Protection, Restitution and Support. Criminological Research Reports* 51. Saarbrücken: Max-Planck Institute.

Schulman, Ronca and Bucuvalas, Inc. (1999) *What Do we Want (and What are we Getting) from the Criminal Justice System? Comparing the General Public's Expectations and Perceptions with Crime Victims' Experiences. Conducted for Council of State Governments Eastern Regional Conference, August 10*. New York, NY: Schulman, Ronca and Bucuvalas, Inc.

Sessar, K. (1999) 'Punitive Attitudes of the Public: Reality and Myth,' in G. Bazemore, G. and L. Walgrave (eds) *Restorative Juvenile Justice: Reparing the Harm of Youth Crime*. Monsey, NY: Criminal Justice Press.

Sherman, L., Strang, H., Barnes, G., Braithwaite, J., Inkpen, N. and The, M.M. (1998) *Experiments in Restorative Policing. A Progress Report on the Canberra ReIntegrative Shaming Experiments (RISE) to the National Police Research Unit*. Australian National University, June (www.aic.gov.au/rjustice/rise/).

Sherman, L., Strang, H., Barnes, G., Braithwaite, J., Inkpen, J. and The, M.M. (1999) *Experiments in Restorative Policing. A Progress Report on the Canberra ReIntegrative Shaming Experiments (RISE) to the National Police Research Unit.* Australian National University, July (www.aic.gov.au/rjustice/rise/).

Sherman, L., Strang, H. and Woods, D. (2000) *Recidivism Patterns in the Canberra ReIntegrative Shaming Experiments (RISE).* Centre for Restorative Justice, Research School of Social Sciences, Australian National University, November (www.aic.gov.au/rjustice/rise/).

Stead, D.G. (1986) 'The effectiveness of Criminal Mediation: An Alternative to Court Proceedings in a Canadian City. Dissertation, University of Denver. Ann Arbor, MI: University Microfilms International.

Strang, H. (1999) Restorative Justice: Current Developments and Research findings. Paper presented at the third National Outlook 'Symposium on crime in Australia: Mapping the Boundaries of Australia's Criminal Justice System', Canberra, 22–23 March (www.aic.gov.au/rjustice/rise/).

Timboli, L. (2000) *An Evaluation of the New South Wales Youth Justice Conferencing Scheme.* Sidney: NSW Bureau of Crime Statistics and Research, Attorney General's Department (www.lawlink.nsw.gov.au/bocsar1.nsf/pages/reports_new).

Trenczek, T. (1990) 'A Review and Assessment of Victim–Offender Reconciliation Programming in West Germany' in B. Galaway and J. Hudson (eds) *Criminal Justice, Restitution, and Reconciliation.* Monsey, NY: Criminal Justice Press.

Umbreit, M. (1993) 'Juvenile Offenders Meet their Victims: The Impact of Mediation in Albuquerque, New Mexico,' *Family and Conciliation Courts Review,* 31(1): 90–100.

Umbreit, M. (1994a) 'Crime Victims Confront their Offenders: The Impact of a Minneapolis Mediation Programme', *Journal of Research on Social Work Practice,* 4(4), 436–47.

Umbreit, M. (1994b) *Victim Meets Offender: The Impact of Restorative Justice and Mediation.* Monsey, NY: Criminal Justice Press.

Umbreit, M. (1995) 'The Effects of Victim–Offender Mediation', in M. Tonry and K. Hamilton (eds) *Intermediate Sanctions in Over-crowded Times.* Boston, MA: Northeastern University Press.

Umbreit, M. (1996a) 'A Humanistic Mediation Model: Moving to a Higher Plane,' *VOMA Quarterly* 7(3).

Umbreit, M. (1996b) 'Restorative Justice through Mediation: The Impact of Offenders Facing their Victims in Oakland', *Law and Social Work,* 5(1): 1–13.

Umbreit, M. (1996c) 'Restorative Justice through Mediation: The Impact of Programmes in Four Canadian Provinces', in B. Galaway and J. Hudson (eds) *Restorative Justice: International Perspectives.* Monsey, NY: Criminal Justice Press.

Umbreit, M. (1997) 'Humanistic Mediation: A Transformative Journey of Peace-making', *Mediation Quarterly,* 14(3), 201–13.

Umbreit, M. (1998) 'Restorative Justice through Victim–Offender Mediation: A Multi-site Assessment, *Western Criminology Review,* 1(1): 1–29.

Umbreit, M. and Coates, R. (1992) *Victim–Offender Mediation: An Analysis of Programmes in Four States of the US.* Minneapolis, MN: Minnesota Citizens' Council on Crime and Justice.

Umbreit, M., Coates, R., Kalanj, B., Lipkin, B. and Petros, G. (1995) *Mediation of Criminal Conflict: An Assessment of Programmes in Four Canadian Provinces. Executive Summary Report.* St. Paul, MN: Center for Restorative Justice and Mediation, University of Minnesota.

Umbreit, M. and Fercello, C. (1997) *Woodbury Police Department's Restorative Justice Community Conferencing Programme: An Initial Assessment of Client Satisfaction.* St. Paul, MN: Center for Restorative Justice and Mediation, University of Minnesota.

Umbreit, M. and Warner Roberts, A. (1996) *Mediation of Criminal Conflict in England: An Assessment of Services In Coventry and Leeds.* Minneapolis, MN: Center for Restorative Justice and Mediation, School of Social Work, University of Minnesota.

Victim–Offender Reconciliation Resource Center (1984) *The VORP Book: An Organisational and Operation Manual.* Valparaiso, IN: PACT Institute of Justice.

Walker, J. (1992) 'Mediation in Divorce: Does the Process Match the Rhetoric?' in H. Messmer and H.-U. Otto (eds) *Restorative Justice on Trial: Pitfalls and Potentials of Victim–Offender Mediation – International Research Perspectives.* Dordrecht: Kluwer Academic.

Walker, L. (2001) 'Conferencing: A New Approach for Juvenile Justice in Honolulu.' Unpublished paper, Hawaii Friends of Civic and Law Related Education, Waialua, Hawaii.

Wandrey, M. (1992) 'Organisational Demands on Mediation Programmes: Problems of Realisation', in H. Messmer and H.-U. Otto (eds) *Restorative Justice on Trial: Pitfalls and Potentials of Victim–Offender Mediation – International Research Perspectives.* Dordrecht: Kluwer Academic.

Warner, S. (1992) 'Reparation, Mediation and Scottish Criminal Justice', in H. Messmer, H. and H.-U. Otto (eds) *Restorative Justice on Trial: Pitfalls and Potentials of Victim–Offender Mediation – International Research Perspectives.* (Dordrecht, NETH: Kluwer Academic.

Warner, S., Knapp, M. and A. Netten, A. (1992) *Making Amends: Justice for Victims and Offenders: An Evaluation of the SACRO Reparation and Mediation Project.* Aldershot: Ashgate.

Warner-Roberts, A. and Masters, G. (1999) *Group Conferencing: Restorative Justice in Practice.* Minneapolis, MN: University of Minnesota, Center for RJ and Mediation, School of Social Work.

Weitekamp, E. (2000) 'Research on Victim–Offender Mediation: Findings and Needs for the Future', in the European Forum for Victim–Offender Mediation and Restorative Justice (ed.) *Victim–Offender Mediation in Europe: Making Restorative Justice Work.* Leuven: Leuven University Press.

Wright, M. (1996) *Justice for Victims and Offenders: A Restorative Response to Crime.* (2nd edn). Winchester: Waterside Press.

Wundersitz, J. and Hetzel, S. (1996) 'Family Conferencing for Young Offenders: The South Australian Experience' in J. Hudson, J. *et al.* (eds) *Family Group Conferences: Perspectives on Policy and Practice.* Monsey, NY: Criminal Justice Press.

Wynne, J. (1996) 'Leeds Mediation and Reparation Service: Ten Years' Experience with Victim–Offender Mediation', in B. Galaway and J. Hudson (eds) *Restorative Justice: International Perspectives*. Monsey NY: Criminal Justice Press.

Yarn, D. (1999) *Dictionary of Conflict Resolution*. San Francisco, CA: Jossey-Bass.

Zehr, H. and Umbreit, M. (1982) 'Victim–Offender Reconciliation: An Incarceration Substitute?' *Federal Probation*, 46(4): 63–8.

APPENDIX
Restorative Justice Program Assessment Samples

program	program start yr	clients	most freq offense	annual contacts	participation (direct)	agreements	compliance	victim-max	offender-max	source
COMMUNITY GROUP CONFERENCING										
Wagga Wagga AU-CGC	1991	juvenile	assault	186	67%		95%	100%	91%	Moore 1995
South Australia-CGC	1993	indictable juvenile	assault	1,397	90%		86%	87%	95%	Daly 2000; Wundersitz & Hetzel 1996
Canberra AU d.driving-CGC	1994	adult	drink drive	326	69%		97%		86%	Sherman, et al 1998, 1999; Strang 1999; Sherman, et al 2000
Canberra AU p.property-CGC	1994	juvenile	personal property	38	89%				94%	Sherman, et al 1998, 1999; Strang 1999; Sherman, et al 2000
Canberra AU retail-CGC	1994	juvenile	retail theft	32	81%		77%		89%	Sherman, et al 1998, 1999; Strang 1999; Sherman, et al 2000
Canberra AU violent-CGC	1994	youth <30	youth violent	15			94%		88%	Sherman, et al 1998, 1999; Strang 1999; Sherman, et al 2000
Woodbury MN-CGC	1995	juveniles		44						Umbreit & Fercello 1997
Sparwood CGC	1995	youth	theft	48	100%	95%	100%	94%		Bouwman 1997
Minnesota 12 site-CGC	1995	juveniles	shoplifting	129		100%		100%	98%	Fercello & Umbreit 1998
Bethlehem PA property-CGC	1996	juvenile	retail theft	37	50%	98%	98%	98%	100%	McCold & Wachtel 1998
Bethlehem PA violent-CGC	1996	juvenile	disorderly	16	32%	100%	92%	100%	94%	McCold & Wachtel 1998
Indianapolis IN-CGC	1996	<15 yr old	retail theft	91	78%		83%	98%	93%	McGarrell, Olivares, Crawford & Kroovand 2000
Calgary CA-CGC	1997	juvenile	robbery	14	64%			94%	88%	Calhoun 2000
Canadian-CGC	1997	juveniles	theft	54			85%	97%	87%	Chatterjee 1999
Virginia 4 site-CGC	1998	juveniles	assault	81	43%	98%		100%	100%	McCold 1999
Honolulu HI-CGC	2000	juveniles	assault	146	64%	100%	87%	89%	88%	Walker 2001
FAMILY GROUP CONFERENCING										
New Zealand-FGC	1990	indictable juvenile	burglary	5,000	41%	95%	58%	49%	86%	Maxwell 1993; Maxwell & Morris 1994,1998
New South Wales-FGC	1998	juvenile	theft & burglary	885	69%		94%	94%	95%	Trimboli 2000
Queensland 3 site-FGC	1997	juvenile	theft	66	78%	100%	98%	98%	100%	Hayes & Prinzler 1998
-Ipswich AU-FGC	1997	juvenile	theft	35	84%	100%	94%	94%	100%	Hayes & Prinzler 1998
-Logan AU-FGC	1997	juvenile	theft	31	69%	100%	90%	94%	100%	Hayes & Prinzler 1998
-Palm Island AU-FGC	1997	juvenile	theft	9	100%					Palk, Hayes & Prenzler 1998
VICTIM OFFENDER MEDIATION										
Elkhart IN-VOM	1979	juvenile		190	60%		78%			Coates 1990; Roy 1994
Winnipeg CA-VOM	1979	adults	assault	327	34%	89%	98%	98%	100%	Umbreit 1996c; Umbreit et al.1995; Umbreit & Coates 1992
VORP 5 site IN-VOM	1980	juvenile	burglary	24	51%	98%	91%	97%	100%	Coates 1985;Coates & Gehm 1989; Roy 1993 1994
Norway-VOM	1981	youth	theft	4,752	74%	93%	94%	95%	98%	Paus 2000
Langley CA-VOM	1982	youth	mischief	82	44%	99%		89%	97%	Umbreit 1996c; Umbreit et al.1995; Umbreit & Coates 1992
Braunschweig DE-VOM	1982	juvenile	assault	24	34%		70%			Bilsky, Pfeiffer & Trenczek 1991; Trenczek, 1990
Finland-VOM	1983	both	assault	3,450	70%	60%	68%			Iivari 2000
German juvenile-VOM	1984	juvenile	assault/threat	434	60%	85%				Loschnig & Kilchling 1997; R suter 1996; Bannenberg 2000
German adult-VOM	1984	adult	assault/threat	342	70%	78%				Loschnig & Kilchling 1997; R suter 1996; Bannenberg 2000
Austria juvenile-VOM	1984	adult	assault/threat	2,602	40%		99%			Pelikan 2001
Minneapolis MN-VOM	1985	juvenile	vandalism	179	70%	93%	77%		94%	Umbreit 1994a, 1994b
Calgary CA-VOM	1985	youth	burglary	51	40%	94%			100%	Umbreit 1996c; Umbreit et al.1995; Umbreit & Coates 1992
English 2 site VOM	1985	both	burglary	39	37%		94%	100%		Umbreit & Warner-Roberts 1996
-Coventry UK-VOM	1985	both	burglary & theft	18	9%	80%		84%	86%	Umbreit & Warner-Roberts 1996
-Leeds UK-VOM	1985	both	burglary	21	13%	80%			62%	Umbreit & Warner-Roberts 1996
Scottish 2 site-VOM	1985	16+ years old	minor crimes	42	8%	80%				Warner 1992; Warner, Knapp & Netten 1992
German multisite youth DE-VOM	1985	juvenile	larceny	64	55%	94%	89%			Hartmann 1992; Netzig & Trenczek 1996; Dunkel & R suter 1989
German multisite adult-VOM	1985	adult	agg.assault	317	34%	93%	96%			Sch ch & Bannenberg 1991; Wandrey 1992
Oakland CAL-VOM	1986	juvenile	agg-assault	50	47%	85%	95%			Sch ch & Bannenberg 1991; Wandrey 1992
Kettering UK-VOM	1986	juvenile	vandalism	129	21%	91%			100%	Umbreit 1994b, 1996b
Cologne DE-VOM	1986	adults	property	28	35%	86%				Dignan 1990
Landshut DE-VOM	1986	juvenile	assault	75	35%	88%				Loschnig & Kilchling 1997
Albuquerque NM-VOM	1986	juveniles		38	77%	100%	91%	67%		Loschnig & Kilchling 1997
Orange CAL-VOM	1987	juvenile	burglary	108	74%	99%		86%	90%	Umbreit 1993, 1994b
Belgium-VOM	1987	juvenile		211	28%	97%	93%		70%	Aertsen 2000
Santa Clara CAL-VOM	1988	both	property	4,360	71%	53%	90%	68%		Evje & Cusman 2000
Ottawa CA-VOM	1989	juveniles	vandalism	69	14%	97%			95%	Evje & Cusman 2000
Austin TX-VOM	1989	adult	assault	114	56%	91%	77%		100%	Umbreit 1996c; Umbreit et al. 1995; Umbreit & Coates 1992
	1990	juvenile	burglary	246	37%	98%	95%		98%	Umbreit 1994b

APPENDIX
Restorative Justice Program Assessment Samples (continued)

Program	program start yr	clients	most freq. offense	annual contf/meds	participation (direct)	agreements	compliance	victim mat.	offender mat.	source
VICTIM OFFENDER MEDIATION (continued)										
Los Angeles CAL-VOM	1992	juvenile	nonviolent	299	48%	100%	70%	98%	99%	Evje & Cusman 2000
Austria adult-VOM	1992	juvenile	assault/threat	2,049	70%		99%		81%	Pelikan 2001
Sonoma CAL-VOM	1993	juveniles	nonpetition	68	49%		84%	81%	81%	Evje & Cusman 2000
Poland juvenile-VOM	1995	juvenile	nonpetition	32	90%	95%	90%			Czar 2000
Mendocino CAL-VOM	1997	juvenile	nonpetition	29	29%	100%	92%	93%	93%	Evje & Cusman 2000
Santa Barbara CAL-VOM	1997	juvenile	mid-property	29	28%	100%	93%	100%	100%	Evje & Cusman 2000
France-VOM	1998	both	assault	8,782	45%	69%				Jaillon 2000
COMMUNITY MEDIATION CENTRES										
Columbus OH-CMC	1971	adults	minor assault	4,548	48%	93%	68%	78%	78%	Garofalo & Connelly 1980
Dorchester MA-CMC	1975	adults w prior relate	assault/harassment	326	66%	89%				Felstiner & Williams 1980
Orange County FL-CMC	1975	adults	assault/harassment	362	55%	80%	52%	59%	69%	Garofalo & Connelly 1980
Venice CAL-CMC	1977	adults	retail	751	32%	69%	71%	85%	76%	Cook Roehl & Sheppard 1980; Roehl & Cook 1982, 1989
Kansas City MO-CMC	1977	adults	assault/harassment	1,333	31%	92%		87%	89%	Cook Roehl & Sheppard 1980; Roehl & Cook 1982, 1989
Suffolk NY-CMC	1977	adults		435	41%	90%	94%	77%	79%	Evaluation Group 1980
Brooklyn NY-CMC	1977	adult felons	felony assault	1,902	56%	99%			70%	Davis 1982; Davis Tichane & Grayson 1980
Dade County FL-CMC	1977	adults	assault/harassment	344	55%	80%				Garofalo & Connelly 1980
Broward County FL-CMC	1978	adults	assault/harassment	540	61%	83%				Garofalo & Connelly 1980
Duval County FL-CMC	1978	adults	assault/harassment	1,632	51%	90%				Garofalo & Connelly 1980
Pinellas County FL-CMC	1978	adults	landlord/tenant	1,586	58%	78%				Garofalo & Connelly 1980
Atlanta GA-CMC	1978	adults	retail		40%	81%	74%	61%		Cook Roehl & Sheppard 1980; Roehl & Cook 1982, 1989
New York State-CMC	1984	adults	harassment	15,780	39%	77%	78%	89%	96%	NYS Unified Court System 1985; 1999
-Rochester NY-CMC	1973	adults		876	38%	73%				NYS Unified Court System 1999
-Bronx NY-CMC	1975	adults		898	27%	73%				NYS Unified Court System 1999
-Rockland NY-CMC	1977	adults		128	53%	64%				NYS Unified Court System 1999
-Long Island NY-CMC	1977	adults		3,710	70%	83%				NYS Unified Court System 1999
-Rensselaer NY-CMC	1979	adults		86	37%	98%				NYS Unified Court System 1999
-Harlem NY-CMC	1981	adults		91	44%	84%				NYS Unified Court System 1999
-Ogdensburg NY-CMC	1981	adults		231	28%	81%				NYS Unified Court System 1999
-Syracuse NY-CMC	1981	adults		454	38%	81%				NYS Unified Court System 1999
-NY/Kings Co. NY-CMC	1981	adults		1,831	41%	76%				NYS Unified Court System 1999
-Schenectady NY-CMC	1982	adults		147	34%	73%				NYS Unified Court System 1999
-Albany NY-CMC	1982	adults		428	64%	93%				NYS Unified Court System 1999
-Buffalo NY-CMC	1982	adults		492	7%	82%				NYS Unified Court System 1999
-Goshen NY-CMC	1982	adults		639	71%	92%				NYS Unified Court System 1999
-Staten Island NY-CMC	1982	both		824	61%	69%				NYS Unified Court System 1999
-Binghamton NY-CMC	1982	both		826	43%	60%				NYS Unified Court System 1999
-Amsterdam NY-CMC	1983	adults		101	36%	86%				NYS Unified Court System 1999
-Ithaca NY-CMC	1983	adults		270	27%	92%				NYS Unified Court System 1999
-Saratoga NY-CMC	1983	adults		277	41%	63%				NYS Unified Court System 1999
-Poughkeepsie NY-CMC	1983	adults		409	63%	83%				NYS Unified Court System 1999
-Ulster/Sullivan NY-CMC	1984	adults		453	66%	88%				NYS Unified Court System 1999
-Watertown NY-CMC	1984	adults		463	39%	83%				NYS Unified Court System 1999
-Yonkers NY-CMC	1984	adults		247	23%	87%				NYS Unified Court System 1999
-Herkimer NY-CMC	1985	adults		31	9%	75%				NYS Unified Court System 1999
-Delhi NY-CMC	1985	adults		76	21%	93%				NYS Unified Court System 1999
-Auburn NY-CMC	1987	adults		67	41%	73%				NYS Unified Court System 1999
-Oneonta NY-CMC	1990	adults		221	48%	84%				NYS Unified Court System 1999
-Catskill NY-CMC	1992	adults		208	33%	85%				NYS Unified Court System 1999
-Queens NY-CMC	1995	adults		1,061	39%	96%				NYS Unified Court System 1999
-Utica NY-CMC	1996	adults		235	40%					NYS Unified Court System 1999
Rotterdam NL	1998	both	noise	54	33%	96%				de Jong 2001

APPENDIX
Restorative Justice Program Assessment Samples (continued)

Program	clients	annual conferrals	participation (direct)	compliance	victim max	offender max	source
CRIMINAL JUSTICE SYSTEM							
Canberra AU d.driving-nonreferred	match	349	96%			81%	Sherman, et al 1998, 1999; Strang 1999; Sherman, et al 2000
Canberra AU p.property-nonreferred	match	72	84%		47%	92%	Sherman, et al 1998, 1999; Strang 1999; Sherman, et al 2000
Canberra AU retail-nonreferred	match	41	89%			81%	Sherman, et al 1998, 1999; Strang 1999; Sherman, et al 2000
Canberra AU violent-nonreferred	match	33	90%		58%	83%	Sherman, et al 1998, 1999; Strang 1999; Sherman, et al 2000
Bethlehem PA property-nonreferred	match	30	91%		84%	100%	McCold & Wachtel 1998
Bethlehem PA property-referred	decline	20	73%		90%	85%	McCold & Wachtel 1998
Bethlehem PA violent-nonreferred	match	16	86%		77%	88%	McCold & Wachtel 1998
Bethlehem PA violent-referred	decline	13	69%		75%	85%	McCold & Wachtel 1998
Albuquerque NM-nonreferred	match	28		69%	63%	71%	Umbreit 1994b
Albuquerque NM-referred	decline	36			52%	86%	Umbreit 1994b
Minneapolis MN-nonreferred	match	71		55%	63%	77%	Umbreit 1994b
Minneapolis MN-referred	decline	40			64%	81%	Umbreit 1994b
Oakland CAL-nonreferred	match	12			56%	100%	Umbreit 1994b
Oakland CAL-referred	decline	19			63%	78%	Umbreit 1994b
VOM 4 site US-nonreferrals	match	110		58%	62%	74%	Umbreit 1994b
VOM 4 site US-referred	decline	95			57%	82%	Umbreit 1994b
Langley CA-referred	decline	42			57%	69%	Umbreit 1996c; Umbreit et al. 1995; Umbreit & Coates 1992
Ottawa CA-referred	decline	12			52%	47%	Umbreit 1996c; Umbreit et al. 1995; Umbreit & Coates 1992
Winnipeg CA-referred	decline	67			41%	48%	Umbreit 1996c; Umbreit et al. 1995; Umbreit & Coates 1992
English 2 site referred	decline	23				56%	Umbreit 1996c; Umbreit et al. 1995; Umbreit & Coates 1992
Brooklyn NY-nonreferred	match	206	75%			67%	Davis 1982; Davis Tichane & Grayson 1980
Brooklyn NY-referred	decline		48%				Davis 1982; Davis Tichane & Grayson 1980
NIJ 3 site US-nonreferred	match	45		86%	56%	67%	Cook Roehl & Sheppard 1980; Roehl & Cook 1982, 1989
9 Northeastern states-public	general public	4,015			16%		Schulman, Ronca & Bucuvalas 1999
9 Northeastern states-victims	crime victims	483			48%		Schulman, Ronca & Bucuvalas 1999

Chapter 5

Evaluating the practice of restorative justice: the case of family group conferencing

Nathan Harris

Restorative justice has grown increasingly popular, such that one current debate within restorative justice circles concerns the degree to which it can replace mainstream forms of justice (McCold 2000; Walgrave 2001). Informal interventions, such as victim–offender mediation, family group conferences and healing circles, are largely responsible for the success of restorative justice and are still the primary mechanisms by which restorative justice is transacted. Despite this, only limited empirical research has examined the dynamics of restorative interventions so as to explain how and why they are successful, though perhaps more than has occurred in relation to courtroom processes. This chapter takes some tentative steps towards considering these issues by identifying four aims that appear central to the practice of one restorative intervention: family group conferences.[1] These broad procedural aims indicate which characteristics a successful conference should have and are used to propose a model for evaluating conferences[2]. Identifying the aims of a restorative intervention also has implications for how the relationship between restorative justice and restorative interventions is conceptualised.

Conferences are a restorative intervention that first came to prominence in New Zealand and then rapidly spread to many countries around the world. The process is used at a number of stages of the criminal justice system (although it is also used in schools and other settings) but has primarily attracted attention as an alternative to formal cautioning or court proceedings. The conferencing process consists of a meeting of those people who have been affected by an offence. This usually includes the offender(s), their supporters, the victim(s), their supporters and a facilitator. Although conferences vary slightly in different locations, the meeting usually follows a fairly simple format which involves the offender explaining what occurred, the victim telling their side of the story, followed by the victim's and offender's supporters discussing the consequences of the offence. A conference will usually end with a formal agreement that includes a plan to resolve any outstanding issues, such as reparation to the victim. Attendance at a conference is voluntary for all participants, although offenders will usually face other action if they refuse to attend. Outcome agreements from conferences are usually decided unanimously and have to be agreed to by the offender.

There have now been several evaluations of conferencing programmes (Maxwell and Morris 1993; Moore and Forsythe 1995; McCold and Wachtel 1998, Strang et al. 1999). Although methodologically robust comparisons of recidivism rates are scarce and results from some existing studies are ambiguous (Sherman et al. 2000), these evaluations tend to show that conferences compare favourably with traditional court processes on a range of outcome measures, such as perceptions of fairness and victim satisfaction. Growing theoretical and political interest in restorative justice can in large part be attributed to the apparent success of conferencing and related interventions, such as victim–offender mediation and healing circles. However, despite the apparent importance of these interventions to restorative justice, much less emphasis has been placed upon understanding the processes that occur within restorative practices. As a result there is still relatively little known, beyond practitioners' experience, about which processes within a conference lead to positive outcomes. Little empirical work has examined what characteristics are important for a successful conference nor how conferences produce them. A greater understanding of these processes is important for both ensuring the quality of restorative justice programmes and if restorative justice is to continue to develop.

Although processes within interventions are difficult to test empirically, one approach is to examine the specific aims that inform their practice. In the case of conferencing, it is possible to identify a number of philosophies or beliefs that guide the way in which conferences are conducted. These can also be interpreted as theories about what is important for a conference to be successful. In practice they present what might be called procedural or intermediate aims, which define in broad terms those qualities of the process itself that are perceived as important to achieve. One example is the goal of empowering those people directly affected by an offence to make decisions about how to resolve problems caused by it. This procedural aim, which we will return to, is supported by a number of beliefs about its effectiveness in preventing reoffending and its desirability as a means for achieving justice (e.g. acknowledging the central role of victims).

Identifying these procedural aims should assist in our understanding of restorative practices because, theoretically, they should mediate between the very specific behaviours of facilitators and outcomes, such as measures of perceived fairness. The techniques used by facilitators in conferences have been developed precisely so as to achieve these goals. At the same time, the practice of conferencing is based on the belief that achieving these aims will lead to positive outcomes. Thus, identifying these procedural aims enables us to address two important questions: do restorative interventions achieve their own aims, such as empowerment, and are these aims related to positive outcomes in criminal justice interventions?

Identifying the procedural aims of family group conferencing

In the following discussion it is proposed that four procedural aims (empowerment, restoration, reintegration and emotional resolution) help to explain the practice of conferencing. These aims are identified from unstructured observations of conferences and facilitator training sessions in Australia and Belgium, discussions with facilitators and programme co-ordinators, training manuals and other literature on the conferencing process. Identifying the procedural aims for conferencing is bound to be controversial. Just as there are many different restorative interventions, conferencing programmes have developed in a variety of places and over more than a decade. These programmes will have emphasised different goals to different extents and as a result the procedural aims identified here will vary in their applicability to different contexts.[3] Broader influences, such as Maori traditions, may also have influenced the way in which conferences occur that are not explicitly reflected in these goals. Despite these difficulties, the process as first developed in New Zealand is still the basis of conferencing programmes around the world. The aims identified here also resonate throughout much of the restorative justice literature, and will be discussed in reference to this broader context.

Empowerment

One of the strongest themes in the development of conferencing is the importance of empowering those people who are directly affected by an offence. This is most obviously seen in practice by the way conferences attempt to involve all those who are connected to the offence, including offenders and victims, and those who are close to them. These parties are then able to discuss how the offence affected them and contribute to decisions about how these issues should be resolved. As Terry O'Connell, one of the leading practitioners who introduced conferencing in Australia, recalls: 'The idea was simple: get everyone affected by a crime together, confront offenders with what they've done, give all those involved a voice, and work towards positive outcomes in terms of personal responsibility and future behaviour' (*Sydney Morning Herald*, 13 June 2000). Empowerment in conferencing is also associated with notions of legitimacy, because it is through empowering the key participants that conferences come to focus upon concrete harms as identified by those who suffered them, as opposed to abstract harms as defined by laws. It is also through this direct interaction that outcomes are directly linked to the wishes of victims and the harms caused by offenders.

Empowerment is also a central theme in broader thinking on restorative justice, which involves a rejection of the way in which traditional forms of justice disempower the parties most affected by an offence. This is probably best illustrated in the classic 'Conflicts as Property' by Nils Christie (1977). Christie highlights the way in which modern legal systems have excluded to various degrees the primary parties involved in an offence from its resolution. This is done either through representation of the parties by the state or lawyers, or through redefinition of the conflict as an event that requires treatment of the offender. Although Christie talks generally about the significance of disempowerment he particularly highlights its impact on victims. As he says, victims are ' ... a sort of double loser; first vis-à-vis the offender, but secondly and often in a more crippling manner by being denied rights to full participation in what might have been one of the more important ritual encounters in life' (1977: 3).

This critique of the court process for victims appears to have been a significant motivation in the early development of victim–offender mediations in North America (Zehr 1990; Van Ness and Strong 1997).

Although not as prominent as empowerment of victims, concern to give offenders a chance to take responsibility is also evident in conferencing processes. In the case of offenders, empowerment has often been conceptualised as the opportunity to understand the effects of their actions, as well as to take responsibility by acknowledging the harm caused and seeking to repair it. It is argued that it is actually better for offenders, and particularly young offenders, to be empowered in this way because it assists their own restoration (Zehr 1990; Harris 2001). Of course, when offenders take responsibility it can also be positive for victims.

Restorative interventions that have emerged more recently, such as conferencing and healing circles, have also emphasised the importance of empowering the community. By community these approaches have usually referred to those who were directly involved in the incident or their families and friends. As Morris and Maxwell (1993: 76) identify, this was an important goal in the introduction of conferencing in New Zealand: 'The underlying intention is to empower families to deal with offending themselves and to restrict the power of professionals, in particular the power of social services.'

A final form of empowerment worth mentioning is empowerment of indigenous peoples. Again, this is particularly seen in the development of family group conferences in New Zealand and healing circles in Canada (LaPairie 1992; Morris and Maxwell 1993; Shaw and Jané 1998). These processes draw directly on traditional practices and in doing so attempt to facilitate a process in which indigenous people feel more comfortable. Perhaps more important is that by giving decision-making powers to the participants, these interventions provide greater opportunity for specific communities to make decisions that are appropriate to themselves.

Restoration

A second procedural aim of conferences is to repair the harm done by an offence. Harm can be either material or relational and, although it is usually seen as having happened to specific victims, it is sometimes also seen as having impacted upon a broader community (Karp 2001). Restoration is action taken by the offender, and sometimes others, to address this harm.

An emphasis on restoration in conferences is evident in the way that they are organised, first around exploring the effect the offence had on those present, and then to finding solutions for this harm. Consistent with this, facilitator training emphasises the importance of focusing discussion on the consequences of an offence rather than on blaming or disapproving of the offender (McDonald et al. 1994). Thus, although responsibility for the offence is clearly acknowledged, the process is less focused on the offender and his or her culpability than on how it might be repaired. Ideally, it is problem and repair focused rather than person and punishment focused.

Proponents have argued that restorative justice is a new paradigm of justice that can be contrasted with retributive models, which emphasise the punishment of offenders based upon 'just deserts' (von Hirsch 1993), but also models of justice that focus upon rehabilitation of offenders. In a defining work, Zehr (1990) argues that restorative justice has a different understanding of crime, justice and accountability. Whereas the present criminal justice system defines offending as a violation of abstract rules, restorative justice defines offending as concrete harms against specific individuals. As a result, justice in a retributive framework is a determination of blame and the imposition of retribution. In contrast, restorative justice involves the identification of problems caused by an offence and their restoration.

The distinction between restoration and retribution, as described here by Zehr (1990), is now the subject of some debate. For example, Walgrave (2001) has argued that a critical characteristic of restoration, in contrast to punishment, is that the intention is not to inflict harm upon the offender. For others (e.g. McCold 2000) restoration must also be voluntary. Ironically, a number of scholars have argued that restoration is not a defining feature of restorative justice and have pointed out that conferences sometimes also result in retributive outcomes (Barton 2000; Daly 2000, 2002). These critiques are more consistent with an approach to restorative justice that emphasises its inclusive process rather than restoration as a core value (see Braithwaite 1999).

However, when we look at the practice of conferencing, the process is clearly orientated to identifying and repairing relational and material harms that resulted from the offence. For example, in some programmes facilitators are encouraged to raise the topic of an outcome by asking what participants 'want out of today's conference', rather than implying that the conference participants should decide what will happen to the offender (O'Connell, *et al.* 1999). Thus, it might be concluded that the process is focused upon the harm caused and encourages outcomes that are focused upon repairing this harm.

Reintegration

A third procedural goal that has been influential in the development of conferencing is the reintegration of participants. This was particularly evident in Australia where those developing conferencing programmes explicitly drew on reintegrative shaming theory (Braithwaite and Mugford 1994; McDonald *et al.* 1994; Moore and Forsythe 1995; Hyndman *et al.* 1996). However, as Van Ness and Strong (1997) suggest, reintegration of both offenders and victims into positive communities is an important aim of restorative interventions more generally.[4]

Reintegrative shaming theory (Braithwaite 1989, 2001) argues that a critical factor in explaining the success of criminal justice interventions is how disapproval of offending is expressed. While the theory argues that disapproval of offending behaviour is important if we want to reduce or prevent crime, it distinguishes between stigmatising and reintegrative forms. Stigmatising shaming is disapproval of the person as well as the act and does not end with forgiveness or ceremonies that decertify the deviant label. In contrast, reintegration shaming involves distinguishing between the person and the act and is resolved with forgiveness of the offender. It is this type of shaming that the theory predicts will be successful. Research examining these propositions (Harris 2001) suggests that reintegration may be a more important factor than explicit disapproval (shaming) in contexts, like conferencing, that by their very occurrence indicate disapproval. This emphasis is reflected in conferencing practices.

Conferences place an emphasis on the reintegration of offenders in a number of ways. One important method is by focusing discussion on the harm caused by an offence, which reduces the potential for labelling and denigration of the offender's person. Where this fails, facilitators tend to intervene to prevent overly aggressive or disrespectful communication by participants. Conferences are also structured to encourage, where it is possible, apology and forgiveness in their conclusion. Creating an environment in these ways, which enabled the reintegration of offenders, was an explicit aim of the conferencing process developed in Wagga Wagga, Australia. Indeed, the training manual for facilitators says that a successful conference '... threatens the young person with social disapproval. But in making the distinction between unacceptable behaviour and the potentially good young person or young people responsible for that behaviour, the Conference offers the possibility of social reintegration' (McDonald *et al.* 1994: 6).

Emotional resolution

A final procedural aim apparent in conferencing is the goal of addressing emotional issues that result from an offence. Common to a number of restorative interventions is a philosophy that the emotions victims and offenders feel are as or more important than the facts of the incident, and are often critical to achieving resolution for victims and offenders. This aspect of conferencing is highlighted by a number of practitioners and scholars (Moore 1993; Retzinger and Scheff 1996; Moore and McDonald 2000; Ahmed *et al.* 2001), who argue that an important feature of conferences is that they address symbolic reparation.

Conferences attempt to address emotional hurt caused by an offence partially by focusing discussion on feelings but also through the order in which conferences address particular topics. Although there is some variation between programmes, conferences usually start with an acknowledgement of responsibility by the offender, which is followed by the victim's account of how this affected him or her, which broadens into a discussion of how the incident affected others. It is suggested that in successful conferences this process involves a core emotional sequence (Moore 1993; Retzinger and Scheff 1996). Anger, indignation and resentment felt by victims are reduced by the offender's acceptance of responsibility and acknowledgement of the harms he or she has caused. At the same time the victim's story of harm, and its resonance in others, leads to empathy and remorse in the offender. The increased understanding of each other produced by this interaction increases the possibility of meaningful apology and forgiveness. For this exchange to occur both parties need to feel confident enough to express responsibility and hurt, and thus conference facilitators attempt to create a non-threatening environment (Moore 1993). Whether or not this emotional sequence occurs, an important goal of conferencing is to provide a forum which allows participants to express and resolve emotions arising from the experience. The transformation of emotional states is also believed to be central to changing the social relationships between victims, offenders and their communities.

Tensions and interconnections between procedural aims

Although four procedural goals have been identified as central to conferencing, it is also apparent that there are tensions between these goals. An obvious example is where the goal of empowering participants is in conflict with the goal of providing a forum that is primarily restorative. As Daly (2002) observed, conference participants draw on a variety of rationales when asked how they would like to resolve issues raised in a conference. In some cases participants use an explicitly retributive rather than restorative framework in deciding what should be done as a result of the offence. In these cases the empowerment of participants is clearly at odds with the aim of restoration, which could only be achieved in this situation by interfering with the group's decision.[5] In practice, aims such as restoration and empowerment have to be balanced and may vary in importance depending upon the specific context in which a conference occurs.

On the other hand, the goals identified often facilitate each other, in that they are not always independent. For example, the goal of restoration may be facilitated by emotional resolution. A number of observers (Retzinger and Scheff 1996; Moore and McDonald 2000) have suggested that it is through addressing emotional hurt and 'symbolic reparation' that conferences allow participants to focus on repairing harm as opposed to remaining hostile. Another example is the relationship between empowerment and restoration, despite the already-mentioned tensions that exist between these aims. Achieving restoration requires that the harms caused by an offence are identified, which is assisted by a deliberative process in which participants are empowered to discuss how they have been affected. This is particularly true if relational or emotional harms, as opposed to just material harms, are to be addressed.

A proposed model for evaluating restorative practice

One reason for identifying the procedural aims of conferences is that they provide measures against which conferences, and potentially other restorative interventions, can be evaluated. Rather than testing whether restorative justice works, this is focused on testing whether restorative interventions do what they claim. So it measures whether conferences do in fact empower participants, reintegrate offenders and victims, repair the harm caused by offences, and address emotional issues arising from offences. This approach is particularly focused upon developing a better understanding of why and how restorative interventions work, but might also provide a way of evaluating how well an intervention lives up to goals that are consistent with a restorative approach.

A possible model for evaluating interventions in this way uses the four procedural aims already identified as criteria. However, two further criteria seem necessary for an evaluation of a criminal justice intervention. The first of these is procedural fairness. Respect for procedural and human rights is an essential characteristic of justice interventions and thus seems a necessary starting point. Moreover, work by Tyler (1990) suggests that perceptions of legitimacy by participants, resulting from perceptions of procedural justice, also increase chances of such an intervention being successful. A number of procedural safeguards are used in conferences to protect participants' rights. For example, attendance at a conference is voluntary for all participants including the offender, who can opt to have his or her case taken to a court if he or she wishes. In addition to safeguards like these, conferences also attempt to be impartial, to give everyone a chance to express his or her view and to treat participants with respect.

The second criterion added was achieving a satisfactory outcome. While court processes can be relied upon to reach decisions, more discursive processes like conferences risk not reaching an outcome because of the emphasis on group consensus and agreement by offenders. Thus, it seemed that an important measure of success is whether interventions reach an outcome, and particularly one that is satisfactory to the different parties.

The six aims have been organised, in Figure 5.1, into a hierarchy which

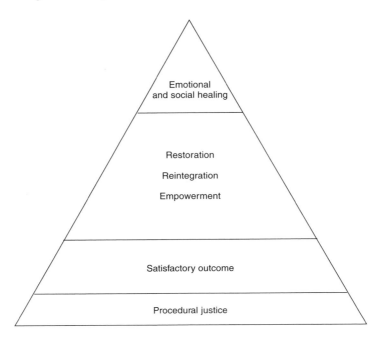

Figure 5.1.   A model for evaluating family group conferences.

reflects expectations we might have regarding conferences. At the bottom is procedural fairness, which as a basic requirement should be expected of all conferences, and indeed all justice processes. Reaching practical agreements that address the basic needs of the participants is the next criterion of success. If an intervention satisfies only these two aims we might still consider it a success in some cases. However, for most conferences to be considered successful, according to the model outlined above, at least three more of the procedural aims need to be achieved to some degree: there needs to be empowerment of the key parties, repair of harm caused by the offence, and the reintegration of victims and offenders. Finally, a higher hope is that justice procedures can heal emotional hurts, repair social bonds and in doing so transform aspects of an offender's life that may have contributed to crime. However, this is an ideal which might only happen in a small number of cases and thus it is represented as a small proportion at the top of the pyramid.

Presenting the procedural goals in this kind of hierarchy does have its flaws as it ignores the way in which they are often interdependent. Emotional healing is distinguished at the top of the pyramid, whereas some degree of it may be necessary for the other procedural aims to occur.

In this respect, the pyramid implies a clear distinction between these aims that is probably false. Nevertheless, this hierarchy does prioritise which objectives seem most important in order for a conference to achieve justice. For example, empowerment of participants should be considered a more basic objective than the repair of social relationships. Given the sometimes exaggerated expectations regarding restorative justice this may also be a useful way of acknowledging that there are degrees of success.

Implications of restorative practice for restorative justice

Current debates in the restorative justice literature concern both the definition of restorative justice and its potential role in the criminal justice system. One critique of restorative justice is that it has a multitude of goals that are broad and undefined, ranging from the offender recognising his or her wrongdoing, to diminishing the fear of crime (von Hirsch *et al.* 2002). This criticism ignores differences between the aims of restorative justice and discussion of its potential benefits. However, it does reflect some uncertainty between restorative justice scholars regarding the way in which restorative justice should be conceptualised. This is evident in the debate as to whether restorative justice should be defined on the basis of its process (i.e. the involvement of key participants) or its core value (i.e. that justice should be about repairing the harm caused by an offence) (Roach 2001). The emergence of this debate possibly reflects the increased interest in, and application of, restorative justice ideas. While Zehr (1990) argued that restorative justice provides a completely different paradigm of justice, it is only more recently that it has been seriously evaluated as a theoretical framework relevant to mainstream criminal justice, as opposed to being simply a range of alternative interventions (Bazemore and Walgrave 1999; Walgrave 2000; von Hirsch *et al.* 2002). Ironically, this increased emphasis upon restorative justice as a theory of justice also demands greater clarity in the definition of restorative justice and its goals.

Discussing the procedural aims of restorative interventions may assist in further clarifying what is important about restorative justice. However, the aims identified here would also seem to raise questions about the importance of defining restorative justice, as such. It at least suggests that the purpose of a definition needs to be clarified. The current debate (Roach 2001) seems focused upon producing a single definition that can define what is and is not restorative justice as well as giving expression to what is important about it. Given the increasing number of domains that restorative justice is currently being applied to, this may not be a realistic or useful objective for proponents of restorative justice. For example, while conferences may fit into a restorative justice framework, and have a restorative focus, they are guided by more than simply a restorative philosophy. I argue that the way in which they are facilitated is determined by at least four separate, if inter-related, concerns. Thus, what is important about the conferencing process may be quite different from what is important about a restorative philosophy. The difficulty of equating restorative practice with the philosophy is even more complex when it is considered that other restorative interventions, such as healing circles, may have somewhat different aims from conferences.

It may also be important for restorative philosophy to be distinguished from interventions themselves. This is most clearly seen where attempts are made to evaluate restorative philosophy on the basis of restorative interventions. For example, Daly (2002) argues that restorative justice should not be seen as truly distinct from retributive justice, partly because conferences often involve retributive ideas and outcomes. While it might be possible to conclude from this that restorative interventions involve elements of retribution, this is not a good basis for forming conclusions about restoration as a philosophy of justice. As the analysis here shows, conferences cannot be regarded as an unproblematic implementation of restorative philosophy. This is important if restorative justice is to be evaluated as a theory of justice in the way that von Hirsch *et al.* (2002) attempt. Indeed, evaluating restorative theory via reference to conferencing processes might be seen as analogous to evaluating retribution theory by observing court procedures. Even where legal systems have embraced just deserts theory (von Hirsch 1993), its translation into practice has to take into account various social and procedural factors. Thus, if restorative philosophy is to be evaluated as a theoretical model of how justice can be achieved (alongside other models such as just deserts theory) it needs to be distinguished from the range of interventions that currently attempt to implement it.

The important differences in the way that the philosophy and practice of restorative justice need to be conceptualised and evaluated cast doubt on the significance that should be given to an all-encompassing definition. Doing so seems to risk concealing the value they potentially bring to different contexts. An alternative approach would be to focus greater energy on thinking about and defining the elements of restorative justice. This would mean that restorative philosophy would be seen as a way of thinking about justice that is not necessarily constrained to the mode in which it is delivered. The advantage of this would be that restoration as a moral and legal framework might be considered without necessarily reverting to the discussion of issues arising from the face-to-face meeting of victims and offenders, for example. These issues would be relevant to thinking about restorative interventions, which could be conceptualised as those practices that implement this ideal of repairing harm as a means of achieving justice. This might also have advantages for the way in which restorative interventions are seen. Rather than simply being subsumed by the label of restorative justice, interventions might be evaluated on a number of dimensions including the degree to which they assist restoration, but also factors such as the degree to which they are empowering or the degree to which they promote emotional resolution. This might help clarify the value that different restorative interventions have in different contexts. Finally, this would leave the term restorative justice as a more general, overarching term referring to those approaches that are concerned with doing justice by repairing harm.

Acknowledgements

This chapter was initially written while I was working at K.U. Leuven on an evaluation of a family group conferencing programme. I am grateful to colleagues at the university and particularly my co-researchers Lode Walgrave and Inge Vanfraechem for their ideas. Helpful comments on an earlier draft were also made by John Braithwaite and Shadd Maruna. Finally, thanks are due to many facilitators and co-ordinators of family group conferencing programmes for their insights.

Notes

1. Family group conferences have been referred to as community conferences and restorative justice conferences, among other things. They will be referred to here as simply conferences.
2. Research evaluating conferences in Belgium will examine how well these aims describe conferences and how well they predict success.
3. Given the background of the author they may reflect the early development of conferencing in Australia more strongly than elsewhere.
4. Conferences would not aim to reintegrate offenders or victims into law-breaking or harmful communities. For example, a conference would not seek to reintegrate a gang member into their gang, but rather attempt to involve other communities which the offender belongs to.
5. Most facilitators would be reluctant to interfere in this decision-making process, beyond making practical suggestions, as long as the outcomes are not outrageous.

References

Ahmed, E., Harris, N., Braithwaite, J., and Braithwaite, V. (eds) (2001) *Shame Management through Reintegration*. Melbourne: Cambridge University Press.

Barton, C. (2000) 'Empowerment and Retribution in Criminal Justice', in H. Strang and J. Braithwaite (eds), *Restorative Justice: Philosophy to Practice*. Aldershot: Ashgate.

Bazemore, G., and Walgrave, L. (1999) 'Restorative Juvenile Justice: in Search of Fundamentals and an Outline for Systematic Reform.' in G. Bazemore and L. Walgrave (eds) *Restorative Juvenile Justice: Repairing the Harm of Youth Crime*. Monsey, NY: Willow Tree Press.

Braithwaite, J. (1989) *Crime, Shame and Reintegration*. Cambridge: Cambridge University Press.

Braithwaite, J. (1999) 'Restorative Justice: Assessing Optimistic and Pessimistic Accounts', in M. Tonry (ed.) *Crime and Justice: A Review of Research. Volume 25*. Chicago: University of Chicago Press.

Braithwaite, J., and Mugford, S. (1994). 'Conditions of Successful Reintegration Ceremonies: Dealing with Juvenile Offenders', *British Journal of Criminology*, 34(2) 139–71.

Christie, N. (1977) 'Conflicts as Property', *British Journal of Criminology*, 17(1): 1–15.

Daly, K. (2000). Revisiting the Relationship between Retributive and Restorative Justice', in H. Strang and J. Braithwaite (eds) *Restorative Justice: Philosophy to Practice*. Aldershot: Ashgate.

Daly, K. (2002) 'Restorative Justice: the Real Story', *Punishment and Society*, 4(1): 55–79.

Harris, N. (2001) ' 'Part II' Shaming and Shame: Regulating Drink Driving', in E. Ahmed *et al. Shame Management Through Reintegration*. Melbourne: Cambridge University Press.

Hyndman, M., Thorsborne, M., and Wood, S. (1996) *Community Accountability Conferencing: Trial Report*. Brisbane: Department of Education Queensland.

Karp, D. (2001) 'Harm and Repair: Observing Restorative Justice in Vermont', *Justice Quarterly*, 18(4): 727–57.

LaPairie, C. (1992) 'Aboriginal Crime and Justice: Explaining the Present, Exploring the Future', *Canadian Journal of Criminology*, 34: 281–98.

Maxwell, G., and Morris, A. (1993) *Family, Victims and Culture: Youth Justice in New Zealand*. Wellington: Social Policy Agency and Institute of Criminology, Victoria University of Wellington.

McCold, P. (2000) 'Towards a Holistic Vision of Restorative Juvenile Justice: A Reply to the Maximalist Model', *Contemporary justice Review*, 3(4): 357–414.

McCold, P., and Wachtel, B. (1998) *The Bethlehem Pennsylvania Police Family Group Conferencing Project*. Pipersville, PA: Community Service Foundation.

McDonald, J.M., O'Connell, T.A., Moore, D.B., and Bransbury, E. (1994) *Convening Family Conferences: Training Manual*. New South Wales Police Academy.

Moore, D., and Forsythe, L. (1995) *A New Approach to Juvenile Justice: An Evaluation of Family Conferencing in Wagga Wagga*. Wagga Wagga: Juvenile Justice, the Centre for Rural Research.

Moore, D.B. (1993) 'Shame, Forgiveness and Juvenile Justice', *Criminal Justice Ethics,* 12(1): 3–25.

Moore, D.B., and McDonald, J.M. (2000) *Transforming Conflict in Workplaces and other Communities.* Melbourne: Transformative Justice Australia.

Morris, A., and Maxwell, G. (1993) 'Juvenile Justice in New Zealand: a New Paradigm', *Australian and New Zealand Journal of Criminology,* 26: 72–90.

O'Connell, T.A., Wachtel, B., and Wachtel, T. (1999) *Conferencing Handbook: The New Real Justice Training Manual.* Pipersville, PA: The Piper's Press.

Retzinger, S.M., and Scheff, T.J. (1996) Strategy for Community Conferences: Emotions and Social Bonds', in B. Galaway and J. Hudson (eds), *Restorative Justice: International Perspectives.* Monsey, NY: Criminal Justice Press.

Roche, D. (2001) 'The Evolving Definition of Restorative Justice', *Contemporary Justice Review,* 4: 341–53.

Shaw, M., and Jané, F. (1998) *Restorative Justice and Policing in Canada: Bringing the Community into Focus.* Royal Canadian Mounted Police, Ottowa.

Sherman, L.W., Strang, H., and Woods, D.J. (2000) *Recidivism Patterns in the Canberra ReIntegrative Shaming Experiments (RISE).* Canberra: Australian National University.

Strang, H., Barnes, G., Braithwaite, J., and Sherman, L.W. (1999) *Experiments in Restorative Policing: A Progress Report on the Canberra ReIntegrative Shaming Experiments.* Canberra: Australian National University.

Tyler, T.R. (1988) 'What is Procedural Justice?: Criteria Used by Citizens to Assess the Fairness of Legal Procedures', *Law and Society Review,* 22(1): 103–35.

Van Ness, D., and Strong, K. (1997) *Restoring Justice.* Cincinnati, OH: Anderson.

von Hirsch, A. (1993) *Censure and Sanctions.* Oxford: Clarendon Press.

von Hirsch, A., Ashworth, A. and Shearing, C. (2002) 'Specifying Aims and Limits for Restorative Justice: a "Making Amends" Model?', in A. von Hirsch *et al.* (eds) *Restorative Justice and Criminal Justice: Competing or Reconcilable Paradigms?.* Oxford: Hart Publishing.

Walgrave, L. (2000) 'How Pure can a Maximalist Approach to Restorative Justice Remain? Or can a Purist Model of Restorative Justice become Maximalist?', *Contemporary Justice Review,* 3(4): 415–32.

Walgrave, L. (2001) 'On Restoration and Punishment: Favourable Similarities and Fortunate Differences', in A. Morris and G. Maxwell (eds) *Restorative Justice for Juveniles.* Oxford: Hart Publishing.

Zehr, H. (1990) *Changing Lenses: A New Focus for Criminal Justice.* Scottsdale, PA: Herald Press.

Chapter 6

Differences in how girls and boys respond to family group conferences: preliminary research results[1]

Gabrielle Maxwell, Venezia Kingi, Allison Morris,
Jeremy Robertson and Tracy Anderson

Introduction

Research from New Zealand, Australia and elsewhere indicates that family group conferences, particularly when they are well run and managed, have the potential to induce remorse in offenders and to assist families and young people to come together to take responsibility for repairing harm to victims and for taking steps to prevent reoffending (Sherman *et al.* 2000; Maxwell and Morris 2001). They can produce outcomes that are judged to be satisfactory by victims, offenders, families and a range of justice professionals. Young people who participate in conferences report that, compared to court, they find conferences fair, inclusive of them, involving them in decisions and providing them with opportunities to repair harm and make a new start (Maxwell and Morris 1999). Victims, also, are more likely to report that conferences, compared to courts, allow them to be included, involve them in decisions and assist them to put the offence behind them (Strang 2001). However, the relatively small number of girls who offend has made it difficult for researchers to answer questions about whether or not there are important gender issues in relation to family group conferencing and whether or not girls respond differently from boys when involved in a restorative process.

We are currently undertaking a large-scale retrospective study of files on 1,000 family group conferences and are interviewing as many as possible of the young people involved who agree to be interviewed. This chapter presents preliminary findings from an analysis of some of the interview and file data that had been collected by the end of July 2001 on this sample of young people who had family group conferences in New Zealand in 1998. Family group conference file data are available on 733 young people: 616 boys and 117 girls. Reoffending information in the adult courts is presently available for 700: 590 boys and 110 girls. Interview data are available from 361 young people of whom 302 are boys and 59 are girls.

Offending patterns

Internationally, previous research has demonstrated that offending patterns are often very different for girls and boys and so are the criminal justice responses to their offending (Anleu 1991; Heidensohn 1996; Chesney-Lind 1997). In this sample, too, we find that girls are more likely to have committed fewer and more minor offences, they are more likely to receive less severe outcomes and they are less likely to reoffend. The data in Table 6.1 confirm most of the findings for our sample. The data in the table show that the girls were referred for different types of offences from the boys. They were more likely to be referred for minor violent offences than boys. They were less likely to be referred for more serious offences of violence, burglaries, car thefts or property damage and abuse. On average, the girls were also more likely than boys to be referred directly for a family group conference rather than being charged in court. All these differences were statistically significant at the 5% level. These findings are consistent with the other data in the table that show that the girls were more likely to have committed offences that were rated as less serious and they committed fewer offences although neither of these findings reached the 5% level of significance.

Previous history

Boys and girls also differ in their backgrounds. Table 6.2 shows the difference in the proportion of girls and boys who had a previous history with the care and protection and youth justice systems. The data show that girls were more likely than the boys to have been previously notified to the Department of Child, Youth and Family as being in need of care and protection (58% of girls compared to 41% of the boys). On the other hand, it is the boys who were more likely to have appeared before in the youth justice system for a family group conference or to answer charges in the Youth Court (although the latter is not statistically significant).

Table 6.1. Comparing boys and girls: type of offence, source of FGC referral, seriousness of most serious offence and number of offences (% or means) (n = 717)[2, 3]

	Girls (n=116)	Boys (n=601)	Total
Nature of offence (%)			
Burglary	**16**	**34**	31
Car theft	**16**	**29**	27
Shop theft and other dishonesty	40	32	33
Property damage and abuse	**9**	**16**	15
Violence minor	**34**	**23**	24
Violence – not minor	**4**	**13**	11
Drugs and anti-social	13	13	13
Other	29	27	27
Source of FGC referral (%)			
Police	50	37	39
Youth Court	50	63	61
Seriousness of most serious offence (%)			
Less serious	41	31	33
More serious	59	69	67
One offence only (%)	41	33	35
Mean number of FGC offences	3.04	3.65	3.55

Table 6.2. Comparing boys and girls: previous history of contact with care and protection (C&P) or youth justice (YJ) systems (%) (n = 733)

	Girls (n = 116)	Boys (n = 601)	Total
Previously notified for C&P	**58**	**41**	**44**
Previously referred for YJ FGC	**47**	**56**	**56**
Previously appeared in Youth Court	28	32	32

Family group conference records

The records show that for 92% of the conferences a victim of an offence was identified and that a victim was present for 42% of conferences. At least 90% of family group conferences had one or more family members present and agreed on the decisions. Recommendations and plans almost

Table 6.3. Records of family group conference attendance by family, agreements and outcomes (%) (n = 464)

	Girls (n = 84)	Boys (n = 380)	Total
A victim identified	87	93	92
At least one victim present	43	42	42
At least one family member[4] present	96	97	97
FGC agreed	86	91	90
Outcomes			
Accountability (any kind)	97	95	95
Apology	85	77	78
Change of residence	16	10	11
Work for community or victim	60	67	66
Reparation/donation	55	58	58
Any minor restriction of liberty	**25**	**39**	37
Supervision	3	7	6
Supervision with activity	2	2	2
Supervision with residence	1	2	2
Transfer to District or High Court	0	3	2
Other provisions to prevent reoffending	48	49	48
Any rehabilitative programme	23	24	24
Education or training	19	23	22

always included some type of accountability, most commonly an apology, work in the community or work for the victim and reparation or a donation. It was uncommon for recommendations for court orders to involve supervision or transfer to the District or High Court. In about half the conferences, there were some recommendations specifically designed to prevent reoffending by providing for a rehabilitative programme or for education or training.

Comparing boys and girls, the data in Table 6.3 show that girls were less likely than boys to have a victim identified for their offending; this difference was almost significant. However, boys and girls were equally likely to have a victim and at least one member of their family present at the conference. When it came to the outcomes of the conferences, some differences can be observed. There was a tendency for conferences for the girls to be somewhat less likely to reach agreement. On the other hand, the recommended outcomes were more likely to involve apologies and a change of residence but less likely to involve work for the community or victim, or restrictions of liberty of any kind including custodial penalties of supervision with residence or transfer to District or High Court for consideration of a prison sentence. However, only the difference with respect to restrictions of liberty reaches significance. These findings about the lesser severity of recommended outcomes are consistent with the findings reported earlier that girls' offences were less serious and fewer in number. Rehabilitative programmes were equally likely to be recommended for both boys and girls but girls were slightly, but not significantly, less likely to have recommendations for educational and training programmes.

Comparing girls' and boys' responses to the family group conference

The most potentially interesting and novel findings in this study are to be found by comparing the responses of girls and boys to family group conferences. The young people were asked about their memory of the conference, the extent to which they were prepared for it and consulted about it, and their participation and involvement during the conference. They were also asked about their responses to the victims and to their own offending, the responses of others to them and for their views on the outcomes. The results comparing the replies of boys and girls are presented in Table 6.4. The data indicate that, on the whole, the young people responded positively. Over half remembered a lot about the family group conference and only 8%[8] indicated that they had little or no memory of it. The differences between boys and girls were not significant. In terms of preparation, over two thirds said that they had been prepared on all issues. Boys more often reported that they were consulted about who should attend and this is the only difference between boys and girls that was significant in this group of items.

At the conference, about 80% felt that they understood what was happening and just under a half reported that they did not feel they had been involved in the decisions. These differences between boys and girls were not significant. However, about three quarters of the boys said that they were able to say what they wanted but only about half the girls reported this. In addition, over half the girls said that they felt too intimidated to say what they wanted to although this was reported by only 40% of the boys; both these differences were significant.

The victim was present at half the family group conferences involving this sample. For this group, about three quarters of the young people reported understanding how the victim felt and seeing the victim's point of view. Three quarters of the boys said that they understood how the victim felt but only half the girls reported this; a difference that was significant.

About three fifths to two thirds reported feeling really sorry for offending, showing that they felt sorry, and that they thought the victim had accepted their apology. Boys were more likely to say these things than the girls although the differences were not significant. About 80% felt that they were able to make up for what they did and again these were more likely to be the boys. This difference was significant.

About half of both the boys and the girls reported feeling ashamed of themselves. However, significantly more of the girls said that in the family group conference they felt that what they did was wrong (71% of the girls compared to 56% of the boys).

A large number of questions was asked that focused on the way the young person felt others responded to them in the family group conference. Generally, at least 80% reported that there had been support for them in the conference and three quarters reported that people had made it possible for them to put things behind them. Two thirds and three quarters respectively reported being treated with respect and treated fairly. However, about half reported being made to feel like a bad person and that they had been treated as though they were a criminal. Over a third said that people did not let them forget what they had done.

Again sex differences emerged on several of these items. It was the boys rather than the girls who were significantly more likely to report being treated fairly, being treated like a trustworthy person, being given another chance and that people made it clear that they could put everything behind them.

The last group of items in Table 6.4 describes the young persons' views of the outcomes. Nearly all (94%) said that they understood what was decided and two thirds agreed with the decisions. Nearly two thirds also said that they thought the outcome was better than they had expected. Over three quarters said that they had decided to keep out of trouble in future. Looking back, 85% said that they now felt that what they had done was wrong. There were no differences between girls and boys on these items.

The young people were asked if the impact of what had happened at the family group conference had helped them stop, or reduce, their offending. A third of those interviewed reported that having a family group conference had helped them to stop or reduce their offending. Girls were only half as likely to report this as boys (19% compared to 35%) and this difference was significant. This finding seems consistent with the differences reported above which suggest that girls were less likely to report being affected by the family group conference than the boys. But what does this mean? Self-report is not necessarily always truthful and those asked questions about their feelings are not always able to analyse them for themselves. Thus, this result could be interpreted as indicating that the boys were more likely to report in a socially desirable way by giving answers they thought were those that people would want to hear. Data on reconviction could be seen as providing one kind of check on the accuracy of reports about the impact of the conference on reoffending.

Reconvictions in adult courts

Information was available on reconviction records for 700 of the sample in the adult courts during the year following their seventeenth birthday. Data

Table 6.4. Boys' and girls' agreement[5] with statements about their involvement in (and views about) the family group conference; percentages from young people's interviews for phase 1 retrospective sample to 1 August 2001 (n = 361)[6]

Statements	Girls (n = 59)	Boys (n = 302)	Total
Memorability			
I remember a lot about it	41	53	51
Preparation			
I was told what would happen	75	77	76
I was told what others might expect of me	63	70	69
I was told about possible outcomes	75	76	76
I was consulted about who should come	**71**	**84**	82
Participation and involvement			
I felt involved in making decisions	43	55	53
I understood what was going on	74	83	81
I felt I had the opportunity to say what I wanted	**52**	**73**	69
I felt too intimidated to say what I wanted to	**55**	**40**	42
Responses to victims[7] and the offence			
Was a victim present?	47	59	57
I could understand how the victim felt	**51**	**75**	71
I felt really sorry about my offending	58	61	60
I showed the victim I was really sorry	52	66	63
I think the victim accepted my apology	59	60	59
I could see the victim's point of view	67	79	77
I was able to make up for what I did	**68**	**81**	79
In the FGC I felt what I did was wrong	**71**	**56**	59
I felt ashamed of myself	53	51	51

continued over

Table 6.4 continued

Statements	Girls (n = 59)	Boys (n = 302)	Total
Responses to them			
People were there who cared about and supported me	90	94	93
In general people were looking out for my best interests	72	65	67
People spoke up on my behalf	79	80	80
People showed they cared about me regardless of what I had done	76	83	81
I was treated with respect	57	70	68
I was treated fairly	**63**	**77**	75
People talked about what they liked about me	43	57	55
People treated me like a trustworthy person	**31**	**50**	47
The way I was dealt with made me feel I was a bad person	53	52	52
I was treated as though I was a criminal	54	52	53
After the FGC people showed me I was forgiven	49	61	59
People gave me another chance	**60**	**83**	79
People made it clear I can put the whole thing behind me	**63**	**78**	76
People didn't let me forget what I had done	41	38	38
Views on outcomes			
I understood what was decided	88	95	94
I really agreed with the decisions	64	66	65
The decision was better than I expected	57	63	62
I decided to keep out of trouble in future	80	76	77
I now feel what I did was wrong	78	86	85

were also available for 585 of the sample for reconvictions over 18 months after their seventeenth birthday (Table 6.5). The data show that, overall, 52% of the sample were recorded as having at least one conviction in the year following the date on which they turned 17 years of age – and 62% were recorded as having at least one conviction in the following 18 months. These overall reconviction rates seem somewhat high but a number of factors account for this: the young people in the sample were those originally referred to a family group conference for relatively serious offences and the reconviction group included young people who were convicted of a range of traffic offences.

When girls and boys are compared it is clear that the reoffending rates were significantly lower for girls at both 12 months (35% of the girls were

Table 6.5. Reconvictions in the adult courts at 12 months (n = 700) and 18 months (n = 585) after the seventeenth birthday showing percentages of girls and boys who were reconvicted of any offence

	Girls (n = 110)	Boys (n = 590)	Total
After one year	35	55	52
After 18 months	43	66	62

reconvicted compared to 55% of the boys) and 18 months (43% of the girls compared to 66% of the boys). There are some apparent contradictions here. Although this finding is consistent with the earlier age of first involvement of boys in offending and the more serious offences they appeared for prior to becoming eligible for the adult system, the girls had a greater probability of having a childhood history of adverse experiences than the boys. The lower reconviction rate for girls also contrasts with the relative lack of responsiveness reported by the girls compared to the boys to what happened in the family group conference.

Two possibilities can be considered. First, it is possible that there are differences in how girls and boys report similar experiences in the conference. These girls, who have often had a history of abuse, may be relatively pessimistic about their future and/or may be more reluctant to admit to softer feelings. It is also possible that there are differences between the boys and the girls in their ability to understand and report their own reactions. Girls may be being more realistic or more honest about their feelings compared to the boys. And, as suggested above, social desirability effects may also play a role.

A second possible explanation is related to the well recognised phenomenon that males are more likely in general to offend than females when other factors are all held constant. Thus, despite less abusive backgrounds and, possibly, more responsiveness to conferences, boys could still be more likely to reoffend.

Summary and conclusions

These data show that, in general, young people attending family group conferences in New Zealand are more likely than not to feel positive about their family group conference experiences. The majority report being prepared for what might happen, understanding what happened, being able to have their say, that people were there who cared about them and looked after their interests and that they were given another chance. Most reported feeling sorry about their offending and seeing the victim's viewpoint. They generally understood the outcomes, decided to keep out of trouble in future and now, two years later, feel that what they did was wrong.

However, nearly half reported some less than satisfactory experiences. These young people did not feel involved in the decision, were too intimidated to say what they wanted to, did not feel that what they did was wrong and were not ashamed of themselves. About half reported that they were not treated as trustworthy, were made to feel a bad person or as though they were a criminal and did not really agree with the decision.

Despite the overall positive responses of both boys and girls, girls were somewhat more likely to report a negative experience of their family group conference than the boys. On most items, differences were not significant but some were. More often it was the girls who did not feel that they had an opportunity to say what they wanted, and that people did not give them another chance and let them put things behind them. Furthermore, although half the girls reported understanding how their victim felt and two thirds reported being able to make up for what they did, the figures for boys were higher. Nearly two thirds of the girls reported being treated fairly and fewer than a third said people treated them as trustworthy – however, these figures were also higher for boys.

On the other hand, when it comes to restorative outcomes, compared to the boys, the girls reported being more likely to experience one outcome that is arguably, more positive from a restorative viewpoint: they were more likely to report that, during the family group conference, they felt that what they did was wrong. However, they were much less likely than the boys to report that attending the conference had helped stop or reduce their offending.

The results reported here appear paradoxical. Why should the girls in this sample report experiencing the family group conference process in ways that are less likely to be restorative? Their pattern of offending suggests that most have committed relatively less serious offences. Relatively more of them were referred directly to their family group conference and relatively fewer had appeared in the Youth Court. They were about as likely as the boys to have had a victim present and to have had family support. Furthermore, compared to the boys, fewer reoffended after their family group conference.

There are a number of possible reasons for these findings. One is that responses to a family group conference differ depending on other factors on which the girls and boys tended to differ: for example, the type of offences they committed, the relative seriousness of their offending and their history of previous victimisation are possibilities.

The RISE study (Sherman *et al.* 2000) found that reduced reoffending compared to control groups, was observed after conferences for offences of violence but not for property offences. Perhaps the impact of meeting a victim and coming to terms with the impact of one's offending is greater when the offence is relatively serious and boys' offending tended to be more serious than girls' offending. Another possible factor is the tendency for co-ordinators to put more effort into arranging conferences and ensuring victims' presence for more serious offences involving personal victims. A relatively cursory conference that was less likely to engage the young person emotionally may have been more common for girls than boys and this may have resulted in more of the conferences having, possibly, less of an impact on girls.

In the sample described here, although the girls were less likely to have a previous history of offending they may have come from families with more adverse backgrounds: more of the girls had previously been notified to the Department of Child Youth and Family Services as being in need of care and protection. This history of greater possible victimisation may be have led to some of the girls being less responsive and empathic with other victims.

Girls also differ from boys in the ways in which they respond to social situations: the way they present in the family group conference when confronted with their offending may affect the responses of others towards them and change the way they tend to experience the conference. Previous research suggests that female offending is generally responded to differently from male offending: sometimes more leniently and sometimes more negatively (Daly 1994; Hedderman and Gelsthorpe 1997), and this could suggest that they were treated differently during the family group conference. We have also suggested that boys may be more readily influenced by social desirability factors and less in touch with their own feelings than the girls. Further analysis and data collection including observations currently being carried out on 100 family group conferences may provide some indication of which, if any, of these hypotheses explain the differences reported here.

Fewer girls than boys reported that what happened at the family group conference was likely to prevent their future reoffending. This contrasts with the finding that girls were less likely to reoffend than boys and underlines the importance of recognising the limited value of self-report statements as predictors of behaviour. What people say about their future actions is often quite unpredictable (Ajzen and Fishbein 1980). Further comparisons on data from family group observations and young people's statements may provide more information.

Whatever the reason for the sex differences reported here, these data indicate that we cannot assume that a family group conference will provide a similar experience for everyone. Differences may lie in the nature and type of offences committed, in how young people are treated in the family group conference and in how young people interpret and react to events in the conference, and in the history and backgrounds of the young people. One thing is certain – in some important respects it appears that girls and boys are responding differently. This could be due to ethnicity differences between the samples or some other factor, and this is being investigated. It is likely that there are a number of underlying factors responsible for the different experiences of boys and girls. We need to know what is really going on.

Acknowledgements

We would like to acknowledge the support in conducting the research of the Ministry of Social Policy, Ministry of Justice, Department of Child, Youth and Family Services, the Ministry of Research Science and Technology, Crime Prevention Unit, Department for Courts, New Zealand Police, Department of Corrections, the Ministry of Pacific Island Affairs and the Department of Maori Development (Te Puni Kokiri) in New Zealand and Professor Lawrence Sherman of the University of Philadelphia. We would also like to acknowledge the efforts of the team of interviewers led by Ron Hooper who were involved in tracking, recruiting and interviewing the young people. Our thanks also to all those involved as advisors, data coders and, in particular, the participants who made the project possible.

Notes

1. An earlier version of this paper was published in the Social Policy Journal of New Zealand (2001, 17: pp 171–182).
2. There are some records where complete information was not available so that the actual n in any particular table or for any particular item can fall short of the possible n of 733.
3. Bolded responses are those where differences between boys and girls are significant at the 5% level using chi-squared tests.
4. Family members include parents, caregivers, siblings, grandparents, uncles aunts and other extended family.
5. Agreement has been defined as responses of 4 or 5 on a five-point scale: 1= disagree and 5 = agree.
6. The number of respondents to the particular questions varies – each person did not answer every item.

7. For the questions about the victims, the percentages have been calculated only for those family group conferences where a victim was present. These percentages are slightly higher than when percentages are calculated for the sample of young people whose offence had involved a victim.
8. This figure comes from inspection of the full data on replies to each point on the five-point scale used for this question.

References

Ajzen, I., and Fishbein, M. (1980) *Understanding Attitudes and Predicting Social Behavior.* Englewood Cliffs, NJ: Prentice Hall.

Anleu, S. (1991) *Deviance Conformity and Control.* Melbourne: Longman Cheshire.

Daly, K. (1994) *Gender, Crime and Punishment.* New Haven: Yale University.

Chesney-Lind, M. (1997) *The Female Offender: Girls, Women and Crime.* Thousand Oaks, CA: Sage.

Heidensohn, F. (1996) *Women and Crime* (2nd edn). London: Macmillan.

Hedderman, C. and Gelsthorpe, L. (eds) (1997) *Understanding the Sentencing of Women. Home Office Research Study* 170. London: Home Office.

Maxwell, G.M., and Morris, A. (1999) *Understanding Reoffending.* Wellington: Institute of Criminology, Victoria University of Wellington.

Maxwell, G.M., and Morris, A. (2001) 'Family Group Conferences and Reoffending', in A. Morris and G. Maxwell (eds) *Restorative Justice for Juveniles: Conferencing, Mediation and Circles.* Oxford and Portland, OR: Hart Publishing.

Sherman, H., Strang, H. and Woods, D.J. (2000) *Recidivism Patterns in the Canberra ReIntegrative Shaming Experiment (RISE).* Canberra: Australian National University.

Strang, H. (2001) 'Justice for Victims of Young Offenders: the Centrality of Emotional Harm and Restoration' in A. Morris and G. Maxwell (eds) *Restorative Justice for Juveniles: Conferencing, Mediation and Circles.* Oxford and Portland, OR: Hart Publishing.

Chapter 7

Juvenile offenders' perceptions of community service

Isabelle Delens-Ravier

What 'community service' embraces

Models of justice and community service

'Community service' has been in operation for many years and is considered by some to offer many possibilities, both of punishment and in terms of rehabilitation:

> Community service had great potential: it soon became popular with courts in that it provided elements of punishment and of reparation: that it satisfied various elements in the community, notably those who gained benefit from work undertaken; that of requiring offenders to give up leisure time rather than be wholly deprived of their liberty. (Cartledge 1986: 15)

Community service can be viewed in different ways, depending upon the legal framework it forms part of: as an alternative to imprisonment under the criminal law; as a special educational tool; as a rehabilitative measure; and as a keystone in a system of restorative justice (Walgrave 1999: 9). And it certainly does seem to be the preferred response to offending when the judiciary resorts to restorative justice processes (Schiff 1999: 327).

In Belgium at the time of writing,[1] legal measures involving young offenders fall under a system of law that is both educational and protective. The 'educational and philanthropic service' provided in the law since 1965 is thus one of the measures a juvenile judge has at his or her disposal when dealing with offences committed by minors. This facet of the law is seen as both a standard-bearer for the new model of justice being sought (Geudens *et al.* 1998; Tulkens and Moreau 20000: 985) and as an alternative to imprisonment or institutionalisation in the traditional criminal justice model. The lack of information on the methods and procedures of community service has made it possible to develop many programmes and practices (Dongier and Van Dosselaere 1992: 503) that fall within the ambit of social reactions to juvenile crime. Thus the implementation of community service within a restorative justice context has not been systematic (Schiff 1999: 341). Community service also means different things to different people. Thus some speak of it as having a retributive function – 'punishment' in response to offence; as having a protective/educational function – treatment for a young person who is demonstrating unsocial behaviour; a corrective function – making a young person aware of his or her responsibilities to society (Walgrave 1999); or a rehabilitative function – symbolic reparation or the restoration of the young person's links with society (Vaillant 1994, 2000).

In Belgium, the debate is still open. While the purely protective model of community service is criticised, guidelines as to future policy cannot be agreed between the two linguistic communities. The position of mediation in community service is still unclear. In the Wallonian community, the rehabilitative approach is quite apparent although, at times, it does adopt different approaches. The Flemish approach, however, is more restorative than rehabilitative (Walgrave 1992: 344).

Generally, and beyond the issue of different models of justice, the response to juvenile offending corresponds to how juvenile offending is perceived. The judicial response varies depending upon whether the emphasis is on the offence committed, the harm done to the victim, the harm done to society or the young person's personality. From another perspective, youth offending can be understood as a breakdown in social links or even the non-existence of social links: 'Delinquency happens when the offender cannot relate to the victim or society, when a link with the harmed person or milieu is nonexistent. [So] restoring or developing a link when one is lacking seemed a plausible answer (Deklerck and Depuydt 1998: 140).

For some, community service is capable of restoring social links as a result of society's reaction to the offence (Vaillant 1994, 2000). Restoration cannot only be understood as reparation of the harm done to the victim, especially through mediation, but also as reparation of the harm inflicted on society and, more broadly, as the reintegration of the young person into society.

Making the minors aware of their responsibilities

Restoring social links means acknowledging the interaction among the minor, his or her act, the victim and – more broadly – society. The concept of the 'social actor' (Debuyst 2002) means we tend to view the concept of responsibility in a relative way. Hence, the subject is considered as having his or her own viewpoint, which in turn depends on the position the subject occupies in the social framework, on his or her background and on his or her personal characteristics. What is 'normal' is, in itself, therefore, problematic if considered as the expression of a 'viewpoint' adopted in a certain context. Consequently, the law itself does not always 'make sense' to everyone and, hence, lies the importance of understanding the different actors involved in the judicial process.

Thus, a young person acknowledging that he or she is someone who has committed a harmful act *and* accepting responsibility for that act are two different things. Young people often acknowledge the wrongful acts they have committed but do not necessarily accept responsibility for such acts in the terms proposed by the judiciary (Delens-Ravier and Thibaut 2001: 56). Being the author of a wrongful act means being able to answer for that act, to assume authorship of that act, as it were. According to Vaillant, 'assuming such a burden is possible for an adolescent only if he can imagine himself not only the author of violent, avaricious or destructive behaviour, but also of other creative, imaginative, useful behaviour' (2000: 55). That is, a responsibility that is a form of encounter, of otherness; being responsible for a wrongful act means being concerned about others. But 'an adolescent who knows only the denials of life can hardly have access to the dimension of the other' (Vaillant 2000: 60).

The idea of *sens vécu*, as developed by Digneffe, is key to understanding the difference between the notion of responsibility and, the notion of experiencing responsibility and therefore, the various aspects of the community service experiment:

Assigning responsibility for a wrongful act to someone means primarily considering that person as the author of the deed, and as such prepared to answer for what he has done. For this feeling to emerge, the subject must perceive a causal link with the wrongful act; must recognise that it was indeed wrongful; and must recognise that he intended to commit it. And it is not sufficient for the person to feel responsible toward the person wronged, the responsibility must also be perceived as equitable. This requirement is presented as a requirement for consistency. The mechanism for assigning respon-sibility and for engendering a sense of responsibility, to coincide, must operate in a common framework into a mutual acknowledgment. This means that each of the parties: judge, parent or other person in authority – and not only the young offender – must be prepared to recognise his errors and his responsibilities, or, more broadly, those of the society which he represents. (Digneffe 1994: 829)

Thus, how a young person perceives the measure, and by that its reparative or restorative nature, will depend largely on the young person's feelings of fairness concerning the judicial decision and on his or her life experiences relative both to his or her wrongful act and to the judicial reaction to it. The young person's perception of community service will therefore be a function of all the relationships he or she has built up with the community. And 'reducing the offence to the contravention of a rule which carries with it a particular punishment entails taking the risk of the punishment being felt as an unjust reaction by society, since it fails to take into consideration the young offender's personal construct' (Digneffe 1994: 833).

Thus, for disaffected young people (as a result of social or family alienation, dropping out of school, etc.) rebuilding social links is sometimes simply rejected while, for others, who find themselves on the 'social integration' side of the equation, some sort of link that existed before the crime through a variety of social institutions (family, school, leisure activities, etc.) might be reparable. The stories we heard from some of the young people we met, and which form the basis of the different interpretations of the community service experience recounted in this chapter corresponds to this understanding of offending as a breakdown or disintegration of social links.

Evaluating the impact of community service

There exist 'few published empirical evaluations of community service programmes in a restorative context and even fewer that have examined the impact of such programmes on offenders' (Schiff 1999: 328). One reason for this lack of evaluations might be that it is especially difficult to assess the impact of community service because the objectives of community service are so varied and diverse.

Normally, when evaluating the service, two elements are taken into account: compensation for the victim and the juvenile offender's reoffending. In so far as community service seeks compensation for the victim, it is logical to ask what sort of compensation the victim does in effect receive through a judicial decision. It should also be possible to measure society's impression of what 'compensation' should entail.

Recidivism, however, is much more complex, and so an evaluation of the effects on offenders is not easy (Walgrave 1992: 350). However, measuring recidivism rates is not our purpose here: here we are interested in offenders' perceptions of community service.

The 'success' of a community service order can be measured on the basis of the effective completion of the work ordered. Hence services rendered correctly, to the satisfaction of the employer, can, upon completion, be considered as 'successful' (McIvor 1992: 82). Even if we limit our evaluation to this aspect only, understanding the perception of young offenders is still of major importance. How a young person sees this service – as a positive, validating experience or otherwise – will have an influence on his or her effective performance of that service: 'Offenders who regard their work assignments as constructive and worthwhile may be more motivated to be attentive to their jobs and may, therefore, have fewer absences from placement and a lower likelihood of breach' (McIvor 1992: 23).

The success of community service can, however, be assessed in other ways: the value of the work to the community; the service's utility in diverting offenders from prison sentencing; and the impact of community service on reoffending . (McIvor 1992: 82).

A typical evaluation of community service, which 'defines itself as focusing on the reparation of the harm done by offenders to victims and communities' (Schiff 1999: 327), does not, in general, concern itself with the impact on the offender him or herself. Even the most ardent of restorative justice proponents (Walgrave 1999: 13) consider the contribution of community service to the rehabilitation of the offender as marginal: 'restorative justice is not primarily concerned with restoring the offender (although this may be a beneficial by-product), but with restoring the harm done by the crime' (Haines 1998: 107).

However, if we take an approach that places the restoration of social links at the heart of community service, understanding the young offender's point of view is a fundamental element of effective evaluation. The reparative sanction itself does not result in the young person acquiring greater self-awareness:

however, [if] justice system interventions are leaving offenders more (or even equally) bitter, angry and violence-prone after leaving the system than when they entered, then something is wrong with the strategy and restorative outcomes must be examined in this context. Moreover, offenders are themselves members of the community and are often victims themselves. (Schiff 1999: 323)

Therefore, the personal and educational impact of community service on young offenders seems capable of constituting a criterion for evaluation, and it is to this aspect of community service this chapter now turns.

Offenders' attitudes towards, and satisfaction with, community service

The varying backgrounds of young offenders, their differing patterns of offending and a multitude of socioeconomic factors all contribute to the difficulties in establishing guidelines for a response to juvenile crime.

Sanctions as a positive experience

For some young offenders, community service can be a positive experience. Research based on juvenile offenders' own experiences (McIvor 1992: 83; Schiff 1999: 342) has shown that most young people consider community service to be a positive, worthwhile sanction: it provides satisfaction at a personal level, the work performed benefits the community and a community service order is a more positive experience than a prison sentence. The work performed is often regarded as interesting and agreeable. It makes it possible for the young people to acquire or extend skills that could prove useful later on and gives them a taste of working in the real world. The relationship the young offender has with the person in charge can be positive and can go some way to rebuilding the young person's self-esteem. A feeling of usefulness to the community is also a positive factor – Vaillant speaks of symbolic reparation and the restoration of social links as a result of work experience born of community service, in terms of concrete achievements, the use of the young person's own initiative and encounters with others: 'Reparation rests on the method of social reconciliation: the young offender and society must each take a step toward the other' (2000: 71).

A less costly solution

Apart from the benefits of the work itself, the less constraining nature of community service can help the young offender because it enables him or her to retain his or her freedom (McIvor 1992: 94) – the relief young offenders often feel at the time the community service order is announced remains with them: relief at not being incarcerated in a confined environment.

However, Vaillant speaks of those young offenders for whom community service has little or no effect (2000: 83). These young people comply with what has been imposed on them – the service is performed satisfactorily and the overall evaluation of their efforts is positive – but they do not commit themselves to the symbolic dimension of this form of reparation. This type of reaction to community service can perhaps be explained in part through the lack of a restorative intent in most community service programmes (Schiff 1999: 343). Some young offenders might also consider the experience as having brought them nothing new – most often because the work did not require any special skills or did not prove 'interesting'. The work and where it is carried out are therefore very important elements of community service. McIvor's study shows that:

> offenders found community service to be more rewarding if they were able to acquire skills during their placement, if they enjoyed a great deal of contact with the beneficiaries of their work or if they were engaged in work that they could perceive as being of considerable benefit to the recipients. (1992: 88)

The apprenticeship aspect of community service is especially valuable for young offenders, as are the opportunities for meeting people.

Hence, if community service is seen solely as a way of escaping from a more severe form of punishment – as boring, of no value and as something to be got over as quickly as possible – it is, in effect, reparation without any element of social restoration. Encounters between adults and young people during the performance of community service represent a form of indirect reparation, constituting a veritable promise by society for youths deprived of human, non-pecuniary relationships, given over to illicit trafficking, scheming, living by one's wits and just managing to survive' (Vaillant 2000: 67).

Refusal

Some young refuse to accept a community service order, even though the alternative might be some form of confinement, just as they would refuse any proposal that came from society at large. Of these young people, Vaillant says that they feel themselves 'victims, victims who are alien to any sense of responsibility. It is a case of "turnaround is fair play": they are totally lacking; everything is owed them; nothing can be asked of them' (2000: 84). It could be said that these young offenders have never had any social links: their relationship with society has been one of exclusion and injustice. This also raises the difficulty of distinguishing between the victim and the offender in complex cases, where the young offender feels him or herself to be the victim of inadequate societal attention and of a very poor family background (Bullock *et al.* 1992: 376).

155

The research: young offenders and judicial measures – young people speak out

The research reported here is based on the findings of a project conducted for the French Community of Belgium concerning the perception by young offenders of two different Youth Court measures: community service and young offenders' institutions (Delens-Ravier and Thibaut 2001). The study included young people who had accepted community service as some form of symbolic restoration as well as those who had refused a community service order. The interpretation presented here of the experiences of these young offenders (which focuses in particular on the extent of their social reintegration) is only exploratory in nature: it should be seen as a starting point for further research.

Methodology

The aim of the research was to ascertain the views of young people whose voices are often absent from debates concerning youth protection even though they are directly involved. To this end, we chose to undertake the research in a qualitative manner, more specifically through focused interviews. The young people interviewed, therefore, spoke of the wrongful acts they had committed, the judicial processes they had experienced (police, prosecuting authorities, juvenile court judges) and of their environment (family, neighbourhood, friends, school). We were not interested in the statistical representatives of these young people's views, it being of little importance that the majority of the young people we interviewed had had the same reaction to the judiciary process.

The Youth Court usually lays down the general framework of a community service order: the specific body in which the service is to be performed defines the content. The work performed must benefit the community, and it can take various forms: manual work, helping people with special needs or administrative work (Tulkens and Moreau 2000: 647). However, it proved difficult to contact young offenders working within the framework of a non-custodial measure such as community service. Although the organisations involved agreed to forward our requests for interviews to the young people concerned, very few young people responded. It seems very few young people are willing to talk about their service once it has been completed. According to the organisations concerned, this is their way of putting the whole experience behind them.

Young offenders' perceptions of community service

Three different types of reaction to community service are presented below. From our research it seems that a young person's perception of the service depends to a large extent, on that young person's relationship with society – in terms of integration or exclusion. It is also clear that the perception of a community service order is broadly linked to the young person's acceptance of his or her guilt and to his or her feelings of fairness regarding the order: 'The successful completion of an Order will prove less likely if the offender perceives the sentence as being unfair or excessive' (Cartledge 1986: 36). Generally once a young offender is caught up in the judicial machinery, he or she acknowledges this fact and recognises that punishment is called for. Community service is, therefore, most often initially greeted with a sense of relief at having avoided something worse (i.e. confinement).

Case 1: sanctions offering the opportunity to turn over a new leaf

The first subject (whom we will call Joseo, aged 18 years) had experienced community service as a punishment meted out by the Youth Court and he saw it as an opportunity to make reparation for his offence. This type of reaction is usually encountered in young offenders who are considered to be socially integrated: students, young people still living fairly amicably with their families, young people who earn a legitimate income, etc. The offence committed is often considered an 'accident' and is regretted. The young person acknowledges the offence, admits to having committed it and, therefore, sees the judicial reaction as justified and logical. To this type of young person, community service is a fair and logical penalty and is not open to discussion: 'I don't know what I knew ... I said to myself that I had gone too far, that's all' ('Louis', aged 16). To return to Joseo, this form of punishment does not seem to be too severe and, in any case, it is better than being sent to a young offenders' institution: 'I was scared of what she (the judge) was going to say. Of what I was going to get. If I was going to be sent away or not ... I was expecting that, I was expecting ... I don't know ... something harder. So this was OK.' To many young offenders, an appearance in court and institutionalisation go hand in hand – they are often unaware of the existence of other types of measures. While being assigned to a young offenders' institution is often viewed as the severest measure a judge can impose, in general, community service comes at the bottom of the scale of penalties, being a less harsh measure than removal from the family environment.

For Joseo, community service was seen as a positive new experience, making it possible for him to explore new horizons, fight boredom and rebuild a self-image damaged by his criminal acts. The work offered a learning opportunity. Both the judge and the young person were 'winners' – the sentence issued by the judge was executed to the full and Joseo learnt something:

> I learnt something and did what I was asked to do, to make up for what I had done ... I already knew it was possible to learn a trade. That instead of sending them [i.e. young offenders] to a boarding school or a prison for a month or two, they asked them to work, for, uh, society ... and at the same time they were doing something good, they were working, they were doing useful work. And all that at the same time, they, uh, ... yeah, they were being punished, OK, but in a different way.

While most young people see the primary purpose of community service as a 'penalty', it also serves as 'reparation', because it is a way of wiping the slate clean after an act that is now regretted: 'I did what the people in charge and the judge expected of me.' This feeling of being able to turn over a new leaf is experienced when the service is actually being performed. Community service was experienced positively by Joseo, who did what was expected of him. His working relationships were good and he felt accepted in spite of the 'stupid thing' he had done. The service offered him the opportunity to learn something new and his encounters with adults were non-stigmatising. Joseo was first and foremost a 'volunteer' or worker rather than a 'delinquent'. The following quotation from Joseo confirms that positive, general impression – the rebuilding of his self-image and, consequently, of sense of social connectedness is undeniable:

> It went well, they accepted me ... And the lady in charge said I was very well mannered, very nice and she couldn't understand how a student like me could end up going before the judge. Because I had ... a good way with words, I spoke well, I was nice. But it's ... anything can happen, as they say.

In spite of having a negative self-image, the experience of community service can help a young offender from equating him or herself with the act he or she has committed, enables him or her to make a fresh start and to retain the esteem of others. Family disappointment and the shame felt by the young person can lead to a dynamic of reparation and a desire to eradicate the incident for ever. Thus, for the parents, community service is an opportunity for them to mobilise at every stage of the procedure: at the initial arrest by the police, at the Youth Court hearings and at meetings with those at the community service placement. For the young person, community service is a chance to prove to his or her family that he or she is capable of doing more than 'stupid things'.

Others have pointed out the effect of community service in increasing awareness of the impact of the offence not only on the victim but also on the young offender's total environment and in terms of the mobilisation of his or her family and friends (Masters 1998: 124). In Joseo's case, reintegration was primarily concerned with his school. Reintegration at school was an important element in the judge's decision, and reacceptance at school is often a deciding factor in a young offender's future life chances. Schools are often tolerant of pupils who behave well, even if they are academically weak. Schools can help to keep those young people in the system and can support the reparation aspect of community service:

> The teachers didn't say anything ... because it wasn't their business ... Because I was liked at school, by the teachers, I didn't have hassles, either from teachers or from ... Yeah, the school mediator, she knew and, uh, she was surprised when she learnt I had done that. Because she knew it wasn't like me and she was really surprised about what I had done.

Young people like Joseo see their encounters with the judicial system as a relief: something that makes it possible for them to acknowledge the illegality of the act, to define the 'deal' and the price to pay. The judgment is confirmation of the rehabilitation process. Court hearings and the judgement help to clarify the situation, are 'fair' and offer the young person the opportunity to make a new start.

Case 2: an unavoidable alternative to institutionalisation

The second subject (whom we will call Benjamin, aged 17 years) saw community service as an unavoidable 'penalty' that was preferable to being sent to a young offenders' institution. Occupying a marginal position in society vastly different from the middle-class background of much of the judiciary, Benjamin considered the judge's decision as yet another aspect of the completely unfair set of relationships he had with society. He nevertheless agreed to it without too much complaint in order to protect his personal plans, which could have been thwarted by incarceration.

Benjamin is typical of many young people on the margins of society: his family did not have a background of stable employment, he had left school early and he had developed 'parallel networks' or illegal circles to support himself. The goal of such young people – which is symbolic of consumerist societies where money is all-important – is to earn lots of money in order to be recognised and respected. Theft, therefore, is seen as a means of survival in a 'hard' society where a young person has the impression he or she will not make his or her way by any other means. Criminal offences are not regarded as infringements of society's rules but, rather, as a sort of game. The fact that some offences mean the young person ends up in court is a 'mistake' – a lost round in a game played between representatives of society (essentially the police) and the young person; a game that represents an important source of income as well as the foundations of social status in a marginal environment.

The first people encountered in this game are the police. Considering themselves to be the 'little guys' and thus stigmatised by their social position, these young people feel particularly hounded by the police.[2] For such young people, a community service order is a punishment like any other, imposed by the rules of a game that always go against the little guy. As mentioned above, it is, nevertheless, the lesser evil in a cost-benefit calculation for a 'business' that must be resumed as soon as possible.

The young person, therefore, 'pretends' to conform to what is expected of him or her, knowing full well what he or she must say and what attitude he or she has to adopt in order to rid him or herself of custodial restraint as quickly as possible while retaining a certain degree of control over the process. Thus, the young person carries out the community service with the minimum compliance possible. He or she will say that he or she goes to the placement but does nothing; that he or she has control of the situation (including where the service is performed) by having established what he or she is willing and unwilling to do – especially considering that the work is unpaid:

> It went well, even very well I would say. Yeah, because considering I wasn't being paid, the first day I went I said: 'OK, look, I don't work, I'm not paid, so it's no good telling me to do something.' He said: 'OK.' And so I went in every day but I didn't do anything (laughs). But in the beginning, yeah, it got on my nerves to have to do service I didn't feel like doing. But since I went there and I saw that things looked calm and … I said to myself: 'It's in the bag.' And that was it. (Benjamin)

The overall assessment of the community service is none the less, positive. Benjamin was satisfied and felt he 'got off pretty well'. The judge was satisfied too. The placement, however, had no voice in the matter, even if it was felt Benjamin was unco-operative and not open to dialogue.

Certain family backgrounds are conducive to young people starting up in 'business': the young person's 'proud' identity is maintained through the illicit trade conducted together by father and son. This represents the intergenerational reproduction of a form of social integration – or rather disintegration – often that is repeated:

> Criminal careers often are interwoven with victim careers. Often the phenomenon spans several generations. Criminals can have parents and grandparents who coped with the same problems, which does not mean that this is hereditary: it is more about the passing from generation to generation of a social, psychological, physical and material context, regenerating the same problems through individual lives. (Deklerck and Depuydt 1998: 150)

If, at the outset, entanglements with the law are seen as an additional injustice, the young person and his or her family soon realise it is better to give in and comply with the judge's demands in order to rid themselves of legal constraint as quickly as possible. Education offers few prospects for this type of young person, who either drops-out or attends sporadically. And school might represent the first institution where the young person experienced a loss of status. Community service can destroy the fragile links a young person has with the education system. Having a police record is likely to lead to the termination of an apprenticeship or vocational training course a young person may be attending as a last desperate effort after numerous suspensions or expulsions from school.

For this type of young person, the Youth Court judge represents, first and foremost, the power of money. The young person is convinced that, if he or she had the money, he or she could pay for the damage, repair the injury to the victim and not have to perform community service. But lacking financial means, the young person has to calculate the costs involved. In this sense, an order to perform community service is a less costly penalty than institutionalisation.

It is nevertheless interesting to note that the moment of judgment, when the official decision is pronounced is a striking one that leaves its mark on the young person. The figure of a judge making a decision – even in the context of a shameful social order – and thus confirming the young person's inferior social status, seems to make an impact.

Case 3: injustice and refusal

It is among the young people sent to young offenders' institutions that we encountered those who had refused to perform community service. More often than not, these young people began community service but quickly refused to continue. One young person thus expressed (hypothetically as it turned out, because the judge gave him no choice) his preference for being locked up rather than being obliged to perform community service, which he considered humiliating and degrading. Another refused to continue doing what he considered a demeaning task. Yet another complained of the multiplicity of measures a judge can take. Community service is therefore considered an additional punishment on top of others – (prison, institutionalisation and so on). It is seen as yet another injustice, exacerbating the young people's feelings of being 'had' by the Youth Court judge.

The humiliating aspect of the service permeates many young people's perceptions, in stark contrast to the judge's attitude to their case. However, some young people (such as Benjamin) redefine the objective of community service, while others (such as Joseo) focus on the dimension of reparation. Whatever the young person's attitude to the service, the simple fact of his or her presence at the placement necessitates a minimum level of social integration – or at least a willingness to make an effort – even if the young person has redefined the nature of community service in his or her own terms.

What can be learnt from these young people?

The question arises as to the impact of community service orders, which are subject to a terminology as diverse and varied as the practices they encompass. If their impact is evaluated on the basis of the few interviews carried out, we see that the dimension of symbolic reparation – the transition from 'debt to gift' (Vaillant 1994) – is barely mentioned by these young people. Reparation is quite 'matter of fact': the young people considered they had made amends for their 'stupid acts' simply by responding to the judge's injunctions. For one young offender, reparation even seemed to constitute an alternative to paying for damages. He imagined the 'salary' he would receive at the end of his service would be paid to the judge so the judge could reimburse the party claiming damages:

> I had to do forced labour. That's, for example, for when you steal something, when you break a window. And the window has to be paid for. The window costs six thousand francs ... the judge gives you work to do. For example, she finds ... oh, I don't know ... in a garden, picking up leaves and all. Instead of being paid, the money goes to her, and she pays for the window. That way, the parents don't have to pay. And I had another ... in a convalescent home, with the

old people, they were a real pain ... They call you with a buzzer ... An hour to get out a single sentence. I don't know ... I did my hours and I left. (Mohammad, aged 17).

But while the aspect of reparation is absent from the young people's accounts they nevertheless mention several positive elements. Where community service is seen as an opportunity to turn over a new leaf it has three important elements:

1. It is an opportunity to make a fresh start. Community service leaves no bitter taste and the young person is given a chance to demonstrate another aspect of himself or herself (to his or her parents, counsellor, siblings, etc.). The young person is not equated solely with his or her wrongful act.
2. The young person can establish positive and status-enhancing relationships with the adults at the placement, without intellectual challenges and labelling of any kind. On the whole, young people say they are surprised by the fact they are accepted – that they have the possibility of showing a different facet of themselves from the one that emerged during the judicial process.
3. Finally, the time spent performing the service is a way of escaping boredom. It is a way of keeping busy during holidays and free time.

Where community service is seen as an unavoidable penalty but preferable to being sent to a young offenders' institution, it enables the young offender to remain free of judicial constraint. Because it is difficult, even impossible, to avoid incarceration once a young person has been sent to a young offenders' institution, community service is much preferable to institutionalisation. Indeed, young people who have been placed in a young offender's institution are very likely to return, and judges will no longer consider community service as an option in such situations.

These young people see the court's judgment as varying according to the social status of the individual concerned – where the poorest are always prosecuted – but a judgment it is best to comply with, given the unequal balance of power. Community service, none the less, offers a young person the opportunity to change his or her image, in his or her own eyes and in the eyes of those around him or her.

Further, community service has parallels with the world of work, from which these young people feel excluded. It is often easier for these young people to fall into unpaid work of this kind than it is to find paid employment. Therefore the fundamental question remains:

> How can we go beyond merely reasserting the rule and securing compensation when dealing with juveniles who are victims of poverty, of second-class status at school, who must be content with reacting in terms of social control for lack of real prospects of being integrated through a productive activity? (De Fraene 2000: 88).

In the eyes of these young people, community service is but an additional measure in a juvenile justice system that they see either as protectionist or penal. This view echoes analyses that highlight the absence of a mechanism within the justice system that would put young offenders back on the right track in society. This view is, after all, quite logical for, as we have seen, the restorative aspect is not always clearly defined.

> However, when community service is imposed as a restorative sanction that meets real victim and community needs, and where input from the victim and the community is included in the sanctioning process, the possibility that community service will benefit offenders, victims and the community is considerably increased. (Schiff 1999: 343)

The impact of community service can only be truly understood in terms of what the young offender experiences as the meaning of rules, and consequently of their violation, which is specific to each young person in terms of his or her history and life experiences. The service belongs to the judicial system, and so it is the entire system and the young person's interaction with it and, consequently, with society as a whole that needs to be considered. A young person's debt to society can only be transformed into a gift if there is some kind of pact of recognition – a sort of 'social gift', a contribution from society.

The current tendency to focus on the crime and to couch responsibility primarily in the terms of the wrongful act committed runs the risk of obscuring society's collective responsibility for bringing up young people: 'In a certain sense, crime is always a collective event' (Deklerck and Depuydt 1998: 150). The components for a new system of justice seem at the moment to be used more as tools to legitimate a form of penalising juvenile offending under the disguise of a diversification of sanctions. We seem to be far from funding the social and political conditions necessary for society to move towards the 'republican society' (Walgrave and Bazemore 1999: 368) that is so essential if we are to find a solution to the paradoxes of the doctrine of reparation (Bazemore and Walgrave 1999).

Notes

1. In Belgium the law on the protection of young people is currently being changed.
2. It is important to address the experiences young people have with the police as this is a theme that recurred in all the interviews. Even if the youth in question admitted he or she deserved to be arrested, young people often voice indignation at the excessively humiliating attitude of the police (violence, insults, handcuffs, 'you'll get yourself a bad name', etc.). Most young people, however, submit obediently to police interrogations.

References

Bazemore, G. and Walgrave, L. (1999) 'Reflections on the Future of Restorative Justice', in G. Bazemore and L. Walgrave (eds) *Restorative Juvenile Justice: Repairing the Harm of Youth Crime*. Monsey, NY: Criminal Justice Press.

Bullock, R., Little, M. and Millham, S. (1992) 'Applying Restitutive Justice to Young Offenders: Observations from the United Kingdom', in H. Messmer and H.-U. Otto (eds), *Restorative Justice on Trial*. Dordrecht: Kluwer Academic.

Cartledge, G.C. (1986) 'Community Service in England/Wales – Organization and Implementation of Community Service: an Evaluation and Assessment of its Outcomes', in H.J. Albrecht and W. Schädler (eds) *Community Service, a New Option in Punishing Offenders in Europe*. Freiburg: Criminological Research Reports by the Max Planck Institute for Foreign and International Penal Law.

Debuyst, C. (2002) 'La Délinquance comme interaction', in L. Mucchielli and P. Robert (eds) *Crime et Sécurité, l'État des Savoirs*. Paris: Editions La Découverte.

De Fraene, D. (2000) 'La Réponse Réparatrice … Quelle était la Question?', *Mille Lieux ouverts*, 4(24): 77–89.

Deklerck, J. and Depuydt, A. (1998) 'An Ethical and Social Interpretation of Crime through the Concept of "linkedness" and "integration–disintegration". Applications to Restorative Justice', in L. Walgrave (ed.) *Restorative Justice for Juveniles: Potentialities, Risks and Problems*. Leuven: Leuven University Press.

Delens-Ravier, I. and Thibaut, C. (2001) *Jeunes délinquants et Mesures judiciaires: la Parole des jeunes* (rapport d'une recherche qualitative sur le point de vue de jeunes délinquants à propos de leur prise en charge judiciaire). Bruxelles: Communauté française.

Digneffe, F. (1994) 'Les Jeunes et la Loi pénale, les Significations de la Sanction pénale à l'Adolescence', *Revue de Droit pénal et de Criminologie*, 7/8: 825–39.

Dongier, S. and Van Dosselaere, D. (1992) 'Approaching Mediation in Juvenile Court: Rationale and Methodological Aspects', in H. Messmer, H. and H.-U. Otto (eds), *Restorative Justice on Trial*. Dordrecht: Kluwer Academic.

Dubet, F. (1987) *La Galère, Jeunes en survie*. Paris: Fayard.

Geudens, H., Schelkens, W. and Walgrave, L. (1998) 'A la Recherche d'un Droit sanctionnel restaurateur', *Journal du Droit des jeunes*, 173: 3–21.

Haines, K. (1998) 'Some Principled Objections to a Restorative Justice Approach to Working with Juvenile Offenders', in L. Walgrave (ed.) *Restorative Justice for Juveniles: Potentialities, Risks and Problems*. Leuven: Leuven University Press.

Masters, G. (1998) 'The Importance of Shame to Restorative Justice', in L. Walgrave (ed.) *Restorative Justice for Juveniles: Potentialities, Risks and Problems*. Leuven: Leuven University Press.

McIvor, G. (1992) *Sentenced to Serve*. Aldershot: Avebury.

Schiff, M.F. (1999) 'The Impact of Restorative Interventions on Juvenile Offenders', in G. Bazemore and L. Walgrave, L. (eds.) *Restorative Juvenile Justice: Repairing the Harm of Youth Crime*. Monsey, NY: Criminal Justice Press.

Tulkens, F. and Moreau, T. (2000) *Droit de la Jeunesse. Aide, Assistance, Protection*. Bruxelles: Larcier.

Vaillant, M. (ed.) (1994) *De la Dette au Don*. Paris: ESF.

Vaillant, M. (2000) *La Réparation : de la Délinquance à la Découverte de la Responsabilité*. Paris: Gallimard.

Walgrave, L. (1992) 'Mediation and Community Service as Models of a Restorative Approach: Why would it be Better? Explicating the Objectives as Criteria for Evaluation', in H. Messmer and H.-U. Otto (eds) *Restorative Justice on Trial*. Dordrecht: Kluwer Academic.

Walgrave, L. (1999) 'La Justice restaurative: à la Recherche d'une Théorie et d'un Programme', *Criminologie*, 32(1): 7–29.

Walgrave, L. and Bazemore, G. (1999) 'Reflections on the Future of Restorative Justice for Juveniles', in G. Bazemore, L. Walgrave (eds), *Restorative Juvenile Justice: Repairing the Harm of Youth Crime*, Monsey, NY: Criminal Justice Press.

Part III

Extending the Scope of Restorative Approaches

Chapter 8

Researching the prospects for restorative justice practice in schools: The 'Life at School Survey' 1996–9

Valerie Braithwaite, Eliza Ahmed, Brenda Morrison and and Monika Reinhart

Restorative justice practices are being regarded increasingly as attractive options for dealing with wrongdoing in school communities. Traditional punishments of a social kind, such as suspension or expulsion, are being sidelined as tools of last resort as researchers and practitioners document the negative consequences of allowing children 'to be at a loose end' in the community (Hirschi 1969; Jenkins 1997; Cunningham and Henggeler 2001). Geographically and socially separated from family and friends who are enmeshed in education and employment networks for most of their day, children who are suspended or expelled are even more at risk than they were previously to being trapped within subcultures that operate at the fringe of, if not outside, the law.

Alternative strategies for dealing with children who find themselves in strife in the school community take a variety of forms (Rigby 2001). Some interventions focus on changing the behaviour of such children through counselling and rehabilitation programmes; others focus on teaching more effective parenting; and still others focus on the school, with the intention of shaping school norms about appropriate behaviour and teaching children to identify wrongdoing, mediate conflict and find peaceful solutions. The whole of school approach of building a culture that rejects actions that involve the domination and exploitation of others is now widely endorsed as a means of reducing school bullying and violence, and creating a safe learning environment for children (Smith *et al.* 1999).

Restorative justice nestles comfortably as an idea within these broad social trends of best practice in school management. Restorative practices focus on maintaining and strengthening social bonds to prevent children, either bullies or victims, from feeling isolated from or rejected by the school community. At the same time as the child is encircled in this community of care, the issue of accountability and responsibility for wrongdoing is placed centre-stage for discussion and resolution. Offenders and victims meet, with care and support available to both sides. Restorative justice practices share the common feature of recognising and discussing the harm done and helping the wrongdoer work towards acknowledgement and commitment to make amends. The approach accepts human weakness in the sense that every person is capable of hurting others, but at the same time affirms human dignity, through recognising each person as a valued member of the community who can make amends and be reintegrated with forgiveness.

How restorative justice practices are best integrated into an educational environment is a complex question. For the most part it is likely to be a reflexive process of action learning and research. Adapting restorative practices to the context is critically important if they are to be effective as a means of social regulation. At the heart of successful restorative practices is commitment and emotional engagement. Neither is possible unless community members feel that the restorative justice process provides safe space to explore the issues that are troubling the group. Having advocated a process of adaptation and diversification in bringing restorative justice to the school context, there are nevertheless some basic processes that are fundamental to its effectiveness.

One social-psychological process that offenders must work their way through in restorative justice settings is the management of shame-related emotions (these include guilt and remorse) (Braithwaite 1989; Ahmed *et al.* 2001). The disapproval of another for failing to meet a standard or for breaking a code of conduct commonly gives rise to shame-related emotions and can be broadly referred to as the process of shaming another for wrongdoing. Yet shaming covers a broad spectrum of disapproving behaviours ranging from those that are highly respectful of the offender (reintegrative) to those that are disrespectful (stigmatising) (Braithwaite 1989). Adaptive shame management is the expected outcome from a process that is reintegrative, and not stigmatising. Under conditions of reintegration where an individual feels supported and valued, the wrongdoing can be acknowledged, the harmful consequences accepted, plans can be made to make amends and forgiveness and repaired social bonds can pave the way for a fresh start. Under conditions of stigmatisation, shame is likely to be all-encompassing and overwhelming for the individual, leading to responses such as withdrawal, avoidance or an attack on self or on others (Nathanson 1992). Once the wrongdoer cuts him or herself off from the community psychologically and socially, the shame and the harm done can be disowned, or at the very least justified, providing the individual with temporary respite from the painful shame emotion. At this point, social regulation has broken down.

While traditionally reintegrative shaming theory embedded effective shaming within a reintegrative framework, understanding how offenders manage and work through their feelings of shame has been a more recent development (Ahmed *et al.* 2001). For instance, despite all the support in the world, do some offenders fall apart psychologically when confronted with their wrongdoing, drowning in a shame experience from which they can see no escape? Alternatively, is the self-protective mechanism so strong in others that they are unable to relate to the harm that they have caused, deflecting the shame experience adroitly away at every turn? And if there can be a win-win solution in the shaming-shame management process, what are the psychological mechanisms that ensure this outcome?

Nathan Harris (2001) and Eliza Ahmed (2001) have focused on such questions from the wrongdoer's perspective. Harris argues that feeling shame means that one's ethical identity has been thrown into question by others whom one respects, as well as by oneself. Self-reflection may be a state that one arrives at through the disapproval of respected others, but at the end of the day, the self-doubt about one's own ethical identity is real: it is not an emotional response that is simply about feeling uncomfortable with the disapproval of others. Given the salience and depth of this emotional response, how does the individual cope? Is the social space provided by Braithwaite's (1989) reintegration philosophy enough? Ahmed argues that it can be enough if the individual can be encouraged to adopt adaptive shame management skills. Adaptive shame management requires two kinds of responses from the wrongdoer. The first is shame acknowledgement. Shame acknowledgement means that the individual can admit and come to terms with any wrongdoing, can take responsibility for the harm done, and is willing to embark on a course of action to make amends. The second desirable set of responses is that the wrongdoer resists the all too human tendency of blaming others, of making excuses for the action, of being angry, and using one's energy to find ways of 'placing' the shame elsewhere. In other words, offenders must have, or be helped to have, the resilience and wisdom to stay away from shame displacement. Ahmed concludes that while shaming is a societal mechanism for regulating social life, adaptive shame management is an individual mechanism for self-regulation. Restorative justice practices therefore are likely to be most effective when they harmonise regulatory mechanisms found in the society with those found in individuals.

If adaptive shame management is crucial to behaviour change and to community reintegration, the question must be asked: is non-adaptive shame management at the heart of repeat offending? Many have argued that unresolved shame is a prime trigger for violence (Lewis 1971; Scheff 1994, 1996). The research of Scheff (Scheff 1987; Scheff and Retzinger 1991) and Retzinger (1987, 1991) describes the relationship in dynamic terms as a shame–rage spiral where one fuels the other at increasing levels of intensity. If poor shame management skills are implicated as a source of the problem, and if adaptive shame management skills are necessary for effective resolution of the problem in restorative justice, then the context in which restorative justice is practised must be one that is capable of eliciting adaptive shame management in place of poor shame management.

Researching the basics for a restorative justice intervention programme

The above issues formed the basis for our deliberations on how best to build a restorative justice programme in schools. Our preferred intervention was to tackle the notion of shame management, both from the perspective of the individual and the school. Could adaptive shame management skills assist children in saying no to bullying, and could a school culture be built where children felt safe acknowledging wrongdoing and resisting the temptation to displace their shame on to others through displays of bravado and machismo? Before walking this path of active intervention, further research was required to test out some of the more fundamental assumptions.

In 1996, Eliza Ahmed had involved 32 schools in Canberra in a 'Life at School' survey. Children from ages 9 to 13 years ($n = 1401$) completed a questionnaire in class about themselves and their school experiences under the supervision of the researchers. The children were given a companion survey to take home for their parents to complete. Parents returned a completed, sealed questionnaire to a collection box at the school at their convenience ($n = 978$). Parent and child surveys had matching identification numbers so that they could be paired later for purposes of data analysis. At the end of the parental survey, families willing to take part in a follow-up survey were asked to provide their name and address. This group formed the sample for a 1999 'Life at School' survey. The combined 1996 and 1999 datasets (comprising 333 parents and 341 children) were used to seek answers to three questions:

1. How relevant and malleable are shame management skills in the context of reducing school violence across different age groups?
2. If relevant, is it possible for schools to strengthen shame management skills as part of the school's behaviour management programme, or are such practices learnt primarily from parents, perhaps even before children go to school?
3. If shame management skills are relevant and can be developed in the school context, how accepting are parents of a restorative justice approach that relies on shame management for dealing with school bullying and conflict among students?

All these questions needed to be answered before we could recommend intervention programmes for schools based on restorative justice principles.

Shame management: still relevant and malleable after three years?

In 1996, Ahmed (2001) demonstrated that two aspects of shame management – shame acknowledgement and shame displacement – were important predictors of bullying behaviour. Shame acknowledgement and displacement are measured through presenting children with a set of different scenarios in which one child is described bullying another and is caught in the act by the teacher. In each case, the child is asked to imagine him or herself as the wrongdoer and to answer a series of yes (2)/no (1) questions. For shame acknowledgement the questions are as follows:

1. Would you feel ashamed of yourself?
2. Would you wish you could just hide?
3. Would you feel like blaming yourself for what happened?
4. Do you think others would reject you?
5. Would you feel like making the situation better?

For shame displacement the questions are:

1. Would you feel like blaming others for what happened?
2. Would you be unable to decide if you were to blame?
3. Would you feel angry in this situation?
4. Would you feel like getting back at that student?
5. Would you feel like doing something else, for example, throwing or kicking something?

Ahmed's analyses showed that children who bullied other children were more likely to adopt a shame management pattern of low acknowledgement and high displacement, and that this pattern explained variation in bullying behaviour even after controlling for a number of other variables that had previously been linked with bullying. Among the list were measures of family disharmony, stigmatising and harsh child-rearing practices, indicators of school performance and school satisfaction, perceptions of a bullying culture in the school, and personality variables such as impulsivity, empathy, self-esteem and internal locus of control (see Ahmed 2001 for details).

Knowing that children involved in bullying others were less likely to acknowledge shame over such actions and were more likely to displace shame was consistent with our basic assumption that, if we could change children's shame management strategies in relation to bullying, we might be able to halt the repeated pattern of bullying, that was so destructive for both victims and offenders. Ahmed's (2001) data suggested that children who bullied others did not have the self-regulatory mechanism needed to think that this was not something they would want to do again. At the same time, these data were cross-sectional and were collected among primary school children: as such, they could not shed light on the possibility that shame management was a deeply entrenched behavioural pattern that could not be readily changed. Moreover, it was not clear that shame management would continue to be important later on. In 1996, all participants were pre-adolescent. With the transition to secondary school, it was possible that shame management would lose its potency as a predictor of bullying. By adolescence, bullying may have become a regular part of life.

In order to establish whether or not shame management was both relevant and malleable, the 1999 'Life at School' Survey dataset was analysed. Some 314 parent–child dyads had completed the survey in both 1996 and 1999.

First of all, a core set of measures taken in 1996 and 1999 were correlated across time. Children's survey responses were used to form the following measures:

1. self-reported bullying behaviour;
2. the number of friends at school;
3. hassles and worries at home;
4. hassles and worries at school;
5. hassles and worries with others socially;
6. empathy;
7. impulsivity;

8. perceptions of a bullying culture in the school;
9. shame acknowledgement; and
10. shame displacement.

All measures, with the exception of shame acknowledgement and shame displacement, were based on previously used survey instruments (see Ahmed 2001 for a description of measures).

Also included were parent's likely responses to seeing their own child bully another. Our interest in parental attributions about bullying grew out of our second question: how important are parents as socialising agents who influence whether or not children develop adaptive shame management skills? In order to measure parental attributions about a child's behaviour, parents were given the same bullying scenarios presented to the children and were asked how they would respond if they saw their child behaving in this way. Parents judged their child on:

1. the future likelihood of his or her behaving in this way;
2. the intentionality of the act;
3. responsibility for the act; and
4. controllability of the act.

These measures were developed specifically for this purpose and are described in full in Ahmed (2001).

The correlations across the three-year timespan were positive and significant in all but one case (the range was .17 to .39). The strongest correlation emerged for the measures of impulsivity ($r = .39$) and family hassles ($r = .39$). Children who were impulsive and reported family hassles in 1996 were more likely to be relatively high scorers on these dimensions in 1999. Also of note was the finding that children who were engaged in bullying others in 1996 were significantly more likely to be bullying others in 1999 ($r = .26$). Similarly, measures of shame acknowledgement in 1996 and 1999 were inter-related ($r = .31$) as were those of shame displacement ($r = .23$).[1]

While these results suggest a degree of stability on a range of psychological, social and behavioural attributes over time, they do not answer the question of their relative importance in predicting the future bullying activities of the child. More specifically, do the shame management skills acquired in primary school limit a child's capacity to turn away from bullying behaviours at secondary school, or do other factors come into play as children mature?

This question was addressed using ordinary least-squares regression analysis. The outcome variable was involvement in bullying others in

1999. The first set of predictors entered into the equation were the control variables of age, sex and bullying behaviour in 1996 (the same bullying measure as had been used in 1999 so that we could interpret the findings in terms of the prediction of change in bullying behaviour). After this the 1996 measures were entered for the number of friends the child had at school, the child's reports of hassles and worries at home, at school and socially, the personality variables of empathy and impulsivity, perceptions of a bullying culture in the school, the shame management skills and parental interpretations of bullying behaviour should it occur in their child.

The results appear under Model 1 in Table 8.1. Bullying behaviour was likely to increase over time for children who, in 1996, scored high on impulsivity, experienced hassles in relation to their academic perform-ance, reported having lots of friends and perceived their school as harbouring a bullying culture. It is of note that neither shame ack-nowledgement nor shame displacement in 1996 played a direct role in shaping future bullying behaviour. In other words, whether or not a child had adaptive shame management skills in 1996 was not a predictor of whether or not he or she would be drawn to bullying others later on.

The next stage of the analysis substituted the measures taken in 1999 for the 1996 measures with three exceptions – age, sex and bullying in 1996 (see Model 2, Table 8.1). This time, bullying in 1996 emerged as a predictor (in the absence of other 1996 measures), together with the 1999 measures of impulsivity, the degree to which the child perceived the school as harbouring a bullying culture, shame acknowledgement and shame displacement. These findings suggest that school culture and shame management within that culture at the time the bullying is occurring are important factors in unravelling bullying behaviour. At the same time, past involvement in bullying behaviour is not irrelevant – past offending increases the likelihood of future offending.

Finally, the 1996 and 1999 measures were entered together (see Model 3, Table 8.1). Children whose bullying behaviour increased over time had significantly higher levels of impulsivity in 1996 and 1999. Their views of their circumstances in 1999 were protective of their bullying status. They perceived a flourishing and accepted bullying culture in the school and they showed a greater resistance to shame acknowledgement over hypo-thetical bullying incidents, along with a readiness to displace shame.

These findings show shame management skills as being relevant during the period when bullying is taking place. The shame management skills shown in relation to bullying episodes three years earlier do not appear to have a direct bearing on later bullying behaviour. By the same token, the importance of shame management is not bound by the

Table 8.1. Beta coefficients with adjusted R squared for three regression models predicting bullying behaviour in 1999

Predictors[2]	Model 1	Model 2	Model 3
Control variables			
Age	.08	−.01	.01
Sex	.09	.03	.02
Bullying in 1996	.11	.14**	.09
1996 measures			
Number of friends	.13*		.05
Family hassles	−.03		−.02
School hassles	.14*		.06
Social hassles	−.02		−.02
Impulsivity	.18**		.14*
Empathy	.01		.02
Perceptions of a bullying school culture	.12*		.07
Shame acknowledgement	−.09		.01
Shame displacement	.07		−.02
Future likelihood from parent	.01		.00
Intentionality attribution from parent	.07		.03
Responsibility attribution from parent	−.02		−.04
Controllability attribution from parent	−.07		−.04
1999 measures			
Number of friends		.05	.05
Family hassles		−.01	−.02
School hassles		.10	.08
Social hassles		−.05	−.03
Impulsivity		.18***	.13*
Empathy		−.05	−.06
Perceptions of a bullying school culture		.12*	.12*
Shame acknowledgement		−.30***	−.28***
Shame displacement		.16***	.17**
Future likelihood from parent		.08	.09
Intentionality attribution from parent		−.02	−.01
Responsibility attribution from parent		.01	.03
Controllability attribution from parent		.00	.00
R squared	.21***	.36***	.39***
Adjusted R squared	.17***	.32***	.32***

$*p < .05, **p < .01, ***p < .001.$

innocence of childhood. Ahmed's findings with 9–12-year-olds were replicated in Model 2 with the same children, now in their teenage years (12–16 years). Children not involved in bullying were more likely to manage shame adaptively in their teenage years.

Shame acknowledgement and displacement appear to be reactions to bullying that are contained by space and time. This is encouraging from the perspective of a school intervention. If children's bullying actions were traced primarily to shame management skills learnt years before in primary school or in the family, prospects of a successful social intervention at the time bullying was occurring would be reduced. At the same time, these findings should not be interpreted as showing that shame management is a will-o'-the–wisp phenomenon. Ahmed (2001) describes adaptive shame management skills as akin to having a conscience. If this is so, learning to manage shame well in early childhood should give the child a head start in applying shame management skills in a range of different contexts later on.

In summary, shame management does not appear to be an aspect of temperament like impulsivity that leaves some children dispositionally vulnerable to getting into trouble from childhood through adolescence. If shame management is conceived as a situational response, there may be some possibility of altering it through re-examining the bullying context with offender and victim. Also of importance in these analyses is the consistent finding that children who bully others perceive their school environment as being tolerant of bullying. In other words, such children fail to perceive school disapproval for the harmful actions in which they engage. Interventions for bullying need to be sensitive to the disposition of the child, particularly impulsivity, mindful of the poor shame management skills that accompany bullying, and critically aware of the school culture in which the bullying incident has taken place. The next question to ask is: what are the antecedents of shame management skills? How much are they shaped by past events and how much by the present, how much by the home and how much by the school? If we want to elicit acknowledgement and discourage displacement, what are the points of leverage, and where are we likely to be blocked in a restorative justice intervention?

Shame management: learning to be adaptive

Ahmed's (2001) research showed that if a school was to control bullying it needed to encourage acknowledgement of its harm and discourage displacement of blame on to the victim or the situation that gave rise to the incident. Ahmed pointed to two personality variables that were relevant to the realisation of this goal. Empathy among students for children who were bullied was a factor conducive to what we call the adaptive shame management pattern of high acknowledgement and low displacement. The personal characteristic that was least likely to be associated with adaptive shame management was impulsivity. Impulsive children were more likely to display low acknowledgement and high displacement. These findings suggest that a restorative justice intervention might be successful in dealing with school bullying if it creates a safe space for children to learn to see things from the perspective of others, and for impulsive children to develop adaptive shame management skills.

In order to find out if a restorative justice intervention was likely to improve shame management skills, a further set of regression analyses were tested in which the 1996 and 1999 measures were used to predict, first, 1999 levels of shame acknowledgement and then 1999 levels of shame displacement (see Table 8.2). Children's capacity to acknowledge shame in 1999 was predicted by both earlier experiences and attributes (as measured in 1996) and by more contextually relevant measures taken in 1999. First, it is of note that acknowledgement was less likely to occur among boys and older children. Acknowledgement of shame was aided by being able to acknowledge shame earlier in primary school.

Other factors measured in 1996 that were important predictors of shame acknowledgement in 1999 were tolerance of a bullying school culture and parental rejection of the idea that their child would intentionally bully another in a scenario context. This latter finding contradicted our hypothesis in an important way. Our initial thinking was that accusing one's own child of intentionally hurting another would be stigmatising to that child, and therefore damaging to self-esteem and confidence. On reflection, however, we realised that our measure asked parents to interpret an imaginary situation where they actually saw their child bully another child. Therefore, what we were measuring was a parent's willingness to accept evidence that appears before their eyes and to face up to a situation where their child intentionally engages in a harmful act. Interestingly, parents who were prepared to confront rather than avoid the problem in 1996 were more likely to have children who were able to acknowledge shame three years on. We now interpret this finding as showing that adaptive shame management involves parents in not only setting limits on what behaviour is appropriate or not in the abstract, but also being prepared to call children to account for inappropriate behaviour when it occurs. Parents who allow their children to wriggle out of difficult situations with excuses and 'on technicalities' are likely to have children who fail to develop adaptive shame management skills. In these findings

Table 8.2. Beta coefficients with adjusted R squared for regression models predicting shame acknowledgement and shame displacement in 1999

	1999 outcome variable	
Predictors[3]	Shame acknowledgement	Shame displacement
Control variables		
Age	−.11*	−.04
Sex	−.11*	.01
Acknowledgement 1996	.24***	−.04
Displacement 1996	−.09	.21***
1996 measures		
Number of friends	−.04	.11
Family hassles	−.05	−.13
School hassles	.02	.08
Social hassles	.02	.04
Impulsivity	.01	−.01
Empathy	−.08	−.03
Perceptions of a bullying school culture	−.13*	−.02
Future likelihood from parent	−.04	.05
Intentionality attribution from parent	.15*	−.16*
Responsibility attribution from parent	.03	.11
Controllability attribution from parent	−.09	.06
1999 measures		
Number of friends	−.04	.04
Family hassles	−.01	.24***
School hassles	−.13*	-.04
Social hassles	.14*	.02
Impulsivity	−.04	.08
Empathy	.37***	−.09
Perceptions of a bullying school culture	−.10	.14*
Future likelihood from parent	−.02	−.08
Intentionality attribution from parent	−.04	.07
Responsibility attribution from parent	−.05	.00
Controllability attribution from parent	−.05	−.02
R squared	.41***	.19***
Adjusted R squared	.36***	.11***

* $p < .05$, ** $p < .01$, *** $p < .001$.

we are possibly catching a glimpse of the parental and school actions that contribute to the development of conscience in children in the domain of bullying behaviour.

The contemporaneous measures that affected shame acknowledgement were having empathy for other children and having hassles at school. Shame acknowledgement was higher among children who expressed empathy for others and who were having difficulties at school socially. Acknowledgement was lower in cases where the difficulties were associated with school work.

In sum, past socialisation and contemporary social context appear to join forces in shaping a capacity to acknowledge wrongdoing in relation to bullying. The most important of the contemporary context variables was empathy. If children in a school share strong positive social bonds with each other, shame acknowledgement is more likely to occur. This finding fits into our general thesis that safe space is important for shame acknowledgement and provides essential background for effective reintegrative shaming interventions in schools.

While the prediction of shame acknowledgement was quite strong from these data, prediction of shame displacement was poor. A tendency to displace shame in 1996 predicted later displacement and, again, parents who were unwilling to accept that their child intentionally hurt another in a scenario context were more likely to have children who later displaced shame in the bullying context. Contemporary measures that affected displacement were related to home and school. Displacement was more common when children reported hassles at home and when they perceived bullying as being tolerated at school.

The findings from this research suggest the following:

1. Bullying behaviour does not disappear as children get older.
2. Bullying behaviour is accompanied by poor skills in being able to acknowledge wrongdoing and a tendency to displace blame and anger on to others. Such tendencies are interpreted as part of the self-regulatory system that we commonly refer to as conscience.
3. Schools that are seen to tolerate bullying provide a fertile ground for the expansion of bullying activity and weaken the shame management skills that might lead children to desist from bullying.
4. Parents have a role to play in developing shame management skills in their children. Parents who were unable to accept intentional wrongdoing in their child in an imaginary situation had children who, three years later, had poor shame management skills.

Together, these findings support current best practice of adopting a 'whole of school' approach to bullying. Teachers, students and parents work together to create a culture in which bullying is not condoned and one in which children can expect to feel safe from predatory behaviour of any kind. The findings also warn, however, that children who step outside the rules and bully others in this culture are not going to be helped by exclusion or marginalisation. The temperament of impulsivity, for instance, will always leave some children vulnerable to a hasty, thoughtless act. Furthermore, hassles created at school, by friends or in the family, will always be occurring and will leave some children emotionally fragile and insecure, despite the prevailing supportive culture. Such children at times may engage in anti-social activities of various kinds. Rejecting such children through suspension and expulsion from a cohesive and generally supportive school community is likely to do more harm than rejecting them from a fragmented group full of competing, mutually hostile sub-cultures. If the 'whole of school' approach is adopted, dealing with acts of wrongdoing through restorative justice practices appears to be the optimal solution. Not only is it in the best interests of the child but also, through being consistent with the school philosophy, the restorative justice approach adds to the integrity of the school culture.

Would parents accept a restorative justice intervention?

As one of the two major learning environments for children, schools should not be places disrupted by unnecessary change and strife. If restorative justice practices are to be introduced into schools, authorities need to know what parents think, what concerns they are likely to have and how they will view such procedures.

Previous work based on the 1996 dataset of 978 parents provided some important insights into how parents wanted the problem of school bullying controlled by authorities (Braithwaite 2000). These findings were confirmed by Morrison (2001) in her research with teachers and parents on trialling intervention programmes in particular schools. Parents consistently favoured non-punitive strategies, usually to the surprise of teachers. Overwhelmingly, parents believed that the first approach should be dialogic, with resort to more punitive measures occurring only when the dialogic had failed.

None the less, constituencies of support could be found for both dialogic and more traditional punitive strategies. The analysis of the 1996 data (Braithwaite 2000) revealed that preferences for dialogue or punishment for dealing with school bullying were largely a question of ideology. Furthermore, ideology outweighed in importance the experience of having a child who was a victim or offender. Those who supported more punitive traditional strategies prioritised security concerns, they saw the world in competitive terms, looked at individuals as isolated entities and supported action to expel the bad apples. They were of the view that children who were bullies could not be changed. The ideological base was inherently conservative, viewing the triumph of good over evil in terms of authorities using a command-and-control system to deter would-be offenders.

In contrast, a dialogic approach was based upon an ideology that sought security through harmonising the social bonds among members of the society. The approach to regulation was not individualistic but relational, favouring social solutions that would rehabilitate wrongdoers. Children who bullied were seen as basically good kids who had got into trouble. A problem-solving approach offering mutual respect, discussion and support was seen as essential for the effective management of bullying. Fundamental to this position was trust in the democracy.

The combined 1996 and 1999 dataset offered an opportunity to examine further the question of how parents would respond to restorative justice processes being introduced into the school. It also allowed us the opportunity to ask if three basic principles of restorative justice (that is, acknowledgement of wrongdoing, readiness to repair the harm done and reintegration as opposed to segregation of the offender) were ideals that were compatible with the dialogic approach that had already been shown to have a strong following among parents in the schools.

The regression analyses used to answer these questions relied on two outcome variables that captured the kinds of strategies considered by schools to be desirable and practicable at the time the research was conducted. The first comprised actions that illustrated a dialogic relational approach to dealing with bullying, and included strategies such as role-playing and story-telling to explain why bullying was bad, meetings with parents and students to develop anti-bullying guidelines for the school, peer mediation and the signing of contractual obligations to desist from bullying. The second involved the school in prioritising punitive individualised actions such as the taking away of privileges if class rules were broken, sending offending individuals to the principal's office, suspension from school for a week or two and expulsion.

Using ordinary least-squares regression analysis, we predicted preference for dialogic relational actions and preference for punitive individualised actions from three restorative justice attitude scales developed by Brenda Morrison and Monika Reinhart. The acknowledgement scale required parents to state how important the following principles were in dealing effectively with school bullying:

1. Ensuring the bully has the opportunity to express/acknowledge the harm done to others.
2. Ensuring the bully has the opportunity to express/acknowledge the harm done to him or herself.
3. Ensuring the victim has the opportunity to express/acknowledge the harm done to others.
4. Ensuring the victim has the opportunity to express/acknowledge the harm done to him or herself.

The reintegration scale comprised the following principles:

1. Ensuring that the bully has the opportunity to feel like a valued member of the school community.
2. Ensuring that the victim has the opportunity to feel like a valued member of the school community.
3. Developing supportive ties within the school community for the bully.
4. Developing supportive ties within the school community for the victim.
5. Ensuring that the bully has the opportunity to be forgiven by those affected.
6. Ensuring that the victim has the opportunity to be forgiven by those affected.

Reparation involved acceptance of the following principles:

1. Ensuring the bully carries out some form of reparation.
2. The form of reparation should focus on the victim and his or her family.

Finally, a segregation measure was included as this would make the introduction of a restorative justice programme virtually impossible in a school context. The scale comprised two items with which parents were asked to agree or disagree:

1. Bullies must be separated from those they are hurting.
2. Victims must be separated from those who bully them.

In addition to these predictors, a number of variables were included representing ideological position and personal experience. Ideology was represented by four measures taken from 1996 and used in the earlier analysis of what parents want schools to do about bullying (see Braithwaite 2000 for a full description of measures). Included were the basic value orientations of security (involving the competitive pursuit of finite resources) and harmony (involving the pursuit of peaceful and co-operative relations with others through sharing resources), and attitudes to child rearing that represented a command-and-control style (using authority and expecting obedience to achieve results) and a self-regulatory style (encouraging open and honest discussion in a mutually respectful manner). The reasoning behind taking these measures from the 1996 sample was that if people's preferences had an ideological base, that base would contain long-held values and beliefs about how children should be treated and how society should be structured.

The experiential variables included in the regression analyses represented whether or not the parent was aware that his or her child had been accused of bullying or was a victim of bullying. In addition, we measured the degree to which parents trusted the authorities and the community to contribute constructively to the problem of solving school bullying, and the degree to which parents believed that children who bullied could change their ways. All these measures were taken in 1996 and 1999 (see Braithwaite 2000 for a description of the measures). The results reported in Table 8.3 are based on the 1999 experiential measures.

Parents who regarded the relational dialogic approach as essential for dealing effectively with bullying were more likely to subscribe to a value system that emphasised societal harmony and co-operation. Such parents also expressed trust in those in authority to contribute constructively to solving the bullying problem. They believed that the process of resolution should involve acknowledgement of the harm done from the perspective of both victim and bully and should enable both victim and bully to be reintegrated into the school community with respect, support and forgiveness.

In contrast, parents who believed that punitive individualised strategies would be essential to controlling bullying problems held a value system that emphasised competition for resources, playing within the rules and having the status and power to ensure security for oneself and one's group. The philosophy of command and control was evident in preferred child-rearing strategies that were protective and restrictive and that emphasised achievement, self-discipline and obedience. Such parents expressed low trust in the community and believed that principles of segregation and reparation should underlie strategies for dealing with school bullying.

Importantly, the approach that parents wanted schools to take in dealing with bullying was not tied to their beliefs about how their child was being affected by bullying at school. Preferences were shaped by a broader worldview.

Table 8.3. Beta coefficients with adjusted R squared for regression models predicting parental support for dialogic relational approaches and punitive individualised approaches to school bullying in 1999

Predictors	1999 outcome variable	
	Dialogic relational	Punitive individualised
1996 ideology measures		
Security value orientation	.09	.21***
Harmony value orientation	.26***	−.11
Command and control parenting	−.04	.15*
Self-regulatory parenting	−.04	−.03
1999 experiential measures		
Child a victim	−.08	.00
Child accused of bullying	.03	.03
Likelihood of changing bully	.05	−.06
Trust in authorities	.26***	.04
Trust in community	.03	−.14*
1999 restorative justice principles		
Acknowledgement	.15**	.00
Reparation	.02	.20***
Reintegration	.14*	−.03
Segregation	.08	.13*
R squared	.34***	.26***
Adjusted R squared	.31***	.23***

$* p < .05, ** p < .01, *** p < .001.$

Conclusion

The purpose of this chapter is twofold. First, we have used data from the 'Life at School' survey to identify the contextual factors that are fundamental to restorative justice practices working effectively in schools. Our findings support the view that a 'whole of school' approach to establishing a community of care in which bullying is regarded as out of bounds is the foundation for any restorative justice intervention. Disapproval for bullying must first come from the school community and be shared by children, teachers and parents. The shared and open opposition to bullying within the school community is fundamental to establishing school norms that recognise bullying behaviours as harmful (and not playful) activities. Such norms underlie the establishment of a safe school and the cultivation of adaptive shame management skills in children so that they can self-regulate their own and others' tendencies to bully.

The second objective was to describe an approach that allows inter-action between theory building, theory testing and practice, and embraces the interdependency of these endeavours. The first wave of data collection in the 'Life at School' survey and Nathan Harris's work on the Re-Integrative Shaming Experiments (RISE) informed the revision of reintegrative shaming theory (Ahmed *et al.* 2001). The follow-up study enabled us to replicate and extend some of our earlier conclusions in a way that would enable the setting up of a contextually sensitive restorative justice intervention programme. The research also alerted us to sources of concern and opposition from parents, providing us with an approach to introducing restorative justice in an inclusive and non-threatening way. The most strongly supported strategy involving an escalating set of sanctions, with traditional punishment on the menu only when relational strategies had failed, recognised the presence of different voices that often compete for ascendancy in the school community.

In walking the bridge between theoretical understanding and practice, we were able to satisfy ourselves that, contextually, shame management was important, even if we had not reached the stage of unteasing its complex inter-relationships with other variables. We had taken the research to a point where it was clear that the capacity to manage shame adaptively needs nurturing in institutional settings. In this sense we emerged with the conviction that a restorative justice intervention programme to address school bullying was a healthy alternative to a more legalistic approach to the problem.

Of fundamental importance in our coming to this view was the active role of parents and the school in promoting shame management. The research findings confirmed the story that socialisation theorists have traditionally told. Society functions smoothly, in large part, because of agreed standards of behaviour that we learn over a lifetime, that we internalise, and that eventually become part of our belief system of 'shoulds' and 'should nots' – that is, of conscience. What happens to children when they are young affects how they respond in later years. And here the leadership of parents was shown to be critically important. Parents can hold children to account for their actions, particularly in relation to coming to terms with intentionality. The finding that a precursor to poor shame management was a parent not accepting intentionality on the part of the child alerts us to the special role parents play in confronting children with their own misdeeds.

Although this result is not at all surprising theoretically, its implications for the practice of institutional design are of considerable interest. An increasing number of cases of bullying are being arbitrated within the formal legal system in Britain, the USA and, more recently, Australia. As admirable as this development may be in making a statement that bullying is unacceptable in our society, its repercussions for other parts of the social regulatory system need to be monitored diligently and systematically. Schools may respond to the fear of legal action with a greater sense of responsibility and follow the widely recommended 'whole of school' approach. This would be a desirable outcome, but requires adaptive shame management at the organisational level. Some workplaces are not so blessed. It is conceivable that some schools will not acknowledge failing the students themselves, but rather push responsibility down the chain to the parents of those who bully others. If parents see that the legal consequences of bullying can be costly, socially and materially, for the child and the family, they may also come to the view that self-protection through deflection is their best option.

This challenges parental responsibilities in an unexpected way. Parents of children who are prone to bullying others might be wise to limit damage to their family through denying that the child had any intention of hurting another. If denial is seen as the prudent response across institutional settings (that is, the family, the school and the court) children will miss out on the opportunity of being confronted with wrongdoing by their most significant others and learning to deal adaptively with the subsequent feelings of shame in a safe environment. Over-reliance on courts to settle bullying incidents may extinguish some important parent–child dynamics that lie at the heart of curtailing bullying early on.

Ideal practice in institutional design would harness the benefits of using the formal legal system to assert normative standards that oppose bullying while supporting institutions of accountability within families and schools. Through heeding the lessons of research and becoming sensitive to the ways in which children learn the art of managing their shame adaptively, we can protect those family and school institutions that are so important to the transmission of adaptive shame management skills. Unless we do, we may destroy an essential element of social regulation and in its place leave a far more threatening 'catch-me-if-you-can' social order. In this respect, restorative justice practice is a constructive offering, strengthening family responsibility for adaptive shame management and legitimating the role of the school in enabling, rather than stifling, the character development of the child.

Notes

1. All the mentioned correlations were significant at the .001. The correlations were partial correlations in which we controlled for age and sex.
2. Variables are scored such that an increase in score reflects an increase in the attribute being measured. Sex is scored 1 = boy, 0 = girl.
3. Variables are scored such that an increase in score reflects an increase in the attribute being measured. Sex is scored 1 = boy, 0 = girl.

References

Ahmed, E. (2001) 'Shame management: Regulating Bullying', in E. Ahmed *et al. Shame Management Through Reintegration*. Cambridge: Cambridge University Press.

Ahmed, E., Harris, N., Braithwaite, J.B., and Braithwaite, V.A. (2001) *Shame Management Through Reintegration*. Cambridge: Cambridge University Press.

Braithwaite, J. (1989) *Crime, Shame and Reintegration*. Cambridge: Cambridge University Press.

Braithwaite, V. (2000) 'Values and Restorative Justice in Schools', in H. Strang and J. Braithwaite (eds), *Restorative Justice: Philosophy to Practice.* Aldershot: Ashgate.

Cunningham, P.B. and Henggeler, S.C. (2001). 'Implementation of an Empirically Based Drug and Violence Prevention and Intervention Programme in Public School Settings, *Journal of Clinical Child Psychology,* 30: 221–32.

Harris, N. (2001) 'Shaming and Shame: Regulating Drink-driving', in E. Ahmed *et al. Shame Management through Reintegration*. Cambridge: Cambridge University Press.

Hirschi, T. (1969) *Causes of Delinquency*. Berkeley, CA: University of California Press.

Jenkins, P.H. (1997) 'School Delinquency and the School Social Bond', *Journal of Research in Crime and Delinquency,* 34: 337–67.

Lewis, H.B. (1971) *Shame and Guilt in Neurosis*. New York, NY: International University Press.

Morrison, B.E. (2001) 'The School System: Developing its Capacity in the Regulation of a Civil Society', in H. Strang and J. Braithwaite (eds) *Restorative Justice and Civil Society*. Cambridge: Cambridge University Press.

Nathanson, D.L. (1992) *Shame and Pride: Affect, Sex and the Birth of the Self*. New York, NY: W.W. Norton.

Olweus, D. (1994) 'Bullying at School: Basic Facts and Effects of a School Based Intervention Programme', *Journal of Child Psychology and Psychiatry,* 35: 1171–90.

Retzinger, S.M. (1987) 'Resentment and Laughter: Video Studies of the Shame-Rage Spiral', in H.B. Lewis (ed.) *The Role of Shame in Symptom Formation*. Hillsdale, NJ: Lawrence Erlbaum Associates.

Retzinger, S.M. (1991) *Violent Emotions: Shame and Rage in Marital Quarrels*. Newbury Park, CA: Sage.

Rigby, K. (2001) *Stop the Bullying: A Handbook for Schools*. Melbourne: Australian Council for Educational Research.

Scheff, T.J. (1987) 'The Shame-Rage Spiral: A Case Study of an Interminable Quarrel', in H.B. Lewis (Ed.) *The Role of Shame in Symptom Formation*. Hillsdale, NJ: Lawrence Erlbaum Associates.

Scheff, T.J. (1994) *Bloody Revenge: Emotions, Nationalism, and War*. Boulder, CO: Westview Press.

Scheff, T.J. (1996). 'Shame and the Origins of World War II: Hitler's Appeal to German People', in D. Parker, R. Dalziel and I. Wright (eds) *Shame and the Modern Self*. Melbourne: Australian Scholarly Publishing.

Scheff, T.J. and Retzinger, S.M. (1991) *Emotions and Violence: Shame and Rage in Destructive Conflicts*. Lexington, MA: Lexington Books/D.C. Heath.

Smith, P.K., Morita, Y., Junger-Tas, J., Olweus, D., Catalano, R. and Slee, P. (1999) *The Nature of School Bullying: A Cross-National Perspective*. London: Routledge.

Chapter 9

Community mediation, criminal justice and restorative justice: rearranging the institutions of law

John Blad

Community mediation in the Netherlands: some data and experiences

From 1993 onwards, community mediation projects have been introduced and developed in an increasing number of neighbourhoods in Dutch towns and cities (Peper *et al.* 1999). The first project started in Zwolle in 1996. This project was quickly started because it was initiated by a high justice official who managed to win the support of a local welfare agency after a visit to San Francisco to study the workings of the famous San Francisco Community Boards (SFCBs). The Zwolle project was implemented top down and on a city-wide basis. The second project was also inspired by the SFCBs and was developed in Rotterdam in 1993 on the initiative of an important housing corporation (Blad 1996). By 1997 this project had been implemented in three neighbourhoods, after a long period of preparation involving consultations with the city council, the councils of the areas in Rotterdam where the neighbourhoods were selected, the police and the office of the public prosecutor. The Rotterdam projects were implemented in a bottom-up way and at a neighbourhood level.

The basic philosophy and practices of the SFCBs functioned as a model for the initial Dutch projects, which were soon replicated in other cities in the Netherlands such as Gouda and Gorinchem. A comprehensive evaluation study – involving Zwolle, Rotterdam and Gouda – showed the relative success of the projects in terms of dealing with disputes between neighbours in a mediation procedure.

Generally, there were two expectations with regard to the possible effects of community mediation that motivated the various stakeholders to support the projects. First, there might be an 'empowering' effect on the neighbourhood – enhancing the social skills of the residents to deal with their own disputes and contributing to the building of a true 'community' in the neighbourhood. This is an important element of the original philosophy of the SFCBs which appealed to housing corporations and welfare agencies, especially when planning community mediation on a neighbourhood level.

Secondly, there was hope that, by offering community mediation, the level of fear (or concern) about crime could be lowered or that there could even be a 'situational preventive' effect on crime in high-crime city areas. What should have been done to assess these possible effects in a methodologically sound way was to take adequate pre-measurements of the situation before introducing the boards. For various reasons, however, this was not done, one of the most important being that uncontested but 'testable' indicators of a lack of social cohesion (other than the number of disputes) and of criminogenic circumstances would not be found easily. We felt that this lack of analysis of the community (which lies at the heart of the SFCB philosophy) was particularly unfortunate, and that we would have found that city-dwellers live in a multiplicity of communities (ethnic communities, communities of allotment-owners, youth peer groups, etc.; see also Crawford 1997: 299 ff) connected to each other only through their common inheritance.

For this reason, in Rotterdam ethnic and other social networks in the neighbourhoods were directly invited to become involved. We felt we were trying to build a social infrastructure for vital communications between communities and between the members of various communities.

The evaluation study of the SFCB's showed that it would be highly unlikely that community mediation would produce direct social results, given the complexity of social life in urban areas and the multifaceted nature of such an experiment. The SFCBs' main evaluators concluded:

> It would be remarkable to find any evidence of transformation in general public attitudes and behaviour attributable to the continuing presence of SFCB in the loosely organised, large and heterogenous urban areas where the programme operated. No matter how visible and effective in conflict resolution and public education SFCB was, it remained, if anything, only a tiny part of the urban experience for

Table 9.1. Nature of the complaints (%)

	City model (n = 268)	Neighbourhood model (n = 86)	Total (n = 354)	SFCBs (n = 2190)
Noise	40	53	44	18
Insults/harassment/gossip	10	6	9	27
Unacceptable pet behaviour	9	6	8	10
Multiple problems	6	14	8	—
Children/teenagers	6	7	6	—
Garden/fence	6	1	5	—
Litter/dirt	4	1	3	6
Other complaints	19	12	17	39
Total	100	100	100	100

most residents. (DuBow and McEwen cited in Merry and Milner 1993: 165)

Most claims with regard to cultural or even structural changes in society as a result of community mediation are difficult to prove (see Tomasic and Feeley 1982: 215 ff), and some of them are easily disproven. It also appears that, the more ambitious the claims, the greater are the frustrations when the promises are not realised. The conflicts dealt with by the community mediation projects we evaluated are summarised in Table 9.1, which gives comparative data from the SFCBs in its last column.[1] The most obvious function of mediation in neighbours' disputes is to offer a service to people in trouble that helps them resolve disputes that often have a very serious impact on their daily lives and that may lead to severe acts of violence. The criteria for evaluating community mediation, therefore, are essentially moral criteria: we should not ignore serious conflicts but pay attention to them to improve the quality of the individual's life (and, hence, of society at large) by giving him or her the opportunity to express and resolve conflicts in a peaceful and democratic way (Christie 1977).

The fact that paying attention to such disputes is socially constructive was illustrated by the early stages of the mediation process, where people actively sought solutions to their problems, often making the actual mediation session unnecessary. The effectiveness of 'shuttle mediation' has also been demonstrated in other projects, such as the Southwark Mediation Centre (Mulcahy and Summerfield 2001: 128) and the *herstelbemiddelingsproject* (restorative mediation project) in the Netherlands.[2]

Offering a safe and easily accessible service to citizens who feel victimised in order to help them deal with this victimisation in a constructive way (by communicating and negotiating with the wrongdoer with the help of a mediator) is a basic procedure in restorative justice. So how does mediation relate to the criminal justice system in the Netherlands?

Mediation and the criminal justice system in the Netherlands

Under certain, legally defined conditions, a great many neighbour disputes could be dealt with by the criminal justice system (or by the civil law system – such as disputes with regard to gardens and fences). If we look at municipal criminal legislation in the Netherlands (which deals with minor offences only), many cases concerning noise at night and nuisance could fall under criminal jurisdiction, and most cases concerning insults and harassment could constitute punishable acts under Dutch common criminal law. So national criminal procedures could in many cases be used as a means to deal with neighbour disputes. However, this rarely happens. Most people who experience long-term nuisance from their neighbours do nothing (varying between 22 and 33% depending on the area, according to our research) or try to do something about it themselves by complaining to the neighbours in question (48–52% of cases). The police were summoned in a number of cases (5–40%). The police, however, do not as a rule, lodge a formal report in such cases. They are inclined to ignore or to play down the complaint or to take some sort of mediatory action vis-à-vis the neighbour causing the trouble. A formal report can then be used as a way of warning one or both of the parties to change their behaviour.

In social housing areas (where the residents are tenants), tenant law can be used to intervene in cases of 'structural nuisance'. The tenancy agreement can be annulled by the civil court, so the 'culprit' will have to move to another neighbourhood (where he or she may again cause trouble). The police may call for such action when there are repeated complaints about a certain resident.

As far as can be ascertained, the criminal sanction is rarely called upon. There seem to be two inter-related reasons for this. First, such breaches of the law are seen as trivial, which makes criminal sanction appear disproportionate to the offence committed. Secondly, the criminal sanctions that can be imposed are modest fines, which cannot be expected to have much impact on the conduct of neighbours involved in a long-lasting conflict. The imposition of a fine could even aggravate the conflict as such an intervention could be seen as an unfair reinforcement of the opposing neighbour's position, regardless of the legal aspects of the conflict. In many cases neighbour disputes persist even after sanctions have been imposed by the civil courts (e.g. to remove or lower a fence).

Non-intervention by the police is in many cases, not a preferred option because, by reporting the conflict to the police, people are drawing attention to something they themselves experience as serious and perhaps destructive of their peace and happiness. In our research many people experienced some form of important nuisance weekly (varying according to location from 6 to 28%) and about 5% of people in all locations 'often' felt they had been insulted or abused in some way.

In conclusion one could say that many disputes between neighbours who cannot tolerate the nuisance any longer and who have no means of redress are too serious to be dealt with in an abstract way, outside the realm of people's interpersonal relationships. It is only through dialogue and community mediation that resolution can be achieved. Hence, when such conflicts are brought to the attention of the police, referal to a community mediation project is the best way of proceeding, leaving the final settlement to the decision of the mediator and the parties involved.

Threshold principles

The criminal justice statistics in the Netherlands do not contain any data concerning the contexts in which registered crimes have occurred. This means we do not know to what extent neighbour disputes are dealt with by criminal prosecution and conviction. In cases of recurrent physical violence and abuse (which are considered more serious in criminal law than, for example, insults or harassment), the police are often inclined to lodge a report and to record this conflict as a crime deserving prosecution and punishment. In the statistics, such cases appear as cases of violence and the connection to neighbourhood disputes is therefore lost. Cases of minor criminal misconduct are referred to community schemes where these are available. In our study, on average 19% of the caseload of the five community mediation projects was referred by the police; it is not clear in which of these cases a criminal sanction would have been possible.

By deciding not to record the conflict as a criminal offence and by not pursuing it further, the police prevent such conflicts entering the criminal justice system. However, this gateway into the criminal justice system has a certain threshold, which consists of various principles. One of the most important of these seems to be the perceived seriousness of the offence, which means the action taken must be in proportion to the perceived seriousness of the offence – the proportionality principle.

The second is the subsidiarity principle, which states that criminal prosecution should not be used when other social systems are capable of dealing with problem behaviour, and that, when a prosecution is made, one should still strive for the minimum intervention and the minimum sanction. The criminal prosecution is thus a chain of decisions, starting with the police, then the public prosecutors and the courts and finally the agencies responsible for executing the punishment. At each stage the question has to be answered as to what constitutes the optimal sanction. In the liberal tradition, the subsidiarity principle states that the minimum sanction is at the same time the optimal sanction.

The subsidiarity principle is reflected in Dutch criminal law procedure in the important concept of expediency. Until 1970, this principle was interpreted narrowly as meaning there was no obligation to prosecute – the public prosecutor could refrain from prosecuting on grounds related to the common interest (a negative interpretation). Since 1970, the interpretation of this principle has been that prosecution should only take place when common interest demands it (a positive interpretation), allowing public prosecutors much greater discretion in dealing with cases other than by prosecuting ('t Hart 1994).

Dutch criminal procedure has a number of formalised criteria for non-prosecution under the expediency principle, important for our discussion about the relationship between community mediation and criminal justice:

1. Methods other than penal intervention should prevail.
2. The facts of the case are not serious enough to warrant penal intervention.
3. Minor reproachability of the perpetrator.
4. The victim has been redressed for the crime committed against him or her.
5. The offender has been negatively affected by the offence.
6. Only a few people are affected.
7. The victim contributed to the offence in a significant way.

Since the police should base their decisions on the decisions the public prosecutors would probably take (De Doelder and 't Hart 1985), the police are, in principle, permitted to divert conflict between neighbours to the community mediation system when one or more of these criteria are applicable. This is, of course, only relevant if the residents bring their problem to the police in the first place, or when the police intervene at the scene of the conflict. It should also be noted here that, for offences involving neighbour disputes, there is no legal obligation for people to report those to the police.

Criminal justice: different systems under the same umbrella

In the Dutch system of criminal law, there is no legal obligation to punish,[3] no legal obligation to prosecute and even no legal obligation for the police to report every offence.[4] Dutch criminal law has become more and more dependent on policy considerations, which has made the system (in principle) more open and more responsive to changing social convictions, problems and needs. In debates about the relationship between restorative justice and the criminal justice system, it is often overlooked that the criminal justice system is becoming more and more diverse in its practices, and that 'punishment' is only one of the options available to it (Blad 2000). Hence, practices exist that do not have a punitive intent but, rather, the social and personal development of the offender (e.g. a 'self confrontational' or 'victim in view' self-development course – courses that hope to instil in the offender what it is like to be a victim). Many cases dealt with by the criminal justice system have no real 'criminal' content at all but are still part and parcel of everyday law enforcement (e.g. traffic violation). The problem we should therefore focus on is a criminal justice system that prioritises punishment (the deliberate delivery of pain) and subordinates all other measures. This focus on punishment – something *not* to be used except for very good reasons – highlights the conflict between the state charging a citizen with an offence for which he or she should be punished and the citizen him or herself and his or her defence. Framing a conflict in this way implies the legal discourse is more important than the everyday language with which an offence can be discussed. It implies the dominance of legal consequences over social consequences. The social consequences thus become rather irrelevant, and everyday language is important only so far as it can justify the standing in law of the offence and the offender (Löschper (1999: 265).

It is not only this focus on punishment that has its repercussions: being prosecuted, standing trial and being imprisoned also have important socio-psychological implications – being publicly punished means the offender suffers degradation and is officially labelled as a criminal. Here we are at the core of the critique about the stigmatising potential of criminal justice systems proposed by adherents of restorative justice (Braithwaite 1989). The creation of the 'true criminal' – identified as such by both the criminal him or herself and by others – is the result of many subtle symbolic interactions within the criminal justice province of meaning (Little 1990).[5] That the criminal justice system is, in a fundamental way, counterproductive as a social control agency is often exaggerated in the sense that a part is mistaken for the whole. On the other hand, this criticism is often ignored by policy-makers when discussing the need to integrate restorative justice practices (of which community mediation is one) into the criminal justice system.

Co-operation of community mediation and criminal justice?

Mediation and other such schemes are on the increase in the Dutch criminal justice system, and these schemes involve the police as well as public prosecutors working with young people. In consultation with justice officials and project managers it was suggested that, if the conflicts dealt with both within and outside the criminal justice system are, in fact, of a similar nature, it might be appropriate if these conflicts were brought to the attention of one, overall agency. Although which precise agency dealt with a conflict would depend on the type and stage of development of a conflict, the various conflict-solving agencies could be co-ordinated, it was suggested, by the Justice Department or by the local offices of the public prosecution service (B. & A. Adviesgroep 1999: 17–18). There seem to be two drawbacks to this suggestion. First, it ignores the fact that the disputants themselves are – and should be – the people who should decide what the most important issues are: is there a conflict? What is it about? Should I deal with it or ignore it? Whom can I go to for help (Hanak *et al.* 1989)? Secondly, it does not take into account the fact that the nature of a conflict changes as it passes from one agency to another. For example, when a conflict enters the criminal justice arena, the victim is replaced by the public prosecutor and the offending behaviour will be judged primarily in terms of its purely legal meaning: any restorative elements will be subordinated to, or even ruled out by, the punitive orientation of the criminal justice systems. However, there may be occasions when such a change in the nature of a conflict is appropriate, and this is why the idea of the co-ordinating conflict-resolution procedures has some validity. Such a co-ordinating body could advise the justice agencies which conflicts they should allow to enter the justice system (and why, then, *criminal* justice?) and which they should refer to conflict-solving organisations outside the legal system. This is, to a certain extent, nothing other than the question concerning what justice should be.

Competition instead of integration

In the Netherlands, as well as elsewhere in the western world, community mediation does not function as an alternative to penal interventions. As noted, above, however, the criminal justice system is quite capable of incorporating community mediation but, as yet, only minor offences related to neighbour disputes are dealt with by community mediators – and these are offences that would probably have escaped the criminal justice system. Current legal thinking in the Netherlands seems to indicate consolidation of this position: minor conflicts should be referred to community mediation or mediation projects within the criminal justice system itself, whereas serious offences should be treated as 'crimes' and should be prosecuted. While this position goes some way to redefining the punitive model, it does, at the same time, uphold it. It is for this reason that some observers regard community mediation as merely an 'add-on' to the formal system of social control – but widening the net somewhat. I think this misses two important points. First, the net does not remain the same. The elements of community mediation are fundamentally different from those of the penal system and, with the introduction of community mediation (and mediation in penal matters), methods of (formal) social control change, become more differentiated and more constructive options become available. The second point is that it is not evident that when criminal justice ignores a conflict (refuses to or cannot deal with it), *only* positive or constructive consequences follow (a positive consequence, on the other hand, being many cases not having to go through an alienating procedure and perhaps not suffering punishment). Our own and other research suggests that many of the conflicts not dealt with by the criminal justice system are experienced as heavy burdens in the social relations of ordinary daily life. Leaving these conflicts unresolved may lead to prolonged victimisation, social isolation, illness, in some cases, even violence.

Community mediation offers people a way to express, explore and resolve social conflicts in a safe and constructive way. It is therefore a socially desirable service that offers the potential for citizens to experience some form of restorative justice. While community mediation and other methods of restorative justice are undoubted methods of social control, social control is not, in itself, an inherently bad thing (Council of Europe 1980). Social control is only a bad thing when it goes wrong, when it is counterproductive, producing exactly those things it claims to control or reduce. Some aspects of the criminal justice system can be regarded as counterproductive when criminal justice is seen as an instrument of social control – when it imposes a criminal identity on a person and broadcasts news of the newly identified criminal to the world when he or she is sentenced for his or her undesirable conduct. It is such stigmatising procedures that produce the career criminals we so much want to avoid producing.

The net-widening argument is nevertheless important, since the adoption and incorporation of restorative practices into the criminal justice system fit in with the bifurcation within the criminal justice system in general – the harsher, exclusionary punishments are given to 'true criminals' (who are different from us), and the softer, more inclusionary 'community sanctions' are given to the offenders who are more like us, who are not truly criminal (Garland 1996). This net-widening effect should warn us not to try to position the 'market share' of restorative justice practice within the domain of criminal justice in the hope of restricting the use of the traditional prosecution and punishment model to the smallest number of cases possible. We should, of course, at the same time try to maximise the number of restorative practices, but it should also be clear that restorative justice will remain very much in the shade if only a limited number of social practices are developed and the institutional discourse of crime and punishment is not addressed. De Haan (1990) is right in stressing that the concepts of crime and punishment cannot be separated (as was tried by penal abolitionists and left-wing criminologists), and that the only institutional and ideological solution is to step out of this discourse into a discourse of redress. Hence, integrating restorative justice practices into a criminal justice system that is still predominantly informed by a punitive rhetoric may lead to the affirmation of the myth of the true criminal. This could occur if restorative procedures are only available for certain kinds of offenders ('only the young, who can still be reformed') or when restorative practices go wrong and the offender has to be punished instead.

Apart from the debate about the 'myths' of criminal justice, there are practical and legal problems in integrating restorative justice practices into the criminal justice system – problems that would radically alter the nature of restorative justice if it was implemented from a predominantly criminal justice perspective. The following is but one, crucial example.

The right to remain silent about an alleged criminal offence is a crucial right of a suspect involved in a criminal procedure. This right is one of the suspect's first means of defence against a powerful opponent who wishes to charge him or her with a crime and to punish him or her for that crime. That a crime has been committed must be proved by the state's representative, the public prosecutor or by the court. Proof is a condition sine qua non for the punishment of a crime, and a suspect has no legal obligation to contribute to the evidence by making a statement. Restorative justice, in contrast, makes a moral appeal to someone who is seen as a wrongdoer to speak up, to admit to it if the allegation is correct, to make good the harm caused to his or her victim and to society and to acknowledge 'dominion'.[6]

Restorative aims are not served by denials or silence (Groenhuijsen 2000: 446). By being co-operative and constructive in a restorative conference, an alleged offender however, weakens his or her legal position in the penal procedure, especially when a restorative conference is used at the pre-trial stage and when it remains unclear what legal consequences the public prosecutor will attach to the alleged offender's co-operative attitude. The principle that the substance of a mediation in penal matters cannot be used as evidence can only have a symbolic meaning here, since entering a restorative conference implies a willingness to confess to the most important facts of the case. The offender might still be prosecuted and punished. The question is: why should the suspect be expected to run that risk if he or she can avoid the negative consequences by denial or by remaining silent?

Many examples can be given of a tendency to approach restorative justice not on its own terms but in terms of criminal law, and of the supposed superiority of the criminal justice system regarding, for example, the rights of the accused, matters of evidence and public accountability. What we should recognise here is that restorative justice is being conceived as a sort of *criminal* justice, as an alternative system of *punishment* – i.e. how restorative justice can be fitted into the dynamics of punishment. From the punitive angle this approach is logical because we can never do without punishment. In Mathiesen's (1974) terms, the process of 'defining in' is well under way. But restorative justice should be a competing way of reacting to crime in the criminal justice discourse. As discussed above, Mathiesen's suggestion that the criminal justice system remains unchanged when new (initially, ideologically foreign) practices are defined in can be refuted because the system *does* change when it becomes more differentiated. The identity and unity of the system are largely discursive only. Criminal justice may be appropriate to a very small number of damaging behaviours (if only for the protection of the rights of the accused when there is a strong desire to punish. Criminal justice itself is severely damaged because it is used on too large a scale.[7] That is why the introduction of new, restorative practices should be accompanied by discursive, ideological shifts in the boundaries of the criminal justice system, boundaries which should, and can, be drawn much narrower. Only in this way can we hope to make the 'qualitative leap' from criminal to restorative justice: different practices, understood differently.

A place for a restorative justice system of law

What is proposed here are only initial ideas for a strategy for implementing restorative justice as an alternative to the criminal justice system – there are complex political, structural and cultural issues involved in this for which there is not space here for a full discussion. The myth of the criminal is not only embraced by criminal justice officials but it is also part and parcel of contemporary culture, and the process of criminalisation is a social process that has more than simply symbolical functions – the most notable being the reproduction of an unequal social structure (Smaus 1998). Two things, therefore, need to be addressed. The first is to narrow the scope of criminal justice, creating a structural space for a restorative model of justice that does not have any punitive connotations. The second (a necessary precondition for the first) is to create a formal system of public law based on the substantive procedural principles of restorative justice. Both these aims imply an important task for restorative justice proponents, namely to find ways of convincing the public, policy-makers and politicians that restorative justice has something better to offer than criminal justice. While this claim can be substantiated to a certain extent by the results of ongoing restorative justice experiments, these experiments have been conditioned by specific working relationships with the existing criminal justice system, which means that sound theory and a reliable system of procedural rules should make restorative justice a plausible replacement for criminal justice – in other words, restorative justice should be institutionalised.

Redrawing the boundaries of institutional space

Arguing for a redrawing of the boundaries of structural, institutional space implies, I think, a fundamental critique of criminal justice and, at the same time, modesty and prudence. The attacks on the World Trade Center and the Pentagon and the initial reactions to these events by political leaders around the world should have made us acutely aware of the uncertainties we have to deal with. Perhaps the best that can be learnt from this is: when war appears to be the only alternative, international criminal law is the preferable option, but criminal law is not the preferable option when restoration and reconciliation are viable alternatives (nothing other, of course, than the *ultima ratio* idea!).

Arguing for a redrawn structural space also implies the transfer of a number of offences from the criminal to the restorative system of law: the decriminalisation of these offences so that they are dealt with in a civil, civic, restorative way. This would mean the categories of offences restorative justice could deal with would have to chosen very carefully. In this we should go as far as we dare (Christie 1981: 115): whenever the offence and the circumstances of the offence permit for restoration and reconciliation, *de jure* decriminalisation should be required. From this, two suggestions can be made. The first is that it does not seem to make much sense to argue for a restorative approach to all those small, regulatory offences that do not impinge on the quality of social life and that are now dealt with by monetary, fixed penalties. Such offences are an expression of socioeconomic order and committing such offences often has more to do with an individual's position within this order than with his or her attitude towards his or her fellow beings. Traffic violations and such like offences could be decriminalised by transferring them to a system of administrative sanctions – something that has already been done in Germany and the Netherlands.

The second suggestion is that it would perhaps not be wise to argue for a predominantly restorative approach to crimes against human life and to crimes against the political and legal institutions of a democratic state. With regard to crimes against human life, it is perhaps self-evident that the restoration of trust in the offender and the reparation of the harm caused could not be achieved without a retributive element in the punishment. Crimes against a state, by definition, undermine the values of that state, including a restorative element to that state's system of justice. A truly minimal criminal code would be dealing with the most serious crimes only. A restorative system of law, therefore, would have to be situated somewhere between administrative offences and the most serious categories of crimes. Even so, there would be exceptions: if there was but *one* case where it was felt punishment was appropriate, we would want to punish that crime with all the guarantees criminal law imposes. What should be rejected, however, is the categorisation of aspects of the criminal justice system according to the type of offender involved. Such a categorisation is discriminatory and reinforces the myth of the criminal type.

Restorative justice as a civil model in the public domain of law

Criminal justice must ignore for various reasons the interests and needs of the victim, who is only allowed a marginal role as a witness or as a private party in criminal procedures. As long as we uphold such a legal system, which aims at convicting and punishing a citizen publicly for having committed certain prohibited actions, the victim's and offender's interests will be subordinated to the common interest, defended by judiciary agents of the state – particularly the public prosecutor. If we look closely at restorative justice, we can see that its basic procedural model does not comprise penal law but civil law, where the victim's interests and interaction between the victim and wrongdoer are placed at the centre of attention. There is certainly a public aspect to restorative justice in the sense that the victim is not ignored but is supported and facilitated (with public means and by public agencies) in his or her actions when the victim decides to reclaim his or her 'dominion' and to restore the harm done to him or her. Hence this model requires a new mix of civil and public law: a public law system that facilitates a civil law resolution to damaging conflicts – through civil law-like procedures – conflicts that are recognised as more than of private interest only. Helping victims repair the harm done is a fundamental aim of restorative justice. However, helping the victim satisfy his or her needs implies that the wrongdoer must be found if the offender's identity is not known. This brings in another public element, namely, the police, who can help to identify the suspect. Finally, the wrongdoer caught up in restorative justice procedures should be involved on a voluntary basis – he or she has a moral obligation to accept his or her responsibility for the offence and to make up for the damages done.

The point I want to make is that – contrary to what most proponents of restorative justice seem to think – there is no obvious reason to fall back on the use of criminal justice when appeals made through restorative justice are unsuccessful. This is, in fact, contradictory to the fundamental principles of restorative justice.

The civil law system can serve perfectly well as a backup system when restorative practices cannot be used – for example, when the offender refuses to take part in agreements – restorative procedures are not fulfilled. In publicly facilitating both victims and offenders to resolve their conflicts in a restorative fashion, a kind of public solidarity is expressed that differs from the traditional culture of private law – which presupposes autonomous, legally well informed and assertive citizens initiating civil law actions. Women's rights organisations and their clients have reported how empowering and satisfying it is for women to determine in a civil court duties and civil sanctions to be imposed upon ex-partners (Hes 1984; Verrijn Stuart 1992).

If a restorative system of justice were to operate as a type of civil law, backed up by the civil law system and in which the parties are expected to participate actively, a public official representing the public interest would need to establish a civil (although imposed) resolution. This is the mirror image of the citizen participating as a civil party in criminal procedures. It is only if restorative practices are removed from (and remain removed from the criminal justice system) and if restorative justice deals with important decriminalised offences (backed up by civil law in instances of failure) that we can avoid contributing to the reproduction of the ideology of crime and punishment. If restorative justice remains within the domain of criminal law, ultimately it will reconfirm punishment as the way of dealing with those who fail to meet the moral requirements implicit in the restorative justice model (e.g. a willingness to accept responsibility for the offence).

The offences that could be 'civilised' by transferring them to a restorative system of law would be all those offences that involve important (moral, normative) conflicts in the relationships between equal citizens and that have important disintegrating and destabilising effects on social interaction in general. Monetary, sexual and many violent offences belong to this catagory and are therefore suitable for a restorative approach to justice.

Comparisons to other forms of dispute resolution in civil law

As indicated above, a system of restorative justice should be a format of civil, not criminal, law. The question therefore arises as to how far the principles of restorative justice coincide with, or show similarities with, important developments in civil law. It is well known that, in civil law conflicts, the use of alternative dispute resolution (ADR) has grown enormously in recent years in many jurisdictions. While there is not the space here to investigate the similarities and differences between ADR and restorative justice, we can, briefly, compare their principles.

ADR and restorative justice share a number of principles in common. First and foremost it is clear that, although there are different, formal, legal definitions of the conflicts involved, conflict-solving in both processes begins and ends with subjective definitions of the conflict and there is ample space for a contextualised discussion about the conflict in hand. Under both systems at least one of the conflicting parties takes the initiative: under restorative justice this initiative is *supported* by public officials (who run restorative justice centres) and not taken over, as is the case in criminal justice. Mediation figures prominently in both ADR and restorative justice. One of the main reasons for this in civil law is that the face-to-face exchange of subjective meanings through dialogue facilitates the development of an understanding of the conflict in hand. The under-standing serves as a grounding for consensual resolution whereas the written procedures in civil suits (where the parties are represented by lawyers) make this consensual resolution much more difficult and often impossible. Information that is important from an everyday perspective is suppressed or transformed in the legal reconstruction of the conflict and, in this way, is lost. Face-to-face communication, on the other hand, permits a rich (instead of poor) understanding of the dimensions of the conflict.

Finally, from the civil law perspective, there is nothing wrong in giving priority to the resolution produced by the parties involved – provided this resolution is not immoral or is forbidden by substantive civil law. In restorative justice, public support is given to the resolution found in order to express a common interest in conflict-solving undertaken in a peaceful and democratic way, and to show that an admitted wrong has been corrected. The positive benefits derived from conflict-solving and from norm clarification and reaffirmation are then realised fully. This may help us to avoid believing that only criminal law has a public dimension and that, consequently, criminal law should function as the back-up for the failures of restorative justice. For restorative justice, punishment-orientated law is not a backup: it is a contradiction.

Notes

1. More extensive information in English can be found in Peper and Spierings (1999).
2. This service is offered to offenders and victims after trial and conviction have taken place, mostly in cases of serious crime, and it aims at healing the consequences of these crimes. In over two years, a total of 118 requests were dealt with, leading to mediation sessions in 17% of the cases, whereas 23% of requests were dealt with satisfactorily by 'shuttle mediation' (Barlingen *et al.* 2000).
3. Dutch criminal code gives the judge the power to pardon when the gravity of the facts, the personality of the perpetrator or the circumstances at the time of the offence or even after the offence give the judge reasons to do so.
4 The positive interpretation of the expediency principle implies that it is only necessary to notify the public prosecutor's office of offences when prosecution or any other formal action would be of common interest. Public prosecutors regularly give clear indications in guidelines of what kind of reporting they wish to receive from the police, and they also indicate what sort of reports are unnecessary. This is, in a number of respects, problematic since the legality principle (in the sense of the 'primacy of the legislator') implies that public prosecutors can never decide *not* to uphold a certain law.
5. Michael Little (1990) manages to a great extent, to 'prove' this subtle process with his 'episodic' approach to the development of the young criminal. It is the episode of imprisonment that is of central importance, both before imprisonment and after.
6. The concept of dominion is central to the republican theory of criminal justice as developed by Braithwaite and Pettit (1990). It is a combination of positive and negative freedom in the classical liberal ideology of criminal law.
7. Already by the 1960's the debate had arisen about the costs of penal inflation (see, for example, Packer 1968).

References

Barlingen van, M., Slump, G.J., and Tulner, H. (2000) *Tussenevaluatie Herstelbemiddeling.* Amsterdam: DSP.

B. & A. Adviesgroep (1999) *Bemiddeling en strafrecht, Leidraad.* Den Haag: B. & A.

Blad, J.R. (1996) 'Neighbourhood-centered Conflict Mediation: The San Francisco Example', *European Journal on Criminal Policy and Research,* 4: 90–107.

Blad, J.R. (2000) 'Strafrecht en bemiddeling: opkomst en toekomst van herstelrecht in Nederland', *Recht der Werkelijkheid,* 2: 51–71.

Braithwaite, J. (1989) *Crime, Shame and Reintegration.* Cambridge: Cambridge University Press.

Braithwaite, J. and Pettit, P. (1990) *Not Just Deserts: A Republican Theory of Criminal Justice.* Oxford: Clarendon Press.

Christie, N. (1977) 'Conflicts as Property', *British Journal of Criminology,* 17(1): 1–10.

Christie, N. (1981) *Limits to Pain.* Oxford: Martin Robertson.

Council of Europe (1980) *Report on Decriminalisation.* Brussels: Council of Europe.

Crawford, A. (1997) *The Local Governance of Crime.* Oxford: Clarendon Press.

De Doelder, H. and 't Hart, A.C. (1985) 'De zeggenschap van het OM over de opsporing en het politiesepot', in J.H.C. Blom, *et al.* (eds) *Redenen van wetenschap.* Arnhem: Gouda Quint.

Garland, D. (1996) 'The Limits of the Sovereign State: Strategies of Crime Control in Contemporary Society', *British Journal of Criminology,* 36: 445–71.

Groenhuijsen, M. (2000) 'Mediation in het strafrecht. Bemiddeling en conflictoplossing in vele gedaanten', *Delikt en Delinkwent,* 2000 (30): 441–48.

Haan, W. de (1990) *The Politics of Redress, Crime, Punishment and Penal Abolition.* London: Unwin Hyman.

Hanak, G.J., Stehr, J. and Steinert, H. (1989) *Aergernisse und Lebenskatastrofen.* Bielefeld: AJZ Verlag.

't Hart, A.C. (1994) *Openbaar ministerie en Rechtshandhaving.* Deventer: Gouda Quint.

Hes, J. (1984) 'Het straatverbod in kort geding als ultimum remedium', *Nemesis,* 5: 130–9.

Little, M. (1990) *Young Men in Prison, The Criminal Identity Explored Through the Rules of Behaviour.*

Löschper, G. (1999) *Bausteine für eine Psychologische Theorie richterlichen Urteilens.* Baden-Baden: Nomos Verlagsgesellschaft.

Mathiesen, T. (1974) *The Politics of Abolition.* London: Martin Robertson.

Merry, S.E. and Milner, N. (1993) *The Possibility of Popular Justice.* Ann Arbor, MI: University of Michigan Press.

Mulcahy, L. and Summerfield, L. (2001) *Keeping it in the Community: An Evaluation of the Use of Mediation in Disputes Between Neighbours.* Norwich: HMSO.

Packer, H.L. (1968) *The Limits of the Criminal Sanction.* Stanford, CA: Stanford University Press.

Peper, B. and Spierings, F. (1999) 'Settling Disputes between Neighbours in the Lifeworld: an Evaluation of Experiments with Community Mediation in the Netherlands', *European Journal on Criminal Policy and Research,* 7: 483–507.

Peper, B., Spierings, F., De Jong, W. Blad, J. Hogenhuis, S., and Van Altena, V. (1999) *Bemiddelen bij conflicten tussen buren: Een sociaal-wetenschappelijke evaluatie van experimenten met Buurtbemiddeling in Nederland.* Delft: Eburon.

Smaus, G. (1998) *Das Strafrecht und die gesellschaftliche Differensierung.* (Baden-Baden: Nomos Verlagsgesellschaft.

Tomasic, R. and Feeley, M.M. (1982) *Neigbourhood Justice: Assessment of an Emerging Idea.* New York, NY, and London: Longman.

Verrijn Stuart, H.M. (1992) 'Naar een geciviliseerd recht tegen sexueel geweld; een verkenning langs het grensgebied tussen strafrecht en civielrecht', *Ars Aequi.* 41(2): 82–92.

Chapter 10

Restorative justice for adult offenders: the New Zealand experience

Allison Morris and Gabrielle Maxwell

Introduction

In practice, most fully integrated restorative justice processes deal with juvenile offenders. Examples are family group conferences in New Zealand and some Australian states (McElrea 1998; Morris and Maxwell 2000; Daly 2001). And most jurisdictions introducing restorative justice processes tend to do so first for juvenile offenders, as in England and Wales, Northern Ireland and Belgium. It makes sense to do this because the public have long accepted that juvenile offenders can be dealt with differently from adult offenders. In principle, however, there is no reason to restrict restorative justice processes in this way. With increased confidence and over time, it should be possible to extend such processes to adults. This is happening now in New Zealand. Restorative justice processes are gradually being extended to adult offenders there at the discretion of individual judges (Consedine and Bowen 1999) and through a range of pilot programmes (Smith and Cram 1998; Maxwell *et al*. 1999).

There is certainly considerable support in New Zealand for restorative justice for adult offenders: 104 of the 113 submissions made to the discussion paper on restorative justice prepared by the Ministry of Justice (Ministry of Justice 1995) were broadly supportive of a restorative approach (Ministry of Justice 1998). Indeed, the Restorative Justice

Network, an organisation for those interested in restorative justice, has close to 600 members across New Zealand. But it is important to stress here too that New Zealand has a high imprisonment rate. When compared with 10 OECD countries, only the USA had a higher imprisonment rate. At 150 per 100,000, it is higher than England, Scotland, Australia, Canada, Germany and France.

This chapter briefly describes the practice of restorative justice for adult offenders in New Zealand and highlights the fact that two somewhat different approaches are emerging. On the basis of evaluations of one of these approaches,[1] this chapter suggests that the benefits identified with respect to juvenile offenders and their victims can also be seen with respect to adult offenders and their victims. It suggests, in addition, that there are clear benefits to the state in extending restorative justice processes to adult offenders.

Restorative justice for adult offenders

Community panel pilots

In 1995, three pilot schemes – Project Turnaround, Te Whanau Awhina and the Community Accountability Programme – were funded by the New Zealand Crime Prevention Unit in collaboration with the police and local Safer Community Councils to divert adult offenders appearing before the criminal courts. They began operating in 1996 and Project Turnaround and Te Whanau Awhina are still in operation. The Community Accountability Programme ceased operation during its first year but, as we will see shortly, it has since begun operation again. Each of these pilot schemes had aspects of restorative justice.

Project Turnaround is situated in Timaru, a provincial South Island city, and it shares its offices with the Safer Community Council and the Community Police. Most of the offenders referred to it are New Zealand European. On the offender's first appearance at court, judges divert selected offenders to the scheme. There the offender meets with panel members who are volunteers selected from applicants who responded to advertisements and the like and who subsequently received some training in restorative processes. Their role is to represent the community in the meeting and they are the principal decision-makers. A police officer is normally present at most of the panel meetings and the victim is also frequently present.[2] A co-ordinator facilitates the process. At the panel meeting, the offender is confronted with his or her offending and its consequences. While the responsibility for developing a plan resides with members of the panel, the goal of the meeting is, where possible, to come to a consensual agreement among the parties about how the offending should be dealt with. If the offender attends the panel meeting and if the plan agreed to there is completed by the offender, the offender makes no further court appearance and the police withdraw their evidence. This process at Project Turnaround can be contrasted with a fully restorative process where decisions are made by those who are most directly affected by the offending rather than by appointed representatives of the community. However, the plans decided at the meetings usually involved making amends to the victim and to the community and making arrangements of a rehabilitative and, at times, of a reintegrative nature. This focus on reparation to the victim and to the community is consistent with a restorative justice approach.

Te Whanau Awhina is situated on a *marae* (a communal centre including a meeting house and other buildings for customary activities as well as educational and training facilities) in Auckland, the largest city in New Zealand, and the community panel meetings are held in the *wharenui* (a traditional meeting house). Almost all the offenders referred to Te Whanau Awhina are Maori (the indigenous people of New Zealand). As in Project Turnaround, they are referred to the scheme by the judge at a court hearing. At Te Whanau Awhina, the panel which makes the decisions typically consists of three or four *marae* members, including one who takes the role of *kaumatua* (elder) and chairs the proceedings. Other people likely to attend are the *whanau* (extended family) and friends of the offender and the co-ordinator facilitates the process. The police do not attend the meetings at Te Whanau Awhina, nor usually do victims. The focus of this panel meeting is first and foremost one of 'challenge': confronting offenders with the consequences of their offending for them, for their victims, for their family and *whanau*, and for the Maori community. The second main focus of the meeting is that of 'embrace': reintegrating the offender back into family/*whanau* and into the Maori community and finding employment. This is usually reflected in the agreed outcome about how to deal with the offending. Thus outcomes proposed by the panel typically include plans relating to obtaining employment or job training and participation in *marae*-based programmes and activities as well as responses to victims. In contrast to the offenders involved in Project Turnaround, offenders who appear before a panel at Te Whanau Awhina are not necessarily diverted from further court appearances and sanctions. Judges there retain greater oversight. Because victims rarely attend the meetings and because the offender and victim are not central participants in developing the plan, Te Whanau Awhina is not fully consistent with restorative processes.[3] However, the focus on reparation to victims and to the community and reintegration with family and *whanau* and with the

Maori and wider community is consistent with aspects of a restorative justice approach.[4]

The Community Accountability Programme was situated in Rotorua, a city in the middle of the North Island in which a significant proportion of Maori live. This programme is described by Webster (2000) as most closely approximating restorative justice practice because, unlike both Project Turnaround and Te Whanau Awhina, decisions were made by victims and offenders themselves (and their communities of care) with the aid of paid facilitators. It was, therefore, much more like the family group conferences which take place in New Zealand for young offenders (see Maxwell and Morris 1993 for more detail). The aims of the Community Accountability Programme were to provide greater satisfaction to victims as well as making offenders more accountable. Thus it gave victims considerable control over the meeting format and only dealt with cases where victims provided input. For a range of reasons, this pilot, as noted earlier, ceased operation, but has since begun again.

At the time of writing, there were, in total, 14 programmes supported and administered by the Crime Prevention Unit (under the title 'Community Managed Restorative Justice Programmes') and one more is in the final stages of development. It is estimated that they will deal with around 900 such conferences in 2001–2 (Brian Webster, Crime Prevention Unit, Ministry of Justice, pers. comm.).[5] These schemes all follow the format of one or other of the three pilots described above.

Restorative justice conferences

A further four pilots schemes (in Auckland, Waitakere, Hamilton and Dunedin) began operation in October 2001. These court-referred restorative processes (restorative justice conferences) are administered by the Department for Courts and follow a different approach from the schemes using community panels: they are much more like the Community Accountability Programme (and family group conferences) briefly described above in that they rely on victims and offenders (and their support people) to come up with a plan or agreement and not panel members. However, they differ from family group conferences in that restorative justice conferences are voluntary and only take place if both the victim and offender agree to participate. Although the police, a probation officer and the offender's lawyer are usually invited to attend the conference, they may decide not to. The intention is that, at the conference, victims will have a say and offenders will take responsibility for putting things right.

The outcome of most, but not all, conferences will be an agreed plan and the conference facilitator will provide the referring judge with a copy of any such agreements (in the restorative justice report). These may contain rehabilitative or reintegrative features. However, the main purpose of the conference is to provide information to the judge who will take the facilitator's report into account along with any other reports (for example, from a probation officer) and not to recommend a sentence. Judges will choose whether or not to incorporate all or part of any agreement reached into the sentence and sentences are expected to continue to be within the current range for 'similar' offences. The evaluation currently in progress will be able to comment, some time in the future, on what actually happens.

Thus these restorative conferences also differ from family group conferences in that they are less likely to have a profound impact on the eventual sentence and are more centrally and specifically victim focused. The explicit aims of these pilots are to offer better outcomes to victims and to reduce reoffending. To this extent, it is possible that sentences will contain rehabilitative or reintegrative features. A key part of the evaluation is to examine whether or not victims do feel better as a result of participating in the conferences and whether or not offenders are less likely to be reconvicted.[6]

Types of offences covered

As in the youth justice system and in contrast to schemes in other jurisdictions, restorative practices for adult offenders in New Zealand deal with relatively serious offences. Maxwell *et al.* (1999), for example, document that, overall, about half the participants dealt with by the panels in Project Turnaround and Te Whanau Awhina were repeat offenders[7] and most had committed medium-serious offences: these included aggravated robbery, threat to kill, driving causing death, driving with excess alcohol as well as the more 'routine' offences of wilful damage, theft and burglary. In the first year of the operation of the court-referred restorative justice pilots, all property offences with maximum penalties of two years' imprisonment or more and other offences with maximum penalties of one to seven years are eligible for referral to a conference by the judge. Domestic violence offences, on the other hand, are excluded. With respect to ad hoc referrals by judges, Consedine and Bowen (1999) present seven case histories of adult offenders who have experienced restorative conferences prior to sentencing as an aid to the judge; three of these related to sexual or physical abuse within the family and all were serious.

A summary of findings with respect to adult offenders

Maxwell *et al.* (1999) obtained information from a small sample of offenders who had participated in Te Whanau Awhina and Project Turnaround about their experience. These interviews showed that most of the offenders found the experience to be positive and meaningful. They thought that the process provided an opportunity to deal with matters constructively and to avoid appearing in court or receiving court-imposed sanctions. Offenders also said that, as a result of the meeting, they had an increased understanding of the impact of their offending on the victim and that they felt remorse. In the words of one offender: 'It gave me a chance to make things right – to appease my guilt and apologise' (Maxwell *et al.* 1999: 30). Over half those interviewed said they had been involved in the decisions about how to deal with their offending.

However, about one in four of those interviewed at Project Turnaround found the experience a negative one: they said they were not listened to, that decisions were coerced and that they were shamed by the process. They also commented on not feeling comfortable with the large number of people at the meeting or with their selection.[8] On the other hand, the small sample of offenders interviewed from the Te Whanau Awhina programme generally found the process meaningful because it happened on the *marae* and in the meeting house where they were in the presence of their ancestors. Despite the panel at Te Whanau Awhina being often seen as intimidating and demanding, its decisions were accepted by those interviewed. This is an important point given the mono-culturalism of conventional justice processes. The following two quotations come from offenders interviewed by Maxwell *et al.* (1999: 31):

It felt like I was among *whanau* even though it was still being dealt with through the legal system.

It brought out emotions. I felt I was answering to my ancestors.

The majority of those interviewed in both schemes thought that the decisions reached by the panels were fair and that the plan provided help that might prevent them offending again. Looking back, 70% of those interviewed said that the experience had been a good one for them either because it was constructive to be part of the process, because of the consequences of the plan or because they were able to avoid the more damaging effects of the alternatives. One interviewee summed it up as follows: 'it was a good experience. I was very anti to start but I've been won over definitely. Seeing the victims really impacts on you and opens your eyes' (Maxwell *et al.* 1999: 37).

A summary of findings with respect to victims of adult offenders

Smith and Cram (1998) examined the extent to which the 1995–6 pilot schemes responded to victims and reported the views of 20 victims who had attended panel meetings in Project Turnaround. Overall, these victims said that they had had good experiences at the panel meeting and even those who were somewhat critical were nevertheless supportive of the continuance of the programme. Victims gave a range of reasons for agreeing to attend. These included feeling that this was a better way of resolving the situation, giving offenders another chance, not wanting the case to go to court, dislike of conventional court processes, knowing the offender, wanting to have a say and to confront the offender, wanting to see the offender, the effects of the meeting on him or her and the offender's remorse, and seeking reparation. The following quotation from Smith and Cram (1998: 93–4) demonstrate some of these reasons:

It seemed a fair and just way of settling the situation.

I wanted to give the offender another chance. I didn't want it to ruin his life.

I think the old sick system failed, there must be a better way.

I thought it was good to see the offender face to face – being able to confront him and have a say.

It was satisfying to see offenders feeling sorry.

Benefits to the state

Irrespective of these benefits to victims and offenders, governments are unlikely to pay much heed to restorative justice restorative processes and practices unless they are more effective than conventional processes and practices in reducing reoffending and offer cost savings. The following sections set out what we know about this.

Community panel adult pre-trial diversion programmes and reoffending

Maxwell *et al.* (1999) collected information on the reconvictions of 200 participants in the two pilot schemes, Project Turnaround and Te Whanau Awhina. A matched sample of the same size was obtained of offenders who had been dealt with through the courts. Each participant was randomly matched with a control subject who was convicted of the same offence (or the same most serious offence where the participant was charged with committing more than one offence) and dealt with by conventional court processes during 1995.[9] Participants and control subjects were also matched on age, sex, ethnicity, previous offending and number of charges. Convictions were used as the measure for assessing recidivism.

Data on reconvictions showed that, over the following 12 months, those participating in both schemes were significantly less likely to be reconvicted than the matched control groups. Thus, 16% of the participants at Project Turnaround were reconvicted within this period compared with 30% of the matched control sample; the comparable percentages for Te Whanau Awhina participants were 33% and 47%.[10] Clearly, not all participants and controls were 'free' to commit offences for the same length of time and so a 'survival analysis' was carried out. This takes account of the different lengths of follow-ups available for each offender. This too showed that both Project Turnaround and Te Whanau Awhina participants were significantly less likely to be reconvicted than their matched controls. Also, not only was there a reduction in the proportion of participants reconvicted but, for those who were reconvicted, the seriousness of the major offence (as judged by a scale of seriousness based on penalties) was not as great among participants in the schemes as it was among the matched control groups. In addition, those referred to the schemes who were seen as having successful outcomes were less likely to be reconvicted compared to those who were seen as not having successful outcomes (although the small numbers here make it difficult to be confident of this finding). The survival analysis on these sub-samples confirmed this finding.

Overall, then, the findings of this research all point in the same direction: those participating in the pilots were reconvicted less frequently and less seriously than matched controls who were dealt with in courts and those who successfully completed the agreements reached in the pilots were reconvicted less frequently and less seriously than those who did not. It seems clear that something in the pilots made a difference. This research cannot say definitively what this was. But the small group of participants interviewed did refer to the sorts of factors identified by the young offenders in the Maxwell and Morris (1999) research on family group conferencing: the importance of inclusion and the potentially negative effect of shaming.

Cost savings

Restorative justice may contribute to cost savings through both its processes (less reliance on courts) and its outcomes (less reliance on custody). Maxwell *et al.* (1999) reported on the costs of Project Turnaround and Te Whanau Awhina. Over the period reviewed (1997), the costs of the schemes per client were $462 at Project Turnaround and $1,515 at Te Whanau Awhina.[11] This difference between the schemes was largely due to the greater involvement of Te Whanau Awhina in providing programmes for participants in the scheme. At the same time, savings on correctional outcomes for 100 participants compared to the 100 matched controls were $27,811 at Project Turnaround and $168,259 at Te Whanau Awhina. This was due to a larger number of the Te Whanau Awhina controls receiving custodial penalties. There were also more savings at Project Turnaround in court appearances and associated costs and these, together with the savings on correctional sentences, were estimated as $85,325. Although there were no savings in court costs at Te Whanau Awhina, there were savings in the cost of programme provision: the total savings for this programme were estimated at $193,096.

Conclusion

The theme of this book is 'repositioning restorative justice'. This chapter suggests that restorative justice can be positioned centrally within the criminal justice system to deal not only with juvenile offenders but also with adult offenders and to deal with not only minor offences but with relatively serious offences.

The data presented in this chapter point to significant benefits for adult offenders, their victims and the state from the introduction of restorative justice processes and practices in New Zealand. The data demonstrate their potential to increase victims' and adult offenders' involvement in dealing with offending. In addition, both adult offenders and victims frequently reported satisfaction in being able to reach agreements that went some way to repairing the harm that was caused. However, some concerns were raised by the offenders involved in one of the pilots (Project Turnaround) about the type of people who were making decisions about how their offending should be dealt with. This raises crucial questions about the legitimacy of restorative justice processes and who the decision-makers should be. Despite the panel meeting at Te Whanau Awhina being often seen by offenders as intimidating and demanding, the panel's decisions were accepted by those offenders interviewed because of *whanau*, *hapu* (sub-tribe) or *iwi* (tribal) connections to these decision-makers, however remote they might be. The decisions also look place, in the eyes of the Maori offenders, before their ancestors. Thus both the forum and decision-makers confirmed the legitimacy of this process.

Adult offenders who participated in Project Turnaround and Te Whanau Awhina, both of which had restorative features, were reconvicted less frequently and of offences of less seriousness than a matched group of controls who had been dealt with in the courts. Furthermore, comparisons of the subsequent reconviction rates for those who successfully completed the schemes and those who did not suggest that those who carried out the agreements reached were less likely to be reconvicted. This suggests that restorative processes and practices can impact on reconviction.

Added to this is the evidence that suggests that significant cost savings can be made because the use of restorative justice processes enabled less reliance on courts and custody. Indeed, the cost savings could have been even greater if the offenders involved in Te Whanau Awhina had not routinely had to reappear in court even after satisfactorily completing the agreed plan; and they could perhaps be even greater in future if those at risk of custody were targeted for restorative justice processes (as in the new pilots currently being evaluated). Although the savings that result from preventing reoffending cannot be estimated, these are also undoubtedly at least as important as the financial costs that have been calculated. Incalculable, too, are the emotional or human costs of crime which restorative justice addresses. Together these findings make a strong case for the continued expansion of the use of restorative practices for adult offenders.

In New Zealand now, a variety of potentially restorative approaches are being used that hold offenders accountable and aim to increase victims' satisfaction with criminal justice processes. This chapter has presented data only on community panel meetings. The evaluation of restorative justice conferences has just begun. If these different approaches are carefully evaluated, comparisons may be able to be made in future which will help to determine the most effective options for both offenders and victims. But this discussion will have to wait until more data are available.

Notes

1. The other approach is currently being evaluated but there are no findings to date.
2. Smith and Cram (1998) state that 70% of the meetings in their evaluation had victims present; on the other hand, Maxwell *et al* (1999) state that only around half of the meetings in their evaluation of Project Turnaround had victims present and that only one meeting in Te Whanau Awhina had a victim present.

3. According to Webster (2000), the victim's consent is now required for the conference to proceed. This does not seem to have been the case earlier (Smith and Cram 1998; Maxwell *et al.* 1999).

4. It is also consistent with indigenous models of justice and, in particular, with Maori values and philosophy. For more information, see Jackson (1988), Consedine (1995) and the New Zealand Maori Council and Hall (1999), though contrast Tauri (1999).

5. The Crime Prevention Unit also provided start-up funding for the Sycamore Tree programme in prisons – a restorative justice programme initiated by Prison Fellowship International. Offenders and victims meet as a group and discuss matters such as the effects of crime on victims.

6. The evaluation involves interviewing 180 victims who have been involved in restorative conferences and 180 offenders who have been involved in restorative conferences shortly after the completion of the conference, shortly after the court has decided on sentence and one year later. It is also intended to interview 90 victims and 90 offenders from the comparison court samples shortly after the completion of their case in court and one year later. In addition, it is intended to observe 90 restorative justice conferences and to prepare in-depth case studies of 18 restorative justice conferences. Ninety key informants (such as judges, police, prosecutors, probation officers and programme providers) will be interviewed during the first year of data collection and again in the second year. A survey of all of the participants who attended conferences during the first year of the data collection is also being conducted. Information contained on the restorative justice database will be analysed for the cases referred to co-ordinators during the first year of the evaluation along with other documentation held by the co-ordinators (for example, the summary of facts for each referral and the conferences' agreements). Comments made by the judges at sentencing and discharge hearings over a three-month period will be collected by court staff and the operating costs of the schemes will be examined. In addition, the Ministry of Justice will compare the reconviction of the 180 offenders in the restorative conference sample with a matched control sample who will have been dealt with solely in the criminal courts.

7. About a third of the Te Whanau Awhina participants and 10% of those participating in Project Turnaround had at least six previous convictions.

8. This concern emphasises the significance of who the key decision-makers should be in restorative justice processes.

9. The Ministry of Justice researchers collaborating on this project took the view that the two to three year time difference between the processing of participants in 1997–8 and controls in 1995 was unlikely to confound the comparison of recidivism rates between the samples as changes in practice or patterns of offending over that period were not of a magnitude that would be likely to lead to differences in recidivism.

10. The fact that a greater proportion of the Te Whanau Awhina participants and their matched controls were reconvicted is likely to be due to them being more

serious and persistent offenders than the Project Turnaround participants and their matched controls.

11. All figures quoted are in New Zealand dollars.

References

Consedine, J. (1995) *Restorative Justice: Healing the Effects of Crime.* Lyttelton: Ploughshares Publications.

Consedine, J. and Bowen, H. (1999) *Restorative Justice: Contemporary Themes and Practice.* Lyttelton: Ploughshares Publications.

Daly, K. (2001) 'Conferencing in Australia and New Zealand: Variations, Research Findings, and Prospects', in A. Morris and G. Maxwell (eds) *Restorative Justice for Juveniles: Conferencing, Mediation and Circles.* Oxford: Hart Publishing.

Jackson, M. (1988) *Maori and the Criminal Justice System Part II.* Wellington: Department of Justice.

Maxwell, G. and Morris, A. (1993) *Families, Victims and Culture: Youth Justice in New Zealand.* Wellington: Social Policy Agency and Institute of Criminology, Victoria University of Wellington.

Maxwell, G. and Morris, A. (1999) *Understanding Re-offending.* Wellington: Institute of Criminology, Victoria University of Wellington.

Maxwell, G.M., Morris, A. and Anderson, T. (1999) *Community Panel Adult Pre-Trial Diversion: Supplementary Evaluation.* Wellington: Crime Prevention Unit, Department of Prime Minister and Cabinet, and Institute of Criminology, Victoria University of Wellington.

McElrea, F. (1998) 'The New Zealand Model of Family Group Conferences.' Paper presented at the international symposium, 'Beyond Prisons: Best Practice along the Criminal Justice Process', Kingston: Ontario, 15–18 March.

Ministry of Justice (1995) *Restorative Justice: A Discussion Paper.* Wellington: Ministry of Justice.

Ministry of Justice (1998) *Restorative Justice: The Public Submissions.* Wellington: Ministry of Justice.

Morris, A. and Maxwell, G. (2000) 'The Practice of Family Group Conferences in New Zealand: Assessing the Place, Potential and Pitfalls of Restorative Justice', in A. Crawford, and J. Goodey (eds) *Integrating a Victim Perspective within Criminal Justice.* Aldershot: Ashgate.

New Zealand Maori Council and Durie Hall, D. (1999) 'Restorative Justice: a Maori Perspective', in H. Bowen and J. Consedine (eds) *Restorative Justice: Contemporary Themes and Practice.* Lyttelton: Ploughshares Publications.

Smith, L.T. and Cram, F. (1998) *An Evaluation of the Community Panel Diversion Pilot Programme. A Report to the Crime Prevention Unit.* Auckland: Auckland Uniservices Ltd.

Spier, P. (1998) *Conviction and Sentencing of Offenders in New Zealand: 1988 to 1997.* Wellington: Ministry of Justice.

Spier, P. (2000) *Conviction and Sentencing of Offenders in New Zealand: 1990 to 1999.* Wellington: Ministry of Justice.

Tauri, J. (1999) 'Explaining Recent Innovations in New Zealand's Criminal Justice System: Empowering Maori or Biculturalising the State?', *Australian and New Zealand Journal of Criminology*, 32(2), 153–67.

Webster, B. (2000) 'Restorative Justice Developments in New Zealand: Community Managed Restorative Justice Programmes – from Inception to Evaluation.' Paper presented at the Australian Crime Prevention Council, 19th biennial conference, October 1999, updated 25 July 2000.

Chapter 11

Restorative justice in prison?

Ottmar Hagemann

Theoretical reflections

Currently, programmes are being implemented in prisons that could be classified as forms of restorative justice (see Hagemann and Robertz 2000; Umbreit and Vos 2000; Liebmann and Braithwaite 2001; Newell 2001). Belgium has recently introduced so-called restorative justice consultants, and one now works in every prison (D'Hoop and Biermans 2001; Malempre and Hodiaumont 2001). But is the concept of restorative justice compatible with imprisonment? Abolitionists have a long tradition of criticising the retributive (and the rehabilitative) approach to criminal law in general and to prison in particular. Like proponents of restorative justice, they have also argued for alternative ways of conflict resolution.

Abolitionists on conflict, criminal law and the criminal justice system, especially the prison

From a sociological perspective, our current (primarily retributive) system of criminal law is not able to solve social conflicts. Instead, it transforms social conflicts into legal conflicts or, as Nils Christie in his famous article 'Conflicts as Property' (1977) states: 'The criminal justice system steals the conflicts of the people'. Currently, (in many western societies at least), social groups are drifting apart (Bauman 1999) and most of those labelled as delinquents now belong to socially excluded factions. We thus need an alternative form of justice if we are to avoid the further disintegration of society. One theoretical alternative is abolitionism, which aims for a more just and integrated society. Abolitionism presupposes an equal distribution of positive as well as negative goods, the chances of participation in social life and an intense communication between all members of society. Many years ago, Thomas Mathiesen (1974) pointed out that prison is the core element of our criminal justice system, and he argued for the abolition of prisons that are used primarily to inflict disciplinary punishment on an underclass of people. Furthermore, he warned against positive reforms in prisons (such as providing more comfortable cells, for example) that would only stabilise the existing system.[1]

But abolitionism has not succeeded. On the contrary, as Mathiesen's Norwegian colleague, Christie (1993) has demonstrated, there is a steady increase in the use of imprisonment – and not only in America (see Walmsley ICPS 2000; 2002, for comprehensive and current figures). Surely no serious criminologist could claim that we are on the way towards abolitionism (see Cayley 1998).

Restorative justice and abolitionism

An alternative to criminal law that has been developing over the last twenty years and that seems to be promising is restorative justice – a growing, though not clearly defined, movement. Proponents of restorative justice describe its elements as: 'a definition of crime as injury to victims and community peace, a focus on addressing the personal–relational injuries experienced by all parties as well as the financial and legal obligations of offenders, and a commitment to including all parties in the response to the crime.' (Van Ness 1990: 10)[2]. Howard Zehr (1990) sees this as a paradigm shift and stresses the constructive, interactive and future-orientated character of restorative justice.

In a report for the Canadian Law Commission Jennifer Llewellyn and Robert Howse (2001) focus on the social justice aspect of restorative justice. In their attempt to develop a conceptual framework, they state that 'restorative justice is fundamentally concerned with restoring social relationships, with establishing or re-establishing social equality in relationships' (p. 2). Therefore, restoration does not necessarily refer to the status that existed before the wrongdoing occurred (p. 18).[3] It means, however, transformation: a better future is achieved through social dialogue. Thus its method of dealing with conflicts differs in essence from the one used in a retributive approach (pp. 23f.f). According to Llewellyn and Howse, punishment has no place in this approach (p. 48). This form of restorative justice could be said to represent the application of abolitionist thinking. Furthermore, it shares the pro-community and pro-democracy orientation (Braithwaite 1994) of the former abolitionist position. Both the restorative justice and abolitionist positions point out that the state's hegemonic power has been promoting a retributive approach since the middle ages (for the history of restorative justice, see Weitekamp 1999).[4]

In practical terms, a crucial element of a fully[5] restorative justice process is the face-to-face interaction between wrongdoers and the sufferers of that wrongdoing. Although there is some debate about this (see Dignan 2001), most leading restorative justice proponents seem to support Mark Umbreit's statement that the (dialogue driven) communicative process between the parties is more important than the outcome (2000: 6). John Braithwaite (1989) has suggested the concept of reintegrative shaming to encapsulate these dynamics. According to Braithwaite, the wrongdoer obtains a deeper insight into his or her wrongdoing through shaming, which arises from a direct confrontation with the victim and the community, as long as the shaming[6] is followed by reintegration ceremonies that assure the wrongdoer that the other participants are able to differentiate between the wrong of his or her action and this person's good.

If we focus on daily, routine work, it seems that family group conferences in New Zealand have achieved great importance, effectiveness and efficiency (Belgrave 1996; Morris and Maxwell 1998, 2001). However, these conferences display a dual system of conflict settlement, with the retributivists having the final say (see the Clotworthy and Gladue cases as cited in Mason 2000; Morris and Young 2000). As an abolitionist, Thomas Mathiesen would criticise such 'positive reform'. Indeed, this reform has helped the New Zealand criminal justice system to reduce its caseload by almost two thirds and custodial sentences by more than 50% (Morris and Young 2000). Such an outcome must indeed stabilise the system, as Mathiesen has predicted.

Restorative justice's concern with less severe cases in most countries has meant that a fully restorative system has not been established. This may be the result of the work of Stephen Schafer (1970), who advocated a compensation and victim-centred approach to criminal justice. However, if restorative justice is to be seen as an alternative to the retributive system – as Mathiesen and Christie suggest – it must, of course, deal with all types of conflict.

Restorative justice in the most serious cases

In 1999, Ivo Aertsen outlined restorative justice projects that had dealt successfully with the most serious of cases: Langley (Canada), Genesee and Texas (USA) and Belgium. Mark Umbreit and Betty Vos (2000: 63) describe a mediation procedure that involves offenders sentenced to capital punishment:

> [The two cases reported] represent the first examination of any capital murder cases involving a victim–offender mediation/ dialogue session between a surviving family member and the death row inmate facing execution shortly after the mediation session. The 5 participants ... stated that this intervention had a powerful impact on their lives; all had been moved beyond their expectations, all were relieved, all reported significant progress on their healing journeys, and all were grateful for the opportunity...

Umbreit and Vos suggest that practitioners and policy-makers should give cautious but serious consideration to expanding opportunities for restorative encounters that have been initiated by victims and the surviving family members of severely violent crime. The film *Dead Man Walking* (1996) has also illustrated the potential of dialogue and inhumanity of a retributive approach.

From this two things emerge:

1. Even the most serious of crimes (such as murder) can be subjected to a restorative justice process.
2. Restorative justice can be combined with retributive justice.

But is it really restorative justice if the offenders are executed? If equality of relationships is a fundamental consideration in restorative justice, surely the offenders must be considered as well.

Empirical evidence

Self-developed empathy training

The present author has initiated a training programme for serious adult offenders in a sociotherapeutic prison in Hamburg, Germany. Serious offenders in this sense means those who are serving longer sentences[7] because they have been convicted of such crimes as homicide, drug trafficking, robbery, fraud or severe forms of assault.[8]

These inmates have already served a significant part of their sentences in 'regular' detention institutions that do not offer rehabilitative or therapeutic measures other than work. Every three months, a group of

5–12 applicants are interviewed by a committee of prison staff to be transferred to a sociotherapeutic institution for the last 18–24 months of their sentence.

In 1997, the current author began a programme called 'Focus on Victims', which was partly inspired by a similar Dutch initiative (see Groenhuijsen and Winkel 1991; Serkei 1997).[9] Almost 150 prisoners have participated in this scheme even though there has been no official evaluation. A programme that focuses primarily on the victims of serious crime is a new venture in Germany[10] where, usually, the subject of victims is not discussed and where preparation for the release of inmates only concerns such practical matters as finding a place to live and prospects for work.

Inmates participate in the 'Focus on Victims' training programme for the first three months of their stay in the institution. Despite the fact that they were referred to the institution on a voluntary basis, participation in the training programmes is obligatory. The programme consists of eight modules conducted in two four-hour sessions. Each module lasts about one hour, with a short break in between. While this may not be sufficient, it was all the institution could arrange. Inmates who request more intensive training are given single counselling sessions over a period of almost two years. The following is a brief description of the programme, which is described in detail elsewhere (Hagemann and Robertz 2000).

The modules

Module 1: victims

This is a 'warming up' session resembling a quiz game. The prisoners are given the names of a series of victims and are asked to discuss the circumstances of their victimisation. This task includes sorting the names into different categories – for example, victims of crime, accident or disease or victims who are also offenders. This usually ends up in a very lively discussion of what makes someone a victim. The anonimity of this means the inmates do not run the risk of revealing too much about themselves.

Module 2: victimisation of friends and relatives

Because it is impossible to continue such a discussion in the abstract, the participants are asked to tell the story of a victim they themselves know and so focus on their own thoughts and feelings about that victim. This enables us to use a wide variety of real-life examples without mention of the inmates' own cases. All the examples discussed are grouped on a blackboard into categories such as victims of physical, psychological, mental, economic and social crime.

Module 3: the victimisation experiences of group members

In this module the inmates are encouraged to talk about their personal experiences as victims and offenders. Defensive psychological mechanisms (Freud 1980) often emerge, resulting in silence or provocative statements that they themselves should be included as victims because of their incarceration.[11] Even though no one is forced to speak, persistence results in the inmates expressing thoughts about their victimisation and also about their victim(s). These experiences are then linked to the categories listed earlier on the blackboard.

Module 4: Carlisle Fantasy Analysis System

At the end of the first day, a more creative technique is used. A set of schematic black and white paintings by Carlisle (1995) depicting scenes of victimisation is introduced. As these paintings are open to interpretation in different ways, the inmates are asked to study the paintings and to describe what they see. Generally, the paintings are associated with an experienced victimisation. After this, the pictures are ordered into a sequence of increasing emotional intensity all the group members agree with. This prompts them to think about victimisation in general and helps them to relate to this in their own personal experiences. The intention is to make it easier for them to reflect on the content of the training programme in the hope they will remember this in the future.

Module 5: assessing the seriousness of victimisation

During this module the group is divided into three or four smaller groups, each one receiving the same set of four victimisation cases. The descriptions of these cases consist of two or three sentences and provide no clues about the consequences of the victimisation. The groups have about 10 minutes to arrange the cases in order of increasing seriousness. The (usually differing) results are put on the blackboard. The participants are then given another set of cards with the same cases but now containing a short, first-person victim impact statement. They now have to consider whether these statements affect their first ratings and why. From this they realise that not only is it rather difficult to predict the consequences of a crime but also, by putting themselves in the place of these victims, they can work out what form of victimisation is the worst. The assumption that they caused 'no real harm' to their victims often becomes quite shaky at this stage.

Module 6: what happened during the offensive act?

The programme now goes into more detail about their own offending. As one or two of the inmates often talk about their offences on the first day, these stories are taken up. If not, someone is asked to explain what he did. Some, however, are unwilling to explore this. Again, we have to fight against such neutralisation techniques (Sykes and Matza 1957; Fattah 1991: 140). We do not, however, force each member of the group to reveal his past. In this module, on the other hand, group dynamics really work in our favour and the inmates usually refute each others' attempts to deny their own responsibility.

Module 7: the victim's coping techniques

By exploring what victims do to come to terms with the consequences of the crime and to recover from psychological and other wounds, the group learns about very different coping strategies (Hagemann 1993). It is important for them to understand the ongoing nature of being a victim, including the procedures within the criminal justice system and/or the victim being prepared for dialogue or even reconciliation. There are four aspects to this coping process:

1. Coping behaviour is very individual and thus varies from one person to another.
2. Coping behaviour also varies over time – victims change their coping strategies again and again.
3. Time and personal preferences interact, making it almost impossible to predict how someone would react to an attempt at dialogue at any one time.
4. It is not clear when coping processes come to an end. Similar or related experiences can open the wounds again (Hagemann 1993).

Module 8: mediation and reconciliation

The last module introduces the concept of victim–offender mediation. For this, we use a brief role play or simply provide information. The advantages and disadvantages for both parties are then discussed. The main aim is to demonstrate the possibilities offenders have to repair some of the damage they have done and to heal some of the pain they have caused. If the victim is known by the offender, we hope to re-establish some sort of social relationship. Even though we cannot expect them to change their behaviour or persuade them to restore the damage they have done, we can at least hope some of them may consider this option in the future. Thus the victim's perspective must be presented in such a way as not to encourage an offender to take steps that lead towards secondary victimisation.

Summary

The concept of victimisation used here is very broad, including as it does such non-criminal instances of victimisation as disasters, accidents or illness. At the beginning we shy away from personal experiences but, during the course of the training, we get closer to the participants' personal conflicts to create an atmosphere of openness. Of great importance are the group context and the fact that everything said stays within the group. After building a relationship with each participant,[12] we encourage them to empathise with victims in general and their own victims in particular. We look at the consequences of their behaviour not only for the victim and the offender but also for their relationship with society at large. Victims' coping processes are discussed as is the social exclusion of offenders from society – something that happens as a result of the stigmatisation that follows degradation ceremonies (Garfinkel 1956).[13] Finally, mediation is introduced as a means to reverse social exclusion and to re-establish the relationship between the victim, his or her environment and the community. The benefits of victim–offender mediation as well as the problems caused by contradictory coping strategies are investigated in detail, and there is an attempt to devise practical action plans.

Our experience of this programme has confirmed our assumption that there are three relationships that must be restored:

1. The internal (psychological) relationship between the participants' two conflicting identities: their 'criminal side' and their concept of themselves as 'normal' human beings.[14]
2. The social relationship between the prisoner and society, primarily represented by the prison and its agents and secondarily represented by acquaintances, relatives, the media, visitors and other inmates.
3. The social relationship between the prisoner and his victim(s) and the people within the victim's network, which is, of course, the most problematic.

Some problems

The restoration of social relationships is seen as a three-step process based on the above list. Some kind of post-sentencing mediation between the victim and the offender is the final aim. However, from a psychological point of view, it makes no sense to initiate such a process if the offender does not accept his 'dark side' or denies his participation in the offending behaviour or, in the words of Braithwaite (1994) and others, if he does not assume accountability or responsibility for his actions. One difficulty is to make all the participants see the sense of this. Most prisoners are reluctant to be open about themselves, and many become open-minded only to a minor extent. Basically there are three types of prisoners:

1. Those who are aware of the consequences of their actions and who are suffering as a result. People who have caused very serious, long-lasting injuries seem themselves to suffer,[15] while those who have, for example, taken goods are able to see the emotional impact of their actions but are much less motivated to offer restitution. Another aspect is anonymity. In most cases of serious violent crime, the people involved often know each other because they are from the same community or belong to the same social group. As Carlchristian von Braunmühl, a victim of a terrorist attack in which his brother was killed, has said: 'There is something that ties us together – the unknown murderer of my brother and me, something that is only ours' (pers. comm.). This 'something' cannot be defined, but 'tied' people clearly feel it. It is missing from more impersonal cases.[16]
2. Those who have suppressed everything about their actions and who are only concerned with the here and now.
3. Those who do not see the necessity for restitution and dialogue because they are already serving their sentence. Being sentenced is sufficient or – as is frequently stated – is seen as overcompensation for their wrongdoing.

Thus our work is a lot easier when the inmates have undergone another mandatory training session called '*Tataufarbeitung*' (Coming to terms with your offences').

Links between theory and practice

We seem to have been reasonably successful with regard to the first and second relationships: the internal relationship and the relationship with society. In a group training session, the trainers and prisoners represent society – its values, norms and feelings. While there are sympathetic listeners, we have all (including the prisoners) experienced the harm of wrongdoing in one way or another. Therefore no participants are allowed to get away with an excuse. For example, a drug dealer might be confronted by a fellow prisoner whose daughter or sister is a drug addict. There are consequences of this addiction for the woman and her family and there is also the emotional pain the prisoner himself is feeling. What we do not do is moralise. Instead, the group puts pressure on members who refuse to take responsibility. In this way shame arises. Reintegrative shaming is considered a powerful tool in restorative justice. However, Braithwaite (1989) warns us that pure shaming can be destructive, excluding effects on the person concerned. He asks for – at least symbolic – demonstrations of reintegration to allow openness – as opposed to defensiveness – and a cognitive learning process that will help to prevent wrongdoing in the future.

Although not directly present, there is also the influence of non-sympathetic people. We are all aware of the tendency of the media or the public to condemn crime and the people responsible for it. The first and third of the above types of offender are (or can be) well aware of the feelings and sufferings of their victims and co-victims. For example, a young man killed a friend of his in a shooting. This young man knew the this victim's parents almost as well as his own and he was afraid to confront them as he had completely destroyed their lives.

The restoration of the social relationship between the victim and offender can be blocked by the victims. In one of only three cases where the offender felt prepared for such contact it was apparent the victim's mother and sister were only participating to demand a stricter sentence. In such circumstances victim–offender dialogue seems impossible. In another of the three cases, the offender lost his nerve after we had asked a priest to approach his victim. Luckily, the priest had not established contact yet. In the third case the offender finally established indirect contact on his own, via his mother. (There was a fourth case where a female imprisoned for manslaughter wanted to co-operate but her family dissuaded her.) After five years working with about 150 prisoners, not a single direct victim–offender contact was achieved.[17] The success of this work is, then, extremely one-sided: restoration failed in one important relationship but the other two seem to be worth all the effort.

So, clearly, we have not achieved what seems to be possible elsewhere. This may be a result of our inverse way of approaching the people involved – we have contact with the offenders but are convinced that we should not approach a victim unless it can be guaranteed that the offender will not withdraw from the attempt to resolve the conflict. The victim may still be in trauma or may be going through a hard time if his or her coping strategy has focused primarily on repression or some other defence mechanism (Hagemann 1991).

Furthermore, there is a structural component to this limited success. Table 11.1 lists some of the characteristics of mediation as a form of restorative justice and the (side) effects of imprisonment. For prisoners, there is an excessive amount of shaming in the communication they have with people from outside and with the prison officials whose duty it is to deliver pain (Christie 1981). Inmates feel ashamed in situations where they are confronted with the consequences of their actions.

Table 11.1 Characteristics of Retributive and Restorative Justice from the perspective of wrongdoers

The Prison	*Mediation*
Identification of the person with the offence	Separation of the act and actor
	Integration
Exclusion	Going through pain and shame to
Permanent pain delivery and shaming	relief and understanding
Voluntariness	Dominion (in the sense of
Coercion	Braithwaite and Pettit 1990: 58)[18]
Domination	Responsibility for one's own action
Order: no individual responsibility	Fundamental equality
Hierarchy	

As long as an offender is totally identified (Garfinkel 1956) with his or her offence, openness will not emerge. Only when there is a clear distinction between the wrong done and the personality of the perpetrator of that wrong – someone responsible for that but also for a great many socially desirable actions – will this openness develop. Reintegrative shaming and the social learning processes that evolve from it can thus only be achieved successfully outside typical prison structures.

Conclusions

I think the intention of our training is clearly restorative. It focuses on victims as well as community peace and is future orientated. Our aim is to include all the parties to a conflict to enable them to act on their own behalf (not through the criminal justice system). Some prisoners find relief from their psychological suffering and, in some cases, social relationships can be restored. But prisoners who are able to cope with their offending will not be motivated to participate in such a strenuous process as long as the retributive aspect – that is, the sentence – is left out of the focus.

Such programmes as these conducted in prisons should not be classified restorative justice because the imposed punishment forms a structural impediment. So the answer to Bazemore and Walgrave's (1999: 359) question whether this is only an add-on to a retributive approach is 'yes'. According to Llewellyn and Howse (2001). Punishment should not be imposed in a restorative justice setting. This is in accordance with Braithwaite and Pettit's (1990) republican theory of criminal justice. Sykes (1958), Goffman (1961) and others have demonstrated various sources of pressure against inmates. The term 'prisonisation' was devised to describe the process of adjustment and its consequences. According to these studies, prisoners are forced to devote all their energy into preventing serious damage to their identity or even its destruction. In such a situation there is only small chance one will open one's mind to others or to one's own negative side. Despite extensive discussion on rehabilitation and reintegration since the 1960s, the prison, even the sociotherapeutic institution, has retained its non-integrative, excluding character. It still is the whole person who is punished and devalued. In his radical critique, Mathiesen (1974) has proven that this disintegrative wall is constitutive and cannot be overcome.

Notes

1. Interestingly, in an empirical study, he found a strong positive relation between the attitudes of those who support imprisonment and the social distance accorded people who have experienced this form of treatment (Mathiesen 1989: 141f.f). This may be a hint that lawyers in their abstract normative thinking (see Sessar, 1999 on *déformation professionelle*) will find other forms of problem-solving as social scientists, who are in their work more often confronted with real actors in a vivid and concrete way at least in the tradition that Matza (1969) has described as a perspective of understanding.
2. For a more recent definition, see Weitekamp (2000: 103).
3. Thus they propose to rename it relational justice, transformative justice or community restorative justice. See also Weitekamp (2000: 99) for other labels.
4. 'Restorative justice is about limiting the role (monopoly) of the state and transferring power to those most directly involved in the offence' (Morris and Maxwell, 2001: 272).
5. In evaluating different applications of practical restorative justice, McCold (2001) differentiates between fully restorative and partly restorative procedures. A fully restorative procedure, such as conferencing or victim-offender mediation involves the participation of all the parties directly concerned. These procedures have produced better results, both in terms of processes and outcome.
6. Perhaps the idea of shame is misleading. We could replace it with the concept of remorse (a suggestion made by Allison Morris). Braithwaite himself points out that shame unaccompanied by reintegrative symbols or behaviour runs the risk of defensive coping and, in the long term, to stigmatisation. This could block insights and empathic feelings.
7. The average length of a prison sentence in Germany is less than one year. This group of prisoners, however, comprises those who are serving sentences of more than two years and those who are serving very long sentences. (i.e. more than 10 years).
8. Sex offenders are referred to other institutions.

9. Soon after beginning this work, a colleague joined me because such group work requires two trainers.
10. In their investigation of victim awareness in English prisons, Liebmann and Braithwaite (1999: 2) found six programmes.
11. Provocation here means that, sometimes, some of the inmates present themselves as victims of the criminal justice system, claiming they had been falsely convicted. This must not be confused with victimisation by fellow prisoners or prison officers.
12. This is the ideal. In reality, some of them cannot be approached in a deeper, psychological sense.
13. In fact, victims and socially vulnerable groups are in general, all too often excluded from society as well.
14. The latter is mostly shared by their caring others; the majority of society will condemn them.
15. For example, one participant repeatedly dreamt he was stabbing his victim: the victim collapsed with blood running down his chest.
16. However, it is for the victim to decide if the offence is only a nuisance or has caused significant suffering.
17. Since the end of 1999, due to a change of personnel, the aim was no longer victim–offender mediation – so the figures relate to approximately 60 participants only.
18. 'Dominion' is the republican concept of liberty that presumes also the equality of liberty with others in a social world. It is not the 'negative' freedom of isolated atomistic individuals left alone by others.

References

Aertsen, I. (1999) 'Mediation bei schweren Straftaten – Auf dem Weg zu einer neuen Rechtskultur?' in C. Pelikan (ed.) *Mediationsverfahren: Horizonte, Grenzen, Innensichten. Jahrbuch für Rechts- und Kriminalsoziologie.* Baden-Baden: Nomos.

Bauman, Z. (1999) *Das Unbehagen in der Postmoderne.* Hamburg: Hamburger Edition.

Bazemore, G. and Walgrave, L. (1999) 'Reflections on the Future of Restorative Justice', in G. Bazemore and L. Walgrave (eds) *Restorative Juvenile Justice: Repairing the Harm of Youth Crime.* Monsey, NY: Criminal Justice Press.

Belgrave, J. (1996) *Restorative Justice. A Discussion Paper.* Ministry of Justice, New Zealand (www.justice.govt.nz/pubs/reports/1996/restorative/).

Braithwaite, J. (1989) *Crime, Shame and Reintegration.* Cambridge: Cambridge University Press.

Braithwaite, J. (1994) 'Thinking Harder about Democratising Social Control', in C. Alder and J. Wundersitz (eds) *Family Conferencing and Juvenile Justice: the Way Forward or Misplaced Optimism?.* Canberra: Australian Institute of Criminology.

Braithwaite, J. and Mugford, S. (1994) 'Conditions of Successful Reintegration Ceremonies. Dealing with Juvenile Offenders', *British Journal of Criminology,*

34(2): 139–71.

Braithwaite, J. and Pettit, P. (1990) *Not Just Deserts. A Republican Theory of Criminal Justice*. Oxford: Clarendon Press.

Carlisle, A.L. (1995) *Carlisle Fantasy Analysis System (C-FAS)*. Price, Utah.

Cayley, D. (1998) *The Expanding Prison. The Crisis in Crime and Punishment and the Search for Alternatives*. Toronto: Anansi.

Christie, N. (1977) 'Conflicts as Property', *British Journal of Criminology*, 17(1): 1–15

Christie, N. (1981) *Limits to Pain*. Oslo: Universitetsforlaget.

Christie, N. (1993) (2nd edn 2000) *Crime Control as Industry*. London and New York, NY: Routledge.

D'Hoop, M.-N. and Biermans, N. (2001) 'Development of Belgian Prisons into a Restorative Perspective.' Paper presented at the 5th international conference on restorative justice, Leuven, 16–19 September.

Dignan, J. (2001) 'Towards a Systemic Model of Restorative Justice.' Paper presented at the 5th international conference on restorative justice, Leuven, 16–19 September.

Fattah, E. (1991) *Understanding Criminal Victimization. An Introduction to Theoretical Victimology*. Scarborough, Ontario: Prentice Hall.

Freud, A. (1980) 'Das Ich und die Abwehrmechanismen', *in Schriften der Anna Freud. Band 1 1922–1936*. München: Kindler.

Garfinkel, H. (1956) 'Conditions of Successful Degradation Ceremonies', *American Journal of Sociology*, 61: 420–4.

Goffman, E. (1961) *Asylums. Essays on the Social Situation of Mental Patients and other Inmates*. New York, NY: Doubleday.

Groenhuijsen, M. and Winkel, F.W. (1991) 'The "Focusing on Victims Program" as a New Substitute Penal Sanction for Youthful Offenders.' Paper presented at the 7th international symposium on victimology, Rio de Janeiro, 25–30 August.

Hagemann, O. (1991) 'Coping and Mediation. Implications of a Research Study on Victims of Assault and Burglary', in G. Kaiser *et al.* (eds) *Victims and Criminal Justice*. Freiburg: Eigenverlag Max-Planck-Institut.

Hagemann, O. (1993) *Wohnungseinbrüche und Gewalttaten: Wie bewältigen Opfer ihre Verletzungen?*. Pfaffenweiler: Centaurus.

Hagemann, O. and Robertz, F. (2000) 'Prevention of Victimization by Working with Serious Offenders.' Paper presented at the 10th international symposium on victimology, Montréal, 6–11 August (www.fas.umontreal.ca/anthro/varia/ PV_2001/diffusion/textes/defgh_t/Hagemann_Robertz.pdf).

ICPS (2002) *World Prison Brief of the International Centre for Prison Studies*. London (www.kcl.ac.uk/depsta/rel/icps/worldbrief/... (www.prisonstudies.org).

Liebmann, M. and Braithwaite, S. (1999) *Restorative Justice in Custodial Settings* (www.restorativejustice.org.uk/prisons5.html).

Llewellyn, J. and Howse, R. (2001) *Restorative Justice – a Conceptual Framework*. Law Commission of Canada (www.lcc.gc.ca/en/themes/sr/rj/howse/index.html).

Malempre, H. and Hodiaumont, F. (2001) 'Restorative Justice in Prison: Concepts of Victims and Reparation.' Paper presented at the 5th international conference organised by the International Network for Research on Restorative Justice for Juveniles, Leuven.

Mason, A. (2000) 'Restorative Justice: Courts and Civil Society', in H. Strang and J. Braithwaite (eds) *Restorative Justice. Philosophy to Practice.* Aldershot: Ashgate.

Mathiesen, T. (1974) *The Politics of Abolition.* London: Martin Robertson.

Mathiesen, T. (1989) *Gefängnislogik. Über alte und neue Rechtfertigungsversuche* (English edn 1990: *Prison on Trial. A Critical Assessment.* London: Sage.)

Matza, D. (1969) *Becoming Deviant.* Englewood Cliffs, NJ: Prentice Hall.

Maxwell, G. and Morris, A. (2001) 'Family Group Conferences and Reoffending', in A. Morris and G. Maxwell (eds) *Restorative Justice for Juveniles. Conferencing, Mediation and Circles.* Oxford and Portland, OR: Hart.

McCold, P. (2001) 'A Survey of Assessment Research on Mediation and Conferencing.' Paper presented at the 5th international conference organised by the International Network for Research on Restorative Justice for Juveniles, Leuven.

Morris, A. and Maxwell, G. (1998) 'Restorative Justice in New Zealand: Family Group Conferences as a Case Study', *Western Criminology Review* 1(1). (www.wcr.Sonoma.edu/v1n1/morris.html.)

Morris, A. and Maxwell, G. (2001) 'Implementing Restorative Justice: What Works?', in A. Morris and G. Maxwell (eds) *Restorative Justice for Juveniles. Conferencing, Mediation and Circles.* Oxford and Portland, OR: Hart.

Morris, A. and Young, W. (2000) 'Reforming Criminal Justice: the Potential of Restorative Justice' in H. Strang and J. Braithwaite (eds) *Restorative Justice. Philosophy to Practice.* Aldershot: Ashgate.

Newell, T. (2001) 'Restorative Justice in Prisons.' Paper presented at the international conference 'Restorative and Community Justice: Inspiring the Future', Winchester, 28–31 March.

Schafer, S. (1970) *Compensation and Restitution to Victims of Crime.* (2nd edn). Montclair, NJ: Patterson Smith.

Serkei, B. (1997) 'Focus on Victims: a Victim-oriented Crime-prevention Project aimed at offenders.' Paper presented at the 9th international symposium on victimology, Amsterdam, 25–30 August.

Sessar, K. (1992) *Wiedergutmachen oder strafen.* Pfaffenweiler: Centaurus.

Sessar, K. (1999) 'Punitive Attitudes of the Public: Reality and Myth', in G. Bazemore and L. Walgrave, L. (eds) *Restorative Juvenile Justice: Repairing the Harm of Youth Crime.* Monsey, NY: Criminal Justice Press.

Sykes, G.M. (1958) *The Society of Captives.* Princeton, NJ: Princeton University Press.

Sykes, G.M. and Matza, D. (1957) 'Techniques of Neutralization: a Theory of Delinquency', *American Sociological Review,* 22(6): 664–70.

Umbreit, M.S. (2000) 'The Restorative Justice and Mediation Collection: Executive Summary', Office for Victims of Crime Bulletin, July, US Department of Justice.

Umbreit, M.S. and Vos, B. (2000) 'Homicide Survivors Meet the Offender Prior to Execution. Restorative Justice through Dialogue', *Homicide Studies,* 4(1): 63–87.

Van Ness, D.W. (1990) 'Restorative Justice', in B. Galaway and J. Hudson (eds) *Criminal Justice, Restitution, and Reconciliation.* Monsey, NY: Criminal Justice Press.

Walmsley, R. (2002) *World Prison Population List* (3rd edn). London: Home Office.

Weitekamp, E.G.M. (1999) 'The History of Restorative Justice', in Bazemore, G. and Walgrave, L. (eds.) *Restorative Juvenile Justice: Repairing the Harm of Youth Crime.* Monsey, NY: Criminal Justice Press.

Weitekamp, E.G.M. (2000) 'Research on Victim–Offender Mediation. Findings and Needs for the Future', in the European Forum for Victim–Offender Mediation and Restorative Justice (ed.) *Victim–Offender Mediation in Europe.* Leuven: Leuven University Press.

Zehr, H. (1990) *Changing Lenses: A New Focus for Crime and Justice,* Scottsdale, PA: Herald Press.

Part IV

Positioning Restorative Justice in Different Countries

Chapter 12

The possibilities for restorative justice in Serbia

Vesna Nikolic-Ristanovic

Concerns about large-scale victimisation during the conflicts in the former Yugoslavia and about their negative impact for present and future relationships led to public discussion and some very precise steps in the direction of applying of restorative justice as one response to the atrocities and their denial. The main purpose of these efforts in some parts of the former Yugoslavia (including Serbia) was to try to break the cycle of violence and to establish long-term peace and normal relationships between different ethnic groups and political opponents. However, it seems there are many unresolved questions and misunderstandings about it and, in first place, about the role, purpose, tasks and organisation of the Truth and Reconciliation Commission (TRC).

One of main problems obviously lies in the specificity of the socio-historical context as well as in the very nature of conflicts and crimes committed in the former Yugoslavia. This makes it difficult to apply existing models of the TRC. This is further complicated in Serbia where, apart from the denial of crimes committed against members of other ethnic groups, the problem is related to a lack of international recognition of the crimes committed against both Serbs from Serbia (by both Kosovo Albanians and NATO) and Serbs from other parts of the former Yugoslavia (who are now living in Serbia as refugees and displaced persons). Also, there has been a large-scale cover-up of the crimes and human rights violations (within the Serbian community itself) committed against Milosevic's opponents during his dictatorship. Another problem is related to the history of the region, where a series of four national liberation wars (the last one was started in 1991 with the secession of Croatia and Slovenia from what was once Yugoslavia) were waged in the twentieth century. All four wars concerned political control of territory and, in all, civilians were victimised. Moreover, as pointed out by Pavkovic, 'the past cannot offer any model of reconciliation in the Balkans: no reconciliation among national groups has ever been attempted in this region. Thus we shall have to explore models of reconciliation successfully implemented elsewhere' (2000: 105).

The main aim of this chapter is to explore the possibilities for restorative justice in Serbia after Milosevic's rule and to suggest some recommendations for the TRC in Serbia. Thus, up-to-date experiences of restorative justice in societies that have experienced collective violence are reviewed, with a special emphasis on those that may be used as models in Serbia. Then, the characteristics and, especially, the specificity of collective victimisation and the socio-historical context of the former Yugoslavia and Serbia are analysed. An appropriate model of truth and reconciliation is then suggested. The chapter is based on research on war violence and human rights violations in the former Yugoslavia and Serbia I have been doing over the last 10 years, as well as on research on the application of restorative justice in contemporary societies affected by mass violence.

Denial and acknowledgement

Many authors have stressed the limited nature of legal truth and its inadequacy for restoring relationships between victims and offenders (i.e. between enemies) (Arendt 1994; Minow 1998; Cohen 1999; Osiel 1999). This has been known since Nuremberg. Cohen, for example, is perfectly right when he stresses that 'only cultural dummies would think of reading a legal verdict as a historical record of the event, let alone its context and why it happened'. 'Even a complete mosaic of legal truths', he continues, 'cannot create a full or shared knowledge of "what really happened", let alone *why* it happened' (1999: 1). Hence it is not surprising that, in the 1980s and 1990s transitions, many alternative ways of getting at the truth were used, some of which were new (e.g. truth and reconciliation commissions), while others were traditional (devising art and memorials to mark what happened to honour victims, and to communicate the aspiration of 'it will never happen again') or adaptations of existing models (opening up access to secret police files; removing political and military officials and civil servants from their posts and from public benefit rolls; publicising the names of victims and the names of offenders; securing reparations and apologies for victims; making available appropriate therapeutic services for anyone affected by the horrors; public educational programmes intended to convey what happened and to strengthen participatory democracy and human rights) (Minow 1998; Cohen 1999).

Truth and reconciliation commissions are needed in two different kinds of circumstances: the Latin American model where truth was, in many ways, hidden (literal denial – Cohen 2001: 104) and the South African model where, as in the former Yugoslavia, there were multiple truths/ interpretations/justifications of truth as a consequence of the denial of the crimes committed by one's own side/people (literal, interpretative and implicatory denial). A third set of circumstances leads to other forms of restorative justice, such as lustration, the opening of secret files, memorialisation, etc. For example, in post-communist countries the concept of 'cultural denial assumes that we can assess what millions of people actually do know despite their denials' (external knowledge – Cohen 2001: 160) as a consequence of difference/conflict between personal knowledge/experience and officially established truth that existed during communism.

On the other hand, bearing in mind an international role for the TRC, it is possible to differentiate between three models.[1] In El Salvador, for example, a wholly international TRC was established due to the severe polarisation of the society, that prevented this country from undertaking this on its own. More recently in Guatemala, however, it was determined this should be a local process with an international chairman. Finally, in South Africa, the process is wholly domestic but, none the less, one with the extensive involvement of the international community (in consultations, donations and in the provision of staff and technical assistance).

Different truth and reconciliation commissions have been launched in different ways: by the decisions of parliaments, presidents or executive bodies and by the efforts of non-governmental organisations.[2] However, only the South African TRC grew from extensive public debate and public involvement in its design (Minow 1998). As pointed out by Cohen, 'the Commission saw its role as establishing as "complete a picture as possible" of injustices committed in the past, coupled with a public, official acknowledgement of the untold suffering that resulted from these injustices' (2001: 227). The acknowledgement of denied sufferings was enabled by the public nature of the hearings and their intense media coverage, which offered a stage for people (victims and perpetrators) to tell stories that had never been told. The TRC has put an end to those denials because of the information it has received from the testimonies of 25,000 victims and over 7,000 perpetrators. As a result, the main achievement of the TRC was, on the one hand, the coming to a single truth, that replaced previous multiple truths, and on the other hand, the healing and restorative character of this truth (telling). Or, to borrow Cohen's words again: 'the narratives that face the past in order to go forward ... the truth goes beyond a factual record (recovery) towards interpretations (clarification) directed as self-healing, reconciliation and reparation. This requires the acknowledgement that everyone's suffering was real and worthy of attention' (2001: 228).

The most distinctive feature of TRCs, in comparison to prosecutions, is, obviously, their focus on victims and, in the case of the South African TRC, an emphasis on reconciliation and healing through the telling of the truth. However, the South African commission was both a victims' forum and an amnesty-type commission – which means it also granted amnesty to perpetrators of politically motivated crimes in exchange for the truth. The linking of truth with amnesty was seen by some as one of the features that made the South African TRC have 'far and away the greatest internal and international impact' in comparison to other commissions (Sachs 2001: 57). Amnesty was assumed to be the price paid for a relatively peaceful transition to full democracy: 'trading truth for amnesty, and amnesty for truth, the commission was intended to promote the gathering of facts and the basis for the society to move toward a strong democratic future ... It combined a notion of restorative justice with the search for truth' (Minow 1998: 55, 56). Thus the TRC was not a complete replacement for prosecutions and trial but, rather, a kind of institution with complementary, qualitatively different tasks. Those whose applications for amnesty were not accepted since they did not meet the TRC's criteria are left to face criminal prosecutions and civil suits. Also, national prosecutions did not stop and 'the information unearthed by the TRC may lead to some legal charges and trials, but its central direction, enhanced by its power to grant amnesty to perpetrators on the condition that they co-operate fully, moves away from prosecutions toward an ideal of restorative justice' (Minow 1998: 90). Thus, the TRC was committed to repairing the injustices and to restoring relationships and future behaviour and, in that respect, it also included economic and symbolic acts of reparations for the survivors and devastated communities (Minow 1998).

Serbia is not Africa, Africa is not Serbia

The South African model of a TRC is the best known and most often mentioned, both in Serbia and in other parts of the former Yugoslavia (e.g. Croatia and Bosnia) where the question of truth and reconciliation was recently raised and discussed. This it is not surprising, bearing in mind that the South African model is the best developed and most successful model in comparison to other TRCs. It is also possible to find similarities between the South African and the former Yugoslavian situation. For example, the scope of the crimes committed in the former Yugoslavia is such that, as in South Africa, it is difficult to believe that all perpetrators will ever be brought to justice. In addition, for reintegration and the establishment of long-term peace in the whole region, it is crucial that the truth about crimes is told by the victims – who must be encouraged to speak not only for the sake of justice but also for the sake of their own and society's healing through the breaking of the cycle of violence. However, there are significant differences between the political and socio-historical situations in South Africa and the former Yugoslavia (i.e. Serbia) as well, and these differences seem to have created serious problems in the application of some aspects of the African experience to Serbia.

There are three main specificities of the Serbian situation: an interconnection between the past and the present and a high level of complexity in both victimisation and in the contemporary political context (national, regional and international). All these specificities are also strongly embedded in the social context of the region (i.e. in the heritage of a similar cultural context and in historical relationships with other newly established countries of one former (common) country – Yugoslavia). All these specificities had a strong impact on both victimisation and its acknowledgement/denial during and after the wars. Thus, all these specificities have to be taken into account in the search for an appropriate model of truth and reconciliation in Serbia.

Past and present

As already mentioned, the region has a history of wars for national liberation, with people from different ethnic groups waging wars against each other. Moreover, the region also has a history of denials and multiple truths (each ethnic group passing its own truth from one generation to the next) as well as a history of the exploitation of (their own people's) victimisation. The implications of a lack of any attempt to obtain a single (common) truth and reconciliation were obvious in the recent wars, where past and present 'truths' were so interlaced that, as Ignatieff put it, 'reporters in the Balkan wars often observed that when told atrocity stories they were occasionally uncertain whether these stories had occurred yesterday or in 1941, or 1841, or 1441' (cited in Minow 1998: 14). The main danger, however, lies in the fact that these multiple (one sided, partial, which see only their own victims) truths may be best described as 'ghosts in a bottle' – ghosts who can always be taken out and used for the manipulation of national sentiments and the provocation of wars.[3] As Pavkovic (2000: 104) puts it:

> in seeking support from powers outside the region, each national liberation movement presented its 'own' national group(s) as an innocent victim or victims of its opponents' oppression or aggression. The need to aid innocent victims and to stop the aggression – forcefully and vividly presented in the sympathetic media - in all four series of wars justified the military support and, at times, intervention by powers outside the region in aid of national liberation movements of the recognised victims (members of the 'oppressor' national groups were almost invariably not recognised as victims).

A history of multiple (mutual) denials of crimes and sufferings is obviously a necessary precondition for the exploitation of victimisation (i.e. for the periodical reviving and manipulation of national sentiments). Thus, it is not surprising that it was used again as such in the 1990s when, as Blagojevic (2000) puts it, most of the people were not ready to cause the deliberate suffering of others so that it was necessary to prepare for the war by justifying the victimisation of others as a 'defence', as a 'just cause' and as 'inevitable'. This was only possible by identifying the other as different – as so dangerously different that his or her suffering became acceptable since this other became the source of fear for one's own security. By making the other 'dangerous', the authorities managed to convince the majority of the people that the war was inevitable as a defence.[4] This was achieved in all parts of the former Yugoslavia in an almost identical way – through public discourse broadcast by media and including what Blagojevic (2000) calls 'latent narratives about the victimisation of people of one's own ethnic group' or 'an ideology of victimisation'. Narratives about:

- the exclusivity of victimisation ('we are the only victims');
- the hierarchy of victimisation ('we are bigger victims');
- the justification for revenge ('we are giving them back what they did to us'); and
- the preventive aggression ('if we do not do that to them, they will do that to us').

Understanding the ideology of victimisation as a powerful way of distorting the truth and of the further use of this 'rump truth' for the production of fear and real victimisation (i.e. the promotion of hatred and war) is extremely important for understanding the post-conflict situation and the importance of restorative justice in all parts of the former Yugoslavia. As noted by Blagojevic, the above-mentioned narratives created an ideology of victimisation from which it was not possible to escape, since it represented the 'web of inconsistent, emotionally fuelled attitudes, which contain "pieces" of truth.' Thus it was extremely difficult to prove the opposite and 'by elimination of the other side's perspective, it was very easy for colluded sides to "produce" themselves as victims.' The fact that all sides (ethnic groups, nations) chose very different historical points for their 'proofs' resulted in the creation of many 'completely parallel para-realities' (Blagojevic 2000: 7).

An ideology of victimisation was a common denominator in all sides in the wars in the former Yugoslavia. Moreover, in a very similar way (i.e. as scapegoat theory – Blagojevic 2000: 7), the same ideology was used by the western media as well, which resulted in the promotion rather than the prevention of war (in spite of their claims of making victimisation visible and (*sic!*) 'democratically available' as 'CNN instant history') (Cohen 1999: 3). The methods used for the creation of images, which were shown world wide, were astonishingly similar to the methods used by the domestic media: the fragmentation of truth; the simplification of explanations as some sort of 'black/white' or bad/good guys theory; the invisibility of victims from the 'bad' side (identified as the aggressors and always Serbs) and the invisibility of perpetrators from the 'good' side (identified as the victims and not Serbs); the decontextualisation or false contextualisation of conflict; and the exploitation of victimisation to prepare the public for military intervention (justification for political and military decisions); etc.

Bearing in mind all those things so far mentioned in this chapter, putting together pieces of truth and creating a single (shared) truth instead of multiple (confronted) truths should be one of the priorities of the truth and reconciliation process in Serbia and other parts of the former Yugoslavia. This means the telling of what, why and how it happened must be done in an holistic way, not in a manner that represents only a fragmented reality (i.e. deconstructing the narratives of victimisation may be a good way of instigating an understanding of the sufferings of others). This should also help to narrow the social distance among people who were victimised in different ways, at different times and to different degrees, although in a similar context.

The complexity of victimisation

As mentioned above, although 'truth(s)' created by ideologists of victim-isation contained fragments of truth, they were far removed from the reality of victimisation in the former Yugoslavia (i.e. Serbia). In reality, victimisation was a much more complex phenomenon, with various manifestations and of still-unknown scope. In all the wars in the former Yugoslavia, victimisation was widespread and it affected most of the population, regardless of ethnic origin. Also, the victimisation was brutal, had serious, long-term consequences and multiple forms. Apart from immediate and direct victimisation, the people were affected by indirect, postponed, temporary or long-term victimisation. In addition, a great many people suffered secondary victimisation, especially in exile, when applying for asylum or humanitarian aid and when testifying before a court, etc. Moreover, women who had been raped suffered as a result of being rejected by their families, through repeated interrogations about their victimisation and because of inappropriate protection of their identity while, at the same time, their victimisation was exploited by the media or when they were testifying (Nikolic-Ristanovic 2000). All individual victims were also strongly embedded in a wider social context so that understanding of their victimisation was not possible without an understanding of the context.

However, apart from being victims of different forms of victimisation, the multiplicity of victimisation was connected to the fact that many people were victims of more than one war. This is especially true of refugees and displaced people now living in Serbia. Thus, the complex nature of the victimisation of the people of Serbia has the following implications for the truth and reconciliation process:

- Many were victimised by people, belonging to different communities and different ethnic groups (e.g. Serbian refuges from Croatia who later lived in both Bosnia and Kosovo).
- Many people were multiple victims who had memories of victimisation from previous wars (e.g. Serbs from Croatia and Bosnia now living in Serbia).
- There is no clear division within society (as is in South Africa) but, rather, many divisions within the same society (e.g. political and ethnic). There are divisions along ethnic lines which cross borders and prevent the establishment of normal relationships within ethnically mixed communities (e.g. conflicts between Serbs and Albanians in parts of Serbia close to Kosovo, and Serbs and Muslims in parts close to Bosnia).
- The entire population of Serbia (Serbs but also other ethnic groups such

as Roma, Albanians, Muslims, Hungarians, Croats, etc.) was a victim of both the immediate and the long-term consequences of NATO air strikes.

Therefore one of main differences in Serbia (compared to other present-day societies faced with collective violence) is that, as a nation, it should confront the violence within its own borders as well as the violence between its own and other ethnic groups/nations (including those of the former Yugoslavia and those of western countries – i.e. as a result of NATO bombing). This means that, within the population of Serbia, there are both victims of crimes and perpetrators of crimes so that the problem of the denial of crimes as committed by Serbs as well as the healing that will make visible the Serbian people's victimisation should be emphasised during a restorative process. As observed by Blagojevic and elaborated by myself elsewhere, it is a paradox that, in order to acknowledge the suffering of others, it is first necessary that people acknowledge their own suffering (Blagojevic 2000; Nikolic-Ristanovic 2000). As events in Serbia have confirmed this may be very important in the restorative process. For example, the efforts made by the independent Serbian television channel B-92 to show programmes about crimes committed by Serbs, as well as about the digging of mass graves in Belgrade, provoked criticisms and anger rather than helping to overcome denial. Although one could argue that this was the result of the high level of denial of crimes committed by Serbs in Serbia, as proven by a recent survey (Logar and Bogosavljevic 2001),[5] it might also be explained by the very complicated nature of victimisation in Serbia. Consequently, patience and the careful planning of the restorative process are needed (Dimitrijevic, cited in Matic 2000). The acknowledgement of the extremely high level of denial of the suffering the Serbs themselves experienced both locally and internationally is no less important than an acknowledgement of the denial of crimes committed by Serbs. Thus, it is not surprising that TV programmes about crimes committed by Serbs shown in Serbia were seen by many as anti-Serb propaganda rather than the truth (although the programmes were part of B-92's series of programmes called 'Truth, Reconciliation, Responsibility') (Matic 2001). To accept the truth about the crimes committed by Serbs, people have asked that similar programmes be shown about crimes committed in other parts of the former Yugoslavia as well (Matic 2001).

The political context

Political factors further complicate the potential for a restorative process. First, the end of the Kosovo conflict did not bring peace to Kosovo or the surrounding countries. On the contrary, NATO intervention and the peace-keeping mission could not prevent further hostilities breaking out, which spread to the southern part of Serbia and to Macedonia. As a result, conflicts are still going on, and Serbia is still full of refugees whose prospects of returning to their homes are not very good. Peace is also very fragile in Bosnia, where strong ethnic divisions still raise their voices in many issues (Ruxton, presentation at the round table 'Truth and Reconciliation ...' 4 February 2000).[6] Although reconciliation is often mentioned in all parts of the former Yugoslavia, it seems that, in reality, it is not familiar enough either to the political elite or to ordinary people.

However, apart from unfavourable political conditions, an additional complicating factor concerns the international community's pressure to prosecute war crimes. Although understandable, this pressure seems additionally to hinder already-uncertain, unsystematic attempts at restorative justice. This was particularly clear at the round table on truth and reconciliation held in Bosnia, where representatives of the International War Crime Tribunal for the former Yugoslavia expressed their concerns that the establishment of a TRC in Bosnia might counteract the work of the tribunal. Moreover, even those (such as Alex Boraine and Richard Goldstone) who did not have particular concerns regarding the establishment of a TRC were persistent in arguing that an amnesty model for the commission would not be applicable to the former Yugoslavia. The only argument for this they offered was that it would be in contradiction to the existence of the International War Crime Tribunal. In a kind of imperialistic way, they did not allow for a single possibility that amnesty can be discussed by the same people who are affected by the crimes. As a result of the slow prosecutions and the even slower trials, people in all parts of the former Yugoslavia are running out of time: new generations of children are growing up who are carrying with them all the traumas and denials as potential sources of new cycles of violence. As noted by Braithwaite (2001: 24):

> The illusion must be resisted that prosecuting as many war criminals as you can is an accomplishment of justice or deterrence ... Selective prosecution inevitably risks what happened in Argentina – 'sending the signal that whoever is not charged is innocent' – and that there can be impunity for collective and institutional aspects of responsibility that do not throw up soft individual targets.

Instead of a conclusion: the TRC in Serbia

In March 2001, the TRC was established by the President of the Federal

Republic of Yugoslavia, Vojislav Kostunica. Some 19 members were appointed and its main tasks are as following. To:

- organise research to recover records about the social, international and political conflicts that led to the war, as well as to ascertain the causal links between the events;
- inform the domestic and international community about its work and results;
- co-operate with and exchange experiences with similar commissions and bodies in other countries.

The president left it up to the commission to determine its own programme of activities, which is still to be done. However, right from the start the conception (or, better, lack of conception) of the commission's work met with vociferous critics, especially among ordinary people. As noted by Matic (2001), the commission was established unnecessarily quickly and without serious discussion that would have brought consensus about its work. This led to suspicions that the president's aim was to score political points rather than to contribute to truth and reconciliation.

Public discussion, which is absolutely necessary in the complicated political and victimisation context of the Federal Republic of Yugoslavia, started two months later, initiated by the independent media and society at large. First, in May 2001, an international conference on truth and reconciliation was organised in Belgrade by B-92. As a result, B-92 have run weekly programmes and have published books (in translation) about truth and reconciliation. Also, the Victimology Society of Serbia has published a series of articles about truth and reconciliation in its journal *Temida,* and it has started a project on reconciliation intended to generate public discussion about denial and the acknowledgement of truth. September 2001, the victimology society organised a panel about the role of women in the truth and reconciliation process in Serbia. Additionally, on a more or less regular basis, panels and debates about war crimes in the former Yugoslavia (which mainly address crimes committed by Serbs) are held in Belgrade and other cities.

It seems that in the Federal Republic of Yugoslavia as in Croatia and Bosnia, state bodies are still not ready or are too overburdened with other problems to think properly about 'remembering' or 'forgetting' the past (Cohen 1997: 7). Thus it is not surprising that ordinary people are more active. However, what is worrying in both Serbia and Bosnia is that there seems to be no real dialogue (i.e. a co-ordination of efforts between the authorities and society at large). What activities there are seem to go in parallel rather than being co-ordinated. The TRC has no members from non-governmental organisations nor any clear concept of co-operation (i.e. the exchange of information and experiences with other bodies). This is problematic, especially when one remembers that non-governmental organisations were the bodies that collected most of the victims' and, especially, women's accounts[7] about crimes in the former Yugoslavia. It is these bodies that have had more experience than any others in listening to, and otherwise supporting and empowering victims.

Bearing in mind the above analyses, I should like to stress eleven points I consider crucial for the successful implementation of a restorative process in Serbia:

1. Large and comprehensive discussions are necessary within all segments of society. These should be held for as long as necessary in order to come to a consensus about what kind of restorative justice is necessary to end the cycle of violence between both the Serbs themselves and between the Serbs and other nations/ethnic groups. Only when reconciliation through truth telling has become truly accepted by the population as a whole will it be possible to start the process itself.

2. The TRC has to be victim focused, and its main aim should be to serve as a forum for victims to speak as publicly as possible (but not necessarily if this might be damaging for them) about their experiences of war victimisation. Their testimonies, however, should not be limited to crimes (i.e. legal definitions of crimes) but they should, rather, be allowed to speak about whatever it was they experienced as victimisation,[8] as well as about the way they interpreted and felt about what was happening in their country. This approach may better distinguish the TRC from the courts and may also be a better way of understanding the broader context of victimisation. It also helps to deconstruct the ideologies that led to mass violence. It can also function for both the healing of the victims and the shaming of those who were responsible for the war, even though they did not commit crimes (e.g. the intellectuals who were the creators and executors of war propaganda).

3. The TRC should ensure gender-based crimes are included as a part of the testimonies. Women's experiences should be heard, whether they were direct or indirect (through the victimisation of those dear to them) victims.[9]

4. Victims should be given appropriate treatment, support and protection. For this purpose, specially trained personnel should be used for all, and for gender-sensitive testimonies in particular. Also, as in South

Africa, special protection should be assured for victims of gender-based violations.

5. Amnesty is a very sensible option but it should be the topic of serious discussion when less serious crimes, committed under coercion, are also in question (e.g. the policemen who beat opponents of Milosevic's regime or who were forced to commit crimes against Albanians in Kosovo).

6. Apart from victims' accounts, the TRC should offer a forum to make visible positive examples of those people whose activities helped assuage the sufferings of others (i.e. those who opposed violence and denial).

7. The restorative process has to be regional. TRC should be established in all countries of the former Yugoslavia, and they must co-operate in terms of the exchanging of victims' testimonies and their broadcasts, records, and publications, etc. Governments of the countries of the former Yugoslavia should allow the free exchange of this information so that people everywhere can learn about the crimes committed against their own people and by their own compatriots. Also, the victims need to be aware of the fact that their testimonies will be heard and acknowledged in areas where their perpetrators live.

8. The TRC should be a state body, but non-governmental organisations and experts should be represented as well. Strong co-operation needs to be established in all segments of the society, and particularly in society at large. International consultancy and other participation should also be welcomed.

9. If necessary, information collected by the TRC should be made available to the International Crime Tribunal for the former Yugoslavia and national courts. However, this should not be the main but, rather, a secondary purpose of the TRC.

10. The timescale for the TRC's work should be limited and should not exceed 2 years.

11. Apart from the TRC, other forms of restorative justice should be used, such as reparation, recording the names of the victims and offenders, education, memorials and lustration. [10]

Notes

1. Neil Kritz, in a presentation to the round table, 'Truth and Reconciliation: the Imperative of the Bosnian and Herzegovian Future', 4 February, 2000.
2. For example, a group of international non-governmental organisations joined

with Rwandan human rights organisations to create a short-lived commission for Rwanda.

3. Also, as Nada Golubovic, from the United Women's Association of Bosnia and Herzegovina said to the UN Congress on the Prevention of Crime: 'traumas are passed from generation to generation. Three generations ... left their traumas as heritage to their children, maintaining the same attitudes about it' (Wienna, cited in Braithwaite 2001: 5). It is not surprising, then, that, as stressed by Dizdarevic, 'the war started with looking for the missing persons from previous wars and the counting of mass graves and victims in them' (presentation at the round table 'Truth and Reconciliation ...' 4 February 2000).

4. Indeed, this was confirmed in my interviews with many people from different war-affected parts of the former Yugoslavia. Most ordinary people did have only one choice: to leave or stay to fight in order to protect themselves and their families (since, very soon, the danger was not fiction any more). Later on, leaving became more and more difficult, as did the possibility of making a choice.

5. However, this is not unique to Serbia. According to the findings of a survey presented at the international conference 'Forgiveness and reconciliation – the challenge to the Church and Society' held in Zagreb in 2001, a similar situation is found in Croatia (source: Radio B–92).

6. Perhaps the best illustration of this is the description given by Svetlana Broz at the round table 'Truth and Reconciliation ...' (4 February 2000): I am passing down the street every day in Dobrinja, which is a part of Sarajevo, which divides two idiotic formations that are called the entities. I keep doing it for seven months hoping that I will see at least one child who crossed the line and went to the other side to play with other children there. I have not seen it yet.'

7. In this respect, the situation in Serbia is much more favourable than in other war-affected societies (Mckay 2000: 565), since feminists and academics collected many women's stories both during and immediately after the wars (e.g. Nikolic-Ristanovic 1996; Bac and Dragulj 1997; Konstantinovic-Vilic 2000; Nikolic-Ristanovic 2000; Vidakovic 2000).

8. For example, the definition of 'victim' as accepted by the South African TRC may be useful here in that it includes relatives or dependants of the victims. It 'recognises that wives, mothers, sisters and daughters suffered violations of human rights even if they themselves were not the objects of torture' (Graybill 2001: 4). In this way it was realised, as shown earlier (Nikolic-Ristanovic 2000), that it is difficult to separate the psychological pain of a mother who watched the suffering of her child from the pain of the child itself.

9. It is important to note that the experiences of the TRC in South Africa show that, in spite of the fact that women were represented widely among those who testified, they tended to speak about the suffering of men close to them rather than about violence against themselves. Later, as a result of gender advocacy efforts, hearings specifically focused on women's own experiences were established (Minow 1998: 84; Mckay 2000: 568; Graybill 2001: 4).

10. The latter, as well as the opening of secret files, has already started.

References

Arendt, H. (1994) *Eichmann in Jerusalem: A Report on the Banality of Evil*. New York, NY: Penguin Books.

Bac, J. and Dragulj, E. (1997) *Pucanje duse* (*Shuttering soul*). Beograd: Helsinki odbor za ljudska prava u Srbiji and B–92.

Blagojevic, M. (2000) 'Prebrojavanje mrtvih tela: viktimizacija kao samoostvarujuce prorocanstvo' (Counting Dead Bodies: Victimisation as a Self-fulfilling Prophecy), *Temida*, 2: 5–11.

Braithwaite, J. (2001) 'Restorativna i reaktivna regulativa u cilju uspostavljanja mira u svetu' (Restorative and Responsive Regulation of World Peace), *Temida*, 2: 3–29.

Cohen, S. (1999) 'Introduction: Unspeakable Memories and Commensurable Laws.' Paper presented at the international conference 'Legal Institutions and Collective Memories', Onati, Spain, September.

Cohen, S. (2001) *States of Denial*. Cambridge: Polity Press.

Dimitrijevic, V. (2001) 'Izgledi za utvrdjivanje istine i postizanje pomirenja u Srbiji (Prospects for Truth Determination and Achieving Reconciliation in Serbia)', *Rec*, 62.8: 69–74.

Graybill, L. (2001) 'The Contribution of the Truth and Reconciliation Commission toward the Promotion of Women's Rights in South Africa', *Women's Studies International Forum*, 1: 1–10.

Konstantinovic-Vilic, S. (2000) 'Izbeglistvo kao trajna viktiizacija' (Exile as Long-term Victimisation'), *Temida*, 2: 91–101.

Logar, S. and Bogosavljevic, S. (2001) 'Vidjenje istine u Srbiji' (Looking at the Truth in Serbia'), *Rec*, 62(8): 7–34.

Matic, V. (2001) 'Odbacivanje istine' (Denial)', *Rec*, 62(8): 75–82.

Mckay, S. (2000) 'Gender Justice and Reconciliation', *Women's Studies International Forum*, 5: 561–70.

Minow, M. (1998) *Between Vengeance and Forgiveness*. Boston, MA: Beacon Press.

Nikolic-Ristanovic, V. (1996) *Zene Krajine: rat, egzodus i izbeglistvo* (Women of Krajina: War, Exodus and Exile). Beograd: Institut za kriminoloska i socioloska istrazivanja.

Nikolic-Ristanovic, V. (2000a) 'Zrtve ratova u bivsoj Jugoslaviji: obim, struktura i obrasci viktimizacije (Victims of Wars in the Former Yugoslavia: Scope, Structure and Patterns of Victimisation)', *Temida*, 2: 11–21.

Nikolic-Ristanovic, V. (ed.) (2000b) *Women, Violence and War*. Budapest and New York, NY: CEU Press.

Osiel, M. (1997) *Mass Atrocity, Collective Memory and the Law*. New Brunswick, NJ: Transaction Publishers.

Pavkovic, A. (2000) 'A Reconciliation Model for the Former Yugoslavia', *Peace Review*, 12(1): 103–9.

Round Table (2000) 'Truth and Reconciliation – the Imperative of the Bosnian and Herzegovian Future', transcript of the presentations, February.

Sachs, A. (2001) 'Truth and Reconciliation: the South African Experience' *Rec*, 62(8): 53–67.

Vidakovic, I. (2000) 'Strategije osnazivanja zena u posleratnom perodu' (Strategies for Empowering Women in the Postwar period)', *Temida*, 2: 55–9.

Chapter 13

Alternative practices for juvenile justice in Flanders (Belgium): the case for mediation

Mia Claes, Frans Spiesschaert, Catherine Van Dijk,
Inge Vanfraechem and Sigrid Van Grunderbeeck

Background

The current law regarding juvenile justice

From the beginning of the twentieth century, as a result of the Children's Act 1912 (i.e. the law concerning juvenile justice), the underlying premise of the Belgian juvenile justice system has been that children do not need punishing but, rather, protecting and (re)educating. As a consequence, the approach to juvenile offending has been similar to the approach to the problem of neglect. In both cases Youth Court judges could resort to almost identical measures. Of all countries that have a judicial reaction to juvenile crime, Belgium has always had a strong tendency to rely on welfare programmes (Walgrave *et al.* 1998). Although there was early criticism of this approach[1] the tradition of rehabilitation was reaffirmed by the Youth Protection Act 1965. After the restructuring of Belgium as a federal state, however, efforts were made to address this problem. An Act was passed in 1994 intended to improve the legal safeguards of young people, and the co-ordinated decrees of the Flemish Community in 1990 aimed at making a clear distinction between social assistance for minors with educational needs and the judicial reaction to juvenile crime. However, the dominant philosophy of the juvenile system still remains one of protection and rehabilitation.

Federalisation transformed Belgium into an entity with several communities and regions. This restructuring has led to a situation in which the judicial reaction to juvenile offending remains a federal matter but the execution of measures ordered by the juvenile court has now become a community matter. In practice, this division of responsibilities has led to a certain amount of confusion but, in theory, at least, it has not changed anything to do with the welfare of young offenders.

This welfare approach has a number of distinctive characteristics. For example, the nature and duration of the social reaction to an offence committed by a young person are not dictated by the seriousness of the crime but by the personal qualities of the young person concerned and the circumstances in which he or she grew up. The objective of this intervention is normalisation (i.e. the young person's character and education opportunity). The means used for this are social assistance and (re)education, and the duration of the intervention is completely dependent on the achievement of these objectives. This often led to lengthy and far-reaching measures that, in the case of putting a young person in care, were very expensive for the community. The young people themselves usually do not experience these interventions as assistance but, rather, as punishment – punishment that is often out of proportion to the committed crime. It is therefore not surprising that great doubts have arisen as to whether these interventions produce the intended effects. As early as the 1970s there was discussion about *Le pouvoir mystificateur du language* ('The mystifying power of language') (see Van De Kerchove 1976–7). The demand for greater clarity gradually became stronger. So far, the Commission Cornelis (which was established with the intention of reforming the juvenile justice system and which has suggested more instructive sanctions) and the report by Walgrave (that has a restorative justice orientation) have not led to changes within the legal framework. In July 2001, a bill was introduced that does not contain a model for juvenile offending but that does try to provide the most appropriate answers for each particular situation and with the utmost respect for the rights of the young person.[2]

This intense discussion has promulgated many models about youth crime and how to deal with it, and a rehabilitative and protective discourse has alternated with more repressive and punitive arguments. This debate has been cross-cut by advocates of constructive yet still educationally orientated sanctions that respect the legal safeguards of young people and, more recently, by advocates of restorative justice. The latter model (which has been promoted as a third line) focuses on the harm caused rather than the offence or the offender. According to this model, the young person does not need to be punished or re-educated but should take responsibility for, and restore the damage caused by, his or her actions. This theoretical shift led to a two-track policy that is also encountered in the adult judicial system: alternative forms of punishment for minor offences but a firm approach for serious offenders and recidivists[3] (Eliaerts and Vansteenkiste 1995).

Children are responsible human beings

Eighteenth-century rationalism promoted a view of a better future for man and society and, within this view, children were considered qualitatively different from adults (Skolnick 1973). Adults:

- were considered to be rational people, whereas children were irrational, emotional beings;
- could think in abstract terms, whereas children thought in concrete terms;
- were sexual beings, but children were asexual;
- had a sense of responsibility, worked and were productive, whereas children were irresponsible, played and were non-productive.

Children's individuality was expressed in terms of not yet being able to do what adults are/can do. This not-yet-being status was considered the most important characteristic of children (Verhellen 1996, 2000) and thus, until they became adults, children spent their time in separate institutions where they were protected, taken care of, educated and moulded. Consequently, as children were regarded as irresponsible beings, the law did not punish them for actions that were considered to be criminal offences but, instead, imposed protective measures, as mentioned above. Towards the end of the twentieth century, this view of children's lack of self-determination came under heavy criticism. In particular the concept of protection often appeared to have other objectives than facilitating young people to develop (Maes 1986). Moreover, it became clear that protection ignores young people's capacities, denying them the right to make their own choices and, therefore, often doing them more harm than good (Verhellen 2000). This view of children's lack of self-determination was sharply criticised, especially from the perspective of children's rights (Mortier 1998); the argument that children are incompetent, and therefore incapable of self-determination, was considered to be irrelevant, invalid and even incorrect (Verhellen 2000). However, if children are not as incompetent as was assumed, they should be able to take responsibility for their behaviour and account for their actions if they commit a crime. This latter is a fundamental premise of the restorative justice view of juvenile offending.

A growing concern for the needs of the victim

Growing concern for the needs of the victim has emerged worldwide and is reflected in initiatives at the level of the United Nations and the Council of Europe. In Belgium, especially towards the end of the last century, several initiatives were taken that aimed at improving the position of victims of crime. In 1994, in response to a request from a plenary meeting of the Chamber of Deputies, the federal government organised a National Forum for Victim Policy. This forum was set up to establish guidelines for the general co-ordination of all bodies involved in helping victims. This increased focus on the victim had resulted in several initiatives aimed at helping victims – by the police and judicial authorities as well as by several public welfare agencies. Local councils for victim policy have now been established by the Minister of Justice in every juridical district.

At the present time, the following trends can be distinguished in this increased focus on the victim:

- Helping victims not only involves victims' welfare and health but should also incudes criminal policy-making and safety issues.
- The rights of the victim are equally as important as the rights of the offender.
- In all actions regarding victims, one should be on the alert for the danger of secondary victimisation.
- Victims have the right to material and immaterial restoration.

Although this increased focus on the victim has resulted in the extension of victims' rights (regulated by law), these principles appear not always to be realised successfully in day-to-day practice.

A growing concern for the rights of juvenile offenders

In Belgium, where children were dealt with outside the law for adults, there were virtually no safeguards to protect young people's rights. A child who had committed a crime should not be punished but, rather, 'guided' and 'treated'. Protective measures were therefore imposed because children who offended were considered to be in a state 'dangerous' to their health, security and morality. The appropriate administration of justice (including such things as the legality principle, the subsidiarity principle and the principle of the presumption of innocence) was either weakly upheld or even completely absent. Moreover, the law provided a young person accused of a crime only limited legal assistance. If a young person did receive assistance, his or her lawyer often considered it his or her duty to seek 'the best interests' of the young person rather than to express the young person's 'opinions'.

As a result of the Beijing Rules and the International Convention on the Rights of the Child, and also because Belgium was sentenced at the European court of Human Rights as a consequence of the Bouamar case, in 1994 the Belgian legislation was amended and an important step was made towards more respect for the legal safeguards of young people. Moreover, the lawyers created a system in the different jurisdictions whereby all young people who appear before the Youth Court are guaranteed legal assistance. This increased focus on young people's rights has led to a call for more clarity and less mystification. Nevertheless, in practice, there is still little enthusiasm for this rough form of juvenile criminal justice. There is still a call for 'meaningful sanctions', where 'sanctions' implies an important educational component. Practical experiments concerning alternative sanctions had already been established in the mid-1980s as a result of these developments (Cappelaere *et al.* 1987).

The restructuring of legal practice

When the protectionist model was at the forefront of the law concerning juvenile justice, there was a vast increase in case load. The number of juvenile files at the level of the public prosecutor increased considerably, and the number of files in which the Youth Court imposed measures also increased to a considerable extent. It was common for people to talk about the 'problematic interventionist character' of juvenile criminal law.[4] In the 1970s the government budget for juvenile justice doubled, and more than 90% of these resources were spent on financing placements. This dissatisfaction gradually increased, not only because of the expense of placements but also because the point of imposing such measures was increasingly questioned. As of 1983, therefore, the Government of the Flemish Communities attempted to reorganise the placement system and to offer a more diversified range of measures. Partly as a result of these factors, initiatives were taken in Flanders to set up mediation services, educational projects and community service.

Experiments in juvenile justice

Although the new bill is still in preparation, experiments have already begun with alternatives to more traditional measures, such as placements and reprimands. However, these experiments often create a feeling of insecurity, especially at the level of the public prosecutor, but problems also occur when they are implemented by the Youth Court. Article 37 of the Youth Protection Act, 1965 provides a legal basis for 'community service and educational projects', but the practical execution and interpretation of this provision vary. Within this provision, the elements of protection, sanctions and restoration are interwoven, and so the emphasis placed on these different elements often depends on the case in question and the personal beliefs of the lawyers involved. This causes legal uncertainty and the unequal treatment of young offenders. Apart from these legal problems, community service and educational projects have experienced difficulties as a result of the rapid and unstructured expansion of these measures and because of the diverse and complex regulatory and funding structures within which they operate.

However, victim–offender mediation experiments have not suffered from such problems as these have been implemented in a more central, structured way. Mediation experiments also have a clear theoretical (i.e. restorative) focus. Their position within the legal system is, however, problematic since they do not operate within an established regulatory framework.

The academic world

Stimulated by the world of academia, there has been growing interest in restorative justice in Flanders. Empirical, theoretical and ethical studies have made an impact on the practical implementation of justice as well as on policy-making in that they have shown how restorative justice can be a valuable alternative to the traditional legal system – an alternative that can offer a way out of the current deadlock in the debate about the reform of juvenile justice. Flanders has also provided international input into the debate about juvenile justice through its membership of (and active participation in) several international forums, such as the International Network for Research on Restorative Justice for Juveniles (with Lode Walgrave of the K.U. Leuven as chairman) and the European Forum (with Ivo Aertsen, also of the K.U. Leuven, as chairman), and through its active participation in several international conferences.

Three restorative initiatives with the Flemish Community

Community service and educational projects

The Youth Protection Act 1965 (art. 37.2) gives judges the power to impose community service and educational projects on young offenders. However, it was not until the end of the 1980s that such measures were first systematically imposed in Flanders (Van Hoof 1996–7).

Community service in Flanders follows the example of the English community service order (CSO). The first experiments began with a pilot project at the Youth Court in Mechelen, which was followed by further initiatives in other districts. In some districts, however, community service has, only recently been established, often in support of other forms of settlement. Some nine community service schemes now operate in Flanders.

Educational projects have evolved in much the same way. The 'intermediate treatment' projects introduced by the UK's Children and Young Persons Act 1969 were an important source of inspiration for the Flemish educational projects. Much of the current expertise in Flanders also originated in the Netherlands – such as the Slachtoffer in Beeld ('Bringing the victim into perspective' project) and social skills training. Apart from these, projects on 'dealing with aggression' and 'coping with drugs are offered, along with coping with drugs' general educational programmes. The Flemish government currently supports some ten services in different county court districts in order to organise such educational projects.

As a result of the 1994 'Global Plan', community service and educational projects have developed rapidly. The Global Plan has enabled municipalities to play a key role in organising and supporting the application of alternative sanctions (Wilderiane and Brutsaert 1997). Of the four alternative measures introduced by the Global Plan, three focus on adults and one on young people. There are now some 25 community service schemes. Organisations of all kinds (social work centres, municipalities, treatment centres for drug addicts, etc.) have also developed various educational projects. The big problem with such schemes is that they are diversionary measures only taken at the level of the public prosecutor. This poses several problems concerning the legal safeguards (especially the presumption of innocence) of minors, and a judgment of the Court of Cassation in 1997 confirmed the illegal nature of this practice (Geudens and Walgrave 1996; Eliaerts *et al*. 1997.

Although, in practice community service means the same thing in nearly every district (i.e. providing unpaid labour for a public or non-profit-making organisation), there are considerable differences in the organisation, funding, legal procedures, etc., involved in the schemes. Although community service is prescribed in the law on juvenile justice, it is still considered to be an alternative measure, often imposed by judges as a substitute for another sanction, such as a placement. Educational projects are also considered an alternative to placements. As their name suggests, educational projects have a pedagogical or rehabilitative orientation, and they are based on the principles of protection enshrined in the 1965 Act. Because of their judicial context, these programmes may also contain punitive measures (their compulsory nature, the giving up of spare time, 'enforced engagement', etc.). These pedagogical, punitive and restorative features vary from project to project and according to the methods used to implement them.

Victim – offender mediation

History and development
The first Flemish mediation initiative for young people was established by Oikoten – a youth-care agency operating in Leuven. Oikoten initiated a series of experiments involving community service for less problematic young offenders, in co-operation with the office of the public prosecutor and Youth Court judges. Several questions were raised about this community service initiative concerning its lack of regard of the young person's responsibility for his or her crime and the total absence of the victim of the crime.

Therefore, from the end of 1987, victims were systematically contacted in all cases of community service. The victims who participated in the scheme in turn effected a change in the mindset of Oikoten social workers. The social workers were forced to abandon their offender-biased approach as victims refused to co-operate with educational goals aimed solely at the welfare of the offender. Instead, they insisted on the full recognition of their victimisation. Observation also revealed that offenders experienced a direct meeting with their victims as a logical and necessary (but not easy) step towards fulfilling their own fundamental needs for taking responsibility for their crimes and for offering apologies. Thus the Oikoten programme evolved from one of pure community service to one where the interests of the victim were incorporated more fully.

The next step (in 1991) was the creation of a compensation fund. This idea originated from the finding that young people often do not have the financial means to pay for the damage done. To encourage young people to take responsibility for their offences and to restore their credibility in the eyes of themselves, their parents and their victims, a method for repairing the damage done to the victim and, simultaneously, to the community was established. When a young offender is not able to restore his or her victim financially, he or she performs a number of hours of volunteer work for a humanitarian, cultural or social organisation. In exchange for this work, the young offender is paid by the fund and, with these earnings, the victim is indemnified. The type of volunteer work is also discussed with the victim. The fund was initially sponsored privately and managed by Oikoten but, in October 1997, it was taken over by the Province of Flemish Brahant through Leuven Mediation Service.

Currently, there are three projects within the Leuven Mediation Service:

1. Mediation for juveniles (the Oikoten project), which offers mediation among juvenile offenders, their parents and the victims.
2. Mediation for redress, which offers mediation between adult offenders and their victims in more serious cases where the public prosecutor has decided to prosecute whatever the outcome of the mediation.
3. Mediation at the police stage, which offers mediation between adult offenders and their victims in cases of minor offences. Under this programme, the police rather than the public prosecutor deliver cases for mediation. However, the public prosecutor is kept informed of the mediation attempt.

For a long time Leuven was the only jurisdiction in Flanders that organised an offender–victim mediation service for young offenders. However, this was followed in 1995 with the establishment of such a service in Brussels.

In March 1999, the Flemish Parliament voted for a resolution that would mean the implementation of such schemes throughout the Flemish Community. Oikoten was given the mandate to implement these schemes and, by the end of 2000, mediation services for young offenders had been initiated in ten Flemish jurisdictions. The thoroughness of the implementation of these schemes has meant that high-quality mediation has been offered right from the start. By means of induction courses for new mediators, the practical experience of Oikoten (which has been built up over many years) was shared among the new mediation services. These courses have been supplemented with monthly training days.

Structure

As noted above, the model used for implementing the programme was based on the Leuven juvenile mediation project and the Leuven mediation service. Under this model, a neutral third party guides the communication process among a young offender, his or her parents and the victim(s) with the purpose of restoring the mental and material harm caused to the victim. If possible, a wider social network is also involved. Cases are referred by the public prosecutor as well by the Youth Court judges. The seriousness of the crime and the fact that a case has been summoned before the court do not weigh against a case being offered for mediation. Mediation is offered to all those cases where certain criteria are met – i.e. the offender must be known and must have admitted to the offence, all information relating to the offence must have been collected and there must be an identifiable victim who has suffered material or immaterial harm. The mediator is guided by the principles of neutrality, voluntariness and confidentiality.

Essential to mediation is its voluntary nature – the victim and offender must decide freely whether or not to start the mediation process with a view to restoring the consequences of the crime. This voluntariness also implies that, at each stage of the process the victim and offender still have the opportunity to end the mediation. While this voluntary aspect of the mediation process requires little explanation with regard to the victim, it is essential the offender participates completely of his or her own free will. In doing so the offender acknowledges that he or she considers it important to take responsibility for the offence committed, which demonstrates to the victim that the offender genuinely wishes to restore the consequences of his or her criminal behaviour. Voluntariness also means the judicial authorities retain their autonomy in decision-making: they are free to choose whether or not they should take into account the outcome of the mediation. However, it often happens that, in cases of successful mediation, they deem further legal measures no longer necessary. Voluntariness, therefore, makes it imperative that mediation remains legal outside formal procedures. Nevertheless, experience has shown that mediation schemes should come under the aegis of a judicial authority – usually the office of the public prosecutor but sometimes a Youth Court judge.

The mediation schemes are organised in the same way in each jurisdiction. A distinct steering group brings together the parties involved in the mediation process. Steering groups comprise representatives of the office of the public prosecutor, the Youth Court, the social services of the Flemish Community at the Youth Court, the bar, the police, the para-judicial field (victim support, the House of Justice, etc.), the Centre for General Welfare Work (which offers services to help offenders and victims), Oikoten and the mediation service itself. Steering groups operate at the local level and offer advice about specific problems that might arise. They oversee the mediation process, ensuring all the information needed for a particular case is available to all the parties involved. Hence steering groups broaden the scope to young offender mediation programmes so that they encompass not only the judiciary but also the social welfare sector (Leynen 1998–9).

Steering groups deal with both adult and young offender mediation schemes as victims would not be much helped by an approach that distinguished between adults and juveniles. Besides the steering group, the support team is of great importance. This team assists in the mediation of individual cases and comprises a number of external experts (e.g. representatives of social welfare organisations or members of the bar).

A uniformity of approach is vitally important if equality and full and legal protection are to be ensured. It is for this reason that there is one mediation service per district. Where a district has more than one service, these are co-ordinated as much as possible. Judicial districts were deliberately chosen as the units of operation as these are of a workable size and are, indeed, the areas within which the various judicial institutions operate. To ensure the standardisation of mediation programmes and co-operation between all the parties involved throughout the whole of Flanders, all procedures and arrangements are in written form so that these can be consulted if there is a dispute or evaluated as and when necessary.

Some reflections on mediation schemes for young offenders

Based on practical work with mediation schemes for young offenders, Claes (2001) offers the following comments:

- Combining punitive sanctions with mediation runs the risk of losing sight of the essence of restorative justice – i.e. giving all the parties involved the opportunity to take a conflict into their own hands (Christie 1977). While there are serious offences for which an immediate intervention is justified, the judicial system should create the space for the parties to a conflict to resolve the matter themselves. Imposing sanctions at the same time as seeking mediation can be confusing.
- When only one young offender involved in a group offence is offered mediation, this can lead to a fragmented approach. This can happen in districts that have several Youth Court judges, who do not look at the case as a whole but deal only with the young person under their authority. It also occurs when young offenders party to one crime live in different districts.
- There can be differences in procedure, vision and approach. Some services operate mainly at the level of the public prosecutor, others at court level. Some are offender focused – more concerned with the pedagogical aspects of mediation – and so are less victim orientated. The methods used, therefore, differ considerably.
- Lawyers appeared to be the most critical of the partners, especially in discussions concerning draft procedures for mediation programmes. Lawyers do not always accept the essence of mediation and sometimes consider it an intrusion. However, a great many lawyers co-operate very positively and have made valuable contributions to the development of the scheme.
- In spite of the attempts to come to a single protocol for all districts, this has not yet been achieved. In most districts, the partners are working without formal procedures. In one district, the absence of a legal framework has prevented the public prosecutor from taking part in that district's programme.

- When the Flemish government released funds for local initiatives, very few guidelines were issued. While the initiatives were to be orientated towards restrictions, no clear definitions were provided. The mandate given to Oikoten to implement the schemes was never clarified, and so no formal links were established between the implementers of the schemes and the new services. This led to great diversity and tension. While implementers strove for co-ordination, uniformity and clarity, this was not supported by official policy.
- Tensions can arise when there is more than one service in the same district. These tensions concern such matters as autonomy, local political interest and competition.
- The Flemish Community considers itself responsible for young offender mediation, whereas the Federal Ministry of Justice considers itself responsible for adult mediation. Mediation, in fact, involves both justice and assistance and presupposes a middle ground between the two. Mediation solely under the guidance of the Flemish Community runs the risk of ignoring the judiciary system. Under the aegis of the Ministry of Justice, on the other hand, mediation runs the risk of becoming a sanction, with a focus on the judiciary, rather than on welfare and assistance. Interdepartmental dialogue and joint financing are therefore necessary to achieve the middle ground between justice and welfare. At the present, mediation for young offenders is in the hands of the Special Youth Care Department. This, too, has raised questions. Mediation involves both the victim *and* the offender, whereas youth care involves only the young offender. Mediation should therefore come under general welfare, where assistance is available to the victim as well.
- Recent policy decisions have separated juvenile mediation from adult mediation (i.e. mediation for redress). While mediation for redress is part of a much wider, international restorative justice movement, there is a risk juvenile mediation will be isolated once more, stuck in a purely pedagogical context. This decoupling of the two forms of mediation has thrown both programmes back into their own territories. As a result there have been immediate repercussions on both programmes. In some districts mediation has become simply one alternative out of many forms of settlement, such as community service and educational projects.

Family group conferences

A family group conference is a meeting between the offender and his or her network, the victim and his and her network and the police (Walgrave

2000b). A neutral facilitator oversees the meeting. In 1989, family group conferences were introduced into New Zealand as a result of the Young Persons and Children Act. Consequently, almost all young offenders now attend family group conferences. Different versions of family group conferences have since been adopted by many countries, tailored to meet local needs.

Experiments with family group conferences began in Flanders in December 2000. This was the result of a process of preparation begun in 1999 when Lode Walgrave and two Youth Court judges[5] visited New Zealand to study the programme in place there. In the following months, several New Zealand mediation services were contacted with a view to introducing family group conferences into Flanders. Allan MacRae, the well-known New Zealand facilitator, ran three-week training courses for mediators, and contact was made with lawyers, Youth Court judges, public prosecutors, social services and the police. After much discussion, a model suitable for Belgium was established (Vanfraechem and Harris 2001). Five Flemish jurisdictions[6] participate in using the scheme, using this model as the basis but adapting it slightly to meet local customs and needs. The programme started on 1 December 2000 and is being evaluated scientifically.

It is the duty of the Youth Court judge to refer cases to conferences. For a case to go to a conference, two conditions must be met: the case must be serious and the young offender must not deny the facts of the case. If the young person denies the facts of the case, traditional procedures will be followed.

Research currently underway aims to investigate whether conferencing can be introduced into the existing juvenile justice system: whether the parties involved are satisfied; whether the rights of the parties involved are respected; whether the young offender's network takes part in the process; and whether the recidivism rate is affected. A final report was submitted to the Flemish Community in November 2002. Referrals started slowly so that, in September 2001, only six conferences had been held and four were in preparation. This slow start has meant the programme has developed carefully but may lead to too few conferences for the purposes of quantitative evaluation. Special efforts are now being made to persuade judges to refer more cases.

What next?

The question remains as to what sort of support should be given to young offender mediation projects and as to what sort of organisational structure they require. A need has been identified for the structural integration of juvenile and adult mediation and, possibly, for a national co-ordinating body. Since the decision was taken to separate juvenile mediation from adult mediation, Oikoten's mandate has been transferred to a newly created organisation, unofficially called the 'Support Platform for Special Youth Care'. This platform comprises about 50 special youth care services. The government of the Flemish Community regards this structure as a means of implementing the Flemish parliamentary resolution of 1999. This platform will provide support for the restorative settlement of youth offending, and community service, mediation, educational projects and (in the future) family group conferences are all on its agenda. The platform is subsidised by the Flemish Community's Department of Special Youth Care.

However, some questions remain unanswered. The lack of a clear distinction between the Flemish Community and the federal state makes it difficult to delineate whom the support platform should work for: all the restorative-justice-orientated projects subsidised by the Flemish Community or the numerous projects and services subsidised by the federal government? For instance, there are currently 35 projects that involve community service but only eight of those are subsidised by the community government. In a recent agreement made between the federal minister and the Flemish minister, a number of proposals were put forward to promote more systematic 'cross-border' dialogue.

At the moment all mediation projects operate on a year-by-year basis but, in the future they should be given a more definitive status and be subjected to clearer regulations.

Notes

1. In 1937, A. Racine published an article that addressed the problem of the legal safeguards of minors.
2. 'Voorontwerp van wet van de Minister van Justitie Marc Verwilghen houdende antwoorden op delinquent gedrag door minderjarigen, 1 juli 2001', *TJK*, 2(4): 1–57.
3. The alternative approach runs the risk of net widening and a lack of legal safeguards; the repressive approach, on the other hand, could compromise the juvenile system of justice by redirecting young people towards the adult system of justice.
4. Verhellen (1996: 373) writes: 'The money so to speak flowed to a swelling army of "rubbish-cleaners" instead of to the down-hearted, small group of primary workers, who had to work preventively according to the law, by "placement". The actual use of the many placements therefore shifted from a problem-solving intervention for the benefit of the child to a problem-shifting activity for the benefit of the institutions and to the disadvantage of the child. This

apparently well concealed meaning of placement was actually never thoroughly recognised.'
5. Judges Raes and Van de Vynckel.
6. Antwerp, Brussels, Hasselt, Leuven and Tongeren.

References

Aertsen, I. (2000) 'Victim–Offender Mediation in Belgium', in European Forum for Victim–Offender Mediation and Restorative Justice (ed.) *Victim–Offender Mediation in Europe. Making Restorative Justice Work.* Leuven: University Press.

Bazemore, G. and Walgrave, L (1999). 'Restorative Juvenile Justice: in Search of Fundamentals and an Outline for Systemic Reform', in G. Bazemore and I. Walgrave (eds) *Restorative Juvenile Justice: Repairing the Harm of Youth Crime.* Monsey, NY: Criminal Justice Press.

Cappelaere, G. Eliaerts, C. and Verhellen, E. (1987) *Alternatieve sanctionering voor jongeren.* Ghent Research and Documentation Centre for Children's Rights, Ghent University.

Christie, N. (1977) 'Conflicts as Property', *British Journal of Criminology*, 17(1): 1–19.

Claes, M. (1998) 'The Juvenile Mediation Project in Leuven (Belgium)', in L. Walgrave (ed.) *Restorative Justice for Juveniles. Potentialities, Risks and Problems.* Leuven: Leuven University Press.

Claes, M. (2001) 'Implementation and Development of Mediation for Juveniles in Flanders (Belgium). A Report Based on Practical Experiences.' Paper presented at the international conference 'Positioning Restorative Justice', Leuven, 16–19 September.

Eliaerts, C. Dumortier, E. and Vanderhaegen, R. (1997) 'Critical Assessment of Community Service and Mediation for Juvenile Offenders in Brussels', in L. Walgrave (ed.) *Restorative Justice for Juveniles. Potentialities, Risks and Problems.* Leuven: Leuven University Press.

Eliaerts, C. and Vansteenkiste, P. (1995) *Proceswaarborgen voo minderjarigen en alternatieve procedures bij de afhandeling van jeugddelinquentie.* Programma Burger en Rechtsbescherming, Federal Services for Scientific, Technical and Cultural Affairs.

Geudens, H. and Walgrave, L. (1994) *'Community Service as a Sanction of Restorative Juvenile Justice. A European Approach.'* Paper presented at the annual meeting of the American Society of Criminology, Miami, November.

Geudens, H. and Walgrave, L. (1996) 'De toepassing van de gemeenschapsdienst door de Belgische Jeugdrechtbanken', *Panopticon*, 5: 499–520.

Leynen, G. (1998–9) 'De betekenis van een Samenwerkingsverband in de aanpak van Criminaliteit. De bemiddelingsdienst van het arrondissement Leuven als praktijkvoorbeeld.' Unpublished thesis, Catholic University of Leuven.

Maes, C. (1986) 'Wet betreffende de jeugdbescherming of betreffende de bescherming van de maatschappij tegen deviante of delinquente jeugd?', *Panopticon*, 36–53.

Marshall, T.E. (1996) 'The Evolution of Restorative Justice in Britain', *European*

Journal of Criminal Policy and Research, 4(4): 21–43.

Mortier, F. (1998) 'Rationality and Competence to Decide in Children', in E. Verhellen (ed.) *Understanding Children's Rights. Ghent Papers on Children's Rights* 3. Ghent: Children's Rights Centre.

Racine, A. (1937) 'Maintien ou abandon de la règle "Nulla poena, nullem crimen sine lege" dans les jurisdictions pour enfants', *Revue de Droit pénal et de Criminologie*, 149–65.

Skolnick, A. (1973) *The Intimate Environment: Exploring Marriage and the Family*. Boston, MA, and Toronto: Little, Brown & Co.

Van De Kerchover, M. (1976) 'Des mesures répressives aux mesures de sûreté et de protection. Réflexions sur le pouvoir mystificateur du langage', *Revue de Droit pénal et de Criminologie*, 4: 245–79.

Van der Laan, P. (1991) *Experimenten met alternatieve sancties voor jeugdigen*. Arnhem: Gouda Quint.

Van Der Minne-Frank, T. (1983) 'Alternatieve Sancties voor minderjarigen', *JV* 5: 5–42.

Vanfraechem, I. and Harris, N. (2001) 'Family Group Conferences in Belgium.' Paper presented at the conference of the International Association for Research into Juvenile Criminology, Greifswald, Germany, June.

Van Garsse, L. (1997) 'Jeugdsanctierecht en bemiddeling' *Agora*, 2: 55–66.

Van Hoof, K. (1996–7) 'Dienstverlening en vorming als gerechtelijk antwoord op jeugdcriminaliteiter.' Unpublished thesis, Catholic University, Leuven.

Verhellen, E. (1979) *Experiment Dendermonde, final report*. Ghent: Department for Youth Welfare and Adult Education, Ghent University.

Verhellen, E. (1996) *Jeugdbeschermingsrecht*. Ghent: Mys & Breesch.

Verhellen, E. (2000) *Verdrag inzake de Rechten van het Kind*. Leuven and Apeldoorn: Garant.

Walgrave, L. (1999) 'Community Service as a Cornerstone of a Systemic Restorative Response to (Juvenile) Crime,' in G. Bazemore and L. Walgrave (eds) *Restorative Juvenile Justice: Repairing the Harm of Youth Crime*. Monsey, NY: Criminal Justice Press.

Walgrave, L. (2000a) *Met het oog op herstel. Bakens voor een constructief jeugdsanctierecht. Samenleving, Criminaliteit & Strafrechtspleging* 18. Leuven: Leuven University Press.

Walgrave, L. (2000b) 'Naar een experiment met Herstelgericht Groepsoverleg (family group conference) in Vlaanderen. Stand van zaken.' Unpublished.

Walgrave, L., Berx, E., Poels, V. and Vettenburg, N. (1998) 'Belgium', in J. Mehlbey and L. Walgrave (eds) *Confronting Youth in Europe. Juvenile Crime and Juvenile Justice*. Kopenhagen: AFK.

Wilderiane, P. and Brutsaert, M. (eds) 1997) *Alternatieve gerechtelijke maatregelen: KB 12 augustus 1994*. Brussels: Ministry of Justice, Social Service, and the Implementation of Criminal Justice.

Chapter 14

Preparing the South African community for implementing a new restorative child justice system

Buyi Mbambo and Ann Skelton

Introduction

South Africa does not currently have a separate statute which deals with children accused of crimes. The Child Justice Bill, when enacted, will be the first such law in the country. The law making process began when the Minister of Justice requested the South African Law Commission to include an investigation into juvenile justice in its programme. A project committee was set up which commenced its work in 1997 and a discussion paper with a draft bill was published in 1998. The final report of the commission, comprising the Child Justice Bill, was completed and released as a public document in August 2000.[1] The Child Justice Bill, includes the following as part of the objectives clause:

> The objectives of the Act are to promote *ubuntu* in the child justice system through –
>
> (i) fostering of children's sense of dignity and worth;
> (ii) reinforcing children's respect for human rights and the funda-mental freedoms of others by a holding children accountable for their actions and safe-guarding the interests of victims and by means of a restorative justice response; and supporting recon-ciliation by means of a restorative justice response;

(iii) supporting reconciliation by means of restorative justice response; and

(iv) involving parents, families, victims and communities in child justice processes in order to encourage the reintegration of children who are subject to the provisions of the Act.

The Child Justice Bill and restorative justice

The draft bill defines restorative justice as follows: `Restorative justice means the promotion of reconciliation, restitution and responsibility through the involvement of a child, a child's parent, family members, victims and communities' (S. 1). The new system includes alternatives to arrest, compulsory assessment of each child by a probation officer and appearance at a preliminary inquiry within 48 hours of the arrest (or the alternative to arrest). The preliminary inquiry will be chaired by a magistrate but will take the form of a case conference, the main purpose of which is to promote the use of diversion. The prosecutor, probation officer and police official will attend this inquiry, as well as the child and his or her family.

Diversion is a core component of the new system, and the draft bill offers three 'levels' of diversion. Level one includes programmes that are not particularly intensive and are of short duration. The second and third levels, however, contain programmes of increasing intensity, which can be set for longer periods of time. The clear intention of setting out a range of options in this way is to encourage those working in the system to use diversion in a range of different situations, even in relatively serious offences. Family group conferences are available at level two and level three, indicating that they are viewed as an intensive diversion option by those drafting the bill. The draft bill also provides a set of minimum standards for diversion and builds in procedural rights protections for children being offered diversion.

With regard to sentencing, the bill also reflects a restorative justice approach. The purposes of sentencing are described as follows:

The purposes of sentencing in terms of this Act are to:

- encourage the child to understand the implications of and be accountable for the harm caused;
- promote an individualised response which is appropriate to the child's circumstances and proportionate to the circumstances surrounding the harm caused by the offence;

- promote the reintegration of the child into the family and community; and
- ensure that any necessary supervision, guidance, treatment or service which forms part of the sentence can assist the child in the process of reintegration.

The bill sets out the sentencing options under four areas, namely: community-based sentences, restorative justice sentences, sentences involving correctional supervision and sentences with a compulsory residential requirement. The postponement or suspension of sentences is linked to a number of conditions, and the list of conditions includes requirements such as 'restitution', compensation or symbolic restitution', and 'an apology'. Children may, in lieu of fines, be required to make symbolic restitution or a payment of compensation to a specified person or group.

The draft bill stipulates that family group conferences can happen as diversion options prior to trial, the court can stop the proceedings in the middle of a trial and refer the matter to a family group conference. The court can also, after conviction, send the matter to a family group conference to determine a suitable plan, which the court can then make into a court order for the purposes of sentencing. In addition to the possibility of referral to a family group conference the draft bill also allows for referral to a victim–offender mediation or 'other restorative justice process'. The idea behind the wording 'other restorative justice process' is to allow for creative or indigenous models of restorative justice procedures to be developed or to re-emerge (Skelton and Frank 2001).

The African philosophy of *ubuntu* and the best interests of the child

The African value and philosophy known as *ubuntu* has been described as an African worldview, which is both a guide for social conduct and a philosophy of life. Archbishop Desmond Tutu (1999) explains in his book about the Truth and Reconciliation Commission (TRC) that:

> *Ubuntu* is very difficult to render into a Western language. It speaks of the very essence of being human. When we want to give high praise to someone we say 'yu, u nobuntu'; 'hey, he or she has *ubuntu*'. This means they are generous, hospitable, friendly, caring and compassionate. They share what they have. It also means my humanity is caught up, is inextricably bound up, in theirs. We belong to a bundle of life. We say, 'a person is a person through other people.'

He further explains how *ubuntu is* linked to the idea of forgiveness:

> To forgive is not just to be altruistic. It is the best form of self-interest. What dehumanises you, inexorably dehumanises me. Forgiveness gives people resilience, enabling them to survive and emerge still human despite all efforts to dehumanise them. *Ubuntu* means that in a real sense even the supporters of apartheid were victims of the vicious system which they implemented and which they supported so enthusiastically. Our humanity was intertwined.

The Child Justice Bill, through its objectives as outlined above, echoes these sentiments. Children who have been accused of crimes should be treated with dignity because our humanity is intertwined with theirs. Traditional African communities had their own ways of raising children. The whole notion of *ubuntu* was translated into child-rearing practices and in this context it meant every person had a non-negotiable responsiblity to:

- ensure the protection and safety of children in the community, regardless of biological connections;
- teach and impart positive values into any and all children in the community and to guide children, since it was believed that 'it takes a community to raise the child'; and
- lead by good example as children were taught to observe and follow the practices of their older peers as well as adults in the community.

There is often a misconception that the notion of communal raising of children implies that adults had power over children which could be used negatively. The African way of raising children had nothing to do with harming children. The thrust was on caring, protection and imparting positive values that would help children grow into contributing citizens in the community. Any harmful behaviour towards any family and its members was not sanctioned by the community – if you harmed or violated the integrity of a family, either by insulting or causing physical harm to a family member (including a child), you would be called upon to cleanse that family.

Traditional approaches to dealing with conflicts

The concept of *ubuntu* underpinned societal harmony in Africa for many years and guided traditional conflict resolution. African customary law has always had traditional mechanisms to deal with problems arising in communities. Allot (1977: 21) has said that 'reconciliation, restoration and harmony lie at the heart of African adjudication' and that the central purpose of a customary law court was to acknowledge that a wrong had been done and to determine what amends should be made (Dlamini 1988). In some communities where traditional practices are still prevalent even today, customary courts, known as *Izinkundla, Izigcawu* or *Makgotla*, are still in operation in some parts of South Africa, mostly in rural areas. These traditional courts are presided over by the chief or the chief's appointed representative (*Ibambankosi*) and different forms of disputes between neighbours including cases relating to domestic violence are still heard and resolved in these courts.

Traditionally, disputes involving children were dealt with by the family concerned, including members of the extended family (Maithufi 2000). It was only when families could not come to an agreement that the matter was taken to the tribal court. One common Zulu expression of resolving disputes between families is that called *'lukuthelelana amanzi'* meaning learning to resolve matters and drinking water from the same calabash as a sign of forgiveness and neighbourliness. Traditionally, it was usually male elders who presided over those family dispute resolution efforts (Van Eden 1995).

The changing socio-cultural context

Apartheid laws, urbanisation and the migratory labour system have been largely responsible for the breakdown of family life and the disintegration of the spirit of *ubuntu* and communality in South African communities (Reconstruction and Development Programme 1996: 11). As male elders began to move to the cities in search of jobs, the task of raising and guiding children as well as mediating in matters of dispute fell on the shoulders of women. Women were left with the challenges of providing for the basic needs of their families. As for men, moving to the cities did not guarantee instant jobs. Women were left to till the lands and had very little support in raising and guiding children. The break away from the carefully structured traditional family life has led to many children being raised in femaleheaded households, rarely seeing their fathers. As women also began to move to the cities in search of jobs to support their families, traditional structures of supporting and guiding children fell apart, leaving children with elderly and even ailing relatives who were ill-equipped to mediate in matters of dispute.

Poverty has also fed on the moral fibre of society. Individual survival has become the norm rather than the traditional communal approach, and people started coveting material possessions. The spirit of sharing with and caring for your neighbour's children as if they were your own slowly dissipated. Education, though a progressive step for African communities, has also divided communities since it has brought with it western individualistic values. Moreover, education created a class system that alienated the elders who were custodians of social values. As the younger generation became more educated and more affluent, the elders who had no education lost their voice and were shifted aside without any meaningful role in retaining traditional values and practices. Middle-income and more affluent African families living in the cities are moving towards nuclear family patterns and have little connection with the communities they live in. Government, through its policies and structures, has also penetrated communities and introduced western ways of dealing with matters that were traditionally dealt with through indigenous structures and processes. Where children were once seen as belonging to the entire community, an attitude has emerged which can be summarised as 'I will take care of my own child and do not bother me with yours'.

Ubuntu under threat

The collective strength of the extended family system, the caring attitude of the community as well as the guiding wisdom of elders have always been seen to be a powerful force of protection for children, but there are signs that this is changing. The idea that 'it takes a village to raise a child' seems to be mutating into 'it takes a village to punish a child' as community members begin to take the law into their own hands. The draft Child Justice Bill clearly promotes community involvement as well as solid partnerships with communities in the provision and supervision of a wide range of diversion and community-based sentencing options. A question which must now be posed is: 'are communities ready to be partners in the implementation of this proposed law?'

Due to the apparent ineffectiveness of the criminal justice system in South Africa, the country has experienced a rise in 'anti-crime' movements which believe that communities have a responsibility to address crime issues. However their methods of dealing with crime often result in gross violations of human and children's rights. One example of such an 'anti crime' movement is called Mapogo a Mathamaga. This name is taken from a Sotho proverb which says that when a leopard is confronted by a tiger, it turns into a tiger itself. The movement is dominant in the Northern Province but is rapidly spreading to other parts of South Africa, with branches being set up in Cape Town where there is also a high rate of crime and gang-related violence (Sekhonyane 2000).

The newspapers carry regular reports of one of Mapogo's one hundred branches arresting and assaulting a suspect. The president of Mapogo, John Mogolego, said at a public meeting on vigilantism held in 2001 that when a suspect is apprehended, some 'medicine' should 'be given to him or her to cure the criminal tendencies'. This 'medicine' comes in the form of beating and public humiliation. If the suspect fails to admit the crime, then according to Mogolego, it is necessary to 'squeeze the sponge and tighten the squeeze until all the water comes out'. Children of course are the most vulnerable of all 'sponges', and inevitably they suffer more than adults. Mapogo believes that its methods are rooted in tradition, says its charismatic leader: 'it is an African way to discipline offenders.' Sentiments such as 'spare the rod and spoil the child', 'the right of a disobedient child is punishment' and 'without corporal punishment in South Africa you will never stop crime' lace the speeches of the Mapogo leader.[2]

Case studies

During the year 2000 South Africa experienced at least four cases in which children accused of offences were assaulted, degraded and, in one instance, killed by community members taking the law into their own hands.[3] Two of these cases are reported below.

Girl painted white

One case of humiliation and degradation was that of 15-year-old Lorraine who went to a departmental store to buy some clothes and while she was in the shop the manager accused her of shoplifting. Instead of calling the police, the manager ordered a male security member of staff to strip her of her T-shirt and paint her white from her head to her waist. The security man did as instructed and then pushed Lorraine out of the shop door. Lorraine still denies the crime she was accused of; she was never brought before the court. Instead she claims that the money she had with her was stolen by the store manager. Lorraine suffered such degradation and humiliation that at school and in the village everyone laughs and points at her whenever she goes out. Lorraine's case attracted media attention. She however did not receive any support or counselling for the injustice she had suffered. She laid charges with the police and the security man was found guilty received a fine and a suspended sentence. The store manager who ordered the punishment she received was found not guilty.[4]

When Lorraine's family was interviewed as part of the research into community perceptions of children accused of crimes, they reported that what made the situation most unbearable for the family was that no one from the shop ever approached the family to offer apologies and to restore the integrity of the family. Not only was Lorraine shamed by this action, the whole family was shamed.

Child burns to death

Another case was that of 14-year-old Kagiso who was accused of breaking and entering a shop. He, together with four other younger children (one of whom was his younger brother), was locked in a store-room by the owner of the business who poured petrol on the children and then lit a cloth. Kagiso caught fire and died of his burns the next day. It was later revealed that the business owner had been to the school and collected the children he suspected of being involved in the thefts from his shop and not a single teacher in the school objected to his taking the children for interrogation purposes.

It also appeared during the research that some members of the community-policing forum were aware of the interrogation, including Kagiso's grandmother. As the interrogation went on behind the closed doors of the warehouse, no adult intervened. At some point the owner went out of the warehouse and came back with a container of petrol, yet not one adult intervened. As the interrogation proceeded, the owner threatened the children by dousing a cloth with petrol. He struck a match and one of the children, Kagiso, caught fire. He died in hospital on the following day. Yet, in an echo of traditional practices, the shop owner in this case visited Kagiso's family and paid for the funeral expenses before handing himself over to the police. He has since been convicted of murder and sentenced to more than 20 years' imprisonment.

As with Lorraine's case, Kagiso's family did not receive any support and counselling services until the researchers reached them and tried to get these families some help. Both families were also headed by females and seen to belong to an inferior ethnic group, therefore not subjected to the rights that the dominant ethnic group in these communities enjoyed.[5] Another common factor in both these cases was economic power and the social standing of the perpetrators of the humiliating and violent acts towards the children, compared to the families of these children. Clearly poor socioeconomic standing rendered these children and their families vulnerable to victimisation.

These incidents and others like them make it absolutely clear that the involvement of communities in restorative justice solutions for young offenders will have to be developed carefully within a framework of minimum standards. Community members will need to be educated about human rights and appropriate justice practice.

Is there hope for restorative justice in South Africa?

The descriptions of these cases may be cause for concern that allowing for greater community participation in the management of children accused of crimes would be tantamount to throwing such children to the 'leopards' and 'tigers' of Mapogo a Mathamaga. Certainly, these cases, and others like them, serve as a warning that unless we address the community perceptions and attitudes towards children accused of crimes, those aspects of the bill which encourage community participation will be difficult and possibly even dangerous to implement. There is a perception that many crimes in South Africa are committed by children, although an examination of the statistics shows that this perception is not based on fact. There is also a perception in some communities that the children's rights movement and the conventions that protect children to which the country is now party balance rights too heavily in favour of children, and that 'nothing can be done' to a child who is accused of a crime. Again, this is not factually true. These incorrect perceptions are definitely feeding in to the community taking a harder line with children, and it is clear that there is much community education that will need to be done to dispel these myths and promote a new approach to children who get into trouble. The issue of the balance of rights and responsibilities is a very important area for community education.

There are promising stories that counter the actions of such groups as Mapogo a Mathamaga. In Alexandra Township, a crime-ridden community near Johannesburg, there is a different form of an 'anti-crime' movement, called the Sector 4 Patrol Group. This is a community-based initiative that has succeeded in working in partnership with the police and members of the community. The methods used by this group are reconciliatory and they try to resolve incidents of petty crime at community level, without resorting to physical punishment and humiliation. Incidentally, the leader of this organisation originates from the Northern Province, where Mapogo is dominant, yet the methods and the underlying philosophies are completely different. The Sector 4 Patrol Group has been more successful for instance in promoting a gun-free community, returning stolen goods and referring suspects to police while at the same time helping to hold the police accountable.

In the past few years there have been demonstration programmes on family group conferencing. Some organisations have also undertaken work in the areas of conflict resolution and community mediation, leading to a modest development of restorative justice processes. One such organisation called the Community Peace Programme has been running a project in Zwelethemba in the Western Cape since 1997. The model uses community forums to undertake problem-solving through peace-making and peace-building (Shearing 2001). The Restorative Justice Centre, an NGO promoting restorative justice based in Pretoria, has developed a model in the municipality of Khayalami near Johannesburg which aims at creating 'a caring Khayalami' in which victims and offenders are sup-ported, cared for and restored. This organisation intervenes through family group conferencing in the criminal justice system and in schools. They have also developed a model which transforms the way conflict and crime are dealt with in schools, where they assist child offenders in schools to be reintegrated into the school. These attempts show that there is a willingness to explore alternative ways of seeking justice in communities and they provide strong models of indigenous community-based restorative justice work that can benefit people accused of crimes in communities.

Conclusion

From the work done so far in promoting restorative justice in South Africa, a number of issues have clearly emerged as challenges that will need to be met as the country prepares for more community involvement in the proposed child justice system.

First, is it important to establish clear and unambiguous political support for the idea of restorative justice. Although policy documents of different departments embrace restorative justice (Skosana 2001), the reality is that the elected politicians feel the need to be seen to be tough on crime. This has led to the promotion in some sectors of a 'zero-tolerance' approach which has found its way into policy and even into law (Skelton 1999). Government will need to be clear about their support for restorative justice, and not send mixed messages. Government commitment should also include the provision of financial resources to promote restorative justice processes and models.

There is a need to change the attitudes of professionals in the criminal justice system towards a more restorative justice approach. At this point restorative justice is being introduced into policy documents but the personnel have very little understanding of how these processes work, nor about their effectiveness. It will be useful to develop strong models of restorative justice practice which prosecutors, magistrates and other critical partners of the criminal justice system can have confidence in. There should be careful documentation of the lessons learnt as well as successes gained from restorative justice practice models. Appropriately skilled people will need to be trained to facilitate effectively family group conferences, victim-offender mediation and other restorative justice processes.

Ways must be found to address the retributive attitudes of communities. This could be fostered through demonstrating the benefits of restorative justice. We will need strong effective models that have been thoroughly researched and documented. The linkages to traditional forms of conflict resolution must be clearly made. The spirit of *ubuntu* must be reclaimed in communities. This is a serious challenge as there is no simple way to achieve it. It requires the concerted effort of civil society and of religious bodies (which in many cases have also proved retributive!), as well as rebuilding strong family and neighbourhood networks.

Community members and community groups must be trained in restorative justice theory and in developing skills in facilitating restorative justice processes. The reality is that many communities are marginalised in terms of the availability of trained professionals. Yet there do exist community structures which serve a crime prevention and community-building function. These are the existing strengths of communities and they should be invested in.

Ways must be sought to use and convert existing community-based informal justice systems such as community courts to promote restorative justice. As South Africa suffers from constraints on resources (both human and material), it is vitally important that maximum use be made of structures and procedures that are already in existence. Structures such as traditional courts and community courts are access points to justice available to many South Africans, and people have faith in them (Nina 1995).

In addition to recognising and utilising what is already there, the development of indigenous models of restorative justice should be encouraged. The model to be developed will need to work with African ideas about raising children while at the same time protecting and promoting children's rights.

Social inequities and injustices will need to be factored in to the way that restorative justice practice is carried out. The unemployment rate in South Africa is very high and many crimes are committed by poor people. Bringing together people from very different socioeconomic backgrounds in a conference to ensure that a poverty-stricken offender should be held accountable and make restitution to a wealthy victim requires a highly skilled facilitator, and may in some instances lead to injustice in itself if not carefully managed (Skelton and Frank 2001).

Finally, a set of minimum standards for restorative justice practice needs to be developed through a participative process, although great care must be taken not to erode existing knowledge of conflict resolution. The purpose of the standards should be to ensure compliance with the human rights standards set out in South Africa's Constitution and other human rights instruments.

For the restorative justice aspects of the Child Justice Bill to be effectively implemented, it is important that the above-mentioned challenges be met. The bill seeks to promote healing and nation-building. Restorative justice should be seen as one method of constructive engagement with communities in matters pertaining to children accused of crimes.

Notes

1. South African Law Commission, *Report on Juvenile Justice*, Project 106, 2000. The report is available at www.law.wits.ac.za/salc/salc.html
2. These quotations are drawn from a speech by the President of Mapogo a Mathamaga, John Mogolego, at a seminar on vigilantism held at the Institute for Security Studies on 8 June 2001, Pretoria. The veracity of the statement that these practices are part of African tradition is obviously questionable. As a starting point, it seems strange that Mapogo a Mathamaga has chosen a tiger as its symbol and part of its name, an animal that does not even live in southern Africa!
3. These are cases which attracted media attention. It is believed that there are many cases of this nature that go unreported and during the study researchers were given anecdotal accounts of victimisation which were not captured by the media.
4. The issue of race also undoubtedly played a role here, as the store manager was white, while the security man and Lorraine were both black. Lorraine made an emotional presentation about her experiences at the International Conference against Racism in Durban 3–7 September 2001.
5. Both Kagiso and Lorraine were described as being 'Shangaan', but were living in a community which was predominantly Northern Sotho.

References

Allot, A.N. (1977) 'The People as Law Makers: Custom, Practice and Public Opinion as Sources of Law in Africa and England', *Journal of African Law,* 1: 21.
Boraine, A. (2000) A *Country Unmasked: The Story of South Africa's Truth and Reconciliation Commission.* Cape Town: Oxford University Press.

Branken, N. and Batley, M. (1998) *Family Group Conferences: Putting the Wrong Right.* Pretoria: Inter-ministerial Committee on Young People at Risk.

Consedine, J. (1999) *Restorative Justice – Healing the Effects of Crime.* Lyttelton: Ploughshares.

Dlamini, C. (1988) 'The Role of Chiefs in the Administration of Justice.' Unpublished LLM thesis, University of Pretoria.

Maithuf, I. (2000) 'The Best Interests of the Child d African Customary Law', in C.J. Davel (ed.) *Introduction to Child Law in South Africa.* Lansdowne: Juta.

Nina, D. (1995) 'Reflections on the Role of State Justice and Popular Justice in Post-apartheid South Africa, *Imbizo* 3: 18.

Reconstruction and Development Programme (1996) *Children, Poverty and Disparity Reduction.* Pretoria: Office of the President.

Restorative Justice Centre (2001) *Retributive Community Justice.* Commissioned by the UN Child Justice Project (ww.rjc.co.za).

Sekhonyane, K. (2000) 'Tracking Vigilante Activity', *Nedbank ISS Crime Index*, (4): 21–5.

Shearing, C (2001) 'Transforming Security: a South African Experiment', in H. Strang and J. Braithwaite (eds) *Restorative Justice and Civil Society.* Cambridge: Cambridge University Press.

Skelton, A. (1999) 'Juvenile Justice Reform: Children's Rights and Responsibilities versus Crime Control', in C.J. Davel (ed.) *Children's Rights in a Transitional Society.* Pretoria: Protea House.

Skelton, A. and Frank, C. (2001) 'Conferencing in South Africa: Returning to our Future', in A. Morris and C. Maxwell (eds) *Restorative Justice for Juveniles: Conferencing, Mediation and Circles.* Oxford and Portland, OR: Hart Publishing.

Skosana, B. (2001) 'Restorative Justice Launched in the Department of Correctional Services.' A speech by the Minister of Correctional Service, delivered at the official launch of the restorative justice approach, 26 November. (www.dcs.gov.za).

South African Law Commission (2000) *Report on Juvenile Justice.* Project 106. Pretoria: South African Law Commission.

Tutu, D. (1999) *No Future without Forgiveness.* London: Rider.

Van Eden, K. (1995) 'What can Indigenous African Customs Teach Contemporary Juvenile Justice?' Unpublished paper, Institute of Criminology, University of Cape Town.

Chapter 15

Positioning mediation in the criminal justice system: the Italian 'justice of the peace'

Grazia Mannozzi

The crisis of the link between 'crime' and 'punishment'

When we speak of 'mediation' the related concept of 'conflict' immediately comes to mind. And conflict leads, in turn, to a number of heterogeneous situations since conflict can arise in the family, at school, in social or economic relations or in the commission of a crime – different situations that require different solutions. If conflict derives from or is expressed as a crime, we can speak specifically of victim–offender mediation as a means of intervention linked to a legal framework – that of *penal law* – that has a 'rigid' structure dominated by very detailed procedural rules and a sound system of guarantees for the benefit of the defendant.

In fact, the distinctive features of almost every criminal justice system are the 'severity' and 'rigidity' of the responses. Even in a justice model with indeterminate sentencing, characterised by flexibility in sentencing, it is always the 'punishment' that represents the system's way of reacting. And the stigmatisation is the effect that follows from the sentence and, even, from being tried. In the Italian penal system in particular, crime and punishment are problematic, for two basic reasons:

- Any definition of crime goes hand in hand with the concept of 'sanction'. In the Italian legal system, the definition of crime is based merely on a *nominal* criterion for identifying what is illegal. Thus the sanction has a *constitutive* function regarding the penal nature of the fact.

* The application of the sanction represents a confirmation of the 'validity of the penal norms' (Jakobs 1991: 9). When a crime is committed, the community 'asks for' the punishment of the offender. When a crime goes without punishment, this is regarded as some sort of 'illness' within the system.

However, for some time, (in Italy at least), the link between crime and punishment has, in practice, become much weaker (Di Martino 1998). Punishment is no longer the inevitable consequence of the commission of an offence, for a number of independent reasons:

1. The 'certainty' of punishment is weakened by the phenomenon of the 'dark number' of crimes.
2. The principle of mandatory prosecution, where provided by law (as in the Italian Constitution), tends in practice to be a sham. Indeed, public prosecutors have a great deal of discretionary power with regard to the prosecution of offences (especially petty offences) and, consequently, they might deflate that considered to be criminal.
3. In Italy in particular, the excessive length of trials leads to the risk of legal prescription and, thus, the nullification of any claims for a punitive outcome.
4. The criminal law itself, at times, provides the means for a quick end to a trial or for a renunciation of the punishment (for instance, the judicial pardon often granted to juvenile offenders).
5. Finally, there is a great deal of uncertainty whether the punishment will, in fact, be carried out. Under the Italian system, only *definitive* sentences are carried out: those that result from cases that have gone through two levels of proceedings, as well as a legitimacy check by the Court of Cassation. The effective punishment, therefore, can change both *qualitatively* and *quantitatively*, according to the inclination of the sentencing judge. Indeed, in Italy, another judge (the 'supervisory judge') deals specifically with punishment matters during the so-called 'enforcement phase of punishment' (Mannozzi 2002).

Therefore when the commission of a crime is not followed by punishment, the justice system appears to be, in the words of *Le petit Prince*, 'the ruler of a planet without subjects'.

Moreover, punishment with respect to the conflict is like a symptomatic drug: it cures the symptoms but not the disease. And symptomatic therapies run the risk of side-effects that should not be underestimated: by making the symptoms bearable, they allow us to live with the disease but do not cure it. Hence, inflicting punishment makes crime more bearable but it only satisfies society's *need* for punishment.

Furthermore, after a while drugs no longer have any effect unless the dosage is increased. This might indirectly confirm the 'more of the same' theory (Paliero 1992): if punishment does not work, increase the dose.

This phenomenon has produced a paradoxical effect in the Italian criminal justice system: on the one hand, the adoption of increasingly more repressive laws and, on the other, more leniency (as a result of the difficulty of concluding trials in a short period of time and of applying too harsh a punishment for offences that are not particularly serious).

This argument does not imply that punishment, according to the (radical) abolitionist perspective (Hulsman 1982), is not useful. It simply implies – to continue with the metaphor – that we should assist or, even, substitute the drug with measures that go to the root of the conflict: mediation and reparation, to be exact. In short, if the crime/punishment nexus is no longer tenable – if the criminal justice system no longer corresponds to the traditional theoretical model of criminal law based on the centrality of 'punishment' – then we have two alternatives. To:

1. adjust the 'traditional' model or
2. recognise that the traditional model of criminal law is a falsification (here I am using Popperean language), as is proved to some extent by the very existence of a 'restorative/mediatory' approach to crime.

It is the second alternative that is discussed here in order to understand how the recent reforms that occurred in the Italian criminal justice profoundly modified the structure and, thus, the representation, of the Italian penal system.

What kind of judicial space for mediation?

In legal systems, several different areas of intervention coexist (criminal law, civil law) and each one can be further divided into specific subsectors (i.e. commercial criminal law, environmental law, etc.). Traditionally, criminal law has tended to regulate specific kinds of conflicts: those characterised as having a detrimental effect on shared fundamental values (i.e. life, personal freedom, physical integrity, property, etc.). When the damage caused by a conflict or is considered to be not particularly serious, the legal system reacts by implementing administrative or civil sanctions. The lines dividing penal sanctions from civil or administrative sanctions and, more generally, the boundaries between 'right' and 'wrong' are complicated functions of numerous political and cultural variables.

Under the Italian legal system, practitioners who wished to implement mediation were forced to use procedures originally introduced for different aims. For example, in the juvenile justice system they had to use measures initially designed to re-educate young offenders. From the perspective of victim–offender mediation, the legislature could follow two different routes:

1. Removing from criminal law certain conflicts that could be settled better by mediation. However, a definition of conflicts valid solely and exclusively for mediation is very difficult to establish. It could also be argued that conflicts that can only be 'mediated' do not, in fact, exist: mediation cannot be 'enforced' by authority. Therefore a link between mediation and institutional solutions to conflicts must be established.
2. The creation of a judicial space for mediation that defines and guarantees its field of operation independently of ad hoc definitions of conflicts. Mediation is seen here as a device applicable to every sector of the criminal justice system when a positive outcome can be envisaged.

The latter option was adopted by the Italian legislator in 2002 when the remit of the office of the justice of the peace was extended to include judicial authority for mediation and reparation for specific offences.

The office of the 'justice of the peace'

Justices of the peace have responsibility for certain crimes included in the Italian criminal code and for several specific laws. Justices of the peace are not professional (or career) judges but honorary judges – that is, they serve for a limited term and are selected for their basic knowledge that guarantees, if not specific experience of judicial practice, at least some understanding of the law and of the problems of the administration of justice. For many years, justices of the peace fulfilled a civil role, and their work contributed to significant reduction in the enormous backlog that has afflicted Italian civil proceedings.

The law that extended the authority of justices of the peace into the penal field (Act 274 of 28 August 2000) came into effect in January 2002. This Act contains the first explicit reference to 'mediation', which generally permits justices of the peace to work towards the settlement of conflicts. It should be noted, however, that this reform falls within the general directive issued by the European Council of 15 March 2001 which encourages, in the context of greater guarantees for victims, recourse to mediation and the right of victims to be informed about criminal proceedings. In particular, art. 10 of this directive provides that: 'Each member state should promote mediation in the context of criminal proceedings for offences that are appropriate for this type of measure. Each member state should guarantee that any agreements between the victim and the offender during mediation regarding criminal proceedings should be taken into consideration'. The Italian Act also introduced a list of sanctions (fines, house arrest, community service) applicable only to offences that come under the authority of justices of the peace. These are to be applied when an attempt to settle the conflict through mediation/ reparation is unsuccessful.

In practice, there are only a few offences that come under the jurisdiction of justices of the peace; as mentioned above, these include offences regulated by the criminal code (threats, assault and injuries) and by certain specific laws. Most of these offences are not serious and, above all, they are subject to proceedings (see Tables 15.1. and 15.2); mediation can only be used for this category of offences.

Table 15.1. Offences contained in the Italian criminal code that come under the jurisdiction of the justices of the peace that are subject to criminal proceedings.

Articles of criminal code	Offence
581	Battery
582/2	(Mitigated) personal injury
590	Negligent personal injury
612	Assault
626	Theft
627	Petty theft
631	Encroachment
632	Illegal water diversion
633	Illegal occupation of land
635	Damage to property
636	Abandonment of flock or herd
637	Trespassing
638/1	Killing of animals (flock or herd)
639/1	Defacement or soiling of property of others
647	Embezzlement of lost property

Table 15.2. Offences contained in the Italian criminal code that come under the jurisdiction of the justices of the peace that are not subject to criminal proceedings.

Article of Criminal Code	Offence	
582/1	Personal injury	
593	Failure to come to the aid of someone in distress	
594	Insult	
595	Libel	
612/2	Assault	
631	Usurpation	if the act
632	Illegal water diversion	occurs on
633	Illegal occupation of land	public property
636	Abandonment (flock or herd)	art. 639 applies
635/2	Damage to property	
638/2	Killing of animals (flock or herd)	
639/2	Defacement or soiling of property	
689	Selling alcohol to minors	
690	Causing another person to become intoxicated	
691	Selling alcohol to individuals who are intoxicated	
731	Failure to fulfill obligation to provide a basic education	
276	Offences against public morals	

The effects of these reforms on the distribution of cases among criminal judges and justices of the peace may be evaluated by measuring the frequency of crimes subject to legal procedures – and thus, in theory, subject to mediation (see Table 15.1). In general, offences that now come under the jurisdiction of justices of the peace represent 12–14% of the offences contained in the criminal code (see Table 15.3).

What is unique about the office of the justice of the peace is that it permits a truly 'flexible' response to crime. Justices of the peace can choose among three alternatives:

1. mediatory/reparative measures;
2. deflective solutions; or
3. punitive measures.

In the last case, the conditional suspension of the punishment is not permitted in order to guarantee the effectiveness of the sanction that is eventually imposed. In the case of mediatory/reparative measures, if the attempt at reconciliation is successful no punishment is inflicted and,

Table 15.3. Frequency rates of crimes coming under the jurisdiction of justices of the peace (1998).

Offence	No.	%
Petty thefts	143	0.005
Trespass to land	266	0.009
Theft	129	0.004
Encroachment	153	0.005
Misuse of property of others	566	0.018
Abandonment of flock or herd	1,937	0.063
Embezzlement of lost property	2,048	0.066
Killing of animals (flock or herd)	2,682	0.087
Total of crimes with a frequency of less than 0.01%	7,924	0.256
Defacement or soiling of property of others	2,813	0.091
Battery	5,178	0.168
Trespassing	7,524	0.243
Assault	34,010	1.100
Personal injury	45,656	1.477
Negligent personal injury	95,021	3.074
Damage to property	229,746	7.433
Crimes coming under the jurisdiction of justices of the peace	419,948	13.587
Crimes not coming under the jurisdiction of justices of the peace	2,663,040	86.157
Total	3,090,912	

hence, there is no sentencing phase. The deflective measures permit the accused to exit rapidly from the trial at the judge's discretion. These measures are mainly aimed at the offence and the offender. As regards sanctions, justices of the peace employ a simplified sentencing model compared to that of the normal criminal justice system – even the justification for a sentence has to be written in an abbreviated form.

Conciliatory/reparative measures

Act 274/2000 provides two different conciliatory/mediatory measures. The first is 'mediation with the aim of reconciliation between the parties'. This measure can be used for offences against which legal proceedings can be taken.

In such cases, the judge can postpone the hearing for up to two months to allow for mediation procedures. Moreover, the judge can act as the mediator or can employ a mediator from outside the judicial system. This is one of the main innovations contained within the Act. However, during their training judges were encouraged to make use of outside mediators. In the event of a positive outcome from the mediation, the judge can acquit the case. One of the problems that arose right at the start of mediation for young offenders concerned the use that would be made of statements given by young offenders whose mediation was unsuccessful. Act 274/ 2000 provides a solution for this in its defence of civil liberties. This Act implies that, in cases where mediation has failed, the statements made by the parties during the reconciliation process cannot be used for purposes of deliberation.

The second measure provided by this Act is the 'acquittal of a case as a result of reparative conduct' (art. 35). Along with recourse to mediation, this is one of innovations of this Act, which at last recognises the importance of reparation. The judge can dismiss a case when the offender can demonstrate, before his or her appearance in court, that he or she has provided for the reparation of the damage done (restitution and compensation) and for the elimination of the damaging or dangerous consequences of his or her conduct. To dismiss a case, the judge has to verify that the reparation of the damage satisfies the requirements for censure (*priprovazione*) and prevention (*prevenzione*) adequately. The judge can also suspend the trial for a period of no longer than three months to allow the offender to make reparations and eliminate the damaging or dangerous consequences of his or her conduct. The victim has the right to be heard before the case is dismissed.

This article is not easy to interpret. It introduces two factors regarding the discretionary powers of judges that cannot be easily verified. How can we ascertain that the requirements for censure and prevention are satisfied? Above all, what are we to understand by 'censure' and 'prevention'? To begin with prevention, this must be understood in terms of both general prevention (the reparation must satisfy the requirement for the reinstatement of social stability) and special prevention (the reparation must lead to full reconciliation between the victim and offender) (Roxin 1987: 20). Prevention should thus lead to a reduction in undesired behaviour by means of so-called 'situational crime prevention' (Clarke 1995).

Censure has many different interpretations (von Hirsh 1993). A rigorous interpretation of censure falls back on classic retributive theory: reparative behaviour should play a role similar to the 'punitive damage' of Anglo-Saxon law. A second interpretation excludes the 'sanctioning' factor. According to this interpretation, the judge must decide whether the offender acknowledges his or her offence and whether it is this that leads to reparation. In particular, judges must decide whether the rehabilitative effort is sufficient to restore social stability (Quattrocolo 2002).

The deflective measure

Act 273/2000 introduced a deflective measure that was already present in the judicial system: acquittal due to the particular tenuity of the fact (art. 34). This device was provided for by art. 27 D.P.R. 448/1988 (Ceretti and Mannozzi 2000) as a means of dealing with young offenders (Gatti and Ceretti 1998). The judge can decide not to inflict a sanction when a series of conditions exist:

1. the offence caused little damage;
2. the offender does not have a serious criminal record;
3. minimal guilt on the part of the offender;
4. there could be a detrimental effect on the offender's work, study, family or health as a result of a sanction.

The decision whether or not to impose a punishment is made during the initial part of the sentencing phase. Judges have a great deal of discretion in deciding to acquit a case, even if the public prosecutor has decided to prosecute. The victim also has the power of veto. Judges can order a trial to proceed if this is in the victim's best interests. However, all parties have the right to challenge the judge's decisions.

The expression 'tenuous fact' refers to the offence as whole. Thus in judging whether a fact is tenuous, careful consideration must be given to the offender's 'guilt'. Thus evaluation of tenuity of the facts is based on the objective and subjective characteristics of the offence, which can be deduced from the criteria listed in art. 133 of the criminal code. This article (and art. 132, which requires the justification of the sentence) provides a general sentencing model: it lays down the criteria that must guide a judge in the application of his or her discretionary powers. The two fundamental criteria are as follows:

1. The 'seriousness of the crime', which is derived from a series of objective and subjective indices (i.e. *actus reus*, *mens rea*, the seriousness of the damage caused, etc.).
2. The 'offender's capacity to commit crimes', which is derived from a series of secondary factors designed to predict the offender's future behaviour.

The sentencing model provided by art. 133 permits so many factors to be taken into account that no real policy has emerged about how to assess the relative seriousness of a case. Moreover, no indications were given regarding the *aims* of criminal punishment. This has meant that, in practice, there is little guidance for judges when exercising their discretionary powers.

In short, in order to evaluate the tenuity of the facts, a judge has to take into consideration objective factors – the amount of damage (see Turin Court of Appeals, sent 13-11-1990) or danger caused and, above all, the nature of behaviour (Di Nuovo and Grasso 1999: 296) – as well as subjective factors (the degree of malice, the degree of guilt, the reasons for committing the crime). Regarding the danger caused by an offence, the Caltenisetta Court of Appeal (see sent. 2-5-1990) disallowed an acquittal based on the tenuity of the facts in the case if a young person who drove a car without a licence: 'which in itself represents a general danger for public safety due to the inexperience and imprudence that derive from a young age … which moreover occurred in a town centre and was carried out by a person with a previous criminal record.'

Article 34 does not directly call for mediation, but neither does it exclude it. However, mediation can be useful for the purposes of judging the tenuousness of the facts since it permits a more accurate evaluation of the entire offence. On the other hand, this implies that judges must be kept informed of the deliberation of mediation processes if they are to evaluate the extent of the offender's guilt. But this contradicts the rules of mediation: the mediator should communicate to the judge only the outcome of the mediation, not the deliberations that led to that outcome.

Conclusion

The law that extends the powers of justices of the peace has, for the first time, expressly provided for victim–offender mediation and has recognised that reparation is an effective means of acquitting an offence. Previously, the judges could only turn to mediation in the area of juvenile justice through a 'broad' interpretation of laws that do not contain any explicit reference to mediation. Mediation, however, under the new law, could also be used as a punitive response to crime. Mediation can also be seen as part of a general strategy to reduce recourse to punishment. However, it can also be considered an expression of the need to promote the 'rehabilitation of a correct model for social relationships' (Picotti 1998: 312) and, in the end, for the restoration of social stability. It should similarly contribute to promoting the idea of a flexible model of conflict resolution. This model does not mean recourse to various forms of punishment (as the sentencing model requires); rather, it requires the rational evaluation of different solutions: not only punishment through trial (i.e. imprisonment, fines suspended sentences, probation, intermediate sanctions) but also pardons, restitution, reparation and mediation.

One problem remains: how do we make the solutions equitable? In other words, we need to avoid disparity of treatment. Indeed, disparities of treatment could be created that are greater than the sentencing disparities of the past. The problems of disparity drove the US justice system to adopt a mathematical sentencing model: sentencing through guidelines. The possibilities for disparities in mediation should be monitored and controlled in the same way as disparities in the infliction of punishment, but such a problem should not deter us from pursuing the ideals of restorative justice. Moreover, the law that has empowered justices of the peace has resolved the problem of the rights of defendants regarding the presumption of innocence. Article 29 states that declarations made by the parties during mediation cannot be used by the prosecutor or judge in the subsequent trial. Mediation, therefore, is no longer two-edged sword since the admission of guilt is disallowed.

References

Braithwaite, J. (1989) *Crime, Shame, Reintegration.* New York, NY: Cambridge University Press).

Ceretti, A. (2000) 'Mediazione penale e giustizia. In-contrare una norma', in *Studi in ricordo di G. Pisapia.* Milano: Giuffrè.

Ceretti, A. and Mannozzi, G. (2000) 'Restorative Justice. Theoretical Aspects and Applied Models', in *Offenders and Victims: Accountability and Fairness in the Justice Process*, proceedings, tenth United Nations Congress on the Prevention of Crime and the Treatment of Offenders. Milano: Centro Nazionale di Prevenzione e Difesa Sociale.

Clarke (1995) 'Situational Crime Prevention', in M. Tonry and Farrington (eds) *Building a Safer Society.* Chicago, IL: University of Chicago Press.

Cotta, S. (1992) 'Il diritto: struttura di pace', *Iustitia*: 379.

Di Martino, A. (1998) *La sequenza infranta.* Milano: Giuffrè.

Di Nuovo and Grasso (1999) *Diritto e procedura penale minorile.* Milano: Giuffrè.

Eusebi, L. (1997) 'Dibattiti sulle teorie della pena e mediazione', *Rivista italiana diritto e procedura penale*: 811.

Gatti, U. and Ceretti, A. (1998) 'Italian Experiences of Victim–Offender Mediation in the Juvenile Justice System', in L. Walgrave (ed.) *Restorative Justice for Juveniles.* Leuven: Leuven University Press.

Jakobs, G. (1991) *Strafrecht – Allgemeiner Teil.* Berlin.

Larizza, S. (1998) 'Profili sostanziali della sospensione del processo minorile nella prospettiva della mediazione penale', in L. Picotti (ed.) *La mediazione nel sistema penale minorile*. Padova: Cedam.

Mannozzi, G. (2002) 'Are Guided Sentencing and Sentence Bargaining Incompatible? Perspectives of Reform in the Italian Legal System', in N. Hutton, and C. Tata (eds) *Sentencing and Society: International Perspectives*. Aldershot: Ashgate.

Mestiz, A. and Colamussi, V. (2000) 'Messa alla prova e restorative justice', *Minori Giustizia*: 223.

Molinari, F. and Amoroso, G. (1998) *Criminalità minorile e mediazione*. Milano: Franco Angeli.

Paliero, C. (1992) 'Metodologie *de lege ferenda*: per una riforma non improbabile del sistema sanzionatorio', *Rivista italiana di diritto e procedura penale*: 510.

Picotti, L. (ed.) (1998) *La mediazione nel sistema penale minorile*. Padova: Cedam.

Picotti, L. (ed.) (2002) *Verso una giustizia penale 'conciliativa'*. Milano: Giuffrè.

Quattrocolo, S. (2001) 'Commento all'articolo 35 L. 28/8/2000', *Legislazione Penale*: 65.

Roxin, K. (1987) 'Risarcimento del danno e fini della pena', *Rivista italiana diritto e procedura penale*: 3.

Silvani, S. (2001) 'Commento alla Legge 4/4/ 2001 n. 154 – Misure contro la violenza nelle relazioni familiari', *Legislazione penale*: 57.

von Hirsch, A. (1993) *Censure and Sanctions*. Oxford: Oxford University Press.

Chapter 16

Anthropological reflections on restoring justice in Norway

Ida Hydle

In a recent analysis of a criminal case in Norway, I studied the performance of legal and medical professionals in the courtroom (Hydle 2001). One of my conclusions after this fieldwork is that there seems to be a troublesome and paradoxical problem of randomness in the legal narrative – in spite of the objective and whole-truth-and-fact approximation claimed by the legal (and medical) professionals, which is exacerbated by the hegemonic position of the presiding judges. I also suggested how African categories for magic and witchcraft might be useful analytical instruments for understanding Norwegian thinking (i.e. turning the colonial direction of the argument the other way round). Looking back at my fieldwork, it becomes clear that the professional actors belong to fields of knowledge from which there is no way of building bridges to each others' understanding. To create 'the other', in the image of oneself or to create oneself in the image of 'the other', both the fields of medicine and law are self-referential. Their ethos lies in the search for knowledge within the medico-judicial image of 'fact', 'truth', 'reality' and 'real'. Such images are myths that exclude the images of belonging to 'the other'. An anthropological view of myths relates them to tales of a general and social, not individual, nature. The practical implications of my ethnography raise questions about criminal court practice and the contemporary Norwegian judiciary.

Med lov skal landet bygges ('The law is the foundation of this land')

Looking back at the history of law in Norway, restorative justice was used as a way of handling crime up to the fifteenth century. The professionalisation of conflicts evolved as a way for the Sovereign and the Church to increase their incomes. Thus there was a shift from 'restitutive justice' and 'community law' to 'punitive justice' and 'state law' (Gatrell *et al.* 1980). A closer look at the history of criminal law, therefore, may afford us a background for understanding some of the contemporary law-and-order problems and the reasons for (re?-)introducing the principles of restorative justice.

During the last few decades, like their colleagues elsewhere, Nordic historians have looked closely at their legal history from (at least) two different perspectives (Österberg 1994): 'the history of human behaviour'[1] (from what I would call an essensialistic[2] perspective) and 'the history of criminalisation'[3] (from what might be called a constructivist or relational perspective). The Norwegian historian, Sandmo, claims that, in the old days, the difference between the terms 'crime' and 'breach of norms', and 'breach of law' and 'offence' were blurred and that the only way to find out the difference is carefully to order different social and discursive[4] levels when investigating historical sources (Sandmo 1999). A theory of 'the judicial revolution' emerged among the supporters of 'criminalisation': a pessimistic view of power and oppression, that took on different forms throughout modern history.

This transformation of Norwegian judicial and criminal procedure throughout the centuries can be seen as a social process – from local and restorative to central/national and punitive[5]. It may be seen as part of general societal changes from the late middle ages to early industrialisation and as dating from a period of Danish dominance, with its development of a professionalised bureaucracy and the construction of a nation-state. During this transformation grew modernity's concepts of time and space, objectivity and absolute truths (i.e. a worldview of essentialised values). Such values grew into law, which borrowed the ideals of rationality and reason from the newly emerging natural sciences.

Restorative justice or restoring justice

Restorative justice in the Norwegian context is well described by Kemény (2000), who has been a leading person within the Norwegian Ministry of Justice urging for the establishment of 'conflict councils':

Contemporary restorative justice has in the western part of the world mostly been initiated either as an academic sociological idea, or as a religiously inspired movement. In Norway, restorative justice has never been associated with the church. It was Nils Christie who introduced the idea of redefining criminal offences as conflicts (Christie 1977). This triggered off the development and establishment of the so-called 'konfliktråd' or 'conflict councils'. Thus the field of restorative justice has been purely secular in Norway.

The Norwegian Act of Parliament regulating the mediation and reconciliation service (as a permanent institution of criminal law) stipulates the following: criminal offences should be defined as conflicts; the mediators must be lay people, the parties (litigants) must meet personally, and lawyers are rarely allowed at the meeting. Direct mediation is fixed by the law and empowerment of the community and of the parties is central to the idea and ethos of the councils (Kemény 2000: 88). The bill was passed in 1991 and the councils were moved administratively from the Ministry of Social Affairs[6] to the Ministry of Justice.

My fieldwork has given me the opportunity to peek into the Norwegian discourse of restorative justice.[7] One of the most conspicuous discussions is the juridical[8] and bureaucratic organisation of 'conflict councils'. Conversations with leading persons within 1) the academic field of criminology; 2) the Ministry of Justice (as the national lead institution of restorative justice; 3) national and local public prosecutors' offices; 4) national and local restorative justice organisations; and 5) local mediation organisations have contributed towards one interpretation: Norwegian restorative justice seems to be a postmodern hybrid[9] construction. Here I see hybridity in terms of time and space. By what may be seen as an application of the old, medieval Norwegian version of justice to modernity's societal form, the contemporary level of confusion, disapproval, continuous reorganisation (throughout the last ten years), local developments of heterogeneous forms, etc., is not at all astonishing. Is it possible to 'force' the principles of forgiveness and reconciliation into a modern criminal legislation that is constructed upon the principle of punity and individual culpability?

Looking back at medieval society, the construction of time, space and personhood seems to have belonged to a different world. God was still part of personhood. Individuality was not perceived as a value. Linguistic constructions of relationship and mutuality were different from what emerged during industrialisation and the invention of the nation-state, upon which contemporary criminal legislation is based. Seen with a postmodern gaze, punitive justice corresponds to an essentialistic worldview ('he or she *is* a criminal – society must get rid of/punish him or her') whereby restorative justice corresponds to a dialogical and situational view of, for example, language and personhood. An event is interpreted as a criminal act by the victim(s) and/or witness(es) as a result of their interpretation of the circumstances and situation. However, at stake is the reciprocal empowerment of the primary performers of the (reconstructed) act – the victim and the perpetrator. This is based on the performers' mutual agreement about reconciliation.

An anthropological approach to mediation implies taking a closer look at the actors involved in a conflict through cross-cultural lenses. Conflicts, or rather the handling of them, are crucial for the formation and of all kinds of human societies. The ways in which such handling is conducted vary to a greater extent than most people/professionals are aware. For an anthropologist this is a unique opportunity to study Norwegian culture in the making. In my work, I endorse the view that conflicts and states are reciprocally related: societies arise out of conflicts and conflicts are socially conditioned (i.e. conflicts are inherent qualities of societies). Focusing on conflict dramaturgies, discourses and fields of knowledge as three important analytical cornerstones, I should like to discuss one particular Norwegian regime – restorative justice – and compare this with criminal justice.

Conflict dramaturgies, discourses and regimes

As a newcomer to the field of conflict mediation, and fresh from my last fieldwork involving a criminal case, I tried to separate the theories underpinning these two approaches. Here I concentrate my preliminary thoughts and experiences concerning the historical, social and political landscape upon which Norwegian restorative justice can be said to be constructed. In doing so I hope to shed some light on general modes of human behaviour and on the ways in which certain behaviour patterns crystallise in conflict resolution rituals – such as criminal justice or restorative justice processes. As an anthropologist I use such terms as ritual, scene, drama, dramaturgy,[10] etc., to describe court proceedings and mediation processes. To most legal practitioners, it sounds strange to use such terms outside the theatre, and many people would find it somewhat denigrating if such terms were used in relation to their own activities or working spaces. Such terms, however, function well as analytical tools in comparative anthropology.[11] There is, in fact, nothing derogatory about these terms. The anthropologist's aim is to compare different worlds and this in itself creates a demand for terms that are useful for comparison.

They belong to anthropological terminology. Concepts such as these 'refer to social roles, frameworks of thought, symbols, systems of morality, axioms, values and sentiments' (Overing 1987: 82). In spite of all the differences, there are comparative elements in which an anthropologist may find empirical or analytical importance.

As Foucault has demonstrated, discourses are expressions and instruments of power, including a whole range of different (levels of) phenomena: people, knowledge, textbooks and institutions (material buildings). The term 'regime' implies a set of rhetorical forms and images, that are implemented in different areas of society and that emerge as hegemonic ways of speaking and acting. Within each area (e.g. fields of conflict such as criminal justice or restorative justice) a conflict regime will define what it means to be a person and what it means to be social. A conflict regime can be said figuratively to have its own vocabulary and grammar (Meyer 2001).

The following analytical models share some basic assumptions:

- There are alternatives to violence and coercion. This is so in private areas, such as street and family violence (where it is possible to be angry or quarrel without beating or killing), as it is public areas, such as war or coercion within prisons or psychiatric hospitals (wars can be omitted by diplomacy; prisoners can work and/or pay back; and most people can receive mental treatment without coercion).
- Conflicts and the handling of conflicts are cultural acts. Conflicts are perceived and handled differently in different social groups as a result of distinctive cultural features, such as language, laws, rules, attitudes and images of right and wrong.
- Conflict-handling often takes the form of a ritual.
- Cross-cultural principles concerning conflicts may be identified and implemented.

I will try to highlight here some theoretical differences between criminal justice and restorative justice as seen from Norwegian victims' and perpetrators' points of view. These are not clear in practice and, in addition they are often contested.

Criminal justice:
- The perpetrators are punished.
- The victims and perpetrators (litigants) are treated as opponents or adversaries in the negotiating process by their juridical representatives.
- The victims want the perpetrators to be punished.
- The victims receive restoration by the mere fact that the defendants are punished.

- The satisfaction of victims' needs is not an issue in criminal proceedings.
- The judges determine what is the best for the victims and perpetrators.

Restorative justice:
- The actors accept responsibility for the act(s) committed.
- The actors and the community (represented by members of the local conflict council) agree upon the harm done.
- The possibility of reconciliation increases if there is a direct co-operation and/or confrontation between the actors.
- The actors must offer repair of the harm done in the form of remorse, restoration, restitution and, eventually, reconciliation.
- The actors are not punished but supported to repair the harm done, to seek help and work on the problems.

An anthropology of violent acts

The anthropologist, David Riches, discusses in *The Anthropology of Violence* (1986) the relationship between the performers of violence (i.e. the perpetrator and victim and (the) witness(es)). He generates a dynamic and relational model 'which captures the fundamental tension in this basic triangle of violence' (1986: 8). In order for anthropologists to see violence as a cross-cultural phenomenon, the act of violence itself must be focused on rather than the roles of the performers. Riches claims that violence must be seen as an act in a relationship involving at least two persons, which is deemed legitimate by the performer and illegitimate by (some) witnesses: 'Once the tension in the relationship between performer, victim and witnesses is drawn out, the vital question of the potency of violence as an act and as an image can be approached' (1986: 9). The basic triangle of violence is illustrated in Figure 16.1. The triangle's lines symbolise the

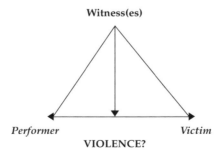

Figure 16.1   The basic triangle of violence

relationships among the performer, victim and witness(es). The line between the performer and victim is seen as the relationship within which the act is committed. The witness(es) look at this relationship in judging whether the act is 'violent', 'accidental', 'deserved', 'legal', 'illegal', etc. Riches describes these relationships as consisting of two elements: 'an element of political competition and an element of competition from the fact that the act of violence never fails to be one of contested legitimacy' (1986: 9). Once legitimacy is brought into the discussion, naming an act as violent will always depend on someone's (the witness's) moral judgement. Legitimacy, however, is also a contested term, not least when the context is a criminal court, or when the military or the police exert violence causing physical hurt or otherwise restricting people's actions by threats of physical force.[12] Thus, there is a need to break down this complexity of meaning into '(acceptable) reason', 'according to the law', and 'grounds for' – which all have different connotations. In my interpretation, violence has a moral dimension. Naming an act as violent is in itself a moral act. There is no space other than morality where one might take refuge from the concept of violence. Or, as Armstrong and Tennenhouse wrote: 'To regard certain practices as violent is never to see them just as they are. It is always to take up a position for or against them (1989: 9).

This perspective for evaluating violence and my distinction between criminal justice and restorative justice are the basis on which the following argument is developed. According to Riches, the differences between restorative justice and criminal justice may be shown using the following two models. Model 1 (see Figure 16.2) demonstrates how we, as witnesses (directly or indirectly), may regard an act (an interaction) between at least two people – based on a moral value judgement of that act – as either violent (i.e. illegitimate) or not violent (legitimate). Witnesses will not always agree as to whether an act is violent or not violent, and neither will the two (conflicting) parties. In criminal proceedings a central premise depicts the two litigants as adversaries (i.e. the disagreements and controversies are central) and, eventually, the extenuating factors lead to the act being interpreted as violent (e.g. a mental illness may be interpreted as the 'reason' for the violent event/act). The negotiations are headed by the parties' 'judicial representatives, the public prosecutor and the defence counsel. In a trial a whole range of opinions will often be expressed concerning guilt and punishment. But there will be an inherent doxic[13] agreement about the phenomena of culpability and punity. Inherence relates to the inevitability or self-evidence of the judgement of a fact – the individually committed criminal act (i.e. a person has been essentialised into being a 'criminal' criminal having committed an act by will and intent). The victim is consequently and likewise essentialised into an individually damaged or injured victimised victim – a passive receiver of evil. And the litigants' representatives build their representations upon a mutual, inimical image.

In a restorative justice process, however, (model 2 – see Figure 16.3), the conflict or violent act will be handled differently. The mediator will not decide or judge upon what has happened or how different witnesses have interpreted an act but base her or his mediation upon the common understanding of reconciliation and restoration the parties themselves may arrive at. In particular cases, 'guilt' or 'cause' may be shared between the two parties as they have not been recognised as adversaries. It is the agreement (not the disagreement) between the two, that is the starting point for mediation. They agree upon the act of illegitimacy but they may disagree upon the degree of it, which is not, however, relevant to the issue of agreement. The two conflicting parties express themselves: they have no representatives (they have a mediator) and no judge.

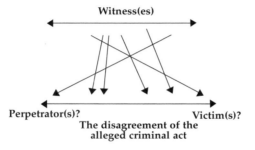

Figure 16.2. An act regarded as violent or not violent (model 1)

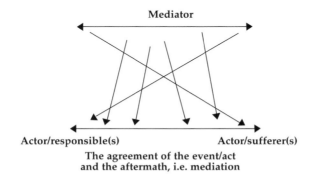

Figure 16.3. An act regarded as violent or not violent (model 2)

Fields of knowledge

The scale of conflicting opinions regarding guilt and punishment is not one-dimensional. The challenge is to recognise its other dimensions[14] within various discourses or conflict regimes (see Table 16.1). The phenomena at stake for the actors in such cases are violence and pain – pain that was suffered by the actors either during the event/act or during the effort with which the actors interpreted the event as a violent act. I, as the observer and anthropological narrator, include rituals as an important phenomenon in this. The anthropological tradition of knowledge provides us with, as I see it, different ways of ordering data: by, for example, cross-cultural comparisons, through analyses of words and acts (e.g. the analysis of rituals) and through variations in the actors' interpretations. The legal actors order speech and events according to the criminal procedure, with its rules and laws, both during the preparation for the trial and during the trial itself. Their knowledge is, at least formally, based upon the premises of law and legal science. I, as participant-observer, have another tradition of knowledge – anthropology, that gives me the possibility of creating a meta-level of comparison, interpretation and explanation.

In suggesting anthropology as an epistemological tool in the outline of legal science, I regard anthropology as embracing the other fields of knowledge at stake in a court case or a restorative justice case – including the lay field of knowledge: the folk theories. This anthropological meta-level includes all the actors as different 'natives.'[16] The mediators are also

Table 16.1. The scale of conflicting opinions

	Lay[15]	Legal	Anthropological
'Cultural stock'	Religious/ 'folk law'	Law/justice	Crossing of lay and scientific categorical boundaries
Theories of knowledge	'Folk theories'	Legal science	Anthropology
Taxonomies	Right/fair, wrong/unfair ...	Criminal law, criminal procedural law ...	Cross-cultural comparison, ritual analysis
Phenomena	Violence, pain, suffering ...	Crime, law, reason, fact, subjective, objective ...	Violence, pain, suffering, ritual, drama, crime, law, reason ...

lay people and, although their specific knowledge base may differ from other lay people (such as the perpetrator or the victim), they refer to a cluster of knowledge different from a lawyer or an anthropologist. Such a model will, in practice, never be as clear and pure as it looks on paper. There will be deep conceptual clefts between some of these traditions and theories, as well as fluent passages between others. In addition, I lean upon such supplementary traditions of knowledge, as European philosophy, the history of ideas and the theory of science (the later two of which may be classified as newer fields of philosophy).

A Norwegian perspective on restorative justice: culture in the making

The re-emerging concept of restorative justice in Norway is multi-faceted,[17] linked as it is to the construction of the nation-state, the emergence of a highly professionalised society and the increasing need for public control of the population now the church is no longer a controlling agent, etc. And not least, the extremely expensive and uncontrolled increase in criminalised[18] activities contributes to a need for 'new' solutions, as seen from both political and bureaucratic points of view. What, then, might be found in modern Norwegian culture that reflects a return to the values of medieval Norway? While I do not want to imply that the proponents of contemporary restorative justice have deliberately looked back on medieval experiences of justice, my aim here is to look for textual or conceptual bridges between old and new practices, which will necessitate a dive into historical sources with an archaeology of knowledge-gaze (Foucault 1969).

While undertaking my former fieldwork into criminal justice I was, first and foremost, a student of juridical discourse as expressed by its actors: police investigators in close co-operation with police lawyers, public prosecutors, the defence counsel, the expert witnesses and the judges. Their script consisted of a 4.6 kg pile of paper produced before trials, in addition to the Norwegian Criminal Procedure Act. Their theatrical performances on stage were readily accessible to me during trials, and they were willing to speak openly to me after the verdict had been finalised. In my new fieldwork, however I have been initiated as a mediator in my own local conflict council. Here I came to learn about rituality and the performative demands placed on the actors. The written script and the oral gestures I experienced were extremely different from those of the criminal justice system.[19] The kinds of public space for handling conflict in Norway fall, therefore, into two different types. The

Table 16.2. The rituals of justice

Ritual	Criminal Justice	Restorative Justice
The owners of the conflict	Adversaries (i.e. the state on behalf of the victim and the perpetrator)	Members/participants
Ritual master	Professional judge, 'central'	Non-professional, local
Ritual actors	Legal counsels (prosecutor, defence counsel)	Participants
Ritual clothing	Long black gowns	Everyday, ordinary clothes
Ritual tools	'Norge's lover', legal textbooks, Norwegian armour, the judge's club	Nothing prescribed
Ritual space	*Strafferetten*, Norwegian court house (*tinghus*)	*Konfliktrådet* (any venue, preferably public space)
Ritual rules of conduct	Impersonal, formal, directed towards strengthening the court's authority according to strict hierarchical rules	Personal, shaking hands and welcoming, directed towards strengthening the dialogue between the participants
Ritual ends	Empowerment of the state by the punitive control of its members	Empowerment of the community by increasing dialogues among its members

rituality of the two 'justices' is also strikingly different and so I will try to emphasise schematically some of the differences (see Table 16.2). I should also like to outline some conflicting areas in contemporary Norwegian culture as these impinge on the matter of justice.

Hospitality and polyphonic dialogue

The criminologist, George Pavlich, was the first person to use the idea of hospitality as a key term in restorative ethics. In his opening address to the Fifth International Conference on Restorative Justice (2001) he said: 'ethics appears as a meta-discourse on how specific instances of hospitality produce ethical subjects who imagine ways to be with others in the future.

This vision of restorative ethics does not claim to be universalisable, or assume a naturally defined ethical subject (e.g. victim, offender, etc.).' The idea of hospitality refers, for example, to Levinas' hosts and guests who are constituted by being given forms of welcome (Pavlich 2001: 13). As a mediator I act as a host. I make it clear the participants in a conflict are welcome to sort out their differences with my assistance. My task is to strengthen their arguments and to make them more specific and concrete so that they can learn about each others' feelings, frames of reference and goals for the future. In the *konfliktråd* they are treated as guests but, instead of a meal, there is an intense yearning for peace and negotiation based upon agreement.

The mediator's position as witness in David Riches' model may be further elaborated by the 'dialogic imagination' as proposed by Mikhail Bakhtin (1981). Bakhtin's theoretical and analytical approach to 'dialogicality' embraces wide fields of knowledge (philosophy, literary theory, linguistics, etc.) and concerns ethics and aesthetics, which are unalterably linked. Every dialogue, be it between persons or between persons and texts, always implies dissimilarity at one or more points. This difference is the key to creativity – to 'creative understanding'. The difference itself is signified or symbolised by a 'witness', a third part. According to Jostein Børtnes' literary interpretation of Bakhtin, 'each dialogue takes place as if against a background of the invisible, but present [is the] "third's" [*superaddressat*] responsive understanding. This "third" is a quality of the word itself; thus the dialogue contains not just the two, but three instances (2001: 10). The third instance is indivisible from the dialogue, as are the two parts – sides (person or text) – creating the dialogue. This 'third' defines the dialogical relation: in addition to I-for-the-other and the-other-for-me comes a 'third' that relates to both and which by its invisible presence yields the dialogical word its open and infinite perspectives of meaning (Børtnes 2001: 11). Bakhtin's musicologic terms 'polyphony' and 'monophony' (as metaphors) refer to his studies of literary texts, especially the novels of Dostoevsky. Bakhtin extends his thoughts (concerning, for example, dialogicality in literature, texts and, especially, novels) towards a social theory, – human interaction (or the philosophy of action). Truth will always depend upon an agreement within the reference of polyphonic dialogue.

In Bakhtinian wording, criminal justice corresponds to a monophonic monologue (of the legal masters), whereas restorative justice may be seen as a polyphonic dialogue (of the various actors in the event that has been interpreted as a criminal act). These differences may be crucial as we seem to find ourselves in a time and place in which there is a growing critical conscience among the people concerning criminal justice (McCold 2001).

This critique poses a threat to the contemporary state of the act of (western/postcolonial) criminal justice of most nations. Using Bakhtin's ideas as Igland and Dysthe have interpreted them (Dysthe 2001), I will try to reformulate the above into a model of monologically versus dialogically organised *justice* (see Table 16.3).

Pavlich divides the way in which restorative justice is conceived into two different fields: the process conception and the value conception. According to a Bakhtinian dialogic perspective, the one is needed for the other: there is no value without a process. I will take the words 'guilt' (representing a criminal domain) and 'responsibility' (representing a restorative domain) as examples of two different terms belonging to the monological versus the dialogical imaginations: Guilt is a 'one-way-term' – there is no way out of it. The word *response*[20] however (or the Norwegian counterpart: *an-svar*), exemplifies a word which, in itself, implies a dialogic relation. There is a question, comment, utterance – and an answer – a response (*et svar*) as an example of the third instance's invisible presence 'which always exerts itself to be heard, always searches for responsive understanding and which does not stay by the immediate understanding, but makes its way continuously forward (boundless)' (Børtnes 2001: 10).

Herein may lie some answers as to why the dialogic relation between participants in restorative justice processes might develop into 'magic' – a term frequently used by mediators when they recall what happened

Table 16.3. The organisation of justice

	Monological/criminal	*Dialogical/restorative*
Paradigm	Professional (legal) Government(ality)	(Non-professionalised) discussion
Communication model	Transmission of legal knowledge	Conversion of insight, comprehension
Epistemology	Objectivism: legal knowledge is taken for granted	Dialogism: knowledge is something created through an interaction between dissimilar voices
Source of appreciated knowledge	Lawyers and legal textbooks and excluding the litigants/ owners of the conflict	Interpretations and personal experiences of the participants, the owners of the conflict

during conferences. People who seemingly oppose each other come, through the dialogue offered by the mediator(s) or the conferencing facilitator(s) to a common understanding of how the event can be interpreted; of the act – in their own wording and with their own rhythm of talk, with anger or anxiety, fury or sadness; of the possibility of forgiveness as an act for the future (Derrida 2001). Thus *restorative* can be taken to mean *restoring Norwegian justice*, both in the sense of *restorative* justice and restoring *justice*.

Acknowledgements

I should like to thank the Programme for Cultural Studies of the Norwegian Research Council and, likewise, Agder University College for financing my research.

Notes

1. Norbert Elias may be said to represent this trend.
2. People *are* criminal or sick, as opposed to a relational/constructivistic perspective – people relate to each other in ways that are dependent upon their context and situatedness as well as the situatedness of the 'witness', the person who interprets and describes what happened.
3. Investigations of those forces that could be said to transform certain events into criminal acts; Michel Foucault represents such perspectives.
4. Defined in a Foucauldian sense.
5. When there were no police, prisons or legal professionals local people had to care for law and order themselves.
6. The Ministry of Social Affairs had been responsible for testing out municipal conflict councils.
7. 'Discourse' as defined according to, e.g., Foucault's directions: persons, textbooks, buildings (institutions) and confrontations/meeting points where emerging values and power relations are at stake.
8. By juridical I mean the idea of the word as given by Bourdieu: 'It [the juridical field] appears to partake of both the positive logic of science and the normative logic of morality and thus to be capable of compelling universal acceptance through an inevitability which is simultaneously logical and ethical' (1987: 818).
9. I use the word 'postmodern' according to Lyotard in *The Postmodern Condition* (1984): 1) views about science as situational; 2) globality as a new way of defining reference, space, time and place; and 3) truth as a differential between a variety of propositions (Lyotard 1979, 1984). By hybrid is meant the construction of a word, or sense with elements from disparate fields of life (in time or

space) or according the *Oxford Dictionary*; 'a composite word formed of elements belonging to different languages.'

10. I use the terms 'drama', 'dramaturgy' and 'dramaturgical' deliberately to emphasise the performative content of the legal and restorative processes described here. In applying these terms I deliberately invoke a comparison with the art and the techniques of the theatre, which I regard as relevant and useful for analytical purposes, and which refer to work of Victor Turner (1974) and Richard Schechner (1994).

11. Anthropologists are not alone in such a comparative metaphorical use of these terms: the Swedish historian Eva Österberg, writes about the courts of fifteenth-century Sweden as the 'theatre of power', (*maktens teater*) (1994).

12. 'Physical hurt' is by no means an uncomplicated term: people my also feel themselves physically hurt by words and texts (e.g. speech acts). Within biomedical reasoning, mental pressure may exert more bodily harm than physical hurt. The whole Carthesian discussion of body vs mind lies in this problematic division. It seems obvious, however, that there is an absolute disruption, biological as well as existential and social, when a violent act causes death or impairment.

13. Here I refer to Bourdieu's notion of those aspects of culture and society that are so obvious to people that they are not even questioned: norms that are so self-evident that they cease to exist as norms.

14. This model presupposes one premise: the existence of a specific praxis that establishes comparability between dissimilar conceptualisations of reality (Larsen 1999: 55).

15. 'Lay' discourse consists of many different things, but here it is used to differentiate from specific professional discourses.

16. They are natives in the sense that they are at home, each in their respective tradition of knowledge – their subculture.

17. This discussion is, of necessity, a simplification of a complex and contested sequence of historical events.

18. In the sense of crime as it is constructed according to contemporary rules and laws.

19. This argument is based partly on Nils Christie's reasoning in 'Conflicts as Property' (1977).

20. Which I define as a feeling or an act answering some stimulus or influence.

References

Armstrong, N. and Tennenhouse, L. (eds) (1989) *The Violence of Representation. Literature and the History of Violence*. London: Routledge.

Bakhtin, M.M. (1981) *The Dialogic Imagination: Four Essays by M.M. Bakhtin*. (ed. M. Holquist, trans. C. Emerson and M. Holquist). Austin, TX: University of Texas Press.

Børtnes, J. (2001) '*Om de kappadokiske fedre og russisk dialogtenking hjå Dostojevskij og Bakhtin*.' Lecture presented at the annual seminar of Hans Skjervheim, Stalheim.

Bourdieu, P. (1987) 'The Force of Law: Toward a Sociology of the Juridical Field', *The Hastings Law Journal*, 38: 814–85.

Christie, N. (1977) 'Conflicts as Property', *British Journal of Criminology*, 17(1): 1–17.

Dean, M. (1999) *Governmentality. Power and Rule in Modern Society*. London: Sage.

Derrida, J. (2001) *Cosmopolitanism and Forgiveness*. London and New York, NY: Routledge.

Dysthe, O. (2001) *Dialog, samspel og læring* (*Dialogue, Interplay and Learning*). Oslo: abstract forlag.

Foucault, M. (1969) *L'Archéologie du Savoir*. Paris: Gallimard.

Gatrell, V.A.C., Parker, G. and Lenman, B. (eds.) (1980) *Crime and the Law: The Social History of Crime in Western Europe since 1500*. London: Europa.

Hydle, I. (2001) *'Murder without Motive. An Anthropological Study of a Criminal Case'*. Doctoral thesis. Department of Social Anthropology, Faculty of Social Sciences, University of Oslo, September.

Justisdepartementet (1999) *Megling som supplement til straff* (*Mediation as supplement to punishment*, my translation). Rapport fra en arbeidsgruppe oppnevnt av Justisdepartementets Sivilavdeling (Report from a working group appointed by the Ministry of Justice, my translation).

Kemény, S.I. (2000) 'Policy Developments and the Concept of Restorative Justice through Mediation', in the European Forum for Victim–Offender Mediation and Restorative Justice (ed.) *Victim–Offender Mediation in Europe*. Leuven: University Press.

Larsen, T. (1999) 'Antropologienes Kulturbegrep' (Anthropologies Concepts of Culture'), in S. Gerrard *et al.* (eds) *Kulturforståelser i fagene. Kulturstudier*, 6: 49–101.

Lyotard, J.-F. (1979) *La Condition postmoderne*. Paris: Les Editions de Minuit.

Lyotard, J.-F. (1984) *The Postmodern Condition: A Report on Knowledge* (trans. G. Benington and B. Massumi). Minneapolis, MN: University of Minnesota Press.

McCold, P. (2001) 'A Survey of Assessment Research on Mediation and Conferencing.' Paper presented at the 'Positioning Restorative Justice' conference, Leuven, September.

Meyer, S. (2001) *Kommunikasjonsregimer* (Regimes of Communication, my translation). Internt notat. Bergen: Senter for Europeiske Kulturstudier.

Österberg, E. (1994) 'Normbrott och Rättspraxis i Norden under Förindustriell Tid. Problem och Positioner (Breaches in Norms and Legal Practice During Preindustrial Times. Problems and Positions'), in K. Tønnesson (ed.) *Det Nordiske historikermøte, Oslo 13.–18. august 1994. Rapporter. 2: Normer og sosial kontroll i Norden ca. 1550–1850: Domstolene i samspill med lokalsamfunnet* (*The Nordic Historian Meeting, Reports. Norms and Social Control in the Nordic Countries, 1550–1850. The Courts in Interaction with the Local Community*). Oslo: IKS, Avdeling for historie, Universitetet i Oslo, og Den norske historiske forening.

Overing, J. (1987) 'Translation as a Creative Process: the Power of the Name', in L. Holy (ed.) *Comparative Anthropology*. Oxford: Blackwell.

Pavlich, G. (2001) *'Towards an Ethics of Restorative Justice.'* Opening address, 5th International Conference on Restorative Justice, Leuven, September.

Riches, D. (ed.) (1986) *The Anthropology of Violence*. Oxford: Blackwell.

Sandmo, E. (1999) *Voldssamfunnets undergang: om disiplineringen av Norge på 1600-tallet (The Decline of the Violent Society: on the Disciplining of Norway in the sixteenth Century)*. Oslo: Universitetsforlaget.

Schechner, R. (1994) *Performance Theory*. London: Routledge.

Turner, V. (1974) *Dramas, Fields and Metaphors*. Ithaca, NY: Cornell University Press.

Chapter 17

Implementing family group conferences in Belgium

Inge Vanfraechem

Introduction

As conferencing is currently being implemented in Belgium,[1] this chapter explores some of the differences between a common law and a legalistic system of Justice. While it is not the intention to try to discuss all these differences, I should like to highlight here the fact that some elements between these two systems are indeed different, and that these differences can lead to the creation of a somewhat different model of conferencing, with different accents. The focus here is on the Belgian model of conferencing rather than on other restorative practices. However, it may well be that differences between practices are a result of differences in the justice systems within which they are implemented. For example, victim–offender mediation is still developing in many European legal systems, while conferencing has been implemented in such common law countries as New Zealand, Australia, the UK, the USA and Canada.

Conferencing

What is conferencing?

Conferencing is a practice within restorative justice, and restorative justice has been described as a 'third way' (Walgrave 2000) of dealing with (juvenile) offending. The first way is the retributive approach, which focuses on punishment and where the punishment is supposed to be proportional to the crime committed. The second way is the rehabilitative approach, which focuses on the offender and how he or she can be treated in order to be reintegrated into society. The emphasis here lies on treatment, supervision and control rather than on punishment. In restorative justice, on the other hand, the focus lies on the harm and how that harm can be repaired. The harm is viewed from a broad perspective: not only the harm to the victim but also the harm to the offender and to society (Goedseels *et al.*, 2001).

Family group conferences are considered to be practices that have a high degree of restorativeness since they include the victim, offender and the broader community (see, among others, McCold 2000). Conferencing can be viewed as a deliberation between the offender and his or her network, the victim and his or her network and the police (Walgrave pers. comm. 2000). In the New Zealand model, the police are present but they do not assume the role of facilitator.

Different models of conferencing

When one studies the available literature on conferencing,[2] one realises it is difficult to make generalisations about all the existing models. Here I would like to distinguish between two main models, namely, the New Zealand model and the Wagga model. In 1989, in New Zealand, the Children, Young Persons and their Families Act led to the implementation of conferencing for almost all juvenile offenders. (The procedures involved in this type of conference are discussed later in this chapter since this is the model used in Belgium.) A youth justice co-ordinator directs the conference and a police officer attends. In the Wagga model, on the other hand, the police act as a facilitator. This model (developed by O'Connell and incorporating Braithwaite's reintegrative shaming theory – (McCold 1999)) was later used in the USA under the name 'Real Justice'. It is currently being implemented in various other countries (for example, in the Netherlands).

The 1989 New Zealand Act focused on the family in general and families' own resources to deal with youngsters' offending. This view can also be seen in wider community approaches that take into account broader networks (Brown 1995). The 1980s saw much discussion about the Maori system of justice. In the Maori approach, collective responsibility is important, and attention is directed towards the broader family. There is also a need to repair the social balance that has been disrupted by the crime. This is done by reintegrating the youngster into his or her family and community and by repairing the damage done to the victim (Morris and Maxwell 1998). From a restorative point of view, three elements are important with regard to the New Zealand Youth Court. First of all, power is transferred from the state to the community. Secondly, conferencing is used as a mechanism for an agreed community reaction. Finally, victims are included as key persons, which makes a healing process possible for both the victim and offender. Conferences are used for almost all juvenile offenders, either as a diversion measure at the level of the police or before the judge makes a decision. In most cases, the agreement reached in the conference is accepted by the judge (McElrea 1998).

Conferencing in Belgium

Origins

In 1999, Lode Walgrave and two youth judges[3] visited New Zealand to study the systems of conferencing in place in that country. In the following months, different Flemish mediation services were contacted to ascertain whether they were interested in implementing family group conferences in Flanders.[4] Once the services expressed their willingness to participate, Allan MacRae, a well-known facilitator in New Zealand, was invited to give the mediators three weeks' training. In the following months, contact was made with the different partners involved in the project: lawyers, youth judges, prosecutors, social services and the police. After much discussion, a model for the Belgian context was established. Five jurisdictions[5] within Flanders would participate, using this model as the basis but adapting it slightly to local customs and structures. The project started on 1 October 2000 and is due to be reviewed after three years.[6]

Practice

Position in the legal framework

In Belgium, family group conferences are at the level of the Youth Court. Family group conferences are not seen as a soft option since they require effort from all the parties involved, and thus are reserved for the more serious cases. Working at the level of the Youth Court should ensure this and it also has the advantage of protecting the parties' legal rights: a lawyer is appointed for the young offender, the victims can bring their lawyer along and the youth judge oversee the process. Most of the existing family group conferences are situated in the common law system of justice, while working within a legalistic system leads to certain peculiarities.

The model

When a young person comes before the youth judge, the judge assesses whether the case would be appropriate for a family group conference. If the young person denies the facts of the case, a conference cannot take place: the case goes through the normal proceedings at the Youth Court. If the young person does not deny the facts, the youth judge asks the Youth Court's social services for advice. Social services then assess the young person's willingness to participate and give him or her more information about what conferences entail. If the case is assessed as appropriate for a family group conference, this fact is relayed to the youth judge within ten days. The latter can then authorise the facilitator to start the family group conference. The facilitator contacts the parties involved: the offender and his or her supporters, the victim and his or her supporters and the police officer.

The offender is contacted first so he or she can offer further explanation and learn whom he or she can bring to the conference as support. Since social services have already checked whether he or she is willing to participate, this is something the facilitator does not have to address. However, the facilitator does have to make sure that the young person does not deny the facts of the case.

The facilitator then contacts the victim to see whether he or she is willing to participate. Even when the victim does not want to attend, the conference can still take place: the victim can still have his or her views represented (e.g. in a letter or by having a friend or relative attend the conference). Of course, the conference will have greater value when the victim is willing to participate, but it is up to the victim to decide. It is important to note that the victim, like the offender, can bring along all the support he or she wants at the conference. This preparation phase is crucial for all the parties involved: it means they know what is going on and what they can and cannot expect. For the offender, it is important to know what his or her rights are and that, if he or she does not agree with the proceedings, he or she can choose to stop the process and have the case taken to court. The victim needs to know what the process is like and what he or she can realistically expect of it in order to prevent secondary victimisation.

As in New Zealand, a police officer attends the conference to make it clear that the conference is dealing with a crime – a serious fact. Also, the attendance of a police officer gives the parties a sense of security and reminds everyone of the fact that harm has been done to society as a whole. A police presence is not so evident in legalistic systems of justice, since they do not have discretionary powers.

The conference meeting itself usually proceeds as follows: first, all the parties are introduced and their respective roles are outlined. This is to ensure that everyone knows what his or her role in the conference will be (for instance, to support the offender or victim). The police officer reads out the facts of the case and checks whether the offender agrees with them. If the offender denies the facts, the conference cannot take place. Then there is a phase of storytelling when the victim, his or her supporters, the offender and his or her supporters explain what effect the offence has had on them. This phase can be seen as the core of the conference: all thoughts and feelings can be shared and a mutual understanding of the harm caused by the offence can be arrived at. This if often the first time the young person realises he or she has hurt his or her own family and friends. This can be an emotional event: when the offender appreciates the harm caused, he or she might apologise spontaneously.

After this process of communication between all the parties, the offender and his or her supporters can have a private time during which they discuss possible solutions for the offence, taking into account the needs and wishes of the victim. Other elements can also be addressed during this private time, such as the underlying reasons for the offending–problems at home, possible drug problems and so on. The main aim of the conference is to address the harm caused by the crime, but the idea is that underlying factors should be addressed as well. In this way there is a greater chance the agreement reached in the conference will be fulfilled. Restoration and reintegration of the offender might also be achieved.

The proposed solution is then presented by the young person to the victim and discussed until an agreement is reached, if possible. The aims of the agreement are threefold: repairing the harm done to the victim, repairing the harm done to society as a whole and preventing such a thing from happening again. The agreement is written down in detail for all the parties (as well as the youth judge) so that all know what is to be accomplished and within what time frame. The people involved in either implementing the agreement or providing follow-up (the offender and his or her support), as well as the victim, sign the agreement.[7]

This agreement is then brought before the judge, who can decide whether or not to accept it. There is an understanding that youth judges, in principle, will accept the agreements, but, as is the case in any legal system, judges make the final decision. The idea is that, when judges accept the agreement, they are acknowledging the work that has been done by the parties involved, thereby empowering those parties.

Once the agreement is accepted it can be put into practice. The agreement includes a means of follow-up and states the period within which the agreement should be executed. The agreement should also be set up in a very concrete manner to make sure follow-up is possible. After the time limit is up, the matter is again taken before the youth judge, who can then check to see whether the agreement has been executed properly. If so, the judge can decide that a decision that the case should be closed and that the young person should not go through any more legal proceedings. If it has not been executed properly, the judge can decide to have a second conference or to impose a different procedure. By bringing the case back to the Youth Court, the victim is sure the young person will undertake what has been agreed, and the youth judge can close the case in a manner positive towards the young person.

The research linked to the project

This conferencing procedure will be evaluated using different methods. Through these various methods, it is hoped to obtain a good idea of what the process of family group conferences entails and wherein its strengths lie. There are five main questions that need to be answered:

1. Can family group conferences be introduced within the existing legal system for juvenile offenders?
2. Are the legal rights of the parties secured?
3. Are the parties satisfied with the process?
4. Is the young person's network strengthened throughout this process?
5. Is there less recidivism?

The question of recidivism will be difficult to address since the project only runs for three years. Furthermore, this experiment does not have a random design whereby different cases would be sent at random to traditional courts or to conferencing. Thus there is no basis for comparison.

Scientific follow-up entails different strands. First, it is based on action research, which means that researchers have close contact with all the professionals involved. Secondly, different methods are used so that a good overview of the steps involved in the whole conferencing process can be obtained. The young offenders' records are studied to get some basic background information, such as family history and previous offending. The family group conference is itself observed, using a standardised observation scheme. The aim is to see what dynamics take place in a conference that may predict its outcome and success.

In addition to the observation, both the victim and offender are interviewed to ascertain whether or not they found the process worthwhile and whether they were satisfied with the way their case was dealt with. The young offender's parents are interviewed to find out whether they, too, found the process worthwhile. They are asked if they feel they have been supported in their role of educating their child, since this is a presupposed effect of the conference.[8] Other people who support the young person might be interviewed as well since, for the young person, his or her parents are not always the most important people present at the conference. The young person is therefore asked who his or her most important support person is and this person is interviewed as well. The police, youth judges, prosecutors, lawyers and social services at the Youth Court will be contacted to find out whether they think conferencing can be introduced into the Belgian legal system and, if so, what conditions must be met. Procedural safeguards are considered to be very important and thus it must be ensured that these safeguards are in place if criminal justice system professionals are to feel confident referring cases to conferencing. This issue is therefore included in the interviews as well.

The first year of the project was dedicated to developing and testing the measurement instruments, using the research methods employed in other countries. The second year of the project focused on obtaining sufficient referrals so the measurement instruments can evaluate the experiment effectively. Partners in the criminal justice system (youth judges lawyers and others) also are asked how they view the project and what should be done differently. The third year focuses on analysing the data, further developing the methodology and solving practical and theoretical questions.

An important research question that needs to be addressed is whether the system can be implemented within the existing youth justice system. Since Belgium is a legalistic system, this is a crucial issue.

The elements of the debate

Working at court level

Working at court level within a legal justice system has resulted in some peculiarities.

First, it is crucial to establish a good referral procedure. Youth judges in Belgium deal with a heavy caseload and do not always have the time to think about new initiatives or to implement them if they are overly complicated. Therefore, a great deal of time has been taken working out a good referral procedure that respects the existing traditions within each jurisdiction as well as legal provisions.

The Youth Court social services have been included in the referral procedure since they are the first people to come into contact with offenders. They also know the young person's family history should the young person have been to court before. As this experiment mainly involves serious cases, most of the young people are known to the Youth Court. Social services can suggest a conference when the judge has not thought of this. Social services can also be involved in the conference and in the follow-up.

Secondly, it is important that conferencing fits into the current structure since the judges have to work within the existing legal framework. For example, since the judges must note a referral to conferencing in their legal documents, we had to find a Dutch phrase for 'family group conferences'.[10] It was also important to protect the young person's legal rights. For example, the judge makes an official judgment when he or she decides whether or not to accept the conference agreement, and this might include community service. The Court of Appeal in Brussels, has judged that community service cannot be imposed unless an official judgment is made. Also, social services follow up the young person since they have a mandate to do so.[11] Working out a good procedure is very important if the young person's rights are to be respected, bearing in mind critiques of rehabilitation approaches as well as of restorative justice.[12]

One of the first cases to be sent to a conference was taken to the Court of Appeal as a result of civil matters (the case was looked at with regard to criminal matters as well). The court commented on the procedure of the case but, at the same time, considered the conferencing process to be positive. A meeting was organised with different youth judges and judges from the Court of Appeal, as well as with facilitators and researchers. This was a very positive meeting. The concept of conferences was clarified and a procedure was sought and found that could be included with the existing Belgian youth justice system. This illustrates the importance of working with judges and other professionals within the justice system if cases are to be referred and if the procedure is to be integrated into the existing system.

A great deal of time must be invested in trying to establish a sound procedure and in working within the existing legal rules and traditions. In this we think we have succeeded. Although this takes up a lot of energy, it might lead to conferencing becoming part of the mainstream. In Belgium it is, of course, too soon to say whether this is the case or not. One hypothesis is that working within the system affects the system and transforms the ideas and attitudes of people working within the system. At the same time, one has to be careful that restorative approaches are not taken over by the system. Such approaches run the risk of being named 'restorative' but, basically, they fulfil different aims, such as rehabilitation and punishment (see, among others, Aertsen 1999; Vanfraechem 2000).

Compared to common law countries, the question can be posed

whether, in legalistic countries, it is more opportune to situate a conferencing procedure at the level of the court. In such a way the legal safeguards that seem to be so important for such countries[13] can be preserved. Another influencing factor is that working at the police level is difficult because the police do not have any discretionary power.

Presence of the police

In certain models of conferencing, the police run the conferences as a facilitator. In Belgium, as family group conferences were implemented at Youth Court level, facilitators[14] run the conferences, yet the police are included. It could be argued that a conference is an intense and emotional event for the parties involved, and that including a police officer could jeopardise the process. However, the presence of the police officer is important for several reasons. First, the presence of a police officer reinforces the fact that the parties have come together because an offence has been committed, which is a serious matter as a social norm has been transgressed. The conference is thus not taken lightly. For the young person, it emphasises the fact that the offence committed has broader social consequences than simply the harm done to the victim. Moreover, the presence of a police officer reassures the victim and enhances the feelings of safety of all the parties present. Finally, the young person and his or her family can get to know the police in a different way – which could change the view they have of the police. All police officers who participate in a conference receive information about what the process entails and what the aim is. In this way they know what their role entails. It is crucial police officers understand the philosophy behind conferences so that they do not take over but still intervene when required. So far, the police have reacted positively: they are glad to be involved even though they felt slightly uncomfortable at the beginning. They receive feedback from the facilitators after the conference so they can evaluate their role. Interviews with the parties involved will establish whether they, too, think it is useful to have a police presence and to find out what they think the role of the police should be at the conferences.

It has, however, to be noted that a police presence at a conference is not an obvious requirement in a legalistic country. In common law countries where the police have wider discretionary powers, their inclusion at a conference can be seen as stemming from this power. In such countries, the police can say whether or not they agree with a conference and, if a conference is implemented at police level, that could be the end of the matter. In a legalistic country, on the other hand, the police have no discretionary power at all. Theoretically, public prosecutors should attend conferences, but this has proved impossible because of constraints on their time. The police uniform lends symbolic importance to the gathering. It is very clear, though, that the police do not have the power to decide whether or not the agreement reached is appropriate. The public prosecutor, therefore, pronounces on the appropriateness of the agreement at the court sessions where, ultimately, the judge will decide.

The role of the lawyer

In Belgium, a young person has the right to be supported by a lawyer at all times at the level of the Youth Court. Thus a lawyer can be present at conferences. In every district, a number of lawyers co-operated with the conferences after they had been informed about what conferencing is, the philosophy behind it and their role as a lawyer in a conference. This way lawyers should realise they are not there to speak for the young offenders and thus should not take over the conference. So far, lawyers seem to have acknowledged the philosophy of conferencing and have played a very positive role.

The presence of a lawyer also protects the parties' rights. As noted earlier, critics of restorative justice initiatives have pointed out that the rights of the young people are sometimes neglected. It is therefore necessary to ensure that the rights of both parties are acknowledged and protected, and so the victims can be accompanied by their lawyers if they so wish. Two problems, however, can arise from this. First, the victim has to pay for his or her own lawyer and cannot always afford to do so. Thus, an unequal situation arises.[15] Secondly, it is the facilitator's role to inform the lawyer of what conferencing is about so that the lawyer does not take over. As noted above, information sessions are being held with lawyers to raise awareness about what the project entails. In this way lawyers can play a supplementary role in explaining to the parties what the process is about and what support they can expect from lawyers at the conference. They can also advise the youth judge when they think a case would be suitable for a conference.

In the literature on conferencing, the issue of a youth advocate is not mentioned very often and, when it is, it is usually stated that the lawyer does not attend the conference. Since in legalistic countries procedure is often very important, including a lawyer in conferences is a crucial matter. In Belgium, where the focus is on serious cases, the presence of a lawyer might be an even more important matter. Also, as critiques of rehabilitative and restorative approaches have often pointed out that the rights of the young person are ignored, we want to prevent this from happening in this project.

More serious crimes

The limited number of conferences[16] so far held have primarily dealt with more serious cases. Working at the level of the Youth Court has, in part, ensured this. Also, as conferencing is a time-consuming process for all the parties involved and is not considered a soft option, it has been reserved for these more serious cases. In most common law countries, however, conferencing is often used as a diversionary procedure and thus includes the less serious cases only. New Zealand is an exception to this, where almost all youngsters go to a conference – including serious cases. Conferences where police officers act as facilitators (for instance, Real Justice in Bethlehem, USA, and the Thames Valley, UK) deal with less serious cases. It could be the case that, in common law countries, the police have more discretionary power and so there is more room for diversion than in legalistic countries.

Cultural relevance

It has often been argued, that Belgian culture is too individualistic and too different from New Zealand or Australian culture for conferencing to be implemented successfully. In New Zealand, conferencing was partly inspired by Maori culture, where it was linked to Maori traditions of giving importance to the family and the community when dealing with crime. Research has shown that conferencing does reflect cultural differences (Maxwell and Morris 1996). Obviously, New Zealand culture is different from Belgian culture but both countries are industrialised and western and individualism is prevalent in both. All young offenders in New Zealand go through conferencing,[17] not only Maori offenders. Therefore, the argument that individualism impedes conferencing in Belgium does not seem to hold. Furthermore, by including not only the close family but also the broader family and other 'significant others' it should be possible to establish an extensive network for the younger person, even when he or she has relatively few close family members. However, it has been noticed that the parents and the young offender are sometimes ashamed of what has happened and do not want other people to know about it. This might, therefore, prevent other support people from becoming involved. This has been noted in New Zealand as well, and so it cannot be considered cultural difference as such. The difference is that, in New Zealand, conferences are regulated by law, which states that family members are 'entitled members'. This means that they are entitled to get an invitation to the conference. However, they can still decide whether or not to attend the conference. This legal requirement might give the facilitator extra powers to persuade parents and the young person to involve more people (Vanfraechem 2002).

Yet there are some cultural differences between common law and legalistic countries. First, conferencing seems to be linked to aboriginal practices in common law countries, as in New Zealand. It has, however, to be noted that there are some critiques of the system from an aboriginal point of view (see, for instance, Tauri 1999). Could it be that, sometimes, aboriginal practices are used as a justification for the system after it has been implemented?[18] In the USA and the UK, on the other hand, such considerations do not seem to apply. Perhaps this was just an important element when the idea of conferencing was first developing.

Another aspect is the concept of community. Common law countries have a tradition of looking to the community rather than the state when dealing with legal matters (Aertsen 2001: 200). Also, volunteers often work in the justice system (for instance as mediators) – a tradition that is not often found in legalistic countries (Aertsen 1994: 4, 2001: 190). Common law countries therefore seem more open to the community when handling criminal cases (Detry 2001).

The last element is the fact that common law countries have a culture of debate which legalistic countries do not (Aertsen 2001: 200). De Smet (1999) compares accusatorial and inquisitorial systems and points out that an accusatorial process is linked to a liberal legal constitution. This means legal safeguards are aimed at protecting a party from the arbitrary action of the state. Thus one could say this has an effect on a country's willingness to implement restorative justice: when there is a fear of the state interfering too much coupled with a tradition of including the community, it might be more logical to implement restorative ideas. Under an inquisitorial regime, on the other hand, procedural safeguards are viewed as preserving the general interest. This means a judge can still deliberate on a case even when the parties have come to an agreement. This way of working can hinder restorative approaches, which aim at involving the parties and letting them decide what the appropriate outcome should be. However, it has often been pointed out that the differences between the systems are not clear anymore. For instance, there is more and more room in a legalistic system for the parties to come to an agreement themselves. The action of the judge is then no longer a procedural requirement but, rather, a means for the parties to come to a solution.

Conclusion

If we want restorative justice to work – if we want to make 'a model' of it – all the factors discussed in this chapter must be addressed. Working within the criminal justice system offers us a unique opportunity to change the system and the attitudes of the people working within that system. At the same time, this process will take a long time and there are a great many barriers to be overcome. However, looking in depth at the differences between common law and legalistic countries, and at their different approaches towards restorative justice, could shed more light on the possibility of creating a truly restorative system of justice.

Notes

1. More precisely in Flanders – the Flemish-speaking part of the country.
2. For instance, Longclaws *et al.* (1996), Moore and Stanway (1997), Fercello and Umbreit (1998), McCold (1998), McCold and Wachtel (1998), Crime Concern (1999), Thames Valley Restorative Justice Consultancy (1999), OKS (2000), Daly (2001), Dignan and Marsh (2001), McKenzie.
3. Youth Judge F. Raes and Youth Judge H. Van de Wynckel, with the support of the King Baudouin Foundation.
4. Mediation services for young people currently exist in various districts in Flanders, as well as in the French-speaking part of Belgium (Wallonia) and Brussels.
5. Antwerp, Brussels, Hasselt, Leuven and Tongeren.
6. The Flemish Community funds this project since, for the Flemish Ministry of Welfare, restorative justice is a policy priority.
7. The words 'declaration of intent' are used to point out that what has been agreed still has to be approved by the youth judge. Thus it is not yet a definitive agreement.
8. This is also considered to be a consequence and strength of including other people in that the young person and his or her parents feel supported in various ways.
9. Others can also suggest a conference – for instance, lawyers.
10. *Herstelgericht Groepsoverleg (Hergo)*.
11. When a judgment is laid down, it is the task of the Youth Court social services to ensure the case is followed up.
12. See, among others, Dumortier (2001).
13. Legal safeguards are, of course, also important in common law countries but they seem to demand more attention in legalistic countries.
14. Victim–offender mediation was already available in several districts in Belgium and so, instead of setting up a new service and training new people, mediators trained in the methodology of conferencing were used in this experiment. Those people were renamed 'facilitators' to emphasise the fact that

they have a different role to play in conferences.

15. This problem can also surface in more 'traditional' procedures.

16. Some 30 conferences in about one and a half years.

17. Unless the police use diversionary measures.

18. Although open to controversy, it is important at least to take this possibility into consideration.

References

Aertsen, I. (1999) 'Restorative Justice in a European Perspective.' Paper presented at the Restorative Justice, Ireland, network 1999 conference (http://www.extem.org/restorative/99-ConfAertsen.htm).

Aertsen, I. (2001) 'Slachtoffer-daderbemiddeling' een onderzoek naar de ontwikkeling van een herstelgerichte strafrechtsbedeling.' Unpublished doctoral thesis, K.U. Leuven.

Brown, M. (1995) 'Background Paper on the New Zealand Youth Justice Process.' Paper presented at the International Bar Association Judges' Forum, Edinburgh, June (http://www.realjustice.org/Pages/NZ.html).

Crime Concern (1999) *An Evaluation of VOICES: Bristol's Victim–Offender Conferencing scheme.* Bristol: Bristol Mediation.

Daly, K. (2001) 'Conferencing in Australia and New Zealand: Variations, Research Findings and Prospects ... Conferencing, Mediation and Circles', in A. Morris and G. Maxwell (eds) *Restorative Justice for Juveniles. Conferencing Mediation and Circles.* Oxford and Portland, OR: Hart Publishing.

De Smet, B. (1999) *Internationale samenwerking in strafzaken tussen Angelsaksische en continentale landen.* Antwerp and Groningen: Intersentia Rechtswetenschappen.

Detry, I. (2001) Restorative Justice: Common Law vs. Civil Law.' Unpublished masters thesis, K.U. Leuven.

Dignan, J. and Marsh, P. (2001) 'Restorative Justice and Family Group Conferencing in England: Current State and Future Prospects', in A. Morris and G. Maxwell (eds) *Restorative Justice for Juveniles. Conferencing, Mediation and Circles.* Oxford and Portland, OR: Hart Publishing.

Dumortier, E. (2001) 'Over het herstel (van het) recht voor kinderen', *Panopticon,* 22(5): 494–511.

Fercello C. and Umbreit, M. (1998) *Client Evaluation of Family Group Conferencing in 12 Sites in the 1st Judicial District of Minnesota* (University of Minnesota) (http://ssw.che.umn.edu/rjp/Resources/Documents/ferumb98.PDF).

Goedseels, E., Vanfraechem, I., Van Grunderbeeck, S. and Walgrave, L. (2001) 'Schade en herstel in herstelrecht', *Tijdschrift voor Herstelrecht,* 1(3): 4–19.

Longclaws, L., Galaway, B. and Barkwell, L. (1996) 'Piloting Family Group Conferences for Young Aboriginal Offenders in Winnipeg, Canada', in J. Hudson *et al.* (eds) *Family Group Conferences: Perspectives on Policy and Practice.* Monsey, NY: Criminal Justice Press.

Maxwell, G. and Morris, A. (1996) 'Research on Family Group Conferences with Young Offenders in New Zealand', in J. Hudson *et al.* (eds) *Family Group*

Conferences: Perspectives on Policy and Practice. Monsey, NY: Criminal Justice Press.

McCold, P. (1998) *'Police-facilitated Restorative Conferencing. What the Data Show.'* Paper presented at the second annual international conference on restorative justice for juveniles, Fort Lauderdale, November.

McCold, P. (1999) *Restorative Justice Practice – The State of the Field 1999* (http://www.realjusti-ce.org/Pages/vt99papers/vtm_mcold.htm).

McCold, P. (2000) 'Overview of Mediation, Conferencing and Circles.' Paper presented at the International Crime Congress, Vienna, April.

McCold, P. and Wachtel, B. (1998) *Restorative Policing Experiment: The Bethlehem Pennsylvania Police Family Group Conferencing Project.* Washington, DC: US Government Printing Office.

McElrea, F.W.M. (1998) 'The New Zealand Model of Family Group Conferences', *European Journal on Criminal Policy and Research,* 6: 537–43.

Moore, L. and Stanway, K. (1997) *Kaslo Restorative Justice Committee. Community Accountability Program* (http://www.kin.bc.ca/Restore Just/report.pdf).

Morris, A. and Maxwell, G. (1998) 'Restorative Justice in New Zealand: Family Group Conferences as a Case Study', *Western Criminology Review,* 1(1) (http://wcr.sonoma.edu/vlnl/morris.html).

OKS (Op Kleine Schaal) (2000) *Echt Recht achtergrondinformatie* (brochure on the project).

Skelton, A. and Frank, C. (2001) 'Conferencing in South Africa: Returning to our Future', in A. Morris and G. Maxwell (eds) *Restorative Justice or Juveniles. Conferencing, Mediation and Circles.* Oxford and Portland, OR: Hart Publishing.

Strang, H. (2001) *Restorative Justice Programs in Australia. A Report to the Criminolology Research Council* (http://www.aic.gov.au/crc/oldreports/strang/index.html).

Tauri, J.M. (1999) *Family Group Conferencing: The Myth of Indigenous Empowerment in New Zealand* (http://www.usask.ca/nativelaw/jah_tauri.html).

Thames Valley Restorative Justice Consultancy (1999) 'The History of the Development of Restorative Justice in the Thames Valley Police', in Thames Valley Partnership (ed.) *Restoring the Balance. A Handbook on Restorative Approaches in Community Safety.*

Vanfraechem, I. (2000) 'Victim's Role in Restorative Justice: is it Worth While for Them? An Analysis of some Restorative Oriented Instruments and what they can Do for Victims of Crime. A Critical Perspective.' Unpublished masters thesis, K.U. Leuven.

Vanfraechem, I. (2002) 'Verslag van een studiebezoek aan Nieuw Zeeland' 16 maart tot 8 april 2000. Unpublished thesis, K.U. Leuven.

Walgrave, L. (2000) *Met het oog op herstel.* Leuven: Leuven University Press.

Young, R. (2001) 'Just Cops doing "Shameful" Business? Police-led Restorative Justice and the Lessons of Research', in A. Morris and G. Maxwell (eds) *Restorative Justice for Juveniles. Conferencing, Mediation and Circles.* Oxford and Portland, OR: Hart Publishing.

Chapter 18

The future of the Japanese criminal justice system

Toshio Yoshida

Introduction

Over the last few decades, victim–offender mediation has become an integral part of criminal justice systems all over the world and is still gaining in importance. In the European Union, Recommendation R(85)11 on the position of victims within criminal law and criminal procedures and R(99)19 on mediation in penal matters have fostered the development of victim–offender mediation. Moreover, the Tenth United Nation Congress on the Prevention of Crime and the Treatment of Offenders (2000), held in Vienna, adopted the resolution that 'we encourage the development of restorative justice policies, procedures and programmes that are respectful of the rights, needs and interests of victims, offenders, communities and all other parties. In some countries that have common law jurisdictions, family group conferencing has also been adopted.

Therefore in certain parts of the world there has recently been a tendency to devise socially constructive responses to criminal acts. However, Japanese criminal justice still relies on its traditional punitive reaction to crime and so, therefore, victim–offender mediation has not been introduced as an alternative measure for either young or adult offenders.

Punitive sanctions

This reluctance to accept other forms of justice is exemplified by Japan's adherence to the death penalty. While the death penalty has been abolished in many countries, in Japan it still has overwhelming popular support.

In an opinion poll conducted by the Information Centre of the Cabinet Secretary (1981, 1990, 1995, 2000), some 80% of those interviewed were in favour of capital punishment. Moreover, the attitude of Japanese people towards the death penalty seems to be hardening. In 1994, almost 75% were in favour of capital punishment, in 1989, 65% and, in 1980, 60%. The reasons given for this hardening of attitude were retribution ('the hated criminal should atone for the act with his or her death'), deterrence ('the abolition of the death penalty will lead to an increase in crime'), the possibility of reoffending ('if the heinous criminal does not forfeit his or her life, he or she will be able to commit another offence'). It is, however, remarkable that 'appeasement' has been named more and more often as a reason for retaining the death penalty, which may have much to do with the growth of the 'victim movement' in the last ten or twenty years.

International victim surveys have also demonstrated the relatively high rate of punishment in Japan when compared to other countries. Respondents were asked which of five types of sentences they considered the most appropriate for a recidivist burglar ('A man aged 21 years found guilty for a second time, this time for stealing a colour TV'). The sentence options were a fine, imprisonment, community service, a suspended sentence or some other form of punishment. Support for imprisonment was strongest in the USA (55.9%), followed by Northern Ireland (53.9%) and Japan (51.0%). It was lowest in Catalan (Spain) (6.9%) (Kesteren *et al.* 2000; Kury 2001). Support for severe punishment to discourage young people from committing serious crimes was highest in Japan (48.1%), with Portugal at 10.2% the lowest. It is clear, therefore, from these figures that Japan has a relatively strong punitive attitude to crime in comparison to other developed countries.

The revisions of November 2000

In November 2000, the law relating to young offenders as enacted in 1948 under the influence of the American legal system was revised. This revision aims to change measures for dealing with young offenders from ones orientated towards punishment. This move was not only supported by the ruling conservative coalition – the Liberal Democratic Party, the

Equity Party and the New Conservative Party – but also by opposition parties, such as the Democratic Party of Japan and the Liberal Party. The new measures, however, will be reviewed five years after taking effect, in accordance with a provision submitted by the opposition parties.

The cause of this new legislation was increasing public concern over a rise in serious crimes committed by teenagers nationwide. The number of serious crimes committed by young offenders has increased sharply in

Table 18.1. The numbers of juvenile offenders and the population rate of juvenile offenders per 100,000 of the population aged 10–20 years.

	Homicide (including certain types of suicide and euthanasia)		Robbery (including murder and robbery and rape and robbery)		Theft	
	No.	*Rate*	*No.*	*Rate*	*No.*	*Rate*
1946	249	1.49	2,903	17.38	87,825	525.85
1948	354	2.06	3,878	22.53	90,066	523.34
1950	369	2.14	2,897	16.78	111,526	645.87
1952	393	2.21	1,956	10.99	104,344	586.34
1954	411	2.25	183	10.00	81,298	444.10
1956	324	1.82	2, 33	11.39	80,770	452.48
1958	366	1.91	2,405	12.56	83,528	436.15
1960	438	2.15	2,762	13.59	110,752	544.88
1962	343	1.68	2,307	11.30	132,096	647.06
1964	361	1.80	1,981	9.90	135,849	677.12
1966	368	1.82	1,901	9.42	117,938	584.51
1968	286	1.54	1,261	6.81	109,266	589.81
1970	198	1.17	1,091	6.45	106,359	628.53
1972	149	0.91	790	4.83	103,451	632.40
1974	102	0.63	677	4.20	116,863	724.30
1976	80	0.50	618	3.85	116,838	727.46
1978	91	0.55	522	3.14	140,611	845.56
1980	49	0.28	788	4.57	172,842	1,003.04
1982	86	0.48	806	4.46	198,701	1,098.78
1984	76	0.40	690	3.66	190,420	1,009.70
1986	96	0.49	708	3.65	177,766	915.68
1988	82	0.43	569	2.97	175,734	917.83
1990	71	0.38	594	3.20	130,802	705.75
1992	82	0.47	713	4.05	103,332	586.49
1994	77	0.47	933	5.65	102,537	621.04
1996	97	0.62	1,082	6.95	103,495	664.31
1998	117	0.79	1,566	10.59	121,261	819.87

Source: Research and Training Institute of the Ministry of Justice (2000).

recent years (see Table 18.1). Fuelled by sensational media reports, there has been a call for tougher sanctions for juvenile offending influenced, to a certain degree, by the economic recession of the past ten years. The new legislation lowers the minimum age at which young offenders can be held criminally liable for their actions from 16 to 14. Punishment for juvenile offenders is now to be administered in a young offender institution.

In addition, all young offenders aged 16 or over who cause death by a deliberate illegal act (including in the course of robbery, rape or personal assault) will, in principle, be tried by the public prosecutor, thereby subjecting them to indictment and trial as adult criminals. However, the public prosecutor can take part in family court proceedings at the perogative of the family court judge, which was not allowed under the old law. In short, the new legislation that came into effect on 1 April 2001 gives great weight to measures aimed towards deterrence and/or retribution, even though research has shown that movements in this direction have a negative social impact (Walgrave 1999).

Restorative justice and criminal law

Penal laws are those devised for those forms of behaviour that are considered to have socially harmful consequences. Such laws formally determine the area of control for infringements of elementary rights and interests (in German, *Rechtsgüter*). However, no legal system can exist without socio-ethical foundations; the law cannot be primarily understood as formal, external norms of order and coercion but, rather, as an expression of social solidarity (Moos 1997). A criminal offence, is therefore, a social conflict that has two dimensions: the state's conflict with the offender, on the one hand, and the (victim's) collective conflict with the offender on the other. As criminal laws apply to human behaviour that severely disturbs the fabric of society and that violates an individual's elementary rights and interests, the general task of criminal justice is, therefore, the maintenance of peace and its re-establishment after a crime has been committed (Baumann 1992 Schöch 1992; Löschning-Gspandl 1996; Rössner 1996; Walgrave 1999). It is therefore the responsibility of 'sensible, legally thinking citizens' to decide whether stability is restored (Dölling 1991).

As a crime violates legally acknowledged values, the primary justification for punishment is not crime prevention but reprimand. However, while punishment reflects society's disdain of the criminal act, it also has preventative intentions in that it aims to stop the criminal from reoffending and is designed to restore social equilibrium. Consequently, the ideology of punishment and the objectives of punishment form a unity (Moos 1997).

Criminal justice can achieve such behaviour control in a number of ways. However, traditional Japanese criminal justice has only a punitive response to crime and has not acknowledged the role socially constructive responses to crime can play – i.e. on effects of an offence.

The concept of restorative justice

What 'restorative justice' means in practice has so far not been answered convincingly, and it is therefore not clear in what way restorative justice is connected with traditional criminal justice. However, it is necessary to define it accurately to clear up misconceptions about what restorative justice means that prevent it from being put into practice. Criminal harm can be repaired through the help of a mediator because crimes are social conflicts, as mentioned above. Much empirical research has shown that victim–offender mediation is widely accepted by the public and offers, therefore, many opportunities for the clarification of social norms (i.e. positive general prevention). On the basis of neutralisation theory (Sykes and Matz 1957),[1] social learning theory (Bandura 1977)[2] and various theories of socialisation (Piaget 1954[3]; Tapp and Levine 1974[4]; Gilligan 1982[5]; Kohlberg 1981/4[6]) one can assume that restorative justice responses to offences are the ones most likely to produce positive outcomes to conflict resolution. Victim–offender mediation could also prevent the continued isolation of those labelled as criminal. Therefore if a conflict can be settled by mediation and reparation (positive special prevention), victim–offender mediation could be effective in lowering recidivism rates. It could therefore, be one of the objectives of punishment.

Victim–offender mediation, however, has another objective: understanding of the position of all parties to an offence and, in addition, reconciliation among the offender, the victim and the community at large – rather than a reduction in the recidivism rate (Bazemore and Walgrave 1999: 57). Through various processes, victim–offender mediation aims ultimately at regret, repentance and, eventually, empowerment (Bush and Folger 1994). Such aims are beyond traditional criminal justice since they contain constructive, interpersonal elements.

In short, conflict management is not foreign to criminal justice but is far more suitable for the restoration of legal equilibrium than punishment. Criminal law, therefore, should give priority to the concept of law, not to the concept of punishment (Kerner 1985). Criminal justice does not simply mean 'penal justice'.

However, restorative justice should not be equated with victim–offender mediation alone, although this is the most important part of it. Restorative justice also allows for such positive activities as paying money to public welfare institutions or doing some form of community service (so-called 'symbolic compensation') (Walgrave 1999: 139) when victims are unwilling to accept reconciliation or the offence was against the public good. Its use, therefore, is not specifically related to the willingness of the victim to co-operate or to the particular offence concerned. Almost all criminal cases could be handled, in principle, in a socially constructive way. In this sense the concept of restorative justice is wider than simply victim–offender mediation. Restorative justice, therefore, is the process through which the offender voluntarily and autonomously accepts his or her responsibility for the offence committed and copes with the effects and consequences of his or her offence in a socially constructive way (Meier 1998). This definition does not deny the harm done; neither does it deny restoring the offender and victim to their former state or the exclusion of the mass of 'victimless' crimes.

Criminal procedures

While the Victim Compensation Act 1980, the Victim Protection Act 2000, and a revised Code of Criminal Procedure 2000 have been enacted in Japan (Yoshida 2001: 995–6), little attention has been paid to the objectives of criminal procedures. In relation to the new perspective of substantive criminal law, there is a need to reconsider the objectives of criminal procedures (Kaiser 1998). One of the principal objectives of criminal procedures is to establish the truth about what happened (i.e. to investigate the suspicion an offence has been committed – to ascertain the material truth). Procedural law should serve substantive law, and procedural law should pursue voluntary reparation beyond the investigation of the material truth. The victim's interests and needs should be taken far more into consideration in criminal procedures. Compensation for the psychological and material harm caused by an offence should become the focus of attention. Victim–offender mediation provides the victim with the opportunity to recover from his or her mental harm quickly and in an informal way. This means that procedural participation alone is not sufficient to satisfy the victim's interests and needs (Moos 1985; Roxin 1986; Peters and Aertsen 1995: 327; Walgrave 2000: 255). The one-way communication of a court trial does not allow for any exchange of views or feelings and is more problematic than victim–offender mediation (Dignan and Cavadino 1998: 145). While a court trial may channel the victim's feelings of outrage and revenge, in the longer term they do little to heal psychological wounds (Walgrave 2000: 253).

In victim–offender mediation, the offender is confronted with the consequences of his or her actions and can eventually take voluntary responsibility for those actions. Such autonomous, socially constructive solutions are often far superior to formal punishment. Autonomous, socially constructive conflict resolution should be an important objective in criminal procedures – i.e. procedures should provide victims and offenders who seek mediation the opportunity to take part in it.

Victim–offender mediation is more successful if it is carried out by extra-judicial bodies or persons independent of the state, such as welfare or social workers or social education workers trained in social work skills. These people play an important role in criminal justice because dealing with crime as a social conflict is not the exclusive domain of public prosecutors or judges.

Before a trial, the public prosecutor may defer a case if the situation is restored by the offender entirely without the intervention of the court and after successful reconciliation (diversionary mediation). In such cases there should be entry in the criminal records. During the trial, efforts towards reconciliation should influence the final decision taken by the court (i.e. have a mitigating, suspending or exempting effect upon the punishment decided), even if punishment seems necessary to prevent the offender from reoffending or to prevent other members of the public from committing similar crimes (Peters and Aertsen 1995: 330). Victim–offender mediation should also be available in cases of very serious crime. Constitutional legal principles could support these measures, and the offender's efforts towards reconciliation should be taken into account at parole hearings. In brief, therefore, restorative justice can be realised at every level of the criminal justice system.

However, the defendant's right not to make a statement regarding the offence conflicts with the expectation the offender should demonstrate positive, socially constructive behaviour. If the offender shows remorse or exhibits a desire for reparation before the trial commences, he or she runs the risk his or her efforts will not be appreciated by the criminal justice authorities and punishment could follow regardless. If the mediation was unsuccessful, any statements made during the mediation process could be turned against the defendant as evidence of his or her guilt.

However, this argument does not seem to make sense (Jesionek 1989; Meier 1998). In the first place, restorative justice requires the offender's willing decision to participate. In addition, voluntariness is only relative as the offender is under pressure of an imminent formal procedure, as in summary proceedings.

Participation in restorative justice measures is also only allowed if the case is clear cut to a certain degree and if enough proof has been found to justify a criminal charge (i.e. a strong suspicion). This does not mean the concept of the presumption of innocence is negated because the findings of an informal procedure (namely, the mediation process) cannot be used as evidence in subsequent formal procedures. It is therefore necessary that the mediator also has a formal right to refuse to give testimony. Finally, restorative justice measures must take place under the overall control of the formal prosecuting authorities. Such bodies are responsible for ascertaining whether the objectives of criminal justice have been met or whether the procedural preconditions of restorative justice were observed.

Conclusions

Social stability can be restored without resort to formal conviction or sentencing. The central task of the criminal law is no longer the imposition of punishment but, rather, control when this is an appropriate response to an offence. Restorative justice cannot be integrated into the existing criminal justice process but needs a new framework with new inter-pretation or perspective although it might perhaps be going too far to say there needs to be e paradigm shift. The Japanese system should move towards a 'criminal justice system based on restorative justice' (Weitekamp 2000: 102), although restorative justice should not be seen as a cure-all for crime. Restorative justice requires new substantive and procedural provisions, such as a community mediation board and a victims' fund financed through fines and donations.

Notes

1. Sykes and Matza (1957) suggest the following five types of neutralisation processes that enable young people to contravene social norms: denial of responsibility, denial of injury, denial of the victim, condemners and an appeal to higher loyalties. Victim–offender mediation or family group conferencing could prevent the operation of these neutralisation processes.
2. Bandura (1977): 12) questions the legal system of deterrence as follows: 'observed punishment can strengthen restraints over forbidden behaviour. Modeling influences, however, can also reduce the deterrent efficacy of threatened legal consequences. The chances of being caught and punished for criminal transgressions tend to increase prohibited behaviour in observers.' He concludes that most law-abiding behaviour derives more from deterrence (through a system of social options) than from threat of legal sanctions.

3. According to Piaget (1954), punishment plays a big role in the establishment of authoritarian morality and can adversely affect a young person's development. In the morality of autonomy and co-operation, law-breakers are condemned for disturbing the fabric of society and, therefore, they should be restored to society through positive adjustment, (for example through compensation).

4. Tapp and Levine (1974) suggest four conditions for legal socialisation: legal knowledge, utilising value conflict positively, participation and valuing multiple legal systems and diverse legal cultures. They emphasise the fact that the vertical system of justice should be supplemented with a horizontal system of justice and they therefore extol the potentialities of mediation.

5. Gilligan (1982: 179) states: 'To understand how the tension between responsibilities and rights sustains the dialect of human development is to see the integrity of two disparate modes of experience that are in the end connected. While an ethic of justice proceeds from the premise of equality – that everyone should be treated the same – an ethic of care rests on the premise of nonviolence – that no one should be hurt. In the representation of maturity, both perspectives converge in the realisation that just as inequality adversely affects both parties in an unequal relationship, so too violence is destructive for everyone involved. This dialogue between fairness and care not only provides a better understanding of relations between the sexes, but also gives rise to a more comprehensive portrayal of adult work and family relationship'. The integrity of justice and care leads to transformative mediation (i.e. considering the needs of both the victim and offender).

6. According to the cognitive-developmental approach of Kohlberg (1981/4), individuals must attain a level of understanding that enables them to interpret ethical principles autonomously and in changing situations. Punishment as reaction to crime will be inevitably reduced in such a view, and so victim–offender mediation will play a much more significant role.

References

Bandura, A. (1977) *Social Learning Theory.* Englewood Cliffs, NJ: Prentice Hall.

Baumann, J. (ed.) (1992) *Alternativ-Entwurf Wiedergutmachung.* Munchen: C.H. Beck.

Bazemore, G. and Walgrave, L. (1999) 'Restorative Juvenile Justice: in Search of Fundamentals and an Outline for Systemic Reform', in G. Bazemore and L. Walgrave (eds) *Restorative Juvenile Justice: Repairing the Harm of Youth Crime.* Monsey, NY: Criminal Justice Press.

Bush, R.A.B. and Folger, J.P. (1994) *The Promise of Mediation.* San Francisco, CA: Jossey-Bass.

Dignan, J. and Cavadino, M. (1998) 'Which Model of Criminal Justice Offers the Best Scope for Assisting Victims of Crime?', in E. Fattah and E. Peters (eds)

Support for Crime Victims in a Comparative Perspective. Leuven: Leuven University Press.

Dölling, D. (1991) 'Der Täter-Opfer-Ausgleich. Möglichkeiten and Grenzen einer neuenkriminalrechtlichen Reaktionsform', *Juristenzeitung*, 47: 493–9.

Gilligan, C. (1982) *In a Different Voice: Psychological Theory and Women's Development*. Cambridge, MA and London: Harvard University Press.

Information Centre of the Cabinet Secretary (1981, 1990, 1995 and 2000). *Yearbook for Public Opinion Polls*. Tokyo : ICCS.

Jesionek, U. (1989) 'Die Konfliktregelung im neuen österreichischen Jugendrecht', in W. Melnizki and C.F. Müller (eds) *Strafrecht, Strafprozeßrecht and Kriminologie (Festschrift fur Franz Pallin zum 80. Geburtstag)*. Wien: Manzsche Verlags- und Universitätsbuchhandlung.

Kaiser, G. (1998) 'Ist die Resozialisierung noch ein aktuelles Thema der Strafprozeßreform?', in A. Eser *et al.*(eds) *Festschrift für Theodor Lenckner zum 70. Geburtstag*.

Kerner, H.-J. (1985) 'Die Wiedereinsetzung des Opfers als Subjekt des (Straf-)Rechts', in H. Jannsen and H.-J. Kerner (eds) *Verbrechensopfer, Sozialarbeit and Justiz*. Bonn: Deutsche Bewährungshilfe.

Kesteren, J.v., Mayhew, P. and Nieuwbeerta, P. (2000) *Criminal Victimisation in Seventeen Industrialised Countries*. The Hague: WODC.

Kohlberg, L. (1981/4) *Essays on Moral Development. Volumes I and II*. San Francisco, CA: Harper & Row.

Kury, H. (2001) 'Zu Sanktionseinstellungen and der präventiven Wirkung (harter) Sanktionen (Teil 1)', *The Hokkaigakuen Law Journal*, 37(1): 215–60.

Löschnig-Gspandl, M. (1996) *Die Wiedergutmachung im österreichschen Strafrecht*. Wien: Verlag Österreich.

Meier, B.-D. (1998) 'Restorative Justice – a New Paradigm in Criminal Law?', *European Journal of Crime, Criminal Law and Criminal Justice*, 6(2): 125–39.

Moos, R. (1985) *Grundstrukturen einer neuen Straprozeßordnung. Verhandlun gen des Neunten österreichschen Juristentages Wien 1985. II/3 Abteilung Strafrecht*. Wien: Manzsche Verlags- und Universitätsbuchhandlung.

Moos, R. *(1997)* 'Der Außergerichtlicher Tatausgleich für Erwachsene als strafrechtlicher Sanktionsersatz', *Juristische Blätter*, 19(2): 337–57.

Peters, T . and Aertsen, I. (1995) 'Restorative Justice: in Search of New Avenues in Judicial Dealing with Crime. The presentation of a Project of Mediation of Reparation', in C. Fijnaut *et al.* (eds) *Changes in Society, Crime and Criminal Justice in Europe*. The Hague: Kluwer Law International.

Piaget, J. (1954) *Das moralische Urteil beim Kinde*. L. Goldmann. Zurich: Rascher.

Research and Training Institute of the Ministry of Justice (2000) *White Book on Japanese Criminality 2000*. Tokyo: RTIMJ.

Rössner, D. (1996) 'Situation, Ethical Grounds and Criminal Political Perspectives of Victim–Offender Reconciliation in the Community', in B. Galaway and J. Hudson (eds) *Restorative Justice: International Perspectives*. Monsey, NY, and Amsterdam: Criminal Justice Press/Kugler.

Roxin, C. (1986) 'Welches Gesamtkonzept sollte der Strafprozeßreform zugrundegelegt werden?', in H.-L. Schreiber and R. Wassermann (eds)

Gesamtreform des Strafverfahrens: Internationales Christian-Broda-Symposion. Bad Homburg: v.d.H.

Schöch, H. (1992) *Empfehlungen sich Änderun gen and Ergänzungen bei den strafrechtlichen Sanktionen ohne Freiheitsentzug?.* München: C.H. Beck.

Sykes, G.M. and Matza, D. (1957) 'Techniques of Neutralisation: a Theory of Delinquency', *American Sociological Review*, 22: 664–70.

Tapp, L.L. and Levine, F.J. (1974) 'Legal Socialization: Strategies for an Ethical Legality', *Stanford Law Review*, 27: 1–72.

United Nations (2000) *Tenth United Nations Congress on the Prevention of Crime and the Treatment of Offenders, Vienna, 10–17 April 2000.* New York: United Nations Publication.

Walgrave, L. (1999) 'Community Service as a Cornerstone of a Systemic Restorative Response to (Juvenile) Crime', in G. Bazemore and L. Walgrave (eds) *Restorative Juvenile Justice: Repairing the Harm of Youth Crime.* Monsey, NY: Criminal Justice Press.

Walgrave, L. (2000) 'Extending the Victim Perspective towards a Systemic Restorative Justice Alternative', in A. Crawford and J. Goody (eds) *Intergrating Victim Perspectives within Criminal Justice.* Aldershot: Ashgate.

Weitekamp, E.G.M. (2000) 'Research on Victim–Offender Mediation: Findings and Needs for the Future', the European Forum for Victim–Offender Mediation and Restorative Justice (ed.) *Victim–Offender Mediation in Europe.* Leuven: Leuven University Press.

Yoshida, T. (2001) 'Geständnis, Entschuldigung, Reue and Wiedergutmachung im japanischen Strafrechtssystem – Ist Japan ein Musterbeispiel?', in G. Britz *et al.* (eds) *Grundfragen staatlichen Strafens (Festschrift für Heinz Müller-Dietz zum 70 Geburtstag.* München: C.H. Beck.

Index